WILLIAM GERHARDIE

A Biography

Dido Davies

Oxford   New York
OXFORD UNIVERSITY PRESS
1991

Oxford University Press, Walton Street, Oxford OX2 6DP

Oxford New York Toronto
Delhi Bombay Calcutta Madras Karachi
Petaling Jaya Singapore Hong Kong Tokyo
Nairobi Dar es Salaam Cape Town
Melbourne Auckland
and associated companies in
Berlin Ibadan

Oxford is a trade mark of Oxford University Press

British Library Cataloguing in Publication Data
Data available
ISBN 0–19–282852–5

Library of Congress Cataloging in Publication Data
Davies, Dido.
William Gerhardie: a biography/Dido Davies.
p. cm.
Includes bibliographical references (p.   ) and index.
ISBN 0–19–282852–5: $12.00 (est.)
1. Gerhardie, William Alexander, 1895–   —Biography.
2. Novelists, English—20th century—Biography.   I. Title.
[PR6013.E75Z65 1991]
828'.91209—dc20   [B]   90–28680 CIP

Printed in Great Britain by
Biddles Ltd.
Guildford and King's Lynn

To Richard Miles Randall Davies

PREFACE

WILLIAM GERHARDIE thrived on the colour and verve of the century's early history. Born in St Petersburg, he grew up amongst the social idiosyncrasies of the English community, against a background of decline and chaos. At 21 he found himself posted to the British Embassy in revolutionary Petrograd. At 23 he was in Siberia, precariously immersed in the cruel vagaries of the Civil War. At 24 he went to Oxford, he published a book, and before he was 27 he was the brilliant young novelist of the age. His delicate humour and a braggadocio that only loosely concealed his diffidence were qualities readily appreciated by society in the twenties and thirties. He was the *outré* Anglo-Russian genius who bewitched, scandalized, and seduced. An Indian princess flew him to her palace. Lord Beaverbrook took him to lunch with D. H. Lawrence, to supper with H. G. Wells, and to breakfast with Marie Stopes. Lloyd George discussed the young novelist's love affairs and his plans for an Algerian harem.

But with the approach of World War II, mood and literary tastes shifted. England lost its gaiety. Gerhardie's humour and irony were perhaps too fine, his writings too far ahead of their time, to take a lasting hold on the reading public of the day. Gerhardie grew increasingly reclusive and by 1940 he had ceased to publish. The post-war world he found drab and disappointing; there seemed no place for him, either personally or on the bookshelves, and he seldom ventured out. Yet throughout it all he maintained a profound belief in his own value as a writer, supported not only by a loyal body of literary admirers—Graham Greene, Evelyn Waugh, Olivia Manning, C. P. Snow, Anthony Powell, L. P. Hartley—but by a stream of unseen readers who at the most unexpected moments would pour out their praise through the post. 'I haven't got a friend who didn't first write to me out of the blue.' Such disembodied contact, ideal and imaginative, delighted one who, though egotistical to a degree, was at the same time nervous and reclusive.

The image of Gerhardie as eccentric egotist has lingered. And in the lingering it has entangled itself with some of his more outrageous public pronouncements—women, he was fond of saying, should be beautiful and stupid, their role in life was to inspire, not to think. But such statements were often—not always—affectations, and they mask a world of complex attitudes towards the sexes. The closest, most loving and unselfish relationships of William's life were all with strong, independent women. He railed against the sexual double standards of the time and urged an end to the 'pernicious' Mrs/Miss distinction. Whilst insisting that no woman could write, he carried on a deeply appreciative literary correspondence with Katherine Mansfield, Edith Wharton, and Rosamund Lehmann.

Unquestionably William Gerhardie would have found it, at the very least, rather *curious* that his longed-for biography should be written by a woman. As a matter of fact Gerhardie approved of me. When he was old and I quite young I was taken to tea in a London flat, where he lived behind closed curtains. 'Which of my books have you read?' he enquired eagerly. I replied 'None' and showed little interest in doing so. Nevertheless he became quickly absorbed in his new guest: he surveyed me from the front, from behind, from the left side, the right side—my eyes he noticed had a plaintive look of the Maharani of Cooch Behar after a particularly taxing night on the razzle. My nose, withal, the muscine point so longingly described by Herr Himmler. He invited me to stand up, turn full circle, extend a limb here and a shoulder there, and he complimented me with enthusiasm. Though my hair was luxuriant, he could see, would I care to guard against future baldness by some of his own lotion, developed over half a century?

Lining the walls in every room were his notes and diaries and manuscripts—of little interest to me then, the occupation of years of my life in years to come. On a second visit, alone together, he demonstrated the proper way to walk on ice, and suddenly recalled a long-forgotten incident with a Bolshevik (I can no longer remember it). He brought out a photograph of his little sister, a handsome edition of *The Memoirs of Satan*, and a letter he had recently received from an admirer, approaching 100, who suggested she meet her idol before time ran out. 'Does she mean my time or hers?'

Years passed and again I visited Rossetti House where he, grown older still, lay on his 81st birthday in a cold bedroom, very weak, distracted, greeting his guests one by one. Eight months later he died.

The paraphernalia of Gerhardie's 81 years at last found their way to the Cambridge University Library: fifty-nine large cardboard boxes full, not merely uncatalogued, not simply unsorted, but—except by himself —unread. The first box yielded a thousand or two letters from his spirited, doting mother Clara; the second, a plaster cast of William's ear. Box 37 revealed Gerhardie on a camel beside the great Sphinx of Giza, and complicated plans and drawings to build his own house, specially designed so that bits could be added on as the anticipated fortunes rolled in. Gradually, box by box, re-emerged Gerhardie: a man given to the occasional hysterical outburst, enthusiastically sincere and unpretentious in his erratic behaviour; a man of unbounded optimism, but above all a writer with a comic gift of genius.

For Gerhardie saw humour not as frivolity, but the most serious aspect of existence. He has aptly been described as a philosopher who treated his philosophy humorously, with a lightness of spirit that sometimes concealed his artistic dedication. For Gerhardie was also an adventurous theorist, constantly looking for new ways to express his ideas. Since the Second World War he has come to be identified with the generation of writers who encouraged him and learned from him, but this has obscured the fact that his fictional innovations, his distinctive concerns with memory, desire, consciousness, and the authorial self align him more accurately with the writers of mainstream Modernism, and with the dramatists of the Absurd. But for all these comparisons his work cannot be labelled. Gerhardie himself, not a modest man, modestly claimed that his most significant contribution to English literature was the development of 'the humorous tragedy, the highest literary expression in our time'.

Gerhardie had precise views on what he thought fit to re-establish his reputation, and in his later years he eyed many of his literary friends as possible biographers, potential resurrectionists. But it would have been impossible to write about him whilst he lived. He remembered himself too vividly. Michael Holroyd, engaged upon short prefaces for the Gerhardie reissue in the early 1970s, received by every post elaborate and insistent instructions to include the toothpaste story, leave out the Oxford scout, modify the girl with the bandy legs, change the first, third, fourth, and eighth words of the second sentence and the seventh word of the fifth, and when he struggled to maintain something of his own, Gerhardie berated him as 'a *smilingly* impenitent, pig-headed, bloody-minded, bigoted, intolerant, unyielding, inelastic, *hard*, inflexible, opinionate, fanatical, obsessed, pedantic, rook-ribbed, *unmoved*, persistent, incurable, irrepressible, intractable, impersuadable, cross-grained ruffian—no offence implied'.

In middle life Gerhardie thought he had discovered the secret of how, plausibly and scientifically, we might imagine a life after death. He viewed his own demise without fear, but sadly, with the dismay one would feel on parting with a dear familiar friend, and he hoped to continue his existence in another sphere. Possibly from there he will read his own biography in a calmer frame of mind. Naturally he will want to delete my criticisms and exaggerate my praises. But perhaps he will not be so unyielding about the Oxford scout scene, which I have included, and resist the temptation to endlessly rearrange, so leaving the book more or less as it stands now, a life of William Gerhardie.

DIDO DAVIES

ACKNOWLEDGEMENTS

I would like to thank the many people who have, in a variety of ways, helped with this book: Julian Amyes, Professor John Bayley, Mary Beard, the Revd John Beech, June Benn, Mr K. F. Bowden of Bacup Public Library, Charlotte Brittan, Sarah Burbidge, Alfred Cohen, Dr Catherine Cook, William Cooper, Sonya Crooks, Timothy Crowe, Austen Davies, Eileen Davies, Maud Diggle, Kenneth Duke, Hilary Ferndale, David Field, Penelope Fitzgerald, Christina Foyle, Joan Gerhardi, Livia Gollancz, Joy Grant, Nathan Graves, Brendan Griggs of the British Council in Tokyo, Bo Gunnarsson, Nora Hartley, Jean Haynes, Dr Frank Holden and Mrs Holden, Dorothy Hopkinson, Tom Hopkinson, Alan Hyman, Richard Ingrams, Michael Ivens, Peter Jones, Yvonne Kapp, the Revd D. H. Kingham, Joanna Lewis, Marie Macey, James MacGibbon, Timothy Mayo, Malcolm Muggeridge, Aleksei Narishkin, Ian Patterson, Penguin Books, Harvey Pitcher, Tony Porter, Anthony Powell, the late John Pudding, Gorley Putt, Miss F. Ratte, Evelyn Roche, John Rothenstein, Annabelle Sally, Sally Sanderlin, Andrew Sixsump, The Society for Psychical Research, The Spastics Society, Dr David Stafford-Clark, the late Oliver Stonor, Mollie Stonor, Frances Streatfield, Elsa Strietman, Snapen Saunders, Harold Speed, Colin Vines, Anina Yaltsin.

Professor Derek Brewer supported the project from the very beginning, at a time when many others were sceptical. I am particularly grateful to the Library Syndicate and the Librarian, Dr F. W. Ratcliffe, for having the foresight to purchase this valuable archive.

Dr Carl Baron of St Catharine's College, Cambridge, was of particular assistance in the early stages. Max Saunders spent scores of hours discussing Gerhardie and offering valuable suggestions.

Throughout the whole long project Anne Amyes has been of inexpressible help, answering my numerous questions and offering me a place to stay when our conversations carried late into the night. Christina Street, also most hospitable, provided many reminiscences of the Gerhardis. Likewise Tamara Tipping offered many valuable insights and anecdotes about the family.

Michael Holroyd has been immensely supportive throughout, talking at great length about Gerhardie, as well as making some valuable suggestions about the typescript.

Patrick Miles has been both enthusiastic and encouraging, and I have benefited considerably from his scholarly and highly sensitive approach to

Gerhardie's Russian works. He has also kindly translated Gerhardie's Russian poems quoted in the text.

I have, on two occasions, received the most generous financial help from the Society of Authors, for which I am immeasurably grateful. My mother Mrs Ingrid Massey bought me a word processor, which great event significantly speeded up this long work.

The staff of the Cambridge University Library greatly assisted me, in particular Margaret Pamplin, Godfrey Waller, and all the Manuscript Room staff who for years on end have been unfailingly cheerful, and who made many otherwise long and boring days pleasant. Miss Pamplin also helped to put the wildly disorganized material into a basic order. Gerry Bye and the University Photographic Department produced some excellent photographic prints for me.

Lastly, for his patient attention, his careful editing, but above all his innumerable helpful and sensitive suggestions which improved the whole tone of the book, Alexander Masters.

CONTENTS

Contents

ILLUSTRATIONS

All photographs are reproduced by permission of
the Syndics of Cambridge University Library

NOTE

William Gerhardie was born William Gerhardi. Late in life he changed the spelling of his name by adding a final 'e'. I have used this altered version (except when quoting) partly in deference to his later wishes, but also conveniently to differentiate him from other members of his family.

For most of his life Gerhardie adopted his own idiosyncratic spelling of 'Anton Chehov' which he considered more accurately reflected the Russian pronunciation. Later in life he came to appreciate that he could never change public opinion on this point, and reverted to the most usual English spelling 'Chekhov'. Except when quoting, I myself have used 'Chekhov'.

All his life Gerhardie had trouble with English spelling, and occasionally with English idioms. To my mind these oddities are an essential part of his appeal, and when quoting him I have retained them.

THE WADSWORTH AND GERHARDI FAMILY TREE

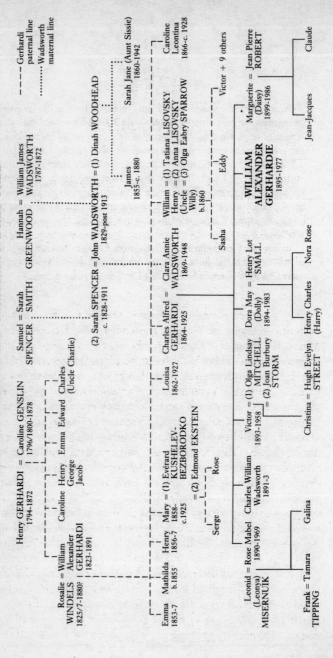

1

ANCESTORS

It is pronounced: Jer (as Ger in Gerald), Hardi is pronounced Hardy with the accent on the 'a'.

This is the way I and my relations pronounce it, though I am told it is incorrect. Philologists are of the opinion that it should be pronounced: Gerhardi as in Gertrude. That is, in fact, how the name is pronounced by most people. I believe they are right. I, however, cling to the family habit of mispronouncing it. But I do so without obstinacy. If the world made it worth my while I would side with the multitude.[1]

William Gerhardie wistfully regretted that he was *not* related to the beautiful Madame de Girardi in Stendhal's *De l'Amour*, nor to the Marchese Gherardi of Lombardy who in 1778 was invited to the same party as Dr Johnson, nor to the Italian singer and hostess named Gerardi who entertained Beethoven. And, though none are known to be direct relations, he wished to point out that an assortment of Italian artists of the sixteenth, seventeenth, and eighteenth centuries bear the name Gerhardi: Cristofano, Filippo, Francesco, Giuseppe. Likewise a sprinkling of Gerhardis published learned works, mostly in Germany, during the seventeenth, eighteenth, and nineteenth centuries: Joannes Cunradus who discoursed on the philosopher's stone; Hermannus on dreams; Fredericus Wilhelmus on dangerous medicines; Gaspar on nutrition; Augustus on dropsy. And, closer still, the museums at Essen and Hagen show works by Ida Gerhardi, born in Germany in 1867, who worked for a long time in Paris. 'I stress the Italian or German origin of the name', William Gerhardie wrote in 1931, 'according to which country we are, at the time, in a state of war with.'[2]

In fact, William's paternal great-grandfather was called Henry. The first Gerhardi in England, he was born in Prussia in 1794 to a family of middle-class *Freiherrs* or *Chevaliers* from Hamburg or Düsseldorf, and sent to work in the London branch of his father's paper mill after having disgraced himself by gambling away his adolescent income. He took for his wife Miss Caroline Genslin, 18 years old and born in Holland but related to the bearer of a prestigious English court office, Gold-Stick-in-Waiting.

Early in his career Henry set up in business: in 1824 the firm of Gerhardi and Hast, Merchants was established at 79 Lower Thames Street, close to Billingsgate and immediately opposite Genslin and Co., Merchants—in both cases the nature of the merchandise is unspecified in contemporary business directories. Eight years later Gerhardi and Hast had disappeared and Henry's profession from then on is variously described as bookkeeper (1851), merchant (1859), commission agent's clerk (1871), bookkeeper (1872), and general merchant (1878). They were a cosmopolitan couple: of their six children Edward was born in Belgium, though as an adult he was employed in London as a telegraph clerk; Emma married a Belgian; Charlie settled in England also as a telegraph clerk; Henry took a French wife and died a naturalized Frenchman; and William Alexander, grandfather of our subject, was born at Tower Hill in 1823, and confirmed at the age of 22 into L'Église Consistoriale Evangelique de Bruxelles. Feeling perhaps that two telegraph clerks were enough for one family, Henry and Caroline envisaged for this boy a more adventurous future and sent him as an apprentice to the cotton mills of Manchester where he qualified as a mechanic and machine-maker. Here he courted Rosalie Windels, a young Flemish governess who had run away from a hated stepmother; and here they were married on Christmas Day, 1851.

Emma, Mathilda, Henry, and Mary quickly followed upon the marriage, and quickly, on a visit to Brussels, Emma and Henry departed —captured by typhus, hastily baptized, and buried together in the Protestant cemetery. A fifth child, Willy, appeared. Shortly afterwards, some time between September 1860 and June 1862, the family left England for Russia, a country at that time virtually unknown to the English.

Whether this move was from choice, or pressed upon them by circumstance can only be guessed. Throughout the nineteenth century Britons emigrated in large numbers—nearly two million during the 1860s alone. Not all were fortunate: the poet Roy Campbell's grandfather, for instance, got an unpleasant surprise when he landed in an extremely primitive Natal in 1850, shortly after Katherine Mansfield's grandfather removed from Highgate to Sydney. Others set out for the United States, Canada, or New Zealand—yet the numbers to Russia were so small as to escape almost all the statistical analyses of the period.

That the Gerhardis travelled over a thousand miles with three young children rather than when still childless and unencumbered suggests that the move was not long premeditated—they may well have been victims of the Cotton Famine of 1861 when the outbreak of the American Civil War virtually ended supplies of raw cotton for four years and mills closed and redundancies soared. Perhaps they were simply exercising an adventurous spirit.

There was developing at just that time a small but significant link between Britain and Russia. In 1855 Tsar Nicholas I had been succeeded by his more forward-looking son Alexander II. A comparatively backward country, Russia was now slowly beginning to reform and modernize: Alexander built railways, encouraged a complex banking system, and in 1861 emancipated the serfs. Just as around the turn of the eighteenth century Belgium and France had developed with British technical expertise, so now the Tsarist government attempted to attract British skills to Russian industry. To the enterprising entrepreneur it was a return to the early days of the Industrial Revolution. Mill workers and foremen could expect a far higher standard of living than at home. They were well paid and their services valued, servants were plentiful and cheap, houses spacious and warm, and there were endless exciting recreational and sporting opportunities. Many families who took the chance later retired to England with substantial savings, and many were able to afford a good education for their children. A number of Scots emigrated, chiefly to Moscow, and from Lancashire there was a steady trickle of managers, foremen, mill-hands.

The Crimean War added the final touch of novelty. By the mid-nineteenth century there was already a small selection of travel literature. Individuals varied considerably in their response to the Russian Empire, but the overall impression was of a vast, ungovernable land, populated by wild animals and outlandish people. William and Rosalie, who purchased an 1849 edition of *Murray's Handbook for Travellers*, read of a tangled country full of colour, charm, and oddities, but potentially vexing to the fastidious English. Russian police regulations were formal and tedious. Murray advises that a *douceur* is expected by officials of all kinds, adding demurely: 'As it will not be the traveller's province to reform abuses, we recommend him, if he values his comfort and quiet, to conform to the customs of the country.' All kinds of articles were liable for seizure and censorship: sealed letters, lottery tickets, playing cards, unworn articles of dress, medicine, and even rhubarb carried as a laxative, though the latter would apparently be returned on assuring the authorities that it is 'not intended for his Imperial Majesty's liege subjects, but for your own sweet self'. Books and maps were also likely to be examined and any 'objectionable work'—(Byron's *Don Juan*, for example)—confiscated. One English lady described her irritation at having a grubby and loutish customs official ransack her luggage, spilling ink, dirtying her clothes, and jumbling up the careful packing. When he came to her portable writing desk she was shocked to observe that he was perfectly *au fait* with the secret drawer, but she cheered up when he cut his finger on some of the steel paraphernalia of the writing equipment.

After a stormy crossing from Newcastle, Gerhardie's grandparents arrived at the Baltic port of Riga, on the very outskirts of the Russian Empire. Founded in the twelfth century by shipwrecked Bremen merchants, the city had since been taken by the Russians, though still populated by German Lutherans, stubbornly Teutonic in their manners and appearance. Even the huge flat-bottomed timber barges were reminiscent of Rhine rafts, built from wood of the fir and pine forests that surrounded the town, and haunt of bears, wolves, and, it was rumoured, rampageous racoons. From the top of a tree one could look down upon the pointed roofs, tortuous streets, town squares, and fine old Cathedral. Here William began work as an engineer in a sawmill on the outskirts of the town, and here his remaining children were born —Louisa, Caroline, and in 1864 the novelist's father Charles. Four years later the family removed to St Petersburg on a steamboat, the *Leander*, full of Germans who, as young Charles clearly remembered, got dreadfully drunk and sang in chorus 'Today to lunch have we a preparation of herrings and Bavarian beer.'

St Petersburg appeared as 'a city of broad thoroughfares, immense squares, wide bridges, lunatic dreams'.[3] 'How often then I dreamed of those white nights of Petersburg, those white mysterious sleepless nights', muses the narrator of *Futility*:

I went home by the silent river. The Fortress of St Peter and St Paul was like a weary watchman. The Admiralty needle seemed lost in the white mist. I sat down on a stone seat of the embankment and rested. The broad milky river was so mysteriously calm in the granite frame of the quays. I sat and wondered; then my thoughts began to drift; and I was lost in this half light, this half dream, this unreal half existence.[4]

Peter the Great created the city in the eighteenth century, importing European architects, landscape gardeners, painters, and craftsmen, before transferring the seat of government from Moscow to this new idyll of painted palaces, pink, pale green, duck-egg blue, and yellow against the snow. Lewis Carroll, who visited Russia in 1867, lauded the new capital, so utterly unlike anything he had ever seen, with its gigantic blue-domed churches covered with gold stars.[5] Mr Murray, however, was more sober in his praise of the droshky, 'a most comfortless conveyance, consisting merely of a bench upon four wheels, on which the fare sits astride, as on a velocipede, and immediately behind the driver, who is not an agreeable person to be in very close contact with; at any rate to those who are not fond of the odours of garlick'. Yet it was not the garlic that alarmed so much as the drivers' reckless speed in the dimly lit streets, seemingly heedless of whom they ran over, and furthermore, for this was Murray's true lament, there was not even a fixed price for such a horse race, 'a most extraordinary thing in a country where the police seem to busy themselves about every thing'; he recommended taking a *calèche*, where the coachman was less likely to be drunk.

Vodka was indeed cheap, and the food palatable on the whole, sometimes delicious. Typical fare consisted of soup, beefsteaks with potatoes, game birds, and *cotelettes* ('which . . . have a most questionable shape'). The pudding, though edible, was 'by no means prepossessing in its outward features'. And the black rye bread was 'very good fare for a Russian or a Spartan, but if the traveller is neither the one nor the other he will find his gastronomic tastes sorely tried'.[6]

Hotels, invariably magnificent and imposing on the outside, were less pleasing within. They were grubby, with a preponderance of unsavoury servants who spoke no English and, worst of all, they were alive with bedbugs. Clean sheets were hard to come by ('it was with the greatest difficulty that we obtained one for each bed; the *fille-de-chambre*, a man, insisting that one was a pair').[7] This particular traveller asked the landlord to remove the bedbugs, and was angrily and contemptuously told this was *capricci Inglesi*. A later, rather more refined, edition of Murray advises: 'Without wishing to detract from the merits of the best hotels mentioned in this Handbook, it is right to advise the traveller to be provided, when travelling in Russia, with remedies against insects of a vexatory disposition.' For those who fell ill (usually diarrhoea and dysentery), a few reliable British doctors could be obtained, and the English Quay also housed a first-rate English apothecary. Yet most found the cold in Russia less offensive than in Britain. At latitude sixty degrees north, roughly that of the Shetland Islands, it was intense, but dry; tuberculosis, rheumatism and asthma—staples of the English constitution at home—were not common here. The Russians were well-prepared for their winters, and walked about literally covered from head to foot in clothing (usually furs), and apparently took a kindly interest in the welfare of passers-by:

'Father, father, thy nose,' one man will cry to another as he passes him, or even stop and apply a handful of snow to the stranger's proboscis, and endeavour by rubbing it to restore the suspended circulation. A man's eyes also cost him some trouble, for they freeze up every now and then.[8]

Inside the houses the temperature was kept high and constant by remarkably efficient stoves built into partition walls, so that they heated two rooms at once. With the onset of winter the double windows were sealed with putty or paper, and several inches of sand or salt placed between the panes to absorb moisture, creating 'a perpetual summer in-doors. No additional blankets are necessary, and no shivering and shaking is to be dreaded on turning out in the morning, as in dear old England, when the north wind drives through every sash in the house. We are acquainted with a lady whose feet and fingers never escaped chilblains until she passed a winter in Russia.'[9]

But when William and Rosalie arrived in St Petersburg they found conditions rather worse than expected. The droshkies, the baths, the beds, and the biting cold of winter were all as Murray had said, but the boss was a 'rough, stingy' Scotsman named Macpherson. William worked hard and long for little money, making steam engines and track for the railway. Yet despite such austere conditions the Gerhardi children lived gaily. Early correspondence between them describes riding and hunting, fishing expeditions, fêtes and festivities.

William, appreciative of his offspring's play, no doubt, but eager also to get some for himself, left, and took another job at a cotton mill in Moscow. Still he worked long and hard. But in place of Macpherson was a friendly English manager, Richard Hill, who gave the family a suckling pig and a goose each Christmas and Easter, as well as a box at the Moscow ballet and the loan of his horse and trap. The family chronicle, written in shaky and slightly imperfect English by Charles and his sisters, shows little surprise at the curious combination of circumstances, though it mentions that the house in which they lived was humble and basic, with only one entrance, through the kitchen, which proved awkward when a Russian princess from the nearby estate (the English had always a certain status in Russia) arrived one day to visit them in a handsome troika.

Eventually they departed once more—for Pereslavl', a small town one hundred miles from Moscow. It was an uncomfortable removal, the Russian roads deep in mud, full of ruts and ditches and hillocks, without fencing or draining, and the coach driver swearing and swigging vodka as he whipped his horses. The quickest mode of transport was by post carriage—it took Lewis Carroll three hours to cover fourteen miles. Alternatively there were public carriages called diligences, but one English traveller helpfully pointed out that he had arrived at his destination with his teeth loose, and his limbs half dislocated.

In Pereslavl' William worked in a large cotton mill managed by a Scotsman named Robert McGill, who later established an iron foundry in Moscow, accumulated immense wealth, and became a pillar of the Moscow British community. Young Charles, now 12 years old, spent his spare time driving himself around in Mr McGill's horse and trap and sneaking into the drunken carding master's 'orgies'. But his greatest adventure was yet to come. His father accepted a post in a remote region of the country reconstructing a mill that had burned down. The Gerhardis spent two weeks in a hotel in Moscow, fêted with great civility by Solovief, the Russian owner, who escorted them to their new quarters. The last hundred miles of the journey had, in true Russian fairy-tale style, to be accomplished by sledge. They rode in two vehicles: a covered troika and an open sledge drawn by a pair, the latter extremely precarious because of the vicious jolts which often ejected the passengers. It was the depths of winter, snowing and blowing, and they stopped at peasants' houses for refreshments. When darkness fell they lost their way. In the eerie silence William unslung the loaded gun from across his shoulders and Rosalie clutched at a Spanish dagger as the wolves began to follow them; Charles remembered them crowding just out of reach, their eyes in the dark shining like lanterns.

At Logino, which they reached safely despite the hounding, William worked for six hard months to re-establish the mill—and was unceremoniously dismissed. The wily Solovief deemed it expedient to replace him with cheaper Russian labour. Thoroughly dispirited the family made the hazardous journey back to Moscow and, through the kind intervention of Robert McGill, returned to Pereslavl'. But by now William was anxious to start on his own. Only months later he entered partnership with a Mr Small, and the family moved, finally, back to St Petersburg.

*

For all their immersion in Russian life, William and Rosalie, in the nostalgic tradition of many of their expatriate friends, and finding indeed that only in Russia could one afford an English education, arranged to send their son Charles back to Britain. Rosalie, daughter of a schoolmaster, had strong views on education. She was opposed to corporal punishment and anxious for her children to be at least bilingual —she herself spoke Flemish, French, English, and Russian. With this in mind she selected Hymans International College in the Finchley Road, and bundled her son off to live with his Uncle Charlie. The manager of the London branch of the Direct Spanish Telegraph Company, he was a jolly and original character, elegant, something of a dandy and, though married, given to disappearing from time to time to his bachelor suite in a hotel. Young Charles rarely spoke of his father, who despite his adventurous life remains a curiously anonymous figure, but he was greatly impressed by his uncle and imbibed something of his style and morals.

Charles (the 'Russian bear', as they nicknamed him at school) contracted scrofula, the school requested his removal and he entered his uncle's office at eight shillings a week. Two years later he was sent as a Morse clerk to Brest in France, where he earned a spectacular £120 a year, a sum which, by dint of poker, beer, and the well-developed teenage daughter of a fellow clerk, quickly disappeared. This freedom was terminated (none too soon, for Charles had just gambled away two months' wages) by the death of his mother Rosalie, and he was recalled to St Petersburg.

The cotton-spinning mill at 41 Vibourg Quay had prospered, with Mr Small in charge of the commercial side, and William responsible for the machinery. While Charles had been cavorting, two of his sisters had married and settled in Antwerp; another had accompanied her husband to Massachusetts; a fourth, the beautiful Mary, had married a Russian aristocrat; a fifth was soon to wed; and Charles's older brother Willy had removed to Smolensk as engineer and manager of a mill.

At first Charles took tuition in mathematics, then entered his father's employ as clerk, at a very small wage. When his father visited France he took over his place and his salary. When Mr Small went abroad Charles did the same for him, and showed a distinct flair for office management. Father and son suggested that Mr Small buy them out of the business, and a figure of 65,000 roubles (about £8,000) was agreed.

Thus, in the spring of 1888 William and Charles set up in business together. Much to the fury of Mr Small they rented an adjacent mill that had previously been used to manufacture red paint, added a third and fourth floor, and ordered the most up-to-date machinery on long credit. The new patent Nobel Brothers' Steam Engine arrived, but did not work, until the deft William devised an alteration. He was also attracted by an entirely new piece of machinery. In the manufacture of cotton, carding is the process of straightening the matted cotton fibres after cleaning and prior to spinning, traditionally done by teasing with a thistle (Latin, *carduus*). Leaving little to chance William befriended carding masters at all the surrounding mills in order to solicit advice, before purchasing not the old type of roller cards but rather the adventurously modern revolving flat cards. Father and son worked from dawn till dusk, but father was never to see completion. One afternoon a pigeon flew into the building. The carpenters chased the bird, captured it, and pushed open a door to let it escape. The bird flew free, but the door had no hinges: it fell heavily on to William who was working below. Despite the devoted attention of his daughter he never recovered. He died three years later, his brain permanently affected by the blow, and was buried in the English Cemetery.

After the accident Charles wrote at once to Smolensk to urge his brother Willy to join him. Two months later the mill was in perfect operation. Profits rose. Charles's gifts were financial, mathematical, and technological. He ran everything with Germanic thoroughness, and if one small thing went wrong he gave vent to an 'almost insane irritability'. He had little sense of humour and the unfortunate knack of 'putting the wind up everyone unwittingly'. But he was at heart kind, and he believed it was important to speak to his Russian employees 'in affectionate terms, in pleasing diminutives: "What is it, my dove?" to a workman. A tender phraseology which, in Russia, contrasting with an equally usual violence of speech, goes straight to their hearts.'[10] An English manager nearby was shot in the eye by an embittered mechanic; it would never have happened, said Charles, if the man had not been so thrifty with his terms of endearment. Each Christmas Charles threw three parties: one for the mill workers, one for the middle management, and one for his own friends.

My father himself was loved by his workpeople with a love that, however, fluctuated at times, for in 1905 his men, who, he thought, regarded him as a father, tied him up in a coal sack and placing him in a barrel wheeled him along to tilt him into the Neva. They were, however, stopped on their way by an elderly workman who put them to shame by asking them what they meant by thus treating the English Socialist Keir Hardie. They then asked my father whether he was the English Socialist Keir Hardie, to which he replied that he certainly was. After which they released him with apologies, helping him out of the coal sack.[11]

Charles's abominable temper soon drove away his brother. Willy sold his share of the business and returned to the remote province of Smolensk to set up a bobbin factory, which articles he then sold to Charles. He established himself as a large provincial landowner on a splendid estate in this rural area of Russia, 'sheer Gogol-land', where it was said you might gallop for a century without reaching a frontier. For years the two brothers vied with each other in prosperity: 'One year it was my father who was ahead, next year it was my uncle; and so for thirty odd years—till the Revolution got the better of both.'[12]

Close to the Gerhardi mill was an even larger concern, the Sampson mill. The carding master John Wadsworth, befriended by his neighbour William Gerhardi, was of good solid English stock. His father—yet another William—after running away at 16 to join the army had fought in many of the Peninsular War battles, suffering such fatigues and privations 'as could scarcely be credited'. After helping to defeat Napoleon at the Battle of Waterloo, he returned to Bacup with his medals and took up his former profession of shoemaker. John (well known for his view that all clergymen were bounders, liars, and parasites) owned a general stores, which failed, and a wool mill, which also failed. He married twice before leaving England: first a millgirl, by whom he had a daughter, Sarah Jane (Gerhardie's Aunt Sissie), and then a local schoolteacher who gave him a second child, Gerhardie's mother Clara—pronounced in the North Country way to rhyme with 'bearer'.

John Wadsworth took care of his old father, who lived on a pension of 6d. a day, but his new wife was restless and ambitious. In 1872, at the age of 85, old Wadsworth finally gave up the ghost, and received a laudatory obituary in the local paper:

DEATH OF AN OLD VETERAN

Another 'heart of oak' has ceased to beat, and Britannia mourns another warrior now at rest . . .

Shortly afterwards, free from family obligations, the Wadsworths moved to Russia. Sissie was then 12 years old, her half-sister Clara 3.

Where John had failed as a boss he excelled as an employee. He tried hard to speak French but never mastered much Russian; he used to say that he was glad he wasn't born a Russian. He knew nothing of literature and never read anything but the *Financial Times* and Smith's *The Peninsular War*, recounting in great detail his own father's military exploits and occasionally producing the medals out of a chest, before locking them up again. He became a cautious, thrifty old man who proffered advice liberally on how not to get cheated and once advised his grandson, when changing buses, not to part with the old ticket obtained on one bus till he had secured a new ticket on another. The child explained to him that the ticket obtained on one bus could be of no use on another. 'Even so,' he said, 'it gets you into good habits.'

The Wadsworths, unlike the Gerhardis, appear to have led a vicissitude-free existence in St Petersburg, and always intended to return to England eventually. They were in time, however, to witness the assassination of Alexander II ('the best, the mildest and the kindest of all the tsars'[13]). As they returned from the English Church one day two sharp explosions sounded nearby, followed by a loud commotion. A bomb had been flung at the tsar's carriage. As he stepped out to see who had been injured a second bomb exploded at his feet tearing off one of his legs, and twisting and shattering the other. He was carried away, and shortly afterwards died. But such political upheavals were of passing importance to the two girls. They visited Yalta and Tiflis (Tbilisi) and Batumi in the Caucasus, and occasionally England, where Sissie was photographed in High Wycombe. She was small, fine-boned, and delicately good-looking; she curled her carrot-red hair tightly overnight with curling papers in a Queen Alexandra fashion. But she had the habit of giggling herself out of marriage; suitors, offended when their proposals were met with an 'ironic astonishment', went away, and Sissie remained forever a spinster.

Clara, larger and more dominant than her sister, was brought up a lady, regardless of expense and sent to school in England. She spoke four languages, was well-read and inquisitive, and also, as later events proved, highly courageous. Although by no means a beauty, she was intelligent, quick-witted, animated, and humorous. Her family thought that had she lived in England she would certainly have been a suffragette. She mixed easily with the Gerhardi sisters and some of their friends, and admired their elegance, while imposing some of her own. Eventually Clara and Charles set eyes on one another. She, 19 years old and fresh from school in England, sat on the steps pretending to play the piano and quite charmed him by singing, 'Come back, come back to me, come back to me, from o'er the sea.'

Clara was not universally popular with the Gerhardis, some of whom considered her pushy and certainly their social inferior. The Gerhardis, established entrepreneurs, moved in rather different circles from the Wadsworths who had but recently emerged from the north of England. None the less, one year after meeting, she married Charles at the palatial English Church in St Petersburg. John Wadsworth provided a handsome wedding for his daughter. After the ceremony the party dined and danced until five in the morning at a restaurant on one of the islands. The following afternoon, a Sunday, Charles and Clara took a picturesque drive to a château in a wooded park, and on Monday Charles returned to work.

2

NIGHTS IN ST PETERSBURG
1895–1913

> *I happen to belong to that elusive class of people knowing several languages who, when challenged in one tongue, find it convenient to assure you that their knowledge is all in another. And I am one of those uncomfortable people whose national 'atmosphere' had been somewhat knocked on the head—an Englishman brought up and schooled in Russia, and born there, incidentally, of British parents (with a mixed un-English name into the bargain!), and here I am.*[1]

William Alexander Gerhardie was born in wintry St Petersburg, shortly before midnight on 21 November 1895. A few months later, his earliest memory, he slapped his mother in the face. There was an uncomfortable pause. 'I became unpleasantly aware that I had spread horror—readily-advertised horror in the nursemaid; subdued, sad horror in my mother; and nicely-balanced horror in my aunt, as who might say: "He cannot be really bad being yours". For some time, the chorus of "Naughty! Naughty!" continued, with which idea I at bottom agreed, but, with the world against me, taciturn, abashed, helpless, I began to cry.'[2] The world he had entered was 'dark, wonderful, fearful', and stretched 'from the distant and mysterious place from which my uncle had arrived to the darkish dining-room at the other end of the world where I sat, engrossed, on my nurse's lap, rapt and spellbound'. Very early in his life he remembered being placed in a wooden frame on wheels 'somewhere high up', in the twilight, watched by his parents and siblings in his attempts to walk, 'ashamed of my poor results'. 'Childhood', he later wrote, 'seemed to last such a long time.'

William, the fifth of six siblings 'all produced within the shortest intervals humanly possible', was the most devoted of all Clara's children, 'the little fellow who followed me everywhere all day long in his childhood', and often desperately unhappy. Timid and sensitive, his intemperate father saw only effeminate ineptitude in his delicate son, inspiring 'a certain nervousness in me', while his mother, one eye on her jewels and dances, seemed not to notice. 'I failed you terribly years ago, dear and it will ever remain a reproach to me', she later wrote. To William, Clara was 'proud, vain, imperious and sanguine'; years later he conjured her image—'She is a young woman dressing for a ball, but when I, now quite a small boy, say to her "Oh, how beautiful you are!" she does not, to my surprise, reciprocate with "And so are you", and I think to myself: That woman, my mother, is cold and strange.'[3] She adored the new-found sophistication of carriages and servants, membership of the prestigious English Club, the Yacht Club, visits to the theatre, opera, and ballet. She entertained regularly and liked to be photographed, heavily ornamented with jewellery, in white lace, velvet, or satin. And she early adopted the habit, when kissing one child, of announcing proudly and gaily to the others, 'Now don't be jealous'.

Yet for all her preoccupation with things social, Clara inspired the greatest affection in her children. Her daughter Dolly described her as 'the centre of all our lives, the animating spirit of us all'. Clara later, somewhat self-deprecatingly, wrote: 'When I look back I have much to be ashamed of. I see now that I did not do my full duty to you children I was just an all round person, never really clever in any particular way and you are still all fond and loving to me and bear me no malice.' Above all, she presented a comforting contrast to the furious unpredictability of her husband, and her letters show an imaginative, humorous, emotional nature, with something of the Russian warmth, spontaneity, and fatalism. Of the death of her 2-year-old son, buried with his grandparents in the Smolenski cemetery, she later wrote: 'In a way I think it is better to die young and leave all the pomps and vanities and sufferings of this world behind. The death of my little Charlie was terrible for me to bear but I have thanked god many times that he was spared the pain and suffering and disillusion that seems to come to most people.' Yet this melodrama was cooled by a certain English pragmatism: she was energetic and efficient, not easily daunted—qualities which emerged most fully later, in adversity. 'Her natural exhuberance . . . was her spirit', said one friend.[4] 'Motherkins is rather bossy', said her daughter Rosie.

Clara was at heart a good deal more English than the Gerhardis, 'inclined to think in terms of Nelsons and Wellingtons', as William put it. She spoke English with a distinct Russian intonation, and in England was often mistaken for a foreigner, yet like many expatriates she maintained an affectionate regard for her mother country, and in particular for the royal family. Close association with William in her later years softened her conservative tendencies, broadened her mind. In

Russia, social status, etiquette, and possessions wove their spell. 'Mama is always proud of something', her daughter once observed; she replied, 'I like everything suitable. I like everything fitting into its place.' Charles appears to have been beguilingly oblivious of such things, and on one occasion he completely ignored the son of a Grand Duke who was visiting, except to ridicule his fastidious preference for tea in a glass rather than a cup. Yet he who did not normally care a rap for custom and tradition, made a great point at Christmas of pouring brandy over his plum pudding and lighting it. And William was greatly surprised to hear him remark to some business colleagues, 'We British have a saying "An Englishman's home is his castle"'.

Despite Charles's appalling temper, he and Clara enjoyed an affectionate though often turbulent relationship; her humour and strength of will enabled her to weather storm after storm. 'He was so busy, nerve-racked, unhappy by nature, that all he could do was to keep his own soul afloat. My mother would say: "Charles, *try* to control yourself! Other men have businesses and enjoy them."'[5] 'Damnation hell!' Charles bellowed at the central heating. In his teens William wrote a number of third-person accounts of his childhood in which he appears under a variety of names, but usually as 'Eddie' or 'Henry'. In one he describes seeing Clara enter her husband's bedroom on his birthday, bearing a present, an ivory statuette of Venus. But she happens to arrive at the moment when Charles has lost his braces, and the present is hurled at the wall. Young Henry 'remembered the damage wrought to the great looking glass. It seemed as if that moment his father wanted something of just that size and weight. And Venus of Milo suffered now additional affliction in limb to that traditionally authorised.' But, just as impulsively, Charles would buy Clara fine jewellery which, after a particularly unsuccessful gambling spree in the South of France, would be quickly sold again. When much later Charles died, William consoled Clara's lingering grief: 'you have been to him all his life, for better or worse, an invaluable . . . *stütze* [support], almost a second leg.'

To some extent William's parents lived independent lives, Clara preoccupied with running the house that Charles had built for her, Charles absorbed in horse-racing, gambling, and European travel. Having made his money he liked to play the *grand seigneur*, and he was not really cut out for family life, which bored and irritated him. A studio photograph shortly before William's birth shows Clara proudly holding two babies, and Charles, ill at ease, forlorn, balancing another on his knee in a very awkward, embarrassed fashion. He was persistently unfaithful, and it is a measure of Gerhardie's own curious moral expectations that he, so devoted to his mother, cheerfully related the following in his memoirs:

When, following on a love affair between my father and the wife of a Russian officer, the husband challenged him to a duel, my father wrote to him explaining that he was attached to life, attached to his own wife and children, and therefore felt that a man who could put forward a proposal having for its object the possible loss of my father's life was too despicable to fight with.[6]

Charles was apparently too preoccupied with his own affairs to notice that Clara, too, had a lover, a great family friend named Mr Fisher, who would lean over the piano gazing adoringly as she played and sang.

To William as a child Charles was remote and terrifying. He could be furious over trifles, or quite unexpectedly (though rarely) kind, and at such times his son's nurtured hatred turned to guilt. His obsessive efficiency, so useful in running the mill, did not go down well with his family who would not be organized like a machine. In his dealings with everybody Charles had 'the uncanny faculty of either talking in a whisper or bringing the roof down with a shout', and he was incapable of repeating anything.[7] Once when he returned home after an absence he completely ignored the 'Welcome Home' garlands so carefully rigged up by the children, and kissed the family peevishly. Fearful of his moods the children kept to their rooms. Yet his nervous irritation and energy were occasionally balanced by 'periods of perfect composure and relaxation . . . when he lay on the sofa and smoked a cigarette in a long holder with the air of one whom nothing in the world could disturb.'[8]

William remembered that he was 'lean, tall, elegant and wore very thin-soled boots with elastic sides, and he had thick beautiful wavy hair, long, slender fingers, and honest dog-like brown eyes'.[9] In photographs he sits, cigarette in hand, elegantly dressed with white shoes and a carnation in his buttonhole, his legs curled nonchalantly round each other. His two sons admired his style and when young tried to emulate it. Later in life William came to appreciate the fact that, though so intimidating, his father had always been liberal with money, free from moralizing lectures, and at heart well-meaning. He would pay them brief but not unsympathetic daily visits when they were ill, but he was always 'a strangely remote being', his mind, and all his adventurous past, quite closed to his children, and probably even to his wife.

They saw him infrequently, passing in the corridor, or at mealtimes where he always insisted on sitting on Clara's right-hand side no matter who was present, and sometimes completely ignored a guest, duke or otherwise. All five children had to say grace at table. It was a practice from which William noticed the adults seemed absolved, and he wondered whether this was because they had contrived to make their peace with God or because God would have nothing to do with grown-ups. At the end of the meal they would say rapidly 'Thank-God-for-a-good-dinner-please-may-I-get-down', and kiss first Clara, then Charles (who one day inadvertently burned William's eye with his cigarette). These meals would include, in the Russian manner, all members of the household: the children, Aunt Sissie, Grandpapa Wadsworth, and the governesses. All were nervous. Charles was normally silent, 'eating his food with the air of a tortured man loathing and struggling with his executioners'.[10] Sometimes in a rage he threw his cutlery on the floor.

While Charles left the care of his children entirely to his wife, she, in order to pursue her hectic social life, relegated them to the care of a nursery governess, a young Fräulein from Reval (now Tallinn) in Estonia, always known as Liebe ('Love'). A slightly startled-looking young woman, neatly coiffured, with a sharp chin, she was the sister of a doctor and unusual in coming from a middle-class family, though as William put it her own 'intellectual expansion had been checked at an early age'. She had been engaged but never married, for having once tactfully ignored her fiancé in the street, believing herself too untidy at the time for presentation to his fancy friends, her betrothed never came her way again. All the children adored her, the boys in particular, each boasting of their plans to marry her. She remained seventeen years with the family, the most cherished soul in the household, 'and there was no worse catastrophe than if she refused to kiss us good-night. The punishment was so barbarous, so unthinkably cruel, that we hated her and carried on like tortured maniacs, howling in sustained volume of protestation: "Liebe! Liebe! Kuss! Kuss!" till she was forced to recant and give in.'[11]

On one occasion when Liebe was on holiday William forlornly asked, 'Who is going to kiss us goodnight?' His brother Victor suggested a pretty young maid, but when she came to kiss William he held up a piece of glass between her lips and his, anxious lest it be unhygienic. Liebe and Clara became devoted friends, indispensable to one another. Though she had two nursemaids under her, Liebe preferred to carry out her duties herself—most memorable to William was her grabbing his neck between her knuckles to wash his ears.

She used to take the five of us for walks and she dressed us so warmly, tying woollen hoods over our heads, that by the time the fifth was dressed and ready for an airing the first was nearly swooning, and either screamed hoarsely with resentment or choked in his padded coat and fur collar raised over the hood. As a result of this we always caught chills.[12]

Beneath the fur they were often dressed in Russian sailor suits, in compliment to Victor's Russian godfather who was an admiral; William possessed a miniature Highland costume, beautifully stitched in velvet and tartan, correct in every detail.

The exquisite pleasure of owning a small ice-cream cart on wheels with a real zinc tub filled with delectable Russian ice cream, and a special long zinc spoon with which to scoop out round balls of it, William never forgot. Likewise a tricycle converted by his brother into a miniature motor-car, and a pair of skis 'which, when the colour came off them, caused me to sob in the night and to feel, perhaps for the first time, that life was a mistake'.[13] All his life the whistle of a train and the smell of pine trees evoked happiness. He recalled with pleasure how as a small boy on Sunday mornings he had walked across the cobbles of the stable-yard to offer sugar-lumps to the horses; then to the cotton-mill where the work people turned round to whisper, 'That is the owner's son'. Charles took the older children to the first cinema in St Petersburg, after which they hurried home to explain to their small brother how strange men had moved jerkily, under continual heavy rain. With the advent of winter the children sailed in ice-yachts across a vast expanse of frozen water, and in December were taken to a big toy shop to shake hands with Father Christmas, who seemed grumpy and irritable. At home there was a Christmas tree, lighted electrically, which they were expected to enjoy, but found in fact that it was 'a torture'. 'Green grow the leaves . . .', sings Clara at the top of her voice, playing the piano and trying to get them to join in: '"What extraordinary, unnatural children. You *should* enjoy yourselves as everybody else!" we hear murmured around us by the grown-ups, who have presumably rigged this nuisance up for our benefit.'

But no experience compared with the rapture evoked by a certain fairy-tale of enchantments and changelings, about a young princess lost in a dark forest who was found by four little bears who played with her during the day and when night came offered her shelter with their father, the old bear, king of the underground kingdom.

They took her down through a hole in the earth, and she was never so surprised. The dark forest, leering trees, a damp hole . . . and suddenly mirrors and chandeliers, gilded chairs, immense lighted halls, and a warm welcome for her from the sad old king of the bears. . . . But on the day on which the little girl was to leave him and her playmates in the underground kingdom, where she had been so loved and so happy, it all came out. The old bear, when the moment of parting approached, broke down, and the little girl, overcoming her natural repulsion, embraced the old king and kissed his weeping old snout . . . and lo! the old bear became a handsome young prince, now free to tell her of his long plight as a bear, into which he was turned by a wicked fairy, a spell which nothing could break but the spontaneous kiss from a little girl like herself with whom henceforth he hoped to share his kingdom.[14]

'I am a changeling', William was heard to say late in life. A changeling in time, taken from the comfort of the past, thrust into the confusion and animosity of the present. And perhaps, too, a changeling in fact—pulled from the imaginative pleasure of fiction; for at 10 years old he fell in love with another fairy-tale heroine, the sombre-eyed, wicked, and thoroughly unmanageable, Eleanora. 'She was so wicked, but she had a heart of gold', and after she had nearly caused the hero to perish, 'the shock revealing how deep was her love for him, she improved beyond recognition; and they loved each other thoroughly after'.[15] 'To this day I have not recaptured the fragrant flower of that love.'

At 6 or 7 years old William visited England for the first time to spend the summer with Clara's parents, John and Sarah Wadsworth, who, now in their seventies, had retired to the little village of Bubwith in Yorkshire. From a quay in St Petersburg Charles waved goodbye to Clara, Liebe, and all five children on board the *Torneo*, a gleaming white boat which carried them across the Gulf of Finland, while they played together with a little boy named Harold. In Hanko they changed to the *Arcturus*, brown and gold and sailing to Copenhagen where William, filled with 'a strange sense of horror', watched a horse cruelly flogged by two men. Of England he later remembered only 'green country and buttercups and a merry-go-round', taking tea with the local schoolmaster, and 'the odd-looking half-crowns which, it was explained to me, were somewhat more than a rouble and bore the face of Edward VII instead of his nephew Nicholas II'.[16] Nearly sixty years later his sister Rosie nostalgically recalled the utter peace and quiet of the village, the old abbey, the little bridge, Victor's kite, and someone saying, 'Should I put the eggs on?' And when the children left, their grandparents gave them handfuls of sunflower seeds to take home and plant along the banks of the Neva.

Shortly afterwards Sarah died. Old Wadsworth, restless and distraught, found himself a prey to melancholy. 'Those who lived many years in Russia found contact with their own lands somehow severed. They never really fitted into Russian life, yet Russia held them, the restless spirit of the plains destroyed their peace and their own countries seemed tame and dull.'[17] He returned to his daughters in St Petersburg, spending his days quietly reading, always very helpful and a model of tact in domestic relations. William, from another room, listened for his strange laughter 'like the sound of distant crying'. As he got older he used to mutter: 'There are many people about who had better be gone.' He always said he would live till he was a hundred, 'but the death of a contemporary suddenly undermined his confidence and he sailed back to England so as to die and be buried in its soil'.[18]

Much of William's early childhood was spent with his younger sister, the dark-eyed Marguerite, always known as Daisy:

I used to delight in buying my young sister little presents. Little pencils and rubbers and note-books and other such things, which she took but found rather useless. I was, however, very fond of her. On one occasion on our removal to the country for the summer I drove a horse van into the yard laden with luggage and my sister climbed up on top and sat at my side. Owing to my skill in driving the van turned over at the gate with my sister beneath it, who, according to all physical laws, should have been killed. But she was completely unhurt. I expected to hear about it from my father. He, however, said never a word; we all dined at the seaside casino, and no reference was made to the incident.[19]

Together they played in a miniature 'villa' set in a little garden with lawns, paths, and a green painted fence, eating strawberries and ice cream and tending the flowers, next door to the 'villa' owned by their older siblings Victor and Dolly. William was impressed by the fact that Daisy would sit fearlessly on her father's knee and ruffle his hair, and remembered with a stab of jealousy how, when she fell ill, Charles sat by her bed enthusiastically describing to his 3-year-old daughter the excitement of Monte Carlo and Nice, where he planned to take her the following year. Eventually Daisy's weak lungs obliged her to attend school in Switzerland.

It was a blow, something I dreaded to think of. We had been taught to play four hands by our French governess—the last of a succession, old, round and small and not unlike Queen Victoria in looks. The last day before my sister went, we played that dreadful Suppé thing together, she at the treble, I at the bass, and the tears welled from our eyes. And in some way her going away for the first time marks the end of my childhood.[20]

With his sister Dolly (christened Dora), a year older than William, 'matter-of-fact and a good sort', he had little in common: 'Somehow we annoy each other, that's all.' She had blue eyes and red hair, and though a very thin child she later grew to resemble Clara in figure. Always a practical girl, they played at barbers together until she cut off all his hair and was punished for it. She was humorous, intelligent, and often critical of William. In his teens he felt himself despised by Dolly, who got on well with Victor. This in itself was enough to alienate William, whose relationship with his brother is eloquently summed up by a comment in a letter Victor wrote many years later to his mother: 'Much love to you and also why not to Willie (for whom I have no loathing but only brotherly love and pride).' The two boys often played together, but William was never able to forget the intense bullying that Victor chose to inflict upon him. Furthermore, Victor, and not he, commanded the approval of Charles and Clara. As adults the brothers frequently quarrelled, though their quarrels were (infrequently) punctuated by such exchanges as this (from Victor): 'I feel a certain personal pride in the great success which you have achieved, a kind of fatherly feeling, don't you know, with an admixture of a certain amount of brotherly deference into the bargain.'

Like his father, Victor possessed little imagination but great practical and technical ability. Both he and William despised the games of soldiering played by children of local army officers, and developed ingenious inventions in which William would contribute the ideas ('the construction of anything with my hands was entirely beyond my competence') and Victor the technical expertise. Once they made a sophisticated cotton mill with newspapers intricately cut and suspended, and wheels from a dismantled tricycle set in motion by a miniature electric motor working belts and pulleys, and using real bobbins and yarn from the real mill. 'I enjoyed the make-believe, the dream and atmosphere and imagination of being in turn the owner of this cotton mill, the proprietor of a theatre, the head of a school, the boss of a tailoring establishment, cutting immaculate tail-coats out of brown paper and selling stiff collars cut out of white cardboard. My brother did not care so much for the game itself, and his interest was exhausted with the invention.'[21]

From his earliest days William's mind was preoccupied with 'make-belief, dream and imagination'. While Marcel Proust, closeted alone in Paris, was beginning the work that years later would so entrance Gerhardie, William was reaching towards 'the appreciation that mortal life, perhaps all life, is lived in a world of illusion'; a world of memory, vision, misconception, anticipation, and desire. 'In regard to the power of hoarding up impressions', wrote Gerhardie's contemporary Vladimir Nabokov, 'Russian children of my generation passed through a period of genius, as if destiny were loyally trying what it could for them by giving them more than their share, in view of the cataclysm that was to remove completely the world they had known.'[22] Nabokov's Russian past remained such a vivid feature of his life that to him its 'robust reality' made 'a ghost of the present'.[23] 'If I had been born four years later, I wouldn't have written all those books.'[24] For both Nabokov and Gerhardie the disjunction of their eventual exile simply enforced the sense of enchantment. 'Do you know the white nights of Petersburg? Do you know their false, unreal, disturbing charm? Then it seems as if heaven were all lit and that the night was made for love', wrote William in his teens, remembering a sledge ride over the snow along the Neva on a starry night, hearing the gypsies sing. Yet like his mother he grew up with a desire for England, the unseen place, his imaginative paradise. He invented a pseudonym and wrote of himself not simply as 'Henry' but 'Henry Esbheornargist', a true Britisher, 'in spite of the delicate irony that clung to his name'.[25] Why he chose this curious name he never revealed, though in parodying the oddity of 'Gerhardi' it evokes espionage, infiltrators, strangers, changelings.

Even as a small child William was captivated by ambiguity and irony. The distinction between real and fictional was hazy, unimportant; the world of his mind, his impressions, was the real world: 'My own dreams have been used by me in my books always to prove, not that dreams were inconsequent, but rather that real life was as inconsequent as dreams.'[26] Early in his career he discarded linear narrative as an unsuitable method of composition:

I have never yet written my books in the ordinary way, from the beginning, by way of the middle, towards the end. . . . I write in little islands—all over the place. I write by indicating certain themes and I develop a paragraph here and there as the whole book gradually gets a firmer hold of my imagination. In this way no door is closed, no thought is shut off, but the whole book grows and extends in a natural way analogous to the normal creative imagination.[27]

And later, the narrative of his own life, his *Memoirs*, heedless of facts, became enmeshed with senses, sounds, associations:

But recently in a hotel at Sousse while spending an April holiday in Tunisia I was suddenly plunged into a sea of pure and reasonless joy by the sound of a small dog yapping, and on analysing the source of this joy identified it with a long forgotten feeling of a summer's day in childhood by a deep black river, resurrected in me because connected by invisible links of time to the little dog we had that far back summer and whose yapping was in the same key as that which now came from next door. In the morning a disturbing-looking young woman stopped me in the corridor. 'I hope my little dog has not troubled you by yapping in the night'. 'Oh, not at all, Madame,' I said with passionate eagerness. '*Vous êtes trop aimable!*' said she.[28]

That William grew up speaking four languages, familiar with the literature of four cultures, only served to compound his sense of indeterminacy. With their French governesses the children conversed (unwillingly) in French; with Liebe in fluent Reval German; amongst themselves and to the servants, always in Russian. Charles and Clara spoke to each other in English, and the odd words addressed to their children were also in English. William, self-conscious, answered 'in that queer tongue in a lame sort of fashion', but to talk English with his siblings would have seemed 'an unpardonable affectation'.

The self-absorbed dreams and fantasies of childhood, so vivid as he trudged home from school in the snow, created an egocentric world from which to escape his father and brother. 'Perhaps it is the subconscious belief of every man that the world is but a crescendo prelude to his own glorious advent', he wrote at an early age of himself and his own feelings of sublimity. Yearning for fame, achievement, and most of all acclaim he envisaged himself in a hundred dramatic roles, each encompassing an incredible intensity of emotion—in love, in anticipation, in self-fulfilment. The *future* was important, 'the present then was an irrelevance sorely out of tune with reality as I understood it; the hope alone was true',[29] he wrote at 39, recalling the St Petersburg ballroom, Clara singing, and 'waiting then, as now . . . waiting for life to begin'. In another image the young William stands by the frozen seashore contemplating the snow, the half-moon, the glaciers, the sun making shadows across the ice: 'Someday', he says to himself, intensely, mysteriously, 'Someday I will write it.' A desperate need to express his overflowing sense of his unique self informs all his childhood writings—and a terrible fear of the inadequacy of his attempts, of the evaporation of all his dreams into nothing more than unsatisfied longing. The suspicion that nothing, not even art, can ever match his feelings, makes oblivion a desperate alternative: 'To be perfectly dead—to think nothing and to feel nothing—is perhaps the most acceptable, merciful end for us all.' Despite the emotional, sometimes mawkish tone of Gerhardie's juvenilia, it shows a sophisticated objectivity and a narratorial irony that later characterized his best fiction. In another scene he envisages himself the author of *The Garden of Eden*, a musical work surpassing in brilliance anything by Skriabin, Rimsky-Korsakov, even Wagner:

Wildly waving a hair-brush and cutting indeed a strange figure in his striped and coloured pyjamas, there stood before the great looking-glass in his bedroom—a ridiculous sight—Henry Esbheornargist. For the brush was an old-fashioned brush with a long handle; and flushed and fluttered, forgetful of the world around him, with that instrument Henry conducted his 'work', knowing only that it was the work the world had always looked for and always missed. He went to bed a happy boy that night, conscious only of a small discrepancy that stood between this work and an eager public—a minor detail, a mere trifle. He had to acquire the art of writing musical compositions.

In all these fantasies it is the desire, the intense, unsatisfied longing that predominates—its object is almost incidental. 'No, the wanton, fiendish absence of a goal that might be at once finite and limitless was what disturbed him . . . [Henry] wanted to be first in everything'—in banking, mill owning, lawn tennis, in composing, conducting, writing ('He left painting to the others'). He wanted to be a famous architect, Ambassador to England, Minister of Foreign Affairs, own a fleet of ships, save the world . . . 'Oh, and still it's not enough, it's not enough.'

And in contrast to the fine savouring of his own existence was the *dread* of extinction: 'I resented the threat of death bitterly all through my childhood,'[30] wrote Gerhardie, for whom the loss of self became associated with the most profound nostalgia. In *Speak, Memory* Nabokov tells of

a young chronophobiac who experienced something like panic when looking for the first time at homemade movies that had been taken a few weeks before his birth. He saw a world that was practically unchanged—the same house, the same people—and then realized that he did not exist there at all and that nobody mourned his absence. . . . Such fancies are not foreign to young lives. . . . Nature expects a full-grown man to accept the two black voids, fore and aft, as stolidly as he accepts the extraordinary visions in between.[31]

It is something that Gerhardie would have understood. Yet death after life held an incomparable fascination for him, as another aspect of illusion, the unseen. Like desire it is something ungraspable, always out of reach. The tragi-comic aspects of death, corpses, graveyards, the half-alive and the nearly-dead, haunted and captivated him. Almost all of Gerhardie's juvenile novels contain deaths, almost always of young and lovely girls. For above all, death is identified with that yearning sense of overwhelming emotion:

When Eddie was a child he mused that his wife would leave him, that he would be left alone with his little daughter, and everybody would pity him. He mused of his wife's death, and of his following the coffin, and of everybody watching him—the great man in grief. In short the mental pictures were always of the great man in something to the great man's advantage.

Two years after William was born the mill was extended and, in the Russian fashion, blessed. Then Charles built a new house for his family; the children, pleasantly aware of the Gerhardi wealth, watched from their old house the construction of the new, rising upon steel girders on a desolate quay overlooking the Neva. The white house, green-roofed and decorative, festooned with fluttering pigeons, offered a bizarre and incongruous contrast to the adjoining mill, and the broad, fast-flowing, steel-grey river, congested night and day with timber barges. 'Through the half opened curtains he could see his father's mill with its many lighted windows like the eyes of some quivering monster', and, when all outside was quiet, it was just possible to hear the throbbing of the machinery. It was, William soon began to realize, a cruel contrast. 'The workpeople, where did *they* live? One didn't even inquire. A family to a corner of some dank room, somewhere, God knew where!'

An early childhood memory: 1905, and from the windows of his father's house William watched a team of mounted cossacks rallying in the mill yard, heard shooting in the streets, and crowds of workmen singing the forbidden 'Marseillaise'. Stones were thrown at the windows of the house, the mill machinery smashed by an infuriated mob—and Charles wheeled off in his sack to the Neva. William remembered his father's preoccupied face at breakfast the next day, and their hurried flight to Finland. Then, well away from danger, he caught threads of conversations with Clara and Liebe about massacres in the streets and the hiding of officers and policemen, of Black Sunday and other dreadful stories from his father who would now and then travel to St Petersburg and return late at night. And at last he heard of the ruthless suppression of the revolution; but he lay awake in the dark, believing that it was not suppressed and that it would break out again soon.

The house displayed an imaginative ornamented baroque façade, tall tower, wrought-iron balconies, caryatids, and silver weathercocks, facing the Botanical Gardens and the small house occupied by the Prime Minister Peter Stolypin, shortly to be murdered in the presence of his sovereign and the Imperial family whilst on an outing to the theatre. Within, above the red-carpeted, curving, white marble staircase of the entrance-hall, a coloured glass window, and the sumptuous high-ceilinged rooms lavishly and ornately furnished: the bronze and dull-green drawing-room with raspberry-red carpet, dark wallpaper, and the smell of oak; Italian tapestries with hunting scenes, a polar-bear rug in Clara's boudoir, a highly polished ballroom floor, and a sophisticated telephone system—'A dream palace as I now look back upon it', Clara wrote wistfully from a small house in Bolton, remembering that there had been fifty-three enormous windows one-and-a-half yards wide and two-and-a-half yards high, of finest quality bevelled plate glass, two panes set a yard apart to keep out the cold. All this was built as a symbol of permanance and stability. 'What a blessing that no one can forsee the future', she declared decades after dismantling piece by piece the home that had taken 'years and years to acquire and collect, and half a morning to empty'.

Inside the house, almost twice as deep as wide, the children had plenty of space of their own. In the wide, long corridor stood a yellow wooden hill with a little cart on wheels which ran down in the grooves, and an enormous hat-stand where William crouched pretending to be a bird. His nostalgic attachment to the home of his childhood never quite left him: 'To die is like leaving the old house in which one has lived since birth.' For much of his adult life, tried by his family yet bound to his family, he dreamed of schemes to re-create something of this world, where all might gather and live, harmonious and independent, beneath one roof.

This mansion absorbed the energy—and sometimes the good temper—of Clara who, ironically, dreamed of a small house in England. In Russia servants were cheap and very plentiful; in the mornings Clara would lie in bed and give orders to a housekeeper. Whilst Charles and Victor liked to leave their clothes and belongings where they had dropped, Clara respected servants. She also managed a chef and full kitchen staff, numerous maids, and two Tartar coachmen: Alexei, old, ill-shaped, and consumptive who smelled of leather and horses and who kept in his room four beautiful wives; and his fine-looking son who got off with the mill girls. Over the decade following William's birth, Charles 'piled on status-symbols': luxurious foreign travel, racing trotters, private carriage horses, and a variety of carriages—a barouche, brougham, landau, victoria, cabriolet, a droshky and two sleighs. Then a very daring innovation:

My father tries his first motor-car, procured at considerable expense from the United States. It has no steering-wheel, but a sort of handle and a bell instead of a horn. My father bids us sit at the back. We climb up, for the motor is about the height of a hansom cab, and we sit with our backs to him, doubled up, since the back of the seat in which he reclines is at a comfortable slope of some sixty degrees and ours accordingly at a reverse angle of thirty. My father, with great expenditure of nervous force, sets the motor puffing, and presently it sets off and runs along over the uneven frozen ground only to land in a bank of snow. We sit there perched behind him like frightened rabbits. My father wipes the snow off his pince-nez and, not knowing what to do with his irritation, applies it to the gears, with indifferent success. My father sends the car to us, at school, and we were terribly proud because it's the first motor to be seen in Petersburg. The motor shambles and bumps over the uneven cobblestones. My brother sits behind holding a bowl of gold-fish he had bought at a bazaar. The gold-fish get so shaken on their first and last motor ride that when we get home they are dead. My father for some time perseveres with the motor-car, but finds himself more and more stuck on the tram lines. The chauffeur in cleaning the engine chops off a finger. My father sells the motor-car and has to pension off the chauffeur for life.[32]

Sometimes at dinner William, watching his father struggling with his food, would look at him and think: 'the man is rich. Why then doesn't he fill all his cupboards with chocolates?'

'Socially we were not entangled—that is, we were looked up to by people we knew, while knowing nothing of any people who might have cared . . . to look down on us.'[33] Gerhardie's evasive account of his parents' status reflected a society where, unlike in England, it was not uncommon for clerks to associate with princes. The Gerhardis never took Russian nationality and scorned those of the English community who did. Where English society would have marked the family as *nouveau-riche* tradespeople, the Anglo-Russian had a status all his own, enjoying respect and friendship from Russians, although always aloof from politics. English nannies were particularly sought after by Russians, and Nabokov describes in his autobiography 'a traditional leaning toward the comfortable products of Anglo-Saxon civilization' that many Russians displayed: Pear's Soap, toothpaste, fruit-cakes, playing-cards, smelling-salts, Golden Syrup, and striped blazers, 'all sorts of snug, mellow things came in a steady procession from the English Shop on Nevski Avenue'.[34] The Anglo-Russian hierarchy, based primarily upon wealth and position rather than birth and education, ensured that the Gerhardis were prominent members of St Petersburg's large and prosperous British colony, maintaining a wide circle of polyglot acquaintances from a broad social spectrum—army officers, Embassy staff, students, bankers and businessmen, and English employees stationed in St Petersburg for fixed terms. English expatriates in Russia seemed rarely to conform to the stereotype, observed by Gerhardie in Hong Kong, of being 'far more *British* than any ordinary Britisher at home need feel'.

The eldest of the Gerhardi children, christened Rose Mabel after the hero of a novel begun by Charles in his youth, was five years older than William. As a small boy he saw her as his beautiful sister, always remote, 'dreamy and poetic and sensitive', with sad dark eyes and heavy hair. Her letters when adult are not unlike William's writings when young: full of passion and intensity, preoccupied with the emotive power of music and literature. As an old lady she described to William her 'unhappy nature' and frequent depression as a child when, believing that nobody understood her, she had wanted to be alone. She adored her father, and accompanied him abroad:

I well remember the places I visited as a young girl with dear papa—the lovely room he had taken for me at the hotel in Nice. A huge bouquet of roses—*Gloire de Dijon*—stood waiting on the table. It was a room for a young girl. The flowers, the view from the window, all was fairylike. He took me to Monte Carlo, then to a restaurant on the Corniche poised on a rock hanging right over the sea. The road of chalk was dazzling white, the olive trees dark green and shady against the radiant sun. I remember it all still. I suppose he felt a little proud of me. He called me 'my white rose'. Well—then I *was* rather pretty, and he wanted to show me all the places he had been happy in. I suppose papa was really in his ways and, to the marrow of his bones, '*grand seigneur*'. His temper, alas, often spoilt his best intentions. But to me he remains a man who was never mean, never close, though he was the one provider for an enormous clan, all with numerous dependants. He loved me.[35]

Though uncomfortable with family life, Charles was proud of his daughters. Victor he tolerated because Victor, quick, sharp, and capable, fitted in unobtrusively. Rosie attributed Victor's hostility towards herself in later life to jealousy of these prosperous years of her youth.

William described the family as 'elaborately, though somewhat superficially educated'. Rosie wrote: 'It was Mama who gave us our education really tho' poor Papa provided for us, but it was dear Mama's wish to see us well equipped for life. My knowledge of 3 foreign languages has enabled me to keep the pot boiling for over 30 years!' All three girls were, at first, taught by governesses: William remembered a hated French 'Mademoiselle' who insisted he make his request for the butter in French, yet would never herself ask for anything at table, but crawl over sideways, reaching with half her body as the children watched, silent and hostile. Later Rosie, Dolly, and Daisy attended a girls' academy, followed by a Swiss finishing school. It was an education typical for girls of their class, inadequate but probably rather better than most English equivalents. Dolly, who earned the distinction of a gold medal for academic achievement, often argued with her brother on political issues and—to his intense annoyance—criticized his work.

The boys were sent first to a preparatory school run by an elderly Baltic lady, Fräulein Kaiser. 'Had it rested with my father', wrote Gerhardie, 'we might have never been sent to school at all. He didn't believe in schools—probably thought there was a snag in it.'[36] (Many years later Clara told one of her grandchildren that she had wanted to go to Cambridge, but that Charles had scorned the idea of her becoming a blue-stocking.) The brothers would travel by horse-drawn tram through the snowy streets, past the coloured Petersburg palaces, dressed in lace-up boots and knee-length knickerbockers: 'Macaroni legs!' the urchins called after them. Often William feigned illness. Clara tended to be gently sympathetic, Charles not so: 'My father, who did not believe in schools, also did not believe in staying away from them.'[37]

Whilst Charles took no interest in education he was once shamed by an English friend whose son had been to Harrow into sending for Victor and demanding abruptly whether he wished to attend public school. Victor, who had read *Tom Brown's Schooldays*, was appalled, and the matter was never raised again. William conceded that he too would probably have been miserable at such a place, but nevertheless deeply resented not having been consulted. Instead, at 11 or 12, he was sent to the Annenschule, an establishment belonging to the Lutheran corporation in St Petersburg and, unlike most Russian schools, not run by the state. In a system that closely mirrored the German, the *Realschule* emphasized mathematics and the natural sciences, at which William proved 'a complete dunce'. Discipline was strict and teaching, usually to a high standard, conducted partly in Russian, partly in German. English was not begun until the fourth year, when it was taught by an Englishman born and nurtured in Russia; and Latin and Greek were not taught at all.

William hated school. 'When I was eleven—*already* eleven!—I felt ashamed of my age. Nothing done—no promise shown, and already eleven.' The Russian boys would invite him to say a few words in English, and then, laughing hysterically, tell him that it sounded as if he had hot potatoes in his mouth. One master, Herr Hauberg, made William the object of his Anglophobia. In the geography class Herr Hauberg, sarcastic about the dimensions of the British Empire (and to William's mind secretly envious), liked to point at the red-marked portions of the map:

'England,' he would say with a sly, side-look at Henry [William], 'is a wily land. She knows the art of helping herself. She does it in an off-hand manner, quietly, without a sound. There is Africa. A fine big country, rich in gold and minerals in the south. "Hm," says England, "I think I'll have this slice. I'll take—all this."' And Herr Hauberg would make a grabbing movement with his hands as if of a thief in the night carrying off South Africa.

'"Then there's America. Not a bad country, you know. What about half of that?" . . .' And he stole Canada.

'"India. Oh, the road to Russia. *Certainly*!"' And Herr Hauberg looked maliciously at Henry, and then invitingly at the Russian boys. And the Russian boys stared at Henry, suspicious and wrathful, and contemplated revenge.

And Hauberg continued until he had disposed of the whole of the British Empire. 'Henry felt that he had to suffer "for his country". Never before did he feel so ultra patriotic.' Yet Gerhardie, arriving at last happily and expectantly in England in 1913, found himself regarded with suspicion as a foreigner. And to William's bewilderment Herr Hauberg regarded him as an authority on England and all things English. One day he pointed to the capital of the United States and enquired of William how it was pronounced:

'*Wedgington*', chanced Henry, whose knowledge of English, history and geography was at that time superbly remote.

'*So*,' said Herr Hauberg, and proceeded: 'The capital of the United States of North America is Wedgington—' He looked at Henry. 'Wedgington? Have I got it right?'

'Yes, quite right,' said Henry.

If challenged as to this pronunciation Hauberg would insist that he had it on the best authority. 'If Herr Hauberg has survived the famine, the pestulence and the Red Terror of Petrograd', William later reflected, 'he must be still insisting on the *correct* pronunciation of the American capital.'

One day the Russian master strode into the classroom and told the boys that today he would not teach. Tolstoy was dead, 'a man towering above his fellow men, a great genius of the human spirit who had lived in their midst and survived, an almost legendary figure, into their own decade'. There would be no Russian literature lesson that afternoon.[38] The education system as a whole bore little resemblance to the English. Pupils came from a wide variety of social types; corporal punishment was forbidden by law and considered a humiliation; nor was there any physical education, and little team spirit. Russian boys tended to despise games as childish, interesting themselves instead in literature, art, music, and (very often) politics. Maurice Baring, who spent years in Russia around this time, considered Englishmen to be 'intellectually immature' but none the less 'nearer to reality and practical life . . . than the intellectually overripe Russian', whose education tended to be intensive in one direction but incomplete in another.[39] William's school career was not a success: he lacked concentration, lacked punctuality, and lacked the art of doing well in examinations.

The religious education of the Gerhardi children was traditionally Anglican, though perfunctory, and church attendance at Christmas and Easter more a social than a religious function. All were baptized and all—with the exception of William, who was by then on his way to London—confirmed. Each week Liebe escorted them in an open victoria to the Mission Hall Sunday School, admonishing the coachman: 'In the name of heaven drive carefully!' Clara throughout her life derived comfort from (perhaps vague) Christian beliefs: 'Not more than others I deserve yet God has given me more', she was fond of intoning. Charles thought religious observance a lot of nonsense.

The family shared a love of music, and Clara, believing it to be a vital part of any child's education, arranged first piano lessons at home, then twice-weekly lessons at a music school where William was taught by a pupil of Rimsky-Korsakov. The family would often assemble in the ballroom, Dolly playing the piano, Victor the violin, William the mandolin, and Daisy the cello, with Clara singing in a lusty voice. And the hall would ring with Caruso's fine renditions of Italian opera, shaky and indistinct on Charles's wind-up gramophone. A visitor once arrived at the house and, making her way to the children's own sitting-room upstairs, was astonished—and slightly horrified—to see William, Dolly, and others marching madly, unsmilingly, and (as it seemed to her) fanatically up and down conducting to the deafening sounds of Wagner. Early in life William learned to associate music with all his violent inarticulate emotion: 'Romance in music is much more real than romance in life. It is pure romance. One really cannot kiss a woman without cutting a ridiculous figure of oneself.' He loved the grandiose seaside concerts of the Czech conductor Josef Suk, son-in-law of

Dvořák, and as a small boy attended not only the daily performances but the rehearsals as well. On the last day of the season he would watch Suk's unforgettable *Tannhäuser* overture, his violent gesticulations, fists and long grey locks shaking, until, on the last note, admirers advanced to the platform bearing shoulder-high an armchair, and in this manner carried off the conductor, to tumultuous applause.

After attending a production of *Faust*, Victor built a tiny opera house: 'This miniature theatre made me conceive a new "Faust" which was to be superior to Gounod's; but wasn't.'[40] After a memorable French play at the Théâtre Michel William was inspired to write drama. Victor duly constructed a 'real' theatre with real footlights, 'but instead of producing a work from my own pen we fell back on Gogol's *Inspector-General*'.[41] There were also frequent visits to the Imperial Ballet (Clara subscribed to standing stalls) and frequent squabbles over who was to go to what and with whom. Victor: 'I don't want to go with Willy.' William: 'And I don't want to go with Victor.'

Just as most well-off Russians passed the summer by the sea or in the country, so at the end of the school year the Gerhardis would pack up and remove to a dacha, first at Terijoki on the Finnish coast, later at the Russian seaside town of Sestroretsk. As a special treat on the first evening, and in order to spare the servants who had not had time to unpack, Charles would take the family to the huge casino restaurant overlooking the sea. William vividly remembered the sunset which lit the table silver, the large unwieldy hard-starched napkins, and the smell of turf, sea, and sand. At the seaside the children had set hours when the hated Mademoiselle would take them for walks to the pine woods, where they sat on a bench and she read aloud in French. At the dacha Charles occupied a small veranda with an armchair and a little table for his coffee and cigarettes. Every morning, dressed in a light grey suit, he would stroll to the hydropathic establishment.

But, ill at ease with the family, Charles preferred the Riviera and would pay only fleeting visits to Sestroretsk before departing to Monte Carlo. There he spent the day at the gaming tables (mostly losing), then retired to his hotel where telegrams would be pushed under his door announcing the movement of shares, or the weather in Egypt with reference to cotton. Sometimes he sent the children baskets of tangerines with the leaves still on them. William, briefly free of the father who intimidated and 'constrained' him, remembered a happy time boating, bathing in streams and in the sea, playing tennis, and, most pleasurable of all, ambling every evening down to the concert hall, whence the music poured out across the sea. 'I cannot work unless I am by the sea', he later wrote, confined in a London flat. At the end of the summer, when the family returned to St Petersburg, the house would have had a brand new coat of white paint.

Such diversions did much to mitigate an increasingly unhappy adolescence, for the older he grew, the more William seemed to disappoint and irritate his father. He was not efficient or useful, on shopping expeditions with Clara he proved more of a hindrance than a help, and when he was sent to find something he came back empty-handed. Small and young for his age, dreamy and rather delicate, he often wore a vague, absent expression ('except when his own affairs are being discussed'), preoccupied by his plans for the future, observant of fine shades of feeling. 'Pure life was of little avail for him; it was in the vibrations and emotions that he lived. He might have been called a dreamer. But if so, was not dreaming the real aim of life for the artist?' Now, with greater independence, he roamed the Russian streets. Easter eve and the advent of Spring: 'I return home from a shop where I had bought an electric torch. The big, stupendous world enshrouds me. The ice is breaking on the Neva. A languid warmth sets in. The stars in heaven shine through the dark.'

At Sestroretsk, where Victor and William shared a bedroom, Victor lingeringly tormented his brother by repeating Mama and Papa's damning and dismissive remarks, describing him as the idiot of the family and despairing of his ever succeeding. 'At bottom this did not distress me because I knew it was not true', Gerhardie wrote confidently in his autobiography, at the period of his greatest achievement. But a dramatized account seventeen years later when again William regarded himself as a failure gives a truer picture: his dramatic persona, 'Jamie Wadsworth', learns that Papa has told Mama he is a fool, and having previously displayed 'a good deal of undergraduate cynicism and superiority' is 'suddenly young, vulnerable, and desperately hurt', anxious above all to know his beloved *mother's* opinion: 'What did *she* say? . . . What did she say about me? . . . [insistently] Please tell me exactly what Papa said. And exactly what Mama replied.' Increasingly agitated, he asks his mother direct. She declines to answer.[42]

As his family's scorn grew more apparent so did William's self-absorption. In contrast to his intensely private passions and dreams he began to cultivate a studied aloofness, an ironic egocentricity, which his little sister found very comical. 'Please tell Daisy I am now still more conceited', William would add to letters home. Literature, both as consolation and inspiration during the 'detested years' of adolescence, occupied more and more of his time: Goethe ('always a hero to me'), Turgenev, Apukhtin, replaced the imaginative games of before and invoked a 'frustrated desire for Russian life existing all around and apart from the isolation of our home life at that time'.[43] At 14 he read Tolstoy and thereafter decided to write. He began with an autobiography, comprehensively entitled *Joys and Sorrows*, chiefly in Russian, which was kept hidden from other members of the family. But Clara noticed him scribbling and later rummaged through his piles of paper. Then, betrayed by Daisy, she hastily defended her action by saying she was afraid that he had become involved in a subversive movement.

From now on William was writing regularly, often simply ideas and observations jotted down: 'To seek meaning, conclusions is to limit one's mind and an absolute error for certain.' He also wrote fictional scenes, strongly autobiographical. One interesting fragment suggests that, despite the fear of his father, he felt a delicate sympathy for, even identification with, the man whom he saw as essentially tired and lonely, remote and out of tune with the rest of the family:

The little girl lay her pale pale face with black hair on the pillow and smiled. 'Yes papa,' she said. He smiled. So nice after the quarrel with Mary. So nice it was now for him together with the little girl, who, he thought, alone loved, who alone understood him, who was not afraid of him. She was the only one he felt who liked his presence. To the others his presence was always tedious, uncomfortable. They pretended to be pleased, pretended to amuse him but he and they themselves felt it was false.

Adolescent love contributed to William's unease. At 15 he became enamoured of a Jewish girl of 16, enraptured by features which appeared to resemble those of a Spanish noblewoman. The beginnings of a novel followed from it: 'Henry' falls in love with a girl in a blue jersey whom he sees whilst playing tennis at the club. He describes the suspense of hearing the click of the gate as she comes on to the court, accompanied by two friends, and the agony of feeling her eyes upon him as she watches him play—apparently quite indifferent herself. At dinner his father begins to talk of the new club members and Henry, 'with his heart beeting itself to death, waited for further revelations'. He dares not ask, but after lying in bed thinking of her he goes into his sisters' room and under threat of a ruthless splash of cold water demands information, feigning indifference. 'But in his heart he knew that he was in love, hopelessly, relentlessly, to the extent of stupefaction, to a degree of madness . . .'

His rival, a Jewish boy of 17, possessed what William most desired—dark hair and an exquisitely pale complexion. So he took himself off to a ladies' *salon de beauté* where, to the stifled giggles of the assistants, his face was given a pale, matt surface by the application of a patent lotion from a bottle. But the mask, less realistic in daylight, cracked when he smiled.

My love had not been furthered by the application of the lotion, and the girl continued to treat me as a child. Everything she said to me—were it only 'How is your sister?'—seemed fraught with secret significance. She was a messenger of the mystery of life. Meeting her one winter day at the Yacht Club in Petersburg, and mentioning, in timidity and for want of something better to say, a common acquaintance about whom I offered an opinion, she reinforced her own by adding: 'I always go by first impressions.' This stuck in my mind as an example of unparalleled profundity.[44]

Always susceptible to infatuation, William would pace the street in which she lived, day after day, for hours on end, hoping to catch a glimpse of her. Once or twice she consented to drive in a carriage up and down the Palace Quay with William at the reins. She inspired him to write Russian poetry, 'musical and elegiac, with notes in it reminiscent of Pushkin, Lermontov and Apukhtin':[45]

> (In memory of Wednesday 9th January 1913)
>
> Why did I see you once again?
> Why did you rouse a bygone passion in me—
> And poison my happiness, my peace, my sleep.
> Why did I fall in love with you again?
>
> I saw you and my restless soul stood still,
> I saw your longed-for, haunting image—
> Pensive, enchanting, kind and tender,
> So dear to me, so eternally precious!
>
> And my heart went flutter in expectancy
> Of welcoming dear words from you,
> I wanted to speak, I languished in silence
> But it was too late: you were hid from my view.
>
> Sepulchral coldness suddenly o'erwhelmed me
> And I understood how passionately, how madly I loved you;
> Come to me, come! Life for me without you is sheer torment
> Speak but one word! Come if only for a moment![46]

Rosie meanwhile was attracting a large number of men, and two or three times a season the Gerhardis gave a ball. The house was taken over by the *maître d'hôtel* of Charles's club together with a host of retainers, and after supper a Master of Ceremonies from the Imperial Ballet supervised the dancing. Charles would sit and watch, playing cards, while Clara gleefully danced everybody under the table. Rosie was courted by an Imperial equerry of cuirassiers, Monsieur Volynsky, a dashing individual with a magnificent uniform, silver helmet, and fine moustache. When Volynsky died of consumption Rosie fell in love with Leonid Misernuik, romantically good-looking and a fine dancer and sportsman. Leonya, then a student, seemed to Charles unpractical and without ambition, an inadequate match for his daughter whom he told to wait three years before marrying. Rosie, heartbroken, never forgot William's comforting words, consoling her with the reflection that in thirty years time it would be immaterial to her whether she had married him then or at any other time. This was typical Gerhardie advice, for though prone throughout his life to affairs of the heart, he could be immensely practical. In 1912 she eventually married Leonya, where-upon Charles bought her a flat and carriage, and sent them on a honeymoon to Paris. In 1914 his first grandchild, Tamara, was born.

Victor and Dolly, patriotic, conservative, and anti-Semitic, were staunch supporters of the British club and colony. Both were excellent tennis players and Victor a skilful rider. William put in an occasional appearance at the tennis club dressed in immaculate white flannels; he once won a leather dressing-case presented by the Austrian Ambassador, who soon after played a not inconsiderable part in causing the First World War. But he found his siblings' friends uncongenial and nurtured a more aesthetic regard for his mother country, looking to England as a place where he might flourish without the constraints of his family. This, too, was partly practical:

Vigorous as was the appeal of the Russian background Henry had to tell himself that interested as he be in all things Russian they were still things in which he could have but little concern as he would have, as a British subject, no voice ever in the management of the country.

When William's infatuation for the Jewish girl was supplemented by a further passion, for Alice, his school work began to suffer. With Clara's sympathetic influence he was moved to the Schule der Reformierten Gemeinden, where he brought his studies to an adequate 'if far from brilliant' conclusion. Now William was summoned to his father's study to discuss his future. At first Charles delivered a lecture to his son, warning him of the dangers of youth, love, and passion, with 'that slow and quiet and somewhat timid, though determined, way he had of speaking, of suggesting rather than advising; (his suggestions though, Henry felt, could be more compelling than an order)'. William, finding it secretly funny, wondered if he had rehearsed this monologue. Then Charles 'after having made up his own mind on the subject' asked what his son intended to become, making it clear that, 'according to the good old English tradition', Victor the eldest was to inherit. William on the other hand held secretly to 'the good old Russian custom' of property equally divided.

William would have liked to go to university, but Charles, after racking his brains, had decided to make a niche on the commercial side of the family firm, and now revealed his plans to his son. For a moment William hesitated: he had often watched his father lying on a sofa near the great window overlooking the mill-yard, with its perpetual noise and suggestion of work, usefulness, and efficiency. Now he envisaged *himself* on the sofa, only more grave and solemn, playing the heavy father with *his* son, 'but perhaps his language more fragmentary, a sort of Asquithian style, speaking in loftily ponderous sentences magnificently framed. The picture that his parent had drawn to him was not without artistic appeal. He perceived himself as a sort of financial and industrial magnet, commanding the resources of the earth.' All this in spite of the great works of literature that he was to write. But the vision faded to reality: commerce! William determined to stick to his original ambitions; instead of opposing the intentions of his parents he adopted a pacifist policy, circumventing and evading, and somehow secretarial college in England was suggested. Hurriedly Charles dashed off some letters. 'This done, Mr Esbheornargist felt confident that he had discharged his parental duties and for the rest of the afternoon he lay on his sofa smoking cigarettes, pleasingly conscious of his excellent qualities of a parent. His valediction over he also reverted to his normal temper and at dinner that night, as a matter of course, terrorized the whole house into panic and submission.'

Victor had been delegated to industry, and bitterly resented it. When he told his father that he wanted to become a surgeon, Charles replied, 'Who do you think is going to run the mill?' And so after leaving school Victor had taken a course in cotton spinning and weaving at Manchester College of Science and Technology, followed by six months' practical experience in Chorley. These were disagreeable times, mitigated only by weekend visits to nearby friends who kept horses. He returned to work as assistant manager at the Gerhardi mill, a post he occupied at the outbreak of the Revolution.

When the brochures arrived, William was allowed to choose his own school. Grandpapa Wadsworth, liberal with advice, read aloud with great relish excerpts from *Pitman's Commercial Correspondence Course*. He thought his grandson should become a banker, or at least marry a rich bride. His own thrifty ways had over the years impressed themselves upon William: 'One of the sentimental illusions', he wrote, 'is that people of artistic temperament are very careless about money. I hope to dispel that illusion.'

Before leaving, he wandered ecstatically around St Petersburg, visiting museums as if for the last time, and taking photographs with a new camera. One day, crossing the Palace Square, he glimpsed the Emperor of Russia at the window of a carriage, all alone, looking through the glass like 'a hot house plant, a wax figure'.

At last, with a new globe-trotting trunk and a lot of expensive linen and clothes, William set off for London. He carried a dark-red, marbled exercise book containing his Russian poems and a Russian prose work, begun at Sestroretsk that summer and simply entitled 'Novel', and a small notebook carefully inscribed with a table of English weights and money to assist him in his new life abroad:

> A farthing, the coin of least value.
> Twelve pennies, one shilling.
> Twenty shillings, one pound.

3

ENGLAND

September 1913–January 1917

*No one wanted the war, no one with the exception of a score of imbeciles,
and suddenly all those who did not want a war turned imbecile and
obeyed the score of imbeciles who had made it.*[1]

Clara and Daisy travelled with William, by train through the Polish
potato fields and German vineyards until, at dead of night, they saw the
lights of Montreux. In the morning William was awoken by the sound of
spitting, and opened the curtains and looked for the first time in his life
upon the mountains. After depositing Daisy at a Swiss finishing school,
he and Clara continued to France. William, engulfed by 'the romance,
the splendour and shabbiness' of Paris, practised his French conversation with an eager prostitute but, with Clara round the corner, resisted
her advances. Besides, his desires lay elsewhere, across the Channel.
And now the long-awaited approach to London 'with its rows of thin,
soot-covered, dingy, incredibly ignoble houses turning their pipes and
backyards on you as you whirled into the greatest of metropolises,
amazed me, astonished my soul'.[2] As their cab horse slithered out of
Charing Cross Station into the Strand William, accustomed to the
'wide, cold, sprung, elegantly poised' St Petersburg, sensed London
'heavy, narrow and growling', 'so heavy that the streets, it seemed,
crumpled under its weight into little hills and valleys', the streets and
trees higgledy-piggledy, and the endless teeming faces 'oscillating with
life'.

Clara did not stay long after having deposited her son in lodgings with
a retired army captain and his wife. He, stalwart of the Empire, talked of
Britain's glorious history, assuring William that England was not Russia,
that here we were free, so free that 'you could go up to any soldier on
guard outside Buckingham Palace and say to him what you liked about
the King, and his smile would imply that it was a matter of opinion'.[3]
Each evening they dressed for dinner and sat long and quiet over their

coffee, which dreary inoffensiveness inspired William to (Russian) poetry:

> *Extempore*
>
> The devil take it! This dump makes me spew.
> O to escape to other places—
> Where I won't see this house, these walls,
> Or these boring damned faces![4]

And he did escape to other places. He paced the streets at night, Finsbury Pavement 'hollow, forlorn' on a rainy Sunday evening, 'Such a spirit world, wasn't it?' A procuress brought him his first, peroxide blonde lover, a crucial encounter only obliquely referred to in his diary. By day he roamed the sprucer regions—Chelsea Embankment, Piccadilly, Pall Mall—pacing the London parks hour upon hour, and after a visit to the National Gallery inspired to more poetry:

> O do not weep, do not sob so insanely, Madonna!
> Though your sorrow is deep and bottomless,
> Understand: He has sacrificed all for others,
> And to Your supplications stayed dumb.
> Life and happiness, all He has given to them!
> But You, sacrifice to them Your Son![5]

Lingering to hear street-corner debates that were so strange after the charged, repressed air of Russia, he admired the casualness of the English towards ideological issues, savoured 'the exquisite joy of being a living representation of a living nation'. And bearing in mind that night would soon follow, he accosted girls in the street, beseeching them to accompany him to the cinema, 'girls who, though they were not prepared to travel the whole length in love, did not disdain the joy of going as far as they decently could without inviting disaster; unlike their sisters of the Continent with whom it was either the kiss complete or no kiss at all. Yes, I admired the national spirit of compromise.'[6]

At Kensington College Gerhardie began his commercial training. The brochure extolled a well-equipped model office and a 'Special Secretarial City Course for the Sons and Daughters of Gentlemen', particularly popular with clergymen's daughters. But he did not take to the director James Munford (nicknamed Mr Bumphill), whose naturally sly face belied the solid front of Edwardian respectability. The discomfiture was mutual, for Gerhardie began by questioning, in the most agreeable manner possible, whether the college—simply a large house with a garden—could truthfully be said to 'stand in its own grounds' as the brochure advertised. Then he thoroughly affronted the director by publishing in the college magazine an article defending (in certain circumstances) the telling of a lie—an outrageous 'philosophy' said Bumphill. 'Your personality has been a great problem to me for a long time. Opinions about you have been warring in my mind, and I feel sure there is like conflict in yours', he wrote three years later whilst informing his ex-pupil, with considerable pride, of the death in battle of seven college members. 'We look forward to that glorious day when we shall all attend that great Muster in the eternal Realms beyond.'

At Christmas William returned to St Petersburg, terrified to admit that he had lost his train ticket and borrowed money from a friend. Charles, languishing on a sofa with a cigarette, inhaled, puffed out the smoke, and said gently: 'It's experience.'

In January he travelled back to London. Twenty-one years later an unknown woman recognized his photograph in the newspaper and wrote telling how she too had been crossing the Channel that day in January, a young and timid French girl leaving home for the first time in order to attend her own wedding the very next day. She had sat quietly on board the empty Calais-to-Dover boat, opposite two ladies dressed in black who looked like sisters. They did not speak but the label on their trunks read 'Tolstoy'. Then a young man approached them, 'very fair and very pale' in a dark overcoat and new red-brown leather gloves. 'He looked English—yet not quite. It was perhaps his clothes which were un-English.' He spoke in Russian to the sisters, but never once looked her way. 'You looked very shy and yet faintly rougish about the eyes.'[7]

To his parents' annoyance Gerhardie's 'abject' English had improved but little. Now, despite uncomfortable recollections of English literature—as a 10-year-old he had, with great difficulty, ploughed through Mrs Craik's *John Halifax, Gentleman* ('I thought John Halifax a great bore')—he picked up Oscar Wilde's *The Picture of Dorian Gray*. 'Something remarkable happened to me then.' Wilde wrote 'exquisitely', and his 'Aesthetic Credo' seemed to coincide with all Gerhardie's beliefs. From Wilde he moved to Shaw, 'incisive and deliberate', then Bennett and Wells, and, emboldened with this new sophistication, gradually began the transition from writing in Russian to writing in English. Later, when he had learned to express himself with effortless delicacy, he recalled his clumsy early attempts and love of long words:

When I could bring out a 'nevertheless' or a 'notwithstanding' I felt instinctively that my command of their language was now such as to allow me to use it like a master ... If a sentence balanced nicely and came down with the awaited emphasis on the last word I deemed it in itself a reason for inclusion. I caressed words like a sculptor, remembered them, used them for their own sake, transposed them indefinitely.[8]

He decided he would be the first person to compose fiction in two languages, and embarked upon *The Guilty Without Guilt*,[9] a fictional work bearing an epigraph from Mme De Staël's *'Corinne*—'To understand is to forgive.' From the fragments that exist it is clear that Gerhardie saw himself as an arbitrator between the two worlds:

Russia was an amazing country, as the Russian people were amazing people. Russia is, always has been, and always will be in a muddle, just as any good Russian. This is a natural state for a Russian to be in. A Russian is not happy unless he is suffering. When he is not suffering he is upset. In other words, if a Russian can't be upset . . . he is upset.

In another scenario a young musician paces the streets of Berlin, so famous that he is in fact wearied by fame, but drawing inspiration from his solitude amongst the crowds. Many scenes are written in a female persona, as 'Nicky', 'Daphne', or 'Julia', dealing in some way with family life, though with fathers and brothers conspicuously absent. Except perhaps for an inclination for death scenes, these passionate, rather feminine adolescent musings have nothing in common with Gerhardie's published novels.

The school year drew to a close. Shortly after William had successfully completed an examination in Elementary Pitman's Shorthand, Archduke Franz Ferdinand of Austria was arranging a military tour of inspection in Bosnia, a small and recent acquisition of the Habsburg Empire. On 28 June 1914 he and his wife Sophie set out in an open car for the capital of Bosnia, called Sarajevo, and here both were killed, shot by a 15-year-old assassin.

For thirty-three days the European powers deliberated, bluffed, miscalculated, and began to mobilize. For Gerhardie, now on his way back to St Petersburg, these off-stage sound effects were quite drowned out by fear of his father, for his college report was mediocre, and a £20 cheque had been stolen by a German waiter. Charles, however, was laid up with a sprained ankle, too preoccupied with his own business problems to take notice of his son. There was a wave of almost tropical heat, with thunder threatening, and forest fires raged in Finland and the surrounding districts, making the air smoky and unfamiliar. The family retired for their annual holiday to Sestroretsk, the last they would ever spend together.

The world war that followed upon the assassination at Sarajevo, in which more than eight million were to lose their lives, began officially in August with Germany's declaration of war upon Russia. Gerhardie described the mood in St Petersburg:

As if at a signal, all the local worthies became patriotic, and marched in processions, united by a feeling that all the shortcomings inherent in the scheme of things, which had hitherto prevented them from being happy, were due to a malignant cancer, now to be eradicated, a cancer which—the newspapers left no room for doubt—was the Empire of Germany. Patriotic wrath was unanimous.[10]

The Russians took it for granted that England would at once join forces against Germany. But for three long days she waited uncommitted. Crowds, angry and perplexed, gathered outside the British Embassy in St Petersburg, cheering, praying, and pressurizing, threatening perhaps a storming of the building. On 3 August the Germans marched into Belgium; the following day Britain declared war upon Germany. At once the English grew more popular than ever in Russia, but it was unwelcome news for Gerhardie who, prevented from travelling back to London, was placed instead as a clerk in his father's head office. These were not happy months: 'I felt I was crowded out and somehow ignored by my father.' The commercial training had not borne fruit. English spelling in particular he found a great tribulation ('it is always a wonder to me why I is rendered in one single letter, why it is not spelt Igh') and even into his twenties he wrote

	instead of	
wheat		wet
uncontious		unconscious
d'ont		don't
habbit		habit
studdy		study
ceized		seized
seize		size
loiterd		loitered

On top of which Charles's impatient mental arithmetic demands —'How much is twenty-seven times twenty-three?'—only flustered an already agitated William. Charles did not mean to be unkind, he simply could not understand why his son could not understand. Once he employed William as his private secretary—an experiment that was not repeated. On another occasion he demanded: 'Today is the 8th of January. How many days till the 9th April?'

'May I look at the calèndar?' asked William, stressing the middle syllable of a word he had never heard uttered in English.

'Calèndar! Calèndar!' shrieked his father savagely in exasperation. 'Oh my God! What have I done to have begotten such a fool of a son!'[11]

But towards Clara William was growing closer. Returning from the office each evening he would sit upon her bed and tell humorous stories of the office people, or read aloud from Chekhov, Gogol, and Dickens, and the adventures of Daudet's comic hero *Tartarin of Tarascon*. To Clara he was 'the dear little man who used to come and sit on my bed-side and we would talk and laugh the hours away'. Charles rarely laughed or even smiled, except on the rare occasions when he would relate an old anecdote of his own; then he laughed so much that though his family had heard the same story many times before, the end remained tantalizingly unknown to them. One, told to Charles by his own father, was especially familiar; a man was training his donkey to eat less and less so that by degrees it would require no food at all; and he had very nearly accomplished his aim when, to his bitter disappointment, the donkey died. Charles, convulsed with mirth, habitually ended his recital in a fit of violent coughing.

In his father's office, scribbling on his lap, William wrote his earliest completed literary work in English, a long play ('like Andreyev, only much worse', as he later described it) completed in February 1915 after four months' work. *The Haunting Roubles* is the story of a handsome Russian, Prince Dmitry Pavlovich Ligin, who,

compelled by his rapacious relatives to marry the daughter of a wealthy merchant, curses his fate and his wife, who he believes has only married him for his title. The idea haunts him and prevents him from confessing his love for her, till, in the last act, she confesses to him that she had been kept back from avowing her love for him by the haunting thought that he had only married her for her money. . . . When their mutual error is discovered there is no further bar or limit to their love and happiness and, as I hoped, the ecstatic tears of the audience.[12]

Gerhardie's own plot summary gives but a modest sense of the play's complexity, humour, vivid Russian atmosphere, and skilful manipulation of its twenty-one characters. As a deliberate and by no means unsuccessful attempt to amalgamate different dramatic forms—the comic, social, farcical, tragic, intellectual, realistic, and romantic—into one work, 'without making the same too meaningless or grotesque', it represents Gerhardie's earliest example of what was to be a lifelong preoccupation.

With *The Haunting Roubles* complete, William was even more determined to return to England, now possible by an elaborate alternative route. Eventually, reluctantly, Charles agreed to resumption of the secretarial school and arranged a family farewell at the station. This was the last time that William ever saw his father on his feet and, in a sense, the very end of their stormy, difficult relationship. As the train pulled out they waved, with vacant faces 'as if they were at a loss to account for my journey to England and, as I thought, for my existence in the world'.[13]

From a Bayswater hotel he settled back to observe the English and —when he remembered—attend the college. Fellow residents, he noticed, held sinister attitudes to Germans. Some old ladies in particular demanded horrid retributions on German babies. Gerhardie was 'not a little shocked, I must confess, at this tardy display of Herodism', and said as much, politely. At which they began to discern unpleasant possibilities in the name 'Gerhardie' that had slipped their attention before. 'Why don't you, rather than make that impossible noise on the piano, go and fight for your country?' asked one old lady.

'Die? That you may live?' retorted Gerhardie. 'The thought's enough to make anyone a funk.'

One by one the hotel residents enlisted, showed themselves proudly and briefly in uniform, went off to France, and died. Sons and nephews of the older residents enlisted, departed for France, and were seen no more. Familiar faces in nearby shops disappeared. Gerhardie was more cautious; his views, even at 20, atypical. In part this was healthy self-regard: he wished to preserve himself long enough to publish his mighty works of literature. He possessed, moreover, a very indistinct sense of his own nationality. Britain he loved, but it was an ideal and imaginative affiliation, and one, moreover, that had been somewhat diluted by a year in class-bound, xenophobic, pre-war England. It was very pleasing to feel that he belonged everywhere; less pleasing when he felt he belonged nowhere. British pragmatism and efficiency he found sometimes admirable, sometimes deplorable, but he could not help but be in awe of her status in the world. Kensington College was particularly dull just then, the street-corner rhetoric of noble self-sacrifice all-pervasive, and besides, it was common knowledge that the war would be over in no time. On impulse one afternoon the Henry Esbheornargist in Gerhardie decided to enlist.

But the recruiting officer, puzzled by his unfamiliar name and convoluted speech—'notwithstanding' and 'nevertheless' and 'hitherto' sprinkled here, there, and everywhere—kindly advised him against joining up for fear that his fellow soldiers might in their ignorance identify him with the enemy. Certainly he must have presented a curious contrast to the average recruit. He had lately acquired a certain air, the elegant pose of Dorian Gray, six foot tall, slender, his hair rather long under a bowler hat, a languid, blasé, aesthetic look in his blue eyes, and an Oscar Wildeish collar and cane—which did not look well with the khaki armband.

'Proud join up King and country', wired his family. William, ambivalent, was disgusted by the sentiment, yet at the same time 'youthfully anxious' to live up to it, and to prove that he too had 'a patriotic heart-beat'. Shortly afterwards Charles and Clara had hasty second thoughts. 'I advise you to pay a visit to the War Office and see Lord Kitchener personally', wrote Charles, 'and tell him that your constitution is not exactly suitable for the rigour and discomfort of the trenches.' A sedentary job with foreign languages was sure to be forthcoming. Clara, meanwhile, determined to use her influence. William, pleased with himself at having made the patriotic gesture, and rather relieved at having got off so lightly, abandoned Kensington College, repaired to another hotel (in pursuit of a good-looking girl whom he had observed on the balcony), and continued to write. Films were the thing of the future, advised a fellow resident. Gerhardie set to work and produced half-a-dozen scenarios, mostly short, Chaplinesque sketches without dialogue. *Charlie the Conscientious Clerk* and *The Modern Handy Andy* each show the comically mismanaged attempts of a well-meaning individual to become a useful and efficient member of society. *Those Who Befell Short of Nature's Gifts: A Comedy for the Cinematograph* expresses Gerhardie's Beckettian inclination for the comically grotesque, being the story of two couples on holiday together: one of the group is 'desperately deaf in both ears. When he sees people speaking to him brings his hand close to his ear; but never hears anything'; another 'stammers, and when trying to speak exhibits her lips in a manner that one may think she is inclined to kiss; but ever fails to produce any sound; is perfectly speechless'; a third 'has rather a disorderly, savage sort of appearance. A smart set of false teeth, that however, continually keep falling out, and at the least movement of his jaw inexorably squeeze his gum, and thus cause pain. In consequence, hates talking much, and is very sulky. Wears pince-nez, for his "short-sightedness" is but a milder expression for blindness'; and the last is 'pigmy; hunch-backed; short-legged; short-necked; lame'. There is a fine attention to details of expressive gesture, and a delicate objectivity towards the characters who, cheerfully oblivious of their own ineptitude, are neither mocked nor sentimentalized.

Gerhardie paid £8 to have *The Haunting Roubles* typed and, encouraged by the old ladies at the hotel, he parcelled it carefully up and delivered it to the Post Office. The talented and elegant Sir George Alexander, actor-manager of the St James's Theatre and a great encouragement to English dramatists, at last returned it. Henry Irving, too, returned the play, and Marie Lloyd, and a dozen others besides.

William was not the only Gerhardie in London. The German invasion of Brussels had exiled Charles's sister Mary who, determined that her family should not be inconvenienced, had arrived in England with her Belgian husband, son, and sundry hangers-on. William became a frequent visitor to their house, storing up details of this curious ménage that he later included in *The Polyglots*. Aunt Mary, 'a beauty in her day: not merely pretty, handsome, or good-looking, but a *beauty* recognised and unmistakable', served as the prototype of the *malade imaginaire* Aunt Teresa, buried beneath medicine bottles, salves, oils, face powder, thermometers, hot-water bottles, old photographs, cushions, cosmetics, and *eau de cologne*, and subject to frequent *crises des nerfs*; 'She took pyramidon for her head, and aspirin for her cold, and pills to counteract the effect of pyramidon on her stomach, and a remedy to counteract the effect of aspirin on her heart, besides which she used lotions.'[14] Cousin Serge, shortly to die at Passchendaele, reappeared as the unfortunate Anatole, and Uncle Edmond as the diminutive and amorous Uncle Emmanuel, strutting about with waxed moustache in a curious uniform of his own devising which he hoped would impress the women.

In St Petersburg Charles was having trouble with his firm and was not sorry to be relieved of the Kensington College fees. He heartily approved his son's budding career in films and promptly withdrew all financial support. William was obliged to sell his astrakhan fur coat to pay his hotel bill, and watch tantalized as hefty sums from his father passed through his own bank account to Aunt Mary. This sudden poverty, together with greatly intensified moral pressure—a new government campaign involving 12,000 organized meetings and 50 million posters brought, in 1915 alone, 1,280,000 new recruits, a figure greater than for any other year of the war—encouraged Gerhardie's further attempt to enlist. In November 1915, just two months before the introduction of conscription, he was successful. 'I suppose my judgement was momentarily warped.'

At York Cavalry Barracks a smart corporal insisted he must join the Scots Greys: the Tsar of Russia was their colonel-in-chief. This distinguished cavalry regiment sounded romantic enough. But Gerhardie's days as a trooper were the worst of his life. His upbringing in Russia had done nothing to prepare him for such conditions: constant damp, barbarous bedding, sleeping in his underclothes on hard boards without sheets or pillow, rising at dawn, obsessive punctuality, 'nauseous' food—made all the worse for his own lack of motivation. And, convinced he was rich, his companions made life unpleasant if he did not lend them money. Unlike the British, who seemed almost perverted on this point, he saw no virtue in physical discomfort, and to one by now obsessively hygienic, the infrequent bathing, stinking urinals, filthy and exhausting fatigue duties, and the constant proximity of sweating bodies were a source of torment.

Worst of all he hated the lack of privacy: 'I am the incessant, the indomitable, extreme, almost *insane* individualist unable to bear the least infringement of his personal freedom', he later wrote.[15] 'In the Army individuality is not encouraged.' From the very first day, when he strolled in and asked to be directed to the 'dining room', he found himself a source of constant curiosity to his companions.

Together with me arrived a freckled East London dairy boy in cap and muffler; and throughout our barrack life together I remained an object which excited spontaneous mirth in him. This took the form of chucking cakes of mud at me in the dark when we slept in a tent; however, in no spirit of malice but through sheer ebullience of humour.[16]

Learning that there was a 'Russian' in their midst, the entire squadron turned out hoping to see him ride his horse Cossack-fashion, only to discover that Gerhardie was hardly capable of mounting at all. He continued to baffle them. He was vain about his appearance, yet did not care for physical strength or muscles. He had no fighting inclination or ability, was neither brave nor competitive and not in the least put out by admitting as much. He could not exactly be described as effeminate, for he took such an active interest in women. But he did not smoke or drink or tell salacious stories, and instead of betting or playing cards he sat with a book.

His companions were in turn a source of curiosity to him. Gerhardie's

Dickensian absorption with individual peculiarities (later used to such good effect in *The Polyglots*), his Chekhovian attention to shades of feeling, and his own sense of the absurd did much to sustain his good humour: 'So interested was I in the expression on the drill sergeant's face that he said: "I've got a picture of meself in me pocket. I'll show it to ye afterwards." In a thundering voice: "And *now* will you look to yer front!"'[17] The uniform, he noted wryly, was designed to fit only 'approximately'; with great solemnity he was given three boards and two trestles which he was instructed to rig up in the barrack room ('And then for some hours [I] sat on these bare boards waiting for developments'). Alternately amused and bemused by his surroundings, he ambled one evening up to the corporal of the guard on the main gate of the barracks and asked what he was doing, as there was absolutely nothing there *to* guard. Repeatedly he failed to keep time on parade: 'When the command "Slope arms!" was rapped out there would come the unanimous sound of the squad's concerted movement, followed two seconds later by the individual sound of my own.'[18]

Despite his background, Gerhardie was rarely ill at ease on account of social or political differences. Though the regiment was almost exclusively manned by professional soldiers he found a few with whom he could pass a congenial evening: Willie Taylor and his friend Willie Taylor, the latter a tailor and a socialist, intelligent and well-read, with whom William played the piano. And he enjoyed the solitary nights 'on guard', pacing silently up and down the silent stables, the rats moving in the dark around him, cats asleep on the horses' backs. But brutality and crudity of sensibility he found harder to forget. 'Jeerady that Chinese puzzle', his squadron sergeant-major habitually taunted him. 'When you go back to your Czar . . .'

The sergeant-major was not the only unsympathetic being. 'My horse and I were not on the best of terms', wrote William, who found him a greedy, bad-tempered beast and moreover, not even grey. 'By the end of the second week I already felt that we were paying too dearly for the war. What indeed had induced me to join the cavalry, where I had to look after a horse, when I could not even decently look after myself!'[19] Once, after missing a week of instruction, he found that in his absence they had learned to ride with only a blanket. The animal was not insensible to his rider's new difficulties: 'My horse, perceiving a troop at a distance and, in his inferior judgement, considering one troop as good as another, would barge into the middle of the closed ranks and set the whole troop agog.'[20] This (indirectly) resulted in two weeks on sick leave, first observing, then escorting local Cadbury's chocolate-factory girls opposite the hospital, and generally benefiting from the sentimental attitude towards war veterans: 'Where were you wounded?' solicitous lady visitors enquired, and Gerhardie—suddenly inspired—replied 'Antibes'. He wrote to ask if he might spend his sick leave in Southport with Aunt Sissie and Grandpa Wadsworth, 87 years old and recently retired from Russia for the last time. 'But mind you I won't require much comfort as anything is too good after the army', he added on the back of a photograph of himself seated so immaculately on horseback that the pair look stuffed. When they met, William, nurtured on stories of his great-grandfather's exploits at Waterloo, was astonished to find that towards his own soldier grandson old Wadsworth seemed indifferent and distracted. He talked again of his father's Peninsular campaigns and tribulations, his long marches in the mud and rain, but the present war seemed unreal. He came to see William off at the station and a few months later he died.

The longer William remained in the Army, the dimmer grew his patriotic spirit. The enemy was, after all, only a collection of beings like himself who had somehow arrived in an uncongenial situation, taught to risk death and to cause death on account of nameless individuals and impersonal ideals. He recalled his night walks through the Berlin streets, the easy hospitality of the Germans, and was angered and dispirited by the anonymity of the conflict. Kipling, he thought many years later, was a fine writer but 'a low-brow ruffian', precisely because of his unforgiving nature:

A man who keeps up an undying hatred for the late enemy because he has lost a son in the war (which (war), one would have thought, was in harmony with his bellicose spirit) does not appear to me to possess a mind compatible with his vivid talent. One must possess both to aspire to the stature of an authentic great poet, like Goethe, for instance.[21]

He particularly loathed the infectious, unthinking hysteria of those who stayed at home. A fellow soldier, something of an idealist, once expressed surprise at the barrack-room dishonesty.

The thieving—'pinching', they called it—that went on in the barrack room appeared to him inconsistent with regimental solidarity, or what is called 'esprit de corps', and seemed indeed to expose the whole idea of a united front to mockery. To me, on the other hand, it seemed more natural, more consistent, that men who presently were to stick bayonet-blades into human beings with whom they were not even on terms of nodding acquaintance, should not be ideal but, if capable of murder, also capable of minor theft.[22]

In spite of all William continued to write home 'cheerful, colourful letters with no reference to my inner well-being'. No one but Clara ever replied.

Due to his general ineptitude Gerhardie's training had taken an inordinately long time. And after a five-day leave in London the prospect of even the trenches seemed preferable to York Barracks; on impulse he wrote and requested a transfer to the Front as soon as possible. At length he was summoned to London, and only after numerous muddles and mismanagements told that he had narrowly missed a prestigious assignment to Russia with Lord Kitchener. The War Office, in a hurry, sent a schoolfriend of his instead. It was on this mission that Kitchener's boat, the *Hampshire*, sank with total loss of life.

He had also applied for a commission and was eventually transferred to the Cavalry Cadet Squadron in Dublin, a city pleasantly reminiscent of St Petersburg. Life as a trainee officer improved very dramatically: both bed and uniform were comfortable and the food delicious—real milk and butter, bacon, eggs, and, best of all, porridge. With his companions, mostly educated young men, leisurely rides around the Irish countryside were punctuated by only the occasional military duty:

Once, a sort of manoeuvre took place. In turn we had to place ourselves at the head of the squadron. I remember galloping and shouting orders with much gesticulation and expenditure of voice, according to what I believed to be the best cavalry style, only to learn at the end of it all that my squadron, by all the rules of the military game, had been annihilated by the 'enemy'.[23]

And here, after the sergeant-major who had incessantly made unkind reference to Gerhardie's foreignness, he remembered with pride an old Irish woman calling angrily after him as he rode past: 'English Swine!'

However, this Irish interlude was brief. Bulgaria had entered the war on the enemy side and, with increased activity in the Balkan regions, the War Office now sought Russian-speaking officers to whom they could teach Bulgarian. Late in 1916 Gerhardie's application for an interpretership resulted in an order to leave Ireland and report to the Royal Horse Artillery Barracks in London. Here, with others he had known in Russia, he was taught Bulgarian, 'a sort of degraded, contorted form of Russian with a few Turkish words thrown in for ornament . . . I confined myself to distorting it at will, which seemed to meet the case.'[24] Quartered comfortably next door to a public house in Finchley, well paid and with few obligations, he again frequented his Aunt Mary's house, and even took the part of Dr Chasuble in a French version of *The Importance of Being Earnest*. To crown his satisfaction, Gerhardie was commissioned as second lieutenant.

Then he was ordered to proceed to Salonika. He packed his kit, bade farewell to the girls in the public house, and reported to the War Office. He was not, they told him, to go to Salonika after all. Someone at the British Embassy in St Petersburg had requested his services, and before he went he had better get hold of a sword—without one no Russian would take him seriously as an officer. With an hour to spare William dashed to the Charing Cross Road and bought second-hand an enormous pre-Waterloo model designed for use with a cavalry charger. Then he embarked at Newcastle. His gesture of Britishness had delivered him back to Russia.

4

PETROGRAD
January 1917–March 1918

Some monarchists now wanted to put down the revolution in order to carry on the war; other monarchists wanted to put down the war in order to put down the revolution; and still other monarchists wanted to put down the revolution and did not care a hang about the war. The Liberals wanted the revolution to carry on the war; the Czar wanted to put down the revolution; the Socialists and workmen wanted to put down the war and to put down the Czar; and the soldiers and sailors wanted to put down their officers.[1]

St Petersburg had ceased to exist. In its stead was a wild, depressed, anarchic city named Petrograd.[2] The Gerhardi family, too, was changing. Victor, recently married, met William at the station and now, eyeing the splendid uniform and trappings, seemed inclined to regard his younger brother with admiration. 'My turnout rather erred, I confess, on the side of the martial and bellicose', Gerhardie admitted later, 'though God knows I was the greatest fake of a soldier alive.'[3]

At home, no Liebe: she had left after a tumultuous row when Aunt Sissie, jealous of her place in the family, accused her of appropriating some silver spoons. No Charles and no Clara. Shortly before the outbreak of war Charles had merged his business with two others into an enormous amalgamation. Two of the directors proved fraudulent and, with the additional strain of war, shares began to decline. Beset with worries, Charles took his dinner one evening, silent as usual and not eating very much. He was served his coffee; he stirred the sugar with a spoon and then, as was his custom, placed his hands on the table and rose, somewhat heavily, to take the coffee into his study. Now he stayed too long in this position—and then he fainted, knocking his head against the chair as he fell heavily, his limbs splayed and contorted.

At first the doctors diagnosed Charles's stroke as a nervous illness, and prescribed complete rest. Clara took him to nearby Lakhta in an open carriage for the fresh air and sun, and in November to Kislovodsk in the Caucasus, a mild climate, where he was given massage and electric treatment. The distortion of his face eventually relaxed; he regained his memory; but the paralysis in the right arm and leg was permanent, and he never walked again.

A few days after William's arrival Clara and Charles returned to Petrograd, and the two brothers drove to meet them at the station. The train drew in and seeing Clara's face at the window William entered the coupé to greet his father:

Already in his overcoat, all buttoned up as if in readiness for removal, his hat at an unfamiliar angle which denoted that it was not put on by himself, sat a patient shrivelled up figure, contrasting so painfully with the man I had known, eager and nervous with initiative. And just because we had never been really intimate, I now felt sorry for him.[4]

And Charles, 'perhaps remembering what a different man he had been when I last parted from him only two years before . . . cried'.[5] William was more deeply moved by the transformation than he could ever have imagined. Here was something worse than the imagined peace of extinction, a terrible vision of slow, living death and decay. His father's legs were twisted, his arms awry, and when he attempted to speak nobody could understand him. 'Charles does not die literally', his son wrote in some notes for a novel, 'but after his stroke he is a dead man. He has been dead ever since that stroke.'

Yet this was probably the happiest period of William's life. He had returned to the city he loved to work amongst 'charming, cultured' diplomats, in an environment ideally combining both Russian and English. Suddenly he found himself no longer the fool of the family, but an object of the greatest respect, quite outshining Victor. To Clara, who valued prestige and success, her younger son's achievement merely strengthened her growing partiality for him. She remained in close contact with her children all her life, visiting each in turn, but it was William, who resembled her in both appearance and temperament, who now received the greatest portion of her love. Every week of his adult life that they spent apart she wrote to him, 'My beloved son Willy', 'My own darling little boy'. Her increasingly dominant role was effected quite subtly, perhaps even unconsciously. And his reliance upon her, even in middle age, was characterized by great affection, but also frequent clashes of will.

Charles's stroke liberated William from the fear of his father, fostering not hatred but compassion and—though nowhere does he openly admit it—guilt. But for a while the illness usurped his mother's attention. In 1917 William began a novel: the main characters, Charles and his wife, who is called Nina, live in a vast baroque house in St Petersburg. One day their two children, left alone briefly, accidentally set alight their wooden dacha and burn to death. Nina, devastated by grief, watches the little coffins lowered side by side into the grave. Nearby, watching Nina, stands the man who loves her, Henry Esbheor-nargist. When Nina goes to Norway, Henry is on the point of joining her in order to consummate their love, but Charles suffers a stroke and instead Nina returns to nurse him. Henry, who reflects that he does not even know what it is like to kiss Nina, is 'grieved, profoundly humiliated, unreasonably jealous of Charles. He almost suspected Charles of having deliberately incurred the stroke in order to frustrate his object.'

William returned not to the room of his childhood, but to his father's old quarters, for the house, too, had altered. Some of the living rooms on the ground floor had been converted into bedrooms for Charles and Clara, and half of the upstairs had been partitioned off to make a flat for Victor and his wife. Dolly had left home to marry Lot Small, descendant of the original Mr Small with whom the original William Gerhardi's partnership had ended so acrimoniously, and now prosperously connected with the Small Mill (a large one). The Gerhardis no longer lived in such opulent style, for Charles's salary, in keeping with the other non-working directors, was severely reduced. In vain he argued that he had lost his health fulfilling his work duties and was therefore entitled to the full amount. Soon the firm refused to meet the expenses of his horses. Clara, never one to give in lightly, now argued with the unsympathetic co-director Mr Bang—again, to no avail. The horses and traps were sold. Rashly, Charles had exchanged the house for shares in the new company, so that when eventually it became clear that he would not recover, and was invalided out of the directorship, the family were obliged to vacate the house he had built for them. They removed first to the country to break the fall, then to a flat. What money Charles had salvaged from his mill shares, he generously distributed between his sisters—40,000 roubles each.

Every day William walked down the great rose-granite Vibourg Quay, past the house belonging to the ballet dancer Mathilda Kshesinskaya, former mistress of the Tsar, across the Troitski Bridge to the British Embassy, housed in a dark-red eighteenth-century palace built by Catherine the Great for her first lover, Sergei Saltikov. The view across the river to the fortress of Peter and Paul was fairylike. Inside the embassy porch three glass doors opened on to a red-carpeted hall with a wide flight of steps to the first landing; the stairs branched into two circular flights leading to the second floor. Here was an anteroom hung with huge portraits of Queen Victoria, Edward VII, Queen Alexandra, George V, Queen Mary. But the ballroom had been turned into a work-room, strewn with sewing machines, bandages, pneumonia jackets, pyjamas, and first-aid dressings for soldiers at the Front. And despite the importance of the embassy, they still retained a very small staff: 'My first impression was of a typing and telegraph bureau conducted by old Etonians',[6] wrote the British agent Robert Bruce Lockhart, surprised that the expensively educated diplomatic secretaries did all the typing, ciphering, and clerical work themselves. When Gerhardie first walked in, 'very perfect young men, very perfectly dressed, were conversing in very perfect intonations about love among monkeys'.[7]

The Ambassador, Sir George Buchanan, had occupied the post since 1910. The son of a former British Ambassador to Vienna, he was the Victorian style of diplomatist: highly courteous, with a gentle, deceptively simple manner and often underrated because of it. Though he spoke no Russian Buchanan was well informed about the country, outspoken and firm in his dealings. A man with 'a fine superiority of distinction', he was thin and good-looking with a handsome moustache, though no longer young. When Lockhart first arrived the effects of war were beginning to show on Buchanan:

a frail-looking man with a tired, sad expression in his eyes came forward to meet me. His monocle, his finely-chiselled features, and his beautiful silver-grey hair gave him something of the appearance of a stage-diplomat. But there was nothing artificial about his manner, or, indeed, about the man himself—only a great charm and a wonderful power of inspiring loyalty, to which I yielded at once.[8]

Though Gerhardie admired Buchanan, his real devotion was inspired by Buchanan's military attaché, Major Alfred Knox, under whom he was to work. Tall, imposing, and much respected by Russians, with powerful sweeping movements, he had the air and voice of a man 'engaged in winning the war while everybody else about him was obstructing him in his patriotic task'.[9] Knox had acted as ADC to Earl Curzon, served in the Indian Army on the North-West Frontier, and on the general staff at the War Office, before being posted to Russia. His diaries are a shrewd, fascinating, often humorous analysis of the situation between

1914 and 1917, and his criticisms of the Russian army (which considerably annoyed Kerensky) were based upon understanding and sympathy.

He had great personality, a fine presence, spoke Russian fluently and, after seven years at the Embassy, still retained a freshness of mind, an eagerness to get in touch with every phase of Russian life, so that he was the real link with the country, the most authentic channel of information for the Ambassador. Though by tradition a Tory, he said *vous* to his Russian batman, not *tu*, like the Russian officers (to give the French equivalent). If a Russian soldier stood to the salute before him, as prescribed, General Knox invariably lowered the man's arm. All of which argued a fine sense of human dignity. He was full of fun, too, and when I showed him a paragraph in the Daily Sketch, describing secretaries of embassies as glorified clerks, General Knox wrote in the margin: 'How true!' and sent it up to the Chancery.[10]

Knox's task was to liaise between the Russian military and the British, assessing strengths and advising on policy. In the early war years the Allies had relied heavily upon the Russian army for victory; with fifty million Russians mobilized, this was not on the face of it unreasonable. But as Knox discovered, numbers alone were not enough: the Russian 'steam-roller' was a myth. He likened the Russian army to 'a heavy-weight, muscle-bound prize-fighter' who, because of his enormous bulk, lacked speed and adaptability and would be intensely vulnerable to a 'lighter but more wiry and intelligent opponent'. Modern equipment was sparse. Despite a population of 180 million, Russia had one factory to every 150 in Britain; for every 100 square miles of land only half a mile of railway, compared to England's 20 miles; and during the first three years of the war the average arrivals of ships in Russian ports numbered 1,250 annually, compared to Britain's 2,200 *weekly*. And discipline was lax: Knox noticed that many Russian officers neglected their duties unless constantly supervised. 'They hated the irksome round of every-day training. Unlike our officers, they had no taste for outdoor amuse-ments, and they were too prone to spend a holiday in eating rather more and in sleeping much more.'[11] As for the ranks, 'It was impossible to hope for individuality in recruits, 75 per cent of whom were drawn from the peasant class. The Tartar domination and serfdom seem to have robbed them of all natural initiative, leaving only a wonderful capacity for patient endurance.' They had 'the faults of their race. They were lazy and happy-go-lucky, doing nothing thoroughly unless driven to it. The bulk of them went willingly to the war in the first instance, chiefly because they had little idea what war meant.'[12]

Thus, against expectation, Russia suffered severe and debilitating defeats. Russian soldiers surrendered in their thousands, freeing almost as many Germans from agriculture and industry to man the trenches in the west. Knox, dismayed but sympathetic, blamed the low education of the Russian peasants: 'A higher type of human animal was required to persevere to victory through the monotony of disaster.'[13] They fought, he believed, not from patriotism or principle but from fear, so that when the Bolsheviks undermined the power of the ruling class they simply gave up.

War took a terrible toll on the civilians, and Petrograd swarmed with refugees. The winters were bitterly cold, with insufficient fuel, disrupted transport, rising prices, food shortages, starvation. Prohibition only served to deepen the people's misery, and the army, with officers killed and thousands of new untrained recruits loitering, grew daily more anarchic. 'I had an impression of senseless *ennui* and *fin de siècle*', observed Lockhart shortly before the Revolution.[14] Yet the Tsar did nothing to alleviate conditions save shuffle his ministers about like a pack of cards, deaf to the advice, supplications, and warnings of those around him. At exactly the time of Gerhardie's return to Petrograd, Knox was chronicling the British dismay at the hard line adopted by the Tsar:

In his interview on January 12th [1917], Sir George Buchanan spoke tactfully, but certainly more strongly than any previous Ambassador had ever ventured to address the ruler of Russia's millions. He implored him to change his policy while there was yet time, pointing out the danger of a starving and exasperated capital. The Emperor listened with scarcely a word of reply, and the Russian Minister, who had an audience immediately following the Ambassador, found him trembling and distrait.[15]

Increasingly the monarchy was blamed for the privations suffered; increasingly it was openly criticized. The relationship of the Empress, a German, with the peasant monk Rasputin fuelled revolutionary propaganda and rumours of her treachery. Gerhardie's less sensational view of Rasputin saw him simply as a man of splendid virility capable of exerting a magnetic fascination upon certain women, and four decades later he wrote a play in which Rasputin is depicted sympathetically as representative of the Russian people pleading for humanity at the Imperial Court.

A few weeks after Gerhardie's return to Petrograd came the Revolution, a modest affair for all its momentous effect upon history. In

March the bread supply in the capital failed almost completely. Pushed at last beyond endurance, those who had queued in the freezing streets began to riot. Soldiers sent to quell the disturbance refused to fire on the starving crowd. The disorders quickly spread, exacerbated by the fact that the Petrograd garrison consisted mainly of untrained reservists, easily swayed. Crowds stormed the fortress of Peter and Paul, releasing political prisoners and burning the hated Secret Police Headquarters with all its incriminating files. Gerhardie and Knox stood by and watched the sacking of the Arsenal by a disorderly mob pressing arms upon a toothless old *babushka* and other unwilling passers-by. Lorry after lorry passed by 'in a kind of wild and dazzling joy-ride' packed with soldiers and workmen, many lying in a 'ready' attitude along the mudguards and waving red flags and revolutionary banners, while street crowds shouted 'Hurrah!' Trainloads of troops arrived from the front to crush the uprising, but went quickly over to the Revolution, and most of the casualties were police: 'Such as were found were brought down and lined up in queues; a hole was hacked in the ice on the river, and they were pushed under the ice one by one with barge poles. No blood was spilled. And the First Revolution was accordingly called "The Bloodless Revolution".'[16]

Nevertheless, observers mingling with the crowds sensed that this was by and large an enthusiastic, optimistic exultation, not a vicious, vengeful one. For forty-eight hours Buchanan sat in his sitting-room transmitting the news to England, whilst Knox was busy with his diary. 'If the officers would only join the movement!' he wrote, and described how walking with a party of British officers (Gerhardie amongst them) from the Embassy to Liteini Prospekt, the District Court blazing in the background, they were stopped by soldiers with rifles and bayonets and asked to surrender their swords, until another soldier (probably drunk) shouted 'These are Englishmen! You must not insult them!'[17] Later, Knox walked with a Canadian railway expert to the Duma, a two-mile tramp through the snow. Half-way there a country sledge passed them, crowded with peasants in holiday dress who waved their arms and cheered. When Knox cheered in reply they stopped the sledge and beckoned the officers to get on, an old soldier, smelling strongly of vodka, turning some others off to make room. Arriving at the Duma their self-appointed guide walked ahead waving his hat and shouting, 'Way for the British representative!' 'I felt a fool, and no doubt looked it', commented Knox.[18]

Shortly afterwards the Tsar signed the abdication papers and thus, quietly, ended the Russian monarchy. There was renewed optimism from almost all quarters, as a Provisional Government of Liberal politicians was established, and, simultaneously, a Soviet of Workers' and Soldiers' Deputies. From the balcony of the British Embassy Buchanan delivered a speech associating Britain with this newly established Russian democracy which, it was believed, would make Russia stronger. The Revolution also gave an important moral boost to the war effort: now that the Tsar was gone there could be no doubt that the Allies were fighting the cause of democracy against autocracy.

Gerhardie was amongst the optimists. He returned from the Embassy late that night and told his family of events, praising the young and charismatic new Liberal leader, Alexander Kerensky. All would now be well in Russia. Victor, who was running the mill with five hundred truculent workers, called William an idealistic fool. 'Now that the Tsar has gone it's time for the Gerhardis to go too', he said.

As it happened Victor was right, though William was not altogether an idealist. The following day he strolled from street corner to street corner, listening to innumerable speeches, 'some of a Liberal loftiness; others of a menacingly proletarian character, threatening death to capital and revolution to the world at large'. Everywhere was flamboyant extravagance and exaggeration. 'Down with Armies and Navies!' shouted one speaker hysterically.

Crossing a bridge I passed a company of soldiers newly revolted. They marched alert and joyous to the sound of some old familiar marching songs till they came to the words 'for the Czar'. Having sung these words they stopped somewhat abruptly and perplexed. '*How* for the Czar?' one of them asked. '*How* for the Czar?' they repeated, looking at each other sheepishly. Then they marched on without singing. There were peasants who did not know the word 'revolution' and thought it was a woman who would supersede the Czar. Others wanted a republic with a czar. And there were others still who interpreted the word republic as 'rezshpublicoo', thinking that it meant 'cut up the public'.[19]

Knox too was bemused and exhilarated by the sudden passion for speech, the right to which had been so long denied, 'and a moment of silence seemed to everyone a moment lost'. A new verb was coined, *mitingovat*, to attend meetings, so that a man might ask his friend what he intended to do that evening, and the reply would be: '*Ya nemnogo mitinguyu*, "I will attend meetings a little".'[20]

Facing the British Embassy on the opposite side of the Neva stood Mathilde Kshesinskaya's house, now empty, looted and abandoned. One day a red flag was hoisted: the professional revolutionaries Lenin and Trotsky had emerged from exile and claimed it as their head-quarters. Few took them seriously. Lenin, from the garden wall, preached against the Provisional Government, promising bread, peace, and the partition of land, but Gerhardie, strolling past in the evenings to listen, found 'nothing in the man's speech or looks to give an inkling of his future career'. When at length the Government, drawing up troops beside the Embassy in preparation for opening fire upon the Bolshevik nest and routing out the revolutionaries, first invited the Ambassador to move to safety elsewhere, he replied: 'Thanks, my wife and daughter want to see it.'

The Revolution notwithstanding, Gerhardie worked hard all that year receiving visitors, writing letters, deciphering telegrams, and accompanying Knox's excursions until nine o'clock each evening. Knox toured the city and environs inspecting and lecturing in an attempt to restore the fighting spirit of the army. It was an uphill task. At one regiment the officers lounged idly about and only reluctantly broke off their game of bridge to receive him. 'What was wanted was games of another type', Knox wrote briskly. 'Some such grand class leveller as football—to bring all ranks together.'[21] In an effort to encourage the recalcitrant troops, a battalion of women was formed, loyal to Kerensky. Few but Gerhardie appreciated them:

I remember these young lasses, as they marched with quivering calves, breasts like cannon balls, inspected closely by a very handsome Circassian colonel on horseback, raising not cheers but jeers from the sloppy soldiers who lounged on street corners with their hands in their pockets, spitting out sunflower-seed husks.

Gerhardie was well at ease with soldiers and politicians of all nationalities, attending meetings and parties. At one such gathering an English colonel, the guest of honour, discovered that as he knew no Russian and the Russian colonel no French, they must converse in the language of the common enemy, 'to whose speedy destruction they raised their glasses'. Other evenings he would return to his parents' flat and work upon his new play *The Khaki Armlet*. Late one night the front door bell rang, but when the maid opened the door she saw only an elaborately dressed, rather elderly figure running down the street. It was—the man later confessed—a commander in the Moscow Guards seeking shelter after his entire regiment had revolted. But at the last minute he felt he could not endanger the family in such a way. Gerhardie later sheltered this man's son by securing him a job at the Embassy as an errand boy, or 'Envoy' as he styled himself, running his missions in great style in a private carriage.

Throughout the summer there was still comparative order. One evening in October Gerhardie was advised by the Minister for Foreign Affairs, Tereshchenko, that there was trouble ahead. British subjects should leave Russia while they could. The permit took ten days, during which time Clara was busy. Undeterred by the wild instability of the rouble she succeeded in amassing £1,000 in cash—chiefly from the sale of shares and a bank loan against valuables deposited. Then, laboriously, item by item, she sewed the rest of her jewels into her clothes, a garnet ring into the lining of her hem, a diamond necklace down the bodice of her frock. When the day for departure dawned she dressed herself in half-a-dozen layers of furs.

The morning of the November Revolution was dark and sleety, Petrograd ominously deserted, 'with mystery behind it and mystery before it' and not a taxi in sight. The family doctor, who had come to see off the Gerhardis, supported Charles on one side and expressed sorrow at their departure. Charles, in no mood for emotion, only said irritably that they must hurry in order not to miss the train. Henry Esbheornargist waves goodbye to Charles and Nina at the Finland Station:

> She had turned round as the heavy door of the vehicle closed upon her and could not help but make the sign of the cross . . . She was glad to leave Petrograd; yet she felt that with Petrograd behind her, her own life was at an end. And when they parted, and the rails where the train had been showed empty, Henry felt that it was the last act of their life that had closed upon them.

It was still early. William walked back to the flat and learned that at eight o'clock that morning the cruiser *Aurora* and three other ships had arrived bearing sailors from the port of Kronstadt and cast anchor on the Neva opposite the Winter Palace. Later in the morning there were barricades in the streets and random shooting began. One by one the Bolsheviks and Red Guards occupied all the vital points in the city: railways, power stations, food stores, banks. They stormed the Military Academy, throwing the young cadets from the windows and roof. The telephone exchange changed hands back and forth. The *Aurora* shelled the Winter Palace where the ministers had collected, which was in turn defended ably by the Womens' Battalion. The Bolsheviks broke through. The ministers were arrested and imprisoned in the Peter and Paul Fortress, and Kerensky escaped in a car flying the American flag.

One hundred and seventy women soldiers taken prisoner were

removed to the barracks of the Grenadier regiment. The chivalrous Knox when he heard of this was greatly alarmed, and without hesitating hurried off to the Bolshevik headquarters to negotiate an agreement to protect the women. He had, he later confessed to Gerhardie, no arguments at hand with which to persuade the Soviet commander to release his prisoners and came out with the first thing that happened to enter his head: 'If you don't let these young women go, I will, I tell you, set the opinion of the entire civilized world against you!'

My chief's eloquence frightened—I think it was Krylenko—out of his not very firm wits. And General Knox was right. For had these girls in uniform been taken to a camp converted into an alternative Luna Park, to provide relaxation from pent-up sexual tension for the soldiery at large, home from the front and welcoming a home from home, it would have furnished the curious inquirer with a more popular topic than even Rasputin taking on all alone the Ladies of the Bedchamber and returning them in an interesting condition.

Gerhardie, exhilarated by the dramatic events taking place around him, cheerfully described the developing chaos: bridges closed, loss of electricity, motor-lorries packed with armed soldiers and workmen careering all over the town, 'and all sorts of lively things'. The Bolsheviks, he assured his parents, 'behave like real gentlemen, and there is really no actual danger living in this place . . . The whole thing is a Gilbert and Sullivan Comic Opera.' Gerhardie was lucky, and protected by his British military status. Other British nationals suffered violence and famine during the Revolution years. On one occasion he and his 'envoy', wandering around the Palace Square, were stopped by a drunken soldier with a bayonet who carefully explained that his duty, coincident with his inclination, was to let out the guts of '*bourguys*' such as themselves.

The presence of mind manifested by our Russian 'envoy' averted in the nick of time a jab of the bayonet. 'That's right, *tovarishch*!' he cried. 'Kill them all, the dirty dogs!'

'I will!' said the soldier, with a curiously dogged nod, as if he thought my friend's encouragement redundant to his set purpose, as he staggered off into the November night.

Gerhardie continued to keep his family informed of events, sending letters by diplomatic bag and enclosing newspapers whenever possible, but warning that most of the news was 'so sensational that one does not dare write it'. Many of his letters were interrupted by the noise of soldiers ransacking nearby flats.

You have no doubt heard of the looting of the Winter Palace. One night some of the garrison decided to 'liquidate' the wine cellars of the Winter Palace, in the interests of the Revolution, of course, and they thought they could not do it better than by drinking the whole lot, or at least as much as they could drink. What they could not, they smashed. A great number of 'volunteers' from the street joined them, and before the night was over a real orgy took place. Drunken soldiers were lying all over the square, and shooting was going on all night. A Fire-Brigade was called out and had orders to break all the remaining bottles and pump the wine out into the Neva. As they arrived they found the cellars flooded with wine several feet high, and many drunken soldiers had been drowned in the wine like flies . . . Before the show was over the fire-brigade had gone over to the rebels and joined them in their orgy. The best wine, 200 years old, was being sold by soldiers at Rs 2–3 a bottle, and there is a very strong smell of wine round the Winter Palace even now, in spite of the stormy weather we are having. Since that night all wine shops are being systematically raided and the crowds usually joins in cheerily, for they are all certain that the 'destruction' of wine is in the best interests of the Revolution.

Shortly afterwards Knox, lunching with friends, was offered some excellent madeira from the Imperial cellar, his hostess's child having found two bottles buried in the snow whilst playing in the Alexandrovski Garden.

Eight young military cadets had been detailed to guard the Embassy, but quickly proved more trouble than help. They appropriated a case of whisky and a case of claret, and were dreadfuly ill in the hallway. 'So far from their protecting us, it is we who are protecting them', wrote Buchanan laconically in his diary.[22] And, when they showed themselves at the window, they incurred the wrath of the mob outside and had to be smuggled out of the building in disguise.

William remained in the flat, along with a soldier called Pidcock. 'Life is only possible in St Petersburg with a flat and a fur coat', he wrote. He was quite comfortable and had obtained a permit which prevented the flat from being searched by the Bolsheviks. Alexei the coachman had sealed up the windows in preparation for winter and they had fixed up the drawing-room portière and a set of white blinds ('the blighter asked Rs 20 for doing it, and P paid him, as he was afraid of an "armed demonstration" if he had not done'). Olga, the cook, remained but complained bitterly that she could not work without a mistress. Gerhardie became an efficient housekeeper. Somehow they had laid in a good stock of provisions, sharing them with Rosie, Leonya, and Tamara, the only ones of the family to remain. From England Victor dispatched a good strong pair of boots for William, and William in turn parcelled up odd parts of Charles's typewriter and sent them in a diplomatic bag along with an urgent request for hair lotion 'lest I should go bald from overwork'. He was regularly visiting his dentist, Mr Goldberg, 'an awful blighter!', who played about jabbing his instruments in at random to the accompaniment of a rehearsal of *Faust* in the upstairs rooms.

William and Rosie paid several trips to the ballet, and struck up acquaintance with some Jewish aristocrats ('I rather like their company and find them very refined'). But he regretted that despite the growing anarchy they had not had a single orgy. He had to content himself with the local brothel, whence he repaired several times a week. His partners varied: a colonel's wife earning extra money and a young girl from the provinces who politely asked him to turn out the light and not to speak so that she might imagine he was the local schoolmaster ('I thought her request reasonable'). The Jewish girl whom Gerhardie had loved years before was now married to a Russian barrister. William dined with them, argued forcefully with her husband and, preparing to depart, was suddenly and unexpectedly at last liberated from her spell:

When I turned to go, she, curious about my unfamiliar uniform, put on my British-warm and looked at herself in the glass as if conscious of the pleasure she must be conferring by this act on the man who adored her. But she looked hateful in it . . . Love, I realized, was subjective and therefore transferable. The recognition that our love does not belong to the being who inspired it is painful but salutary.[23]

Throughout the Revolution Buchanan had remained unruffled. Refusing to have his routine disrupted he walked about the most dangerous parts of the city in his lounge suit, and often calmly addressed angry crowds from his balcony. On Christmas night he gave a party, 'very jolly indeed, and in its style was so perfectly "ambassadorial"'. He stood at the top of the Embassy staircase receiving guests as they came up, his monocle dangling down from his neck on a broad ribbon. After a magnificent supper and concert the party sang 'He's a jolly good fellow', to which Buchanan, modest and charming, replied that he was neither jolly nor good, and all that he could say of himself was that he was a fellow.

With the arrival of the new year life in the flat became increasingly uncomfortable: a battallion of Bolsheviks quartered in the same building were refusing to allow Gerhardie any wood. The situation grew critical; he considered burning the piano and even asked the family to send fuel in a diplomatic bag. Pidcock paced all around the flat singing of southern Italy and tropical climes, while Gerhardie preferred to remain quietly in the drawing-room well wrapped up, imagining that he was reclining in the Summer Gardens. At mealtimes they sat swathed in fur coats, fur gloves, galoshes, rugs round their legs, and scarves wound twice round the neck, 'but in spite of all these precautions, I am sorry to say, Pidcock got his ears frozen during dinner, which dropped into his soup, which, however in these times of great scarcity of good meat, was a source of profit as much as it was of loss to him'.

The possibility of removing money grew remote. Charles's company had, after bitter wrangles, agreed to settle 15,000 roubles upon him, but the Revolution had undermined all hope of payment. Early in 1918 Gerhardie took advantage of his diplomatic status to help his Uncle Willy Gerhardi and family to escape. They arrived from Smolensk, together with innumerable nurses, maids, in-laws, second cousins, fiancés, and scores of small children (Willy was now on to his third wife). 'Quick, quick, quick. No time to waste, quick quick', he urged, shepherding them all into Gerhardie's flat. Pale-faced, red-nosed, with his 'sulky Charlie Chaplin look', Uncle Willy helped himself liberally to William's store of provisions whilst muttering about the 'ruinous' Petrograd prices. When night fell there were several times more human beings than beds, sofas, and chairs, and everyone had to take care not to step on some sprawling little Gerhardie in the dark, which did not deflect William from rushing in every ten minutes to kiss his red-haired cousin goodnight, again and again pretending to have forgotten some item essential to his *toilette*. Two weeks passed in this fashion, the flat a babel of voices from dawn till dusk, until at length they departed safely and thanks to William's intervention were not even searched at the border. 'All the good things I do, makes me believe that I will undoubtedly go to Heaven when I die, unless, of course, as Rosie says, I die unexpectedly of conceit.'

The fate of Rosie, who, in marrying a Russian had forfeited her British nationality, continued to worry Clara, who wished to see the family united. William, who was always irritated by his mother's alarm, and not a little jealous, wrote sharply back:

It is futile your wiring about Rosie and Leonya coming over to England. In the first place no Russian subject is allowed to leave Russia by the Bolsheviks, but what is more, no foreign subjects are allowed by the British Controls Office to enter England; and what is still more, Leonya cannot possibly get any job in England knowing as he does one language only, and even if he does get one to last him for the time of the war . . . he will be hopelessly stranded at the end of the war. Neither Rosie nor Leonya have any desire to go, and even if they had, it would hardly be a desire worth entertaining as it cannot be fulfilled.

Early in the new year Buchanan and Knox began the evacuation of the British Embassy. The Bolshevik officials had refused to reserve them accommodation on the train, but a gift of two bottles of Buchanan's best Napoleon brandy to the station master procured them a sleeping car. Most of the Allied representatives and many members of the British colony gathered at the station to bid farewell, including Gerhardie, who was to remain a little longer.

In parting, General Knox thanked me for my work for him and supposed that when he saw me again I'd be a general. He gave me a mock punch in the ribs and said that if I did not come to see him in England he would kill me. I was so attached, so devoted, to the man that when I was alone in the street I hurried against the biting blizzard, which blinded me as I tore on, and sobbed.[24]

Buchanan was reluctant to leave Russia, his home for the past seventeen years. He had grown visibly older, and for two years after returning to England took no duties. His had been one of the most crucial roles an Ambassador has ever had to play, and he found himself the object of much bitter criticism. Russian monarchists in particular went so far as to blame the Revolution itself upon the conduct of the British Embassy, and a story was circulated of Buchanan in false nose and wig attending revolutionary gatherings. Gerhardie's view, and one held by most informed people at that time, including Lockhart, was very different:

To my mind the British Embassy at Petrograd is a perfect illustration of what can, should, shouldn't and cannot be done by an Embassy. I know the hollowness of corporate emotion which vents itself in some such terms as: 'A more splendid set of fellows I never knew'. But at the Embassy in Russia you had the pleasing spectacle of loyal teamwork under a sensible, intelligent chief . . . Sir George Buchanan, whatever his politics at home, displayed a completely open and flexible mind in regard to Russian politics.[25]

Gerhardie and a few others stayed on until March, before being escorted by train as far as the Finnish frontier. At Tammerfors (now Tampere) the train sat in a siding while they waited, listening to intermittent firing in the town between Finnish Reds and Whites. Gerhardie hurried to the public baths to be scrubbed not, as he had hoped, by a young Finnish beauty but by a skinny old woman. When at last he found his Finnish beauty she attacked him and tried to steal his watch. The following day the party transferred to sledges and two members rode ahead to the frontier waving a Union Jack and a White Flag. A week later they sailed for England, Gerhardie still busily engaged in writing *The Khaki Armlet*.

5

THE GHOST WAR
March 1918–July 1920

By now, 'Intervention' has been relegated to the shelf of history. But I cannot but remember it, not merely as an adventure in futility, as admittedly it was, but as an ever-shifting, changing sense of being alive.[1]

In England Gerhardie was transferred to the 3rd Battalion Scots Guards at Wellington Barracks. He had a 'rattling raw sore throat'. His ears were numbed by the whistling March wind. His feet were swollen from the hammering on the hard parade ground, and he had a fearful collar rash from his new military wear. His days were spent first training with, then training, a squad of recruits; unlearning cavalry drill in favour of what he described as 'pedestrian' drill. He bellowed at the top of his voice at his underlings while children gathered behind the railings to watch and giggle. His were dreary tasks (though the yelling had its charms), yet he found that he had an unexpectedly good time:

Just as the diplomats at the Petrograd Embassy deferred to me because they thought I must have had an adventurous time as a soldier, the guardsmen were charming to me, perhaps because they thought I had gone through hair-raising adventures while with the diplomats. Of this I was glad. For I would sooner be undeservedly than deservedly rewarded, preferring a gift to mere payment.[2]

In the evenings he worked upon *The Khaki Armlet: or Why Clarence Left Home*, which was completed in April. The plot, involving an inheritance, concerns the recruitment into the British Army of Clarence, a not very healthy 68-year-old man. The dialogue, spare and gruff, parodies the English both as individuals and in their attitude to the war; and achieves its comic effects through simplicity and a barely perceived undercurrent of the grotesque. It is unsurprising that such a work should fail to find acceptance in wartime England: the play was returned by everybody who read it. 'If the Army be anything like what you describe', added Miss Horniman of the Manchester Repertory Theatre, 'all the more honour to the Navy and Air Force for keeping the enemy out.'[3]

The rest of the family had by now all reached England safely. Dolly, the first to leave Russia, was living in dull comfort with a fellow exile in Bolton who by chance had offered her accommodation. Victor had obtained a job at the Ministry of Information in London, and Daisy was working for the War-Graves' Commission and lodging with some *nouveaux-riches* friends who decorated their dining table with dainty coloured lights. Charles and Clara, as mild pillars of the English establishment abroad, had been met after crossing the Russian frontier by a very polite, somewhat surreptitious old gentleman representing the British Legation, who solicitously installed them in a Norwegian hotel. Thence, via Bergen and Aberdeen, they made their way to 'hide themselves' from the world in Grandpapa Wadsworth's old village of Bubwith in Yorkshire. In Gerhardie's novel, Henry Esbheornargist, who parallels Gerhardie's thoughts during most of the early years, visits Nina in Bubwith. He sees she has aged, and though he loves her still, congratulates himself on not having married her:

he remembered how years ago he had intended to set out on a mission to make himself worthy of her; and now—the irony of it!—presumably he had exceeded the standard of excellence necessary of attainment and had become too good for her.

Some months later Charles and Clara moved to London, and took lodgings at 95 Oxford Gardens, Kensington, where Uncle Willy from Smolensk paid a long-awaited visit. While Clara made the tea, Willy, the impatient handyman, pulled out a hammer and screwdriver and asked if there was anything by way of a nail anywhere that wanted driving in. He wandered upstairs to William's room 'and, watching my typewriter, said that he could construct a machine which would work by electricity in such a way that if I pressed the keys in my attic the typewriter would actually perform the work in the basement. It seemed a wonderful invention, almost worth patenting.' But when questioned by William as to the actual benefits of the typing being done in the basement while he pressed the keys in the attic Uncle Willy 'agreed that there appeared to be no visible advantage in such an arrangement'.[4] Then, over sweet sticky buns, the two brothers talked excitedly and light-heartedly of their early days building the Gerhardi mill and of the fortunes to be made in England, Willy now deaf and using an ear trumpet, Charles confined to his wheelchair. But while the old competitive spirit had gone from

Charles, Willy, as mettlesome as ever, shortly after opened a machine-tool factory in Great Missenden. Some years later, Willy's son Victor suggested that he would like to start a new life farming in Canada. 'That's a good idea', said his father. 'We'll all go too. But you'd better stay behind and look after the factory.' So Willy established himself on a Canadian cattle and poultry farm, homely and comfortable in a small house with furniture all made by himself next door to his son Eddy's dairy and poultry farm. Victor stayed in England.

In June 1918 Allied victory was far from certain. France, weak and trench-ridden, was vulnerable, and the Germans continued to win ground in Russia, marching their way closer to the vast quantities of war supplies and food sent out from the United States and Britain, and now lying idle in Russian ports. Many observers believed that the Allies also owed brotherly support to the White Russians and Czechs, and though few were as rabid as Winston Churchill, others distrusted Bolshevism, Lenin, Trotsky, and their suspected German sympathies. Churchill, Minister of Munitions since 1917 and from January 1919 Secretary of State for the War Office, was a vigorous advocate of Allied intervention in Russia, and became so insistent that Lloyd George felt obliged to write to him in 'one last effort to induce you to throw off this obsession with Russia which, if you will forgive me for saying so, is upsetting your balance'.[5]

After much feverish debate, Allied Military Missions were established at strategic points in Russia—Murmansk, Vladivostok, and Archangel—ostensibly for the protection of supplies from the Germans. After the signing of the Armistice on 11 November 1918—the Germans thoroughly subdued—the official justification, hastily adjusted, was pronounced to be relief of the distress of the Russian people and restoration of a 'stable' government. Certainly the political, military, and civilian chaos in the vast territory of Russia was now greater than ever, and taking advantage of the plethora of counter-revolutionary pockets throughout the country, the Allies announced that they would supply credits for arms and equipment to help make the peace in Russia.

The man appointed, in June 1918, British Military Representative for Siberia (and thereby one of the most influential men in all Russia) was Alfred Knox, soon to be promoted to Major-General. His task was to establish headquarters in distant Vladivostok ('"Lord of the East"—an unwarranted peerage', he later remarked). Many thousand miles from Petrograd and close to the Chinese border on the south-eastern tip of

Russia, Vladivostok was a vital link in Russia's chain of communications throughout the First World War. Since the Revolution it provided not only asylum for refugees from Bolshevik areas, but soon grew to be the focus of anti-Bolshevik operations from the east and the training ground for White forces.

Knox immediately requested the services of 'Gerhardie the faithful'. He also selected the amiable Colonel James Blair, who had served in South Africa, India, France, and Petrograd, and who was apocryphally said to walk about London with his wife, plus her umbrella, bag, portmanteau, and other items on one arm, and on the other arm his little son Noel who in turn carried in one hand a cage with a canary, and in the other a goldfish bowl. The fourth member was a Russian officer, Paul Rodzianko, pre-Revolutionary aristocrat and an insatiably brilliant story-teller. He was the nephew of the 'pot-bellied' ex-President of the Duma who had, just a year before, telegraphed the final message to Tsar Nicholas II before the Romanov collapse:

FROM PRESIDENT OF THE DUMA, RODZIANKO, TO HIS
IMPERIAL MAJESTY THE EMPEROR QUOTE IT IS TOO
LATE UNQUOTE RODZIANKO.[6]

Early in the war, Paul Rodzianko had been assigned the task of protecting Knox, who with his vast military knowledge would have been a great prize to the enemy. But it had been a nerve-racking task: 'The centre of the firing-line held an incomprehensible attraction', wrote Rodzianko, 'and he constantly led me into the most uncomfortable positions', coolly lighting his pipe and munching his sandwiches in the midst of hails of bullets.[7]

Gerhardie, promoted to Staff Lieutenant 1st Class with a salary (including allowances) of £550 a year, was not displeased at the idea of returning to Russia, though his ardour for intervention was slight: 'the distraction and novelty of travelling in new countries will make us forget about the war. That is the reason for our going as I understand it', he wrote in July. As before, he greatly enjoyed the celebrated company he was keeping, flattered by Knox's affectionate regard. At an introductory luncheon at the Naval and Military Club, Knox (jolly and bright in spite of toothache) introduced him to Harold Williams, the Petrograd correspondent of the *Daily Telegraph*, and teased Gerhardie about his 'Bosch' name. 'I think Knox is about the greatest character I have ever seen', wrote William.

Most of the preparations for the journey were left to Gerhardie. He

rushed eagerly round London in a 'flapper-driven' car arranging pass-
ports, choosing clerks, purchasing kit, wasting six hours a day circumventing red tape at the War Office, and generally throwing himself into
the 'razzle dazzle' of diplomacy. Knox took against his tiny manservant
who smelled more per square inch of person than anyone he knew, and
off Gerhardie rushed post-haste to spend all Sunday afternoon at the
WO entrance stopping every private soldier who passed along and
asking if they wished to go to Russia. An Oxford man in training for the
diplomatic service was procured and this 'servant' was seen off at the
station by his father, tall, dignified, top-hatted, and looking like a lord.
At the Russian Embassy Gerhardie caught a glimpse of V. D. Nabokov
('He looks such a rascal'), the Russian Liberal politician and father of
the novelist, shortly to die at the hands of an assassin; in Bloomsbury he
thought he glimpsed the back of H. G. Wells, and Bernard Shaw went
stalking by in Bond Street. It was, as he pointed out to his mother, a good
week for the 'literaries'. But it ended with a runny nose: 'I think it is what
they call here the "flew".'

The delays were considerable. Gerhardie moved from London to
Liverpool, keeping in regular correspondence with his parents, emphas-
izing happily that the *utmost secrecy* shrouded the whole undertaking. He
also urged the UTMOST SECRECY in their proposed dealings with
Rosie, lest (and this was by then quite a danger) by anti-Bolshevik
references in letters (so frequently intercepted) they endanger her life.
Knox meanwhile tiptoed away a little before the rest of the Mission, in
order to keep an appointment in the United States with President
Wilson.

At last Gerhardie, pale and foot-weary, set sail across the Atlantic in a
luxurious state apartment of the *Aquitania*, in spite of a U-boat scare
which made him feel that at any moment he might find himself 'floating
on the water owing to the disappearance of the boat'. The glimpse of
America was brief and the bustle of crossing the country to prepare for
the Pacific left him little time to write. A genial American slapped him on
the back as they arrived: 'No kings and princes here to lock you up in
prison. No priests and courtiers intriguing against your liberty. Ah, this
is a free country, my friend.'[8]

New York was irresistible: the warm, brightly lit streets, towering
buildings, the sky abuzz with aircraft, and the superb hotel efficiency
that put even the best London establishments to shame. '"Me in
America!" I seemed to be saying to myself. "Me in New York!".' The
cost of living was staggering, but the food worth every cent: 'I know you

would have enjoyed sliced peaches and cream (always first) for breakfast', he wrote home, 'followed by oatmeal and cream, followed by an omlette and tomatoes, followed by poached eggs on toast, followed by cold ham and eggs, followed by eggs and bacon, kidney and sausage and eggs, and corn muffins and cake and crab and salmon and eggs. You can always get more eggs afterwards if you wish.' Gerhardie greatly admired the negro waiters—'they are so very sharp, but of course you have got to take it for granted that their hands are clean', he wrote (he habitually made a note of such things). American pride he found overbearing: 'The Americans are very charming people, but are very great boasters. They mainly talk about dollars.' He admired their egalitarian ways, amused that hotel porters would shake hands and wish him well ('most democratic'). There was no doubt that they were 'very proud of themselves and consider themselves even a little bit superior to us'. War hysteria was rife: 'they are all crazy about uniform. Girls driving cars stop you in the streets and take you for a ride. People shake hands with you in the streets and weep. I was looked upon as a hero when I told them of my daring adventures in France and my experiences in the Trenches in the Dardanelles. We Europeans have grown tired of all this.'

In one American city Gerhardie was mistaken for the Prince of Wales, and on the train between Chicago and Minneapolis got a taste of American snobbery when a lady and her daughter, 'crazy' about the English aristocracy, recited tales of the American 'aristocracy' ('as if there existed such a thing'). After one of the English party made a casual reference to Gerhardie's father 'the Duke', they would not leave him alone, thrilled when he told them his decoration was the Order of the Garter. In Canada Gerhardie embarrassed himself by rather ruthlessly insisting that he *did not want* to buy flowers from a group of women who, it transpired, were dignitaries attempting to make a presentation.

Knox and Blair were in the best of expectant spirits when the two parties united; and at Victoria they boarded a Japanese boat for a fourteen-day trip across the Pacific to Yokohama. The sea was calm, schools of whales passed by, and flying fishes leaped out of the green water. Gerhardie tried to catch one, and almost fell in. The SS *Kashima Maru* was a small boat, but stable and well fitted, and a morning paper printed on board was circulated daily, giving news received by wireless. The dinner menu, in a curious language lying somewhere between Japanese and English, consisted of food enough to grace a Victorian state banquet (including an intriguing speciality 'Parisian Ties'). There were regular concerts, and to the horror of the thrifty Gerhardie an auction which raised $600, 'and we, poor devils, were forced to compete with American millionaires in buying absurd and unnecessary things (sometimes given by ourselves) for the highest possible prices, to keep up the prestige of the British Army!' Knox was not keen on the soldiers talking to girls on board, so Gerhardie, deprived of a pleasing pastime, began work on a play and a novel, the latter almost certainly *Futility*.

As Gerhardie sat down to write what became his first published novel, he was undergoing the experiences with which his second, *The Polyglots*, opens. The hero Georges, like Gerhardie himself, arrives in Japan, a land phantasmal and vivid, a coral reef:

Everything from scenery downwards has that weird look about it, and one fancies that these moving statuettes, as it were, or the weird coloured scenery is merely a scene from some balet or some Japanese picture: so it is unreal. The town is weird and the houses are weird, and the people, men and women and children, all move about on weird bits of wood—as some mechanical dolls and look singularly unhappy in doing so.

Again, Gerhardie's letters give only fleeting images: a little fishing fleet and the fishermen waving, melting heat, strange birds and insects which produced unfamiliar and continuous sounds, the whole effect perfectly unreal, so still and hot and full of colour.

At Yokohama a crowd of reporters rushed on board clicking cameras and led them to 'a royal reception' at the British Embassy; hundreds more photographs taken, flashlights going off continuously 'like a real bombardment'. They put up at the Imperial Hotel in Tokyo, in order for Knox to negotiate the British position in case the Japanese should also decide to intervene in Russia. 'The Japanese, of course, talk English, but unfortunately they are alone who understand it.' Gerhardie was put to work buying dinner sets, kitchen utensils, typewriters, and stationery for the Mission, engaging cooks, and choosing Daisy an embroidered silk kimono. Just before leaving, the Japanese Minister for Defence laid on a banquet in their honour, with the Minister and his staff dressed in *samurai* clothes. All sat cross-legged on the floor, drinking sake and served by geishas, two to a man, who sat upon their knees. Rodzianko thought that the geisha singing sounded like cats yowling. Then they walked home at dawn as the first pink light came up.

Nine days later the SS *Penza* of the Russian Volunteer Fleet sailed into Vladivostok harbour. It was raining heavily, the Pacific beat against the rocky coast, and the port looked grey and hopeless, 'like the Russian situation'. Every kind of vessel bobbed and swayed upon the waters of the Golden Horn and around the bay tiers of low wooden houses rose on the steeply sloping hills. In the town two cobbled avenues lined with stone buildings ran at right-angles to each other, whilst all the other streets were deeply rutted, with rotting wooden sidewalks. Trade in this great eastern city was almost at a standstill. 'Penniless refugees thronged the town', wrote one British officer,

crime and licence grew unchecked, and there was universal and feverish speculation in foreign exchanges. On the streets an extraordinary motley of races, creeds, and tongues passed and repassed. Allied soldiers, carefree and with money to spend—Americans, British, Canadians, French, Italians, Japanese, Chinese, and Serbs—British, French and American sailors, tanned by the open sea and now ashore in search of a girl or a scrap; ex-Tsarist officers in grey greatcoats lined with scarlet silk; Russian soldiers in the homely drab supplied by the British Government; a sprinkling of soberly dressed foreign consuls and businessmen; soldiers of the new nations, Poles, Letts and Czechoslovaks many of them ex-prisoners of war, now clad in fresh uniforms; fat Chinese merchants and lean coolies; Koreans in flowing white with strange stove-pipe hats; bearded Russian priests trailed by numerous offspring; fierce-looking Cossacks in mighty fur caps; tight-lipped American nurses in hard blue hats and billowing cloaks; pretty ladies with scarlet lips, high French heels, and expensive furs, Jews in gabardines and Jews in soiled frock-coats; hook-nosed Armenians; ragged refugees; indescribable beggars; lean-faced Turks, Germans and Austrians—prisoners of war awaiting repatriation; fat speculators; decent bourgeois; hooligans; grey-clad militiamen; a never-ending stream of polyglot humanity.[9]

Knox's advance party set up in temporary headquarters in a deserted house standing in a grim and desolate side-street. Gerhardie shared a room with Rodzianko, who—Rodzianko began a story as soon as he settled for a moment anywhere—had once come across one thousand uniformed skeletons deep in a forest clearing which, when the buttons and bayonets were sent for identification, proved to be those of a Napoleonic troop that had lost its way in the retreat from Moscow nearly one hundred years before. Rodzianko was a fine horseman, and everywhere he went he encountered animals. On his Ukrainian—he rarely seemed to pause between one tale and the next—estate he had had a pet bear, Mishka, who travelled with him in trains, slept in his study, and, standing on his hind legs, drank beer from a bottle. One morning Mishka had wandered into a local shop and stood with his paws on the counter. The shopkeeper, mistaking the bear's grunts for threatening behaviour, had promptly handed over the open beer bottle he held in his hand, after which Mishka repeated this performance daily, so that his master had to arrange for the beer to be put on account. Later Mishka took to vodka 'which he consumed with unholy zeal'. During the war Rodzianko adopted a little pig that he had found wandering in the deserted ruins of a village, and taught it to jump. But the pig was mistakenly eaten by a Red Cross unit.

After a while the Mission headquarters and its nucleus of staff moved to their permanent location in a large school building. Here Knox, Blair, Rodzianko, and Gerhardie lived in considerable comfort with servants and an excellent Chinese cook. Gerhardie's own man, once valet to a millionaire, thought his thrifty new master a poor contrast. 'I daresay he feels the war very painfully', wrote Gerhardie, who was having trouble keeping pace with his servant's tastes.

Knox, punctual, precise, and with too much to do, found Gerhardie indispensible as an assistant and after only a few weeks as a full Lieutenant promoted him to Captain. He also approved of his subordinate's thrift: Gerhardie was one of the very few officers who did not constantly attempt to borrow money (Knox was known to be well-off). The British Military Representative had exacting methods: he rose at 5.00 a.m., entered William's room at 6.00 with work to be done, and would often barge in and continue to add to the pile until as late as 1.00 in the morning. Many of Knox's habits depended on his digestion—bad on account of the poor sanitation and cooking conditions. Never before had the underdone potato held so much sway—on a poor day Rodzianko cursed Knox for keeping him awake by typing until 4.00 a.m., and even the good-natured Blair admitted 'the old devil is sometimes very trying, though, of course he is a d—n good fellow'.

The precise tasks of the Mission were always rather vague—to protect supplies, and, in conjunction with an International Railway Mission with headquarters at Harbin, to operate and protect the Trans-Siberian Railway. The 4,000 miles of track between Baikal and Omsk were guarded in part by the two English regiments, the Middlesex and the Hampshires, but also by Czechs and Russians armed, equipped, and instructed by Knox. There were also two Canadian regiments and an American regiment, together with 80,000 Japanese troops, in residence. Major Phelps Hodges, who arrived in Vladivostok in early 1919, described the task of that one small Mission as the training and equipping of Kolchak's recruits, 'a Russian army of 100,000 men in Siberia alone'. Rodzianko reckoned the figure to be nearer 200,000. Yet the whole affair was run in the most haphazard manner. Officers had been picked at random—Hodges himself was there for no better reason (as far as he could see) than that whilst recovering from a wound received in the trenches he had sent off for a Hugo's Correspondence Course in Russian. Many of the officers knew not a word of the language, and had the near-impossible task of training troops with the help of interpreters. Gerhardie described the following incident: a British officer who considered himself a Russian scholar delivered a speech in Russian to a group of Russian generals. Afterwards he approached one of the generals and asked how he had liked the lecture. This old man, well known for his politeness, replied: 'Well, I regret that in my youth I have rather neglected the study of English and consequently have not caught everything you said.'

The soldiers' living quarters, by contrast with the Mission head-quarters, were atrocious. Numbers had quickly swelled and many lived in railway carriages because of the lack of accommodation in the town. The barracks, as one fellow remarked cheerfully when he arrived, were exactly like the Boche prison camp where he had spent the last four years. 'The senior officers took no notice of us whatever', wrote Hodges, 'and we literally had no idea what we had been sent for. No statement of policy, no instructions as to the aims and objects of the Mission, no information as to our future employment, and no effort to keep us employed, properly housed, or fed. Not even a talk from General Blair, or one of the Staff, on what to do or what not to do.'[10] Knox and his staff were simply too busy elsewhere, their task too great to accomplish properly, the land too huge to control, and their purpose too diffuse to allow for policy. Even Churchill later described it as 'The Ghost War', 'a war in areas so vast that considerable armies, armies indeed of hundreds of thousands of men were lost—dispersed, melted, evaporated'.[11] None the less, Knox battled on. The following year he was knighted for his efforts and Gerhardie had the pleasure of relaying the news to him: 'Sir A. was very pleased, but naturally would pretend that it was "all rot".'

As the Mission mess was not large enough, officers were directed to the Zolotoi Rog Restaurant, known in the barracks as the Solitary Dog. 'William Gerhardie', wrote Hodges, 'at that time a member of Britmis, in his excellent novel *Futility*, has given a very slightly exaggerated description of its "service".'[12] This restaurant was, for most British, their first introduction to the Russians' complete contempt for time. They would order, and then wait. Hours passed. 'Entreaties, prayers, threats, curses, all brought the same answer from the waiter.

"*Seichass*"—immediately'. 'No special arrangements, no bribes, no threats, could lessen the time necessary for ordering a meal. Two hours, almost to the minute, was the recognized period. If one ordered and then went away, expecting to return later and find it nearly ready, one's waiter had probably disappeared or had forgotten all about one. In self-defence, to pass the time, we took to vodka and liked it.'[13] Even Gerhardie, at other times a temperate man, seemed perpetually tipsy. When at last the food arrived it was on a Russian scale: Hodges ordered a cutlet and received four young shoulders of mutton; even the oysters were obese. They learned to order one meal between four.

Soon after arriving at the Mission headquarters, 'incomplete and contradictory' rumours began to filter through to Knox about the murder of the Tsar and his family at Ipatiev House in Ekaterinburg. Not until a few weeks later, when the White forces finally recaptured that town, were they able to start an investigation. Knox and a small party set off to inspect the area, and make a report. Rodzianko examined the basement room where on 16 July the Cheka had set to work: he found ricochet bullet-holes and bayonet stabs in the wooden floor, but the bodies were never discovered. Gerhardie, with a perhaps slightly over-developed sense of the dramatic, has given a lengthy account of the royal family's final hours in *The Romanovs*, and of the butchery that followed the assassin's last speech before he placed his revolver on the Tsar's forehead and fired. The eleven Lett soldiers each took aim at one of the eleven prisoners: seven members of the royal family, the family doctor, two menservants, and a maid. ('Evidently the Revolution was no respecter of persons.') 'It is in vain', Gerhardie concludes, 'to ask why such things are done.' As the Reds had massacred, so the Whites ruthlessly destroyed the assassin, Yurovski, and his family, and the families of his family. 'It is vain to plead "historical necessity". It is these historical necessities which, by placing distant objectives above the suffering unit, are to blame for the long and heartless tomfoolery of history.'[14]

It became increasingly clear that the political objectives in Siberia were futile and misplaced. Hodges thought it was because the Allied Mission was insufficiently committed to either Red or White ideology. 'If the Allies had decided on the downfall of Lenin and Trotsky, they could easily have chased them out of Moscow with Allied troops, but they had to keep up a pretence of neutrality, and armed the White troops to do the work for them.'[15] After visiting Omsk during the summer of 1919 and seeing the results of conflict with Kolchak's forces, Hodges later wrote that most of the interventionist troops including, he hinted, himself, secretly sympathized with the Bolsheviks, so evident was the corruption and cowardice of the Whites: 'It was revolting to see wounded men dragging their way from station to hospital over dirty streets for perhaps a mile or two, while officers rode scornfully by in droshkies or motor cars.'[16] Even the strongly anti-Bolshevik Knox did not greatly admire the Whites.

The experience of British participants in Russia was significantly different from that of soldiers serving on the Western Front during the First World War. There is nothing comic in the 'futility' of the latter: it is evocative of massive and unnecessary loss of life, lack of purpose, inept leadership, and appalling battle conditions. But Gerhardie, viewing the Allied intervention as 'a series of comic opera attempts to wipe out the Russian revolution . . . an adventure in futility', was not alone in assigning to the interventionist 'futility' a humorous twist. Hodges speaks of 'this gigantic struggle, which, for all its tragedy and suffering, contains much that is comic and futile'.[17] Another Mission officer, writing to Gerhardie years later, 'sometimes wondered what became of the various actors in that rather pointless farce'.[18]

The vast size of Russia, its scores of nationalities and political factions, the passionate ideological commitment of a minority versus the chaotic ignorance of the majority, the precarious contingent nature of political success, the often farcical unreliability of the Russian army, even the very magnitude of atrocities committed which rendered verbal expression inadequate: all these factors lent an air of the absurd to life in eastern Russia. Gerhardie's pre-war writing had shown a ludicrously grotesque, though essentially sympathetic, humour. Involvement in the civil war significantly strengthened this bias into an ironic detachment that saw 'futility' as finely balanced *tragi-comedy*. His notebooks are filled with jottings and observations:

Captain McCullagh painted the bolsheviks in colours so black and lurid, made them so horrid and terrible in their atrocities that when the Siberians whom it was his object to stir up by his propaganda to fight the bolsheviks, got his papers, they said 'No: we're off', and fled in disorder.

Then again:

The Siberians ran away over to the bolsheviks, but the latter thinking that they are being attacked retreat in disorder. It was consequently, many a mile that the Siberians had to run after the Bls to give themselves up!

Gerhardie did not fight, but he witnessed brutality—and its after-math—on a massive scale. The morning after an unsuccessful coup by the Czech General Gaida revealed a frozen landscape of massacred bodies. 'The square, the streets, the yards, the rails, and sundry ditches betrayed them lying in horrid postures, dead or dying. Those who were not dead, when discovered were finished with the bayonet by the "loyal" troops, amid unspeakable yells.'[19] Eighty prisoners, he told his parents, some almost green from fright, their hands in the air, were driven down a staircase at the station. There followed a rattle of machine guns from within. A young man, about William's own age, good-looking and gentle, was found hiding in the chimney, and hurried off by his captors to be separately dispatched. When Gerhardie entered the station he saw the boy on the top of the pile, the back of his scalp blown off. The dead men's boots had been removed and appropriated by their executioners. Another man lay wounded in the pile shamming death while a curious mob walked about him. 'This was done by the people whom we are helping, and honestly, with the best intention in the world it is difficult to see any difference in the methods of the bolsheviks and the reaction-aries.' His simultaneous sense of compassion and detachment finds expression in an extract from his diary, which was put almost verbatim into *Futility*: 'The horror of the sight of a dead body is that it brings home to you, stronger perhaps than anything else, the conviction of the *temporary* nature of a human being. What was once a human being is now an object—like a stone, or a stick.'

He was also in not inconsiderable danger. When the fighting in Vladivostok grew particularly fierce the Allied Missions convened a conference, to which Gerhardie accompanied one Colonel Wickham. This involved walking to their motor-car across a square that was being pelted by machine-gun fire. Yet Wickham did not increase his leisurely pace, and Gerhardie was obliged to conform. When at last they drove off in the car, Wickham remarked with a smile: 'My nerves are not what they used to be.'[20] At times events were so momentous that Gerhardie could only write laconically: 'Played tennis in the afternoon; then had a woman; then a bath, and afterwards witnessed a revolution.' Ger-hardie's brief political idealism of 1917 was evolving into a cyclical view of history—revolution was not progressive but circular, the perpetual exchange of one set of values for another. As the most workable compromise for Russia he believed in a form of co-operative socialism: 'It must come', he wrote. 'Only such people who still believe in a kind of divinity of the ruling class will ignore that fact, but soon they will be the only people left who will believe in this divinity; no one else shall.'

The chaos continued. Crime, corruption, and profiteering flourished; half the population starved. Astronomical inflation caused an acute shortage of paper money. The Vladivostok police arrested a Nagasaki steamer passenger carrying two suitcases of 2,000,000 forged Omsk roubles. Owing to diplomatic relations with Japan, the Vladivostok authorities wired to Omsk reporting the case and asking for instructions. The reply came back immediately: 'Urgent stop Deport Japanese subject stop Put notes in circulation immediately.'[21]

With the approach of winter the entire bay froze over and fighting became impossible. A wedding party near Ekaterinburg was caught by wolves and eaten, horses, bridesmaids, and all. The British troops played football when they could, and the Canadians caused considerable interest with their figure-skating. Gerhardie remained in reasonable spirits, while finding Vladivostok 'exceptionally monotonous', a 'god-forsaken part of the world'. He had bought himself a fur coat which, not having been properly cured, shed its hair everywhere, so that he took to wearing a deerskin ('I look in it like a proletariat').

In spring he and the Financial Adviser on the Mission, Captain Sandelson, a well-known London solicitor, took a brief holiday and drove thirty *versts* into the country. Finding no hotels they stopped for the night at a small restaurant where the owner offered them his dining-room to sleep in. Gerhardie was too fastidious to use the blankets which had come from the man's own bed, though he satisfied himself that the 'sheets'—dirty tablecloths from the restaurant—were only stained with jam, coffee, butter, and gravy. On another occasion he set off with a fellow officer to Mukden in quest of several thousand sheepskin coats ordered by Knox, which had simply disappeared. The two delayed as long as possible, travelling in a leisurely way via Harbin, a Russian town on Chinese territory where (as Gerhardie noted) 'every other girl was passable; every third, good-looking; every fourth, a beauty'. And, meeting up with a woman who was searching for her husband, he temporarily took the man's place. 'Meanwhile, the situation as regards the sheepskin coats was vague and obscure. Obscure and uncertain. Uncertain and hypothetical, to quite an extraordinary degree.'[22] The obscurities became a little less prominent when, after some weeks, Knox wired to point out that it was not coats after all, but hats that Gerhardie was supposed to be looking for.

*

At Mission headquarters, Gerhardie's 'meteroic' rise on the staff occasioned not a few petty jealousies, and the efforts of a succession of senior officers to displace him. A fat, flabby Major and a beady-eyed Colonel prowled about the office, intriguing to get his job; while Gerhardie, himself a master of intrigue, schemed to keep his place by letting it be known he would soon vacate the position of his own accord.

One of his chief tasks was to supply précis of the current situation, initiating the higher ranks into the mysteries of the devilishly complicated local politics. Knox, with his impeccable standards of excellence, would enquire (for example) 'if you are aware of the relation between the so-called nationalities such as the Letts, Latvians, Lithuanians, and so forth, and the so-called countries as Lettland, Latvia, Lithuania, Esthonia, Livonia, Esthland, Kurland, Livland, and so forth?' to say nothing of the Poles, the Czechs, the Yanks, Japs, Romanians, French, Italians, Serbians, Slovenes, Jugoslavians, the German, Austrian, Hungarian, and Magyar war-prisoners; the Chinese, the Canadians, the British, 'and many other different nationalities, whose presence rather tends to complicate the situation in view of the several politics they follow'.[23] In spite of all, Gerhardie quickly found himself head of his department, 'viz. the General Office, which is divided into several sub-sections, such as all political, secret and confidential and personal telegrams and correspondence section, all ciphering and coding and typing for the whole of the Headquarters Staff, all central registering of telegrams, etc., and', he continued, he was 'a sort of private secretary to Genl Knox and in his absence to Genl [*sic*] Blair'. Every visitor that looked in he interviewed,

Dictators, Supreme Rulers, Prime Ministers, Ministers, Admirals and some times merely Generals, of whom there is a score here. I have under me in Dept one Major (a 'tame' one), one Captain, (an ex-Oxford Don) one Lieutenant (who had been British Consul in China for 30 years and is twice these years) and one 2nd Lieutenant; also 3 Staff-Sergeants and five privates (who do all the typing and registering). Now if this is not enough to make your head swell, I don't know what is! I need hardly say that nearly every one of my 'subordinates' is at least 10 years older than I am.

He enjoyed intermittent contact with England, writing home when he could spare a moment but having to whisk the sheet out of the typewriter whenever Knox bustled past. Again he warned his mother not to try to contact Rosie, encouraged Charles's idea to write a book on the Russian card game Vint, and asked him to give Clara a kiss. Dolly wrote a letter now and again, Victor never, and Daisy continued to send his play round to publishers.

One memorable autumn Gerhardie accompanied Knox and Rodzianko on a visit to Omsk, travelling the 4,000 miles by Trans-Siberian railway. The 'luxurious train, freshly painted, beautifully furnished, admirably kept' carried arms, ammunition, and food supplies through a 'stricken land of misery', alive with the dead and dying, outcasts, soldiers, the starving and the dispossessed; 'the glamour of innumerable lights within our carriages presenting to a community of half-starving refugees the gloating picture of the Admiral and his "staff" at dinner'.[24] They sat up late drinking pepper vodka and singing gypsy ballads till the dawn broke—and always the threat of guerrilla attacks, trickery, and sabotage. Then the Russian general grew maudlin. 'Tell me you love Russia,' he begged. 'We both love Russia. Tell me you love Russia. She's been degraded and trampled on; but she is a fine country. She will arise. She must arise.' He began to sob. 'Tell me you love Russia. Tell me you love her. We Russians are lazy, drunken, good-for-nothing swine, but we are good people, aren't we? It's a holy land. It's a holy people. Look at her.'[25] He gazed out of the window. Often they almost came to blows, 'for the ordinary Russian does not argue: he shouts, and his opponent, to score a point, shouts louder and quicker'. Gerhardie shared a sleeping compartment with Knox, flattered that he should have been chosen but acutely conscious of Knox's embarrassed discomfort over where to put his false teeth, and finding his English sensibilities a little comic: Knox blushed and giggled like a schoolgirl whenever his wife was mentioned, while Rodzianko, Russian and unabashed, marched boldly into religion and the tender emotions. At Omsk, where they put up in the train, Knox diverted himself by throwing empty tobacco tins at the pigs that dwelt in the surrounding ditches. 'You have no conception what a pig a pig really is,' he said, 'till you see an Omsk pig.'[26]

For Gerhardie one trip was sufficient. Thereafter he insisted that he was indispensable in the office and remained with Colonel Blair. When Blair went away Gerhardie worked under Sir Edward Grogan, a fussy individual blessed with 'a masterly grasp of the inessential' and maddeningly polite: if Gerhardie so much as handed him a piece of paper he responded, in an inimitably English accent, 'Thank you, thank you, thank you so much, thank you very much, so good of you, so very nice of you, thank you, splendid fellow!'

Gerhardie got on badly with NCOs and rather well with the senior officers. Photographs of this period show him well at ease chatting with generals of every nationality. Knox continued to value him highly—'the most practically useful officer on the Mission'. One day Gerhardie walked into his bedroom to find Knox seated with a small man, dark-haired and aquiline-featured, the pair talking like conspirators. The stranger rose with the precision common to Russian officers and shook hands. Gerhardie later learned with pride that this was none other than General Kolchak; some months later the infamous White leader was captured by the Reds and shot.

But for all his value, Gerhardie's egocentricity, intellectual arrogance, and obsession with women made him 'but moderately popular' in the mess. 'I know William used to look on every woman's body as his own property for a time',[27] one Mission member later wrote. Another composed a long Old Testament-style chronicle of the Mission in which Gerhardie appears as Ger the son of Hardi:

> And he set up a graven image in the house of his brethren, and commanded men to worship before it. And the name of the image was Ego.

The chronicle relates how Gerhardie was busily and pleasantly arguing one night with Konni Zilliacus, a brilliant young officer who later did important work in the League of Nations, when three others broke open the door,

> And they spoiled the household stuff of Ger the son of Hardi, and his rubber goods wherein he delighted.
>
> And offered them for a burnt-offering on the threshold of Spencer the Cipherite, according to the word of Higgs the Prophet which he spake unto them.
>
> And the smell thereof was very great.

Gerhardie himself composed and circulated spoof newspaper reports of the Siberian situation: 'Bright Bits From the Baltic; Reds Looking Blue; Petrograd Petrified; Letts Have a Battle (from our Special Correspondent Mr Borham Stiff)'. He was a lively talker, and his literary remarks a familiar, though incongruous, part of office life. Outraged by his intellectual assertiveness and aloofness some officers again burst into his bedroom and hoisted him, bed and all, on to the roof. Gerhardie stayed put, pretending to enjoy it more than they, and was eventually carried back still comfortably tucked up.

He was also viewed as being a little on the stingy side. Prudence he would have called it, and it was moreover a trait manifested with such ironic self-consciousness as to be scarcely offensive. He could also be giving and, if not precisely generous, then at least so humorously almost generous that one could not help but feel charmed; he issued the following memo to a selection of officers:

INSTRUCTIONS

1. You are hereby informed that dinner will be provided for you tonight at 8.30 at the ZOLOTOI ROG at Capt. Gerhardi's expense, which should be regarded by you as a return of the hospitality that in a thoughtless moment he was lead to accept from you on a previous occasion.

2. You are reminded that the strictest possible economy should be observed throughout the meal. We have won the war, but our victory will not be worth having unless we remember that it is our duty to ourselves and our hosts on all occasions to suppress waste wherever we find it.

3. Your attention is drawn to the fact that the dearest dishes are not always the most tasteful, inasmuch as cheap food is not necessarily bad.

4. Many illusions are cherished about wine by people of high credulity who have not the honesty to admit that water is every bit as good. If insisted, however, wine will be provided at Capt. Sandelson's expense.

5. The settling of cloak-room expenses has been delegated to Lieut. Gruner, R.N.V.R.

6. Major F. Graham Powell, Embarkation Staff, will detail Sergt. Hashigan to act as waiter, thus saving unnecessary expense for service, etc.

7. All guests are invited to participate in tips.

> W. A. Gerhardi
> Captain

Vladivostok, 4th April 1919

For all its dreary melancholy Vladivostok was not lacking in spirited entertainment at the various Allied Mission headquarters and on Allied cruisers. 'My tangled memories of Siberia', William wrote years later, 'come to me today largely as a string of dances, dinners, concerts, garden-parties, modulated by the atmosphere of weather and the seasons of the year, with the gathering clouds of the political situation looming always in the background.'[28] There were Hawaiian string bands on the US flagship, brass bands on the British, waltzes, and, as the years progressed, the newly fashionable foxtrot and one-step. Knox enjoyed such entertainment: one Russian woman, he was fond of repeating sagely, is worth ten Russian men.

The officers, well paid, well fed, and clean, were never short of female company. Gerhardie diverted himself with the voluptuous, dark-haired Lina Goldstein who for many years afterwards sent photographs of herself overwritten with provocative messages: 'I am wearing purple hyacinths—for you dear. Don't think that my hair is cut. It is long, and black, and awaits to entangle your soul in its darkness.' Ten years later she turned up in London with her husband to visit Gerhardie, having grown into 'a typical Jewess of extreme dimension'. And it was in Vladivostok that he met Nina, Sonia, and Vera, the mysterious 'three sisters' of his first novel *Futility*. Nina, object of Gerhardie's infatuation, flirted, enticed, charmed, and ultimately rejected him. Despite her central role in *Futility*, she and the rest of the Bursanov family are curiously elusive to the biographer—one finds only a brief mention here and there amongst his archives, a walk one evening together through frosty pine woods on to the frozen seashore, the sky 'grey and fretful' and darkness falling deeper every minute; and a small and tatty photograph of a young, smiling Nina lying in the grass with a dog. From the novel we know that, barely more than a child, she would tease him, jump about on the sofa, take water in her mouth and squirt it in his face. She maddened him considerably—she was quiet and thoughtful; she had a lithe body and disturbing sidelong glance; she was carefree, impetuous, unconstrained: 'I liked you this morning', she sprang on him. 'But *now* . . . ! You are nice and there are days when I like you . . .' Yet she and her family remain a mystery.

As the year advanced Gerhardie grew weary of the perpetually changing but never progressing state of affairs, bemused by the sheer scale and madness of it all. He took to long lonely walks in the dark: 'Who can convey at all adequately that sense of utter hopelessness that clings to a Siberian winter night? Wherever else is there to be found that brooding, thrilling sense of frozen space, of snow and ice lost in inky darkness, that gruesome sense of never-ending night, and black despair and loneliness untold, immeasurable?'[29] 'I sat among my guests, strangely flushed, and the vast sea of Russian life seemed to be closing over me.' As expectations of the outcome of the civil war varied from season to season, month to month, it became clear to almost all at the Mission that Intervention was a waste of time, effort, and money, and, if anything, only served to prolonged the misery of the Russian people. Gerhardie believed that Bolshevism in its militant and objectionable form would only last as long as there was military opposition to it for it was impossible to beat the Bolsheviks, and therefore the Intervention was nothing short of 'insanity'. 'I wish', he concluded, 'Winston would shut up'. It would be much the best for all, 'and us and poor dear Rosie in particular.'

The interventionists grew increasingly unpopular, handsomely cursed by all factions of the population in Russia: 'by those whom we are presumably helping, for not helping sufficiently, for not recognising them, for giving no loans, for withdrawing our troops, etc., etc. etc. By those against whom we are fighting, for doing this for our own ends. And by those who do not think the question of the form of Govt for Russia is a sufficient reason for a lot of apathetic people to continue to slaughter each other.' The hypocrisy inherent in the conflict grew ever greater, and though 'freedom' on one side has always had a tendency to be 'terrorism' on the other, the virulence of the denunciations and the savageries of the denouncers seemed without end or parallel. 'And so it goes on, month after month.' Gerhardie grew impatient with Knox's unbounded efficiency. 'One day in Vladivostok the devil got hold of me . . .' Whilst Knox was sitting quietly in the office typing, William suddenly loosed a flood of invective against the Allied policy, the British government, and above all the 'perverted and romantic' military, 'infants who know no better'. On and on he went, louder and shriller, until Knox rose precipitately—'by the look of it to kick me out of his room'—but got caught, inexplicably entangled, in his typewriter. At which moment Gerhardie made a hasty but dignified exit.

Blair is a much sounder, if less flamboyant, man and is broader in outlook and far less prejudiced. Knox is one of those men who style themselves 'the Englishmen who *know* Russia'—a phrase which means that the Englishman has lived in Russia, associated with a certain class of Russians, acquired all their prejudices —the prejudices of their class, and afterwards calls on his Govt to support his friends and calls them 'Russia'—to support them against the whole of the rest of Russia whom he calls 'swine and blackguards'.

Rodzianko, on the other hand, was bitter when the Allies at last agreed to withdraw, for he believed that a little more help for a little longer would have finally ousted the Bolsheviks. But by the autumn the Mission was being gradually reduced; Gerhardie spent most of the day at his own writing and even Knox began to look forward to leading a quiet life at home. Gerhardie wanted none the less to stay until the end because he had been present from the start, and because he was earning a very good salary—now paid in dollars as the rouble was valueless. 'Our Mission, as the whole of this fantastic scheme of "Intervention", has proved a "wash-out"', he wrote to his parents, deprecating the melodramatic mood of the press, dismissing the descriptions of the

Vladivostok battlefields, and explaining that *coups d'état*, so prestigious in the West, were storms in a teacup in Vladivostok. Besides, 'the bolsheviks here are a much nicer sort of people to deal with than the old regime'.

By February very few remained. The British batmen had left and Gerhardie was now attended by a German prisoner called Gerhard. By April the Americans had departed, and at last Knox telegraphed to London:

GENERAL KNOX PRESUMES THAT HIS FURTHER STAY HERE CAN SERVE NO USEFUL PURPOSE AND RECOMMENDS RECALL TO ENGLAND

The reply came:

GENERAL KNOX'S PRESUMPTION IS CORRECT

'I think the only good Siberia has done to me', wrote Gerhardie, 'is that it has taught me to foxtrot, which I enjoy thoroughly; but to think that for that it should have been necessary to come to Siberia!' To return through Soviet Russia was out of the question. Instead, the very last of the Mission left Vladivostok by special train: Gerhardie, Blair and his wife, and Rodzianko, who carried Joy, the Tsarevich Alexei's little spaniel who had escaped when he and the family were murdered. There was an attempt at a smart military send-off at the station, but the war office had long since withdrawn most of the men, and the parade was not inspiring. A Russian general in a grey coat with scarlet lining stamped up and down in front of the small Japanese guard of honour in red-banded caps, and a meagre Russian military band; the peasants with their faces against the railing simply watched and stared. Mrs Blair blew a whistle which started the train. There was a jerk, another and another. William stood at the window and watched the vanishing scene: a few mills, a few factories, a cemetery, a glimpse of a river, then fields and woods. 'The engine gave a shrill whistle. The train rattled on with increasing speed, swayed at the curve—and all these things had become of the past.'[30]

'Ah! China! How it all comes back: that spell of langour, of pathos in the very animation of Peking at night. I can see Canton with its narrow, crowded streets sheltering beneath the dripping, overlapping roofs and shops, and feel the sombre enigmatic calm of their interior, the lethargic stare of Chinese merchants seated on the floor, and the thudding of the rain upon the roof.' As the train rolled south through Manchuria,

Gerhardie's companions argued heatedly about the relative merits of Oxford and Cambridge.

And I can see the dull and yellow water of the rivers, the swarming multitudes of lives upon the quays, the sampans crowding the canals; and I recall again the din of Nanking, the stench of ancient muddy soil receding from my sight as I watched from the window of the train, the fall of evening and the melancholy of the ages. And, you know, I was made to feel that I was in another age, another world, that somewhere I must have dreamt this or perhaps have known it before I was born on earth, that deep in the recesses of my memory was an imprint of this peculiar light, this noise and din, this languid stillness of the East.[31]

'Peking is, of course, a wonderful old city with queer old palaces and temples and full of all sorts of curios', wrote Gerhardie, but just now he was in the mood for the brilliant modernity of New York or Shanghai. He telegraphed to his parents before leaving Peking, missing by two days the arrival of his Mission mate Major Phelps Hodges who, on a military assignment, had undergone a seven-month trek in the dead of winter on foot and horseback more than 3,000 miles across the Kirghiz steppes and the Gobi desert. Gerhardie and his party continued to Tientsin, Nanking, and Shanghai, where they sank under the relentless hospitality of the British community of merchants and brokers. All had the expatriate's obsession with the mother-country, and were anxious to show their patriotism, but had had little opportunity of helping the war effort so that whenever a party of officers arrived in Shanghai these families would 'bounce' upon them at the station, 'capture' them, and convey them in luxurious automobiles to their palatial retreats where they intrigued and talked scandal all day long. After three days Gerhardie was quite convinced that he had won the war single-handed.

Here he visited the enchantress Nina again, now exiled with her family. For months he had thought of little else but this reunion but, like the hero of *Futility*, he was mortified to find that they all treated him with the greatest indifference. After a blazing row with Nina he marched abruptly out of the front door without saying goodbye, and stepped dramatically into his motor car—only to find that it would not start. He eventually moved off jerkily amidst shrieks of laughter from Nina and her sisters on the balcony. At his host's house he dined alone, ensconced in the patriarchal chair while a succession of butlers and Chinese waiters slipped noiselessly into the room carrying a multitude of dishes and wines. 'They never asked me what I wanted. They studied my expression and tried to divine. I think I impressed them by endeavouring to maintain a grim look—of the "strong silent man", somewhat after the manner of Admiral Beatty.' Afterwards he indicated a desire to write and immediately a host of servants carried in a writing table, until at length, the expensive wines he had chosen for dinner working upon him, he fell asleep. 'When I woke I saw a column of Chinese servants headed by the chief butler standing in perfect symetry behind me, awaiting my further orders. I ordered them to carry me upstairs into my perfumed bedroom when I soon fell asleep on my large, soft bed under the moscito net.'

From Shanghai Gerhardie sailed, heartbroken, to Hong Kong, 'a beautiful port but—ph! what a climate. It is the most damnable combination of heat and dampness that you can imagine. It makes you feel quite sick.' Green mould grew all over his luggage. The Hong Kong inhabitants were horribly 'struck-up' and talked perpetually of 'Society', and vied for the Governor's attention. The officers were invited to a ball at the Governor's residence on King George V's birthday, but could not go as none possessed the correct levee dress.

On board the *Professor* the party sailed via Singapore, Colombo, Aden, Port Said, and Cairo, where Gerhardie rode a camel to see the Sphinx. The boat was comfortable but old, frequently in need of repairs, and very slow: 'We have, I think, beaten a record voyage. It is the slowest voyage across the "high seas" since the sixties.' The novel was nearly finished and Gerhardie settled down to 'bovril and biscuits, deck-tennis and quoits, concerts, dances, cocktails, conversations, fudge, lemon squash' and a fancy-dress ball where he dressed as a Red Guard. But after weeks of monotony, suddenly, lying indolent on deck, he was fired with fierce impatience, 'seized with energy, filled with dread lest I should lose another moment. . . . It was as if these wasted months had tumbled over me and were pressing me down with their weight. I longed to see it finished, printed, an accomplished task embodied in between two cardboard sheets of binding, wrapped in a striking yellow jacket, and sold at so much net. This old decrepit ship was so intolerably slow. She literally went to sleep. I wanted to *do* things, to live, to work, to build, to shout.'[32]

Early next morning land appeared on the dim horizon. Another day and at last England hove in sight, 'quite plainly now as a green island with houses and people and parks. . . . It was doleful in the gathering twilight, and the lights of England blinked at us ruefully, sadly. The gong echoed to the sound of the sea, and the gulls, the wind, and the drizzling rain.'[33]

6

OH, FUTILITY
July 1920–June 1922

I am so glad I went to Oxford because if I had not gone I would have such a tremendous respect for anyone who had been there. As it is, I don't care a damn.

Charles, never demonstrative, suddenly began to display extraordinary impatience when he heard that William had set sail from Shanghai. He studied the shipping intelligence in the papers, and sent Sissie off in search of news. He fretted and grumbled. When at last William walked through the door, Charles urgently demanded to see him privately. Alone together, he confided to his son the agony he had suffered all through the infernally slow progress of the boat, delaying so cruelly his homecoming, as he wished to borrow £25 for a speculation he had in mind.

Investment, or the anticipation of it, had become Charles's consoling pastime.

He had extravagant hopes of making money by sending every penny or ten-shilling note he could lay his hands on to dubious brokers in London, who advertised for likely victims. His old financial perspicacity seemed to have left him and he was invariably cheated by those sharks of the mart. . . . When my mother refused to give him any more money for his speculations, he would keep up a sustained scream at regular intervals to force her hand, or compromise her with the neighbours.[1]

Clara, since the stroke, had become a competent and efficient head of the family, and the energy and spirit which she had formerly put into entertaining, she now directed towards rallying her dependants. She organized their limited finances with the utmost care, was mindful of morale, courageous, cheerful, and above all dependable: 'Duty comes before all', she later wrote to William, 'there can be no life worth living without it.' Though she found England unfamiliar, rather drab, and above all cold ('I really think England takes the cake for discomfort in the houses'), she adapted to this unexpected homecoming more readily than Charles, who dreamed impotently of £100, a manservant, and the Continent. But instead of Vienna, Paris, and Monte Carlo, the Gerhardis moved north to join Dolly in Lancashire. Clara purchased a semi-detached house, 40 Bradford Street, Bolton, in an area populated by the professional and lower middle classes: several dentists, commercial travellers, and teachers of music, a builder, a doctor, and, immediately next door, an NSPCC inspector. Thus the family had a roof—but no income. So Clara, 52 years old, having spent her entire life attended by servants, set to work again: almost single-handed she converted the front room of the house into a small shop, *Madame Claire*, where she sold gowns, lingerie, and elaborate hats sent over from France by Daisy who had recently moved to Paris.

Charles, confined to his wheelchair, his right hand twisted and paralysed, was subject to frequent bouts of gloom: 'There he sat day after day. Formerly he had only read newspapers. Now he began to read books, too. When tired of reading he would begin to brood on the past; and when tired of thinking he read again. He sat there, pulling out his watch at intervals, waiting for the evening paper, restless, anxious to get time on, to "kill time".'[2] At night, after hours of inactivity, he could not sleep. 'Poor Papa eats less and less and is very irritable', Clara wrote to her son. 'I do not think he is feeling well. He enjoyed the opera very much to which I took him last week. He and I alone like Darby and Joan.' Untiringly she cared for him, washing and shaving him, dressing him, manœuvring him up and downstairs every day, cooking for him, reading aloud, and wheeling him on outings. Charles's two or three letters to his wife at this period, written when she was away visiting, and banged out with his left hand on an ancient and rusty typewriter (the same which William had painstakingly dispatched in diplomatic bags from war-torn Petrograd), conjure little of the intimidating, energetic personality of St Petersburg days. They are composed in the informal, semi-educated manner ('well tata for the present') of somebody unaccustomed to writing, or, like many polyglots, perhaps lacking a sophisticated command of any one language:

My Dear Clara,

It is many years since I wrote to you but I suppose it is a case of better late than never. . . . Mr Kay does very well and is one of the rare good sort, the only fault I can find with him is that he is too fond of jawing. He jaws for a ½ hour and more every morning and evening so that instead of 5 minutes he is here for nearly an hour, all the same he is a very interesting original chap and has had a great experience of all sorts of operations and treatments of the wounded in the war both on land and on hospital ships and he relates some most interesting operations such as removing damaged parts and ribs inside, grafting flesh and skin to blown out parts inside and stitching up of wounds of all sorts. He even offered of himself to come and take me out in my bath chair every afternoon but that would be going too far. . . . We all miss you very much and impatiently wait for Saturday when we shall see your dear face again.

Oh yes Mr Kay told me honestly and without complementary exaggerations that he thought you to be a foreigner and not over 40 years old so you can go up 1 . . . This machine is not all right yet and having no more news I will finish with much love to you and Sissie from us all and loving kisses and a good hug to you from your everloving HUBBY.

P.S. Am pleased to see East Rands advanced 6d at the close yesterday it is as I expected and there seems no cause for alarm, a wait and see policy is the best under the circumstances. I see also that as I said they would the german marks have improved from 350 to 290 to the pound. If you want to make money now the good and pretty sure thing is to buy a ton or two of biscuits as after April 12th all articles containing flour will rise considerably such as bread, fancy pastry, buns, biscuits etc.

The profits from *Madame Claire* were modest and highly unpredictable—one week three hats sold, yielding £5, another week nothing. William had saved £1,000, money he intended to spend on what he considered to be a necessary—almost symbolic—start to his English life: an Oxford degree. This was a desire he later (perhaps overdeprecatingly) described as 'dictated by a sense of propriety. . . . Going to Oxford was merely for me a sort of inoculation against future academic snobbery. Degrees were valid only in so far as they would be missed if they were denied oneself.'[3] But his family thought him 'mad', and only Clara, who envisaged a brilliant literary future for her clever son, supported him.

Applying rather late, Gerhardie was accepted to read English Literature at Worcester College—home of the opium-eating De Quincey. Clara took great pleasure in packing for him. ('What a confounded lot of socks there are in my baggage', he remarked. 'It seems *all* socks. What are they all for?') He went up to Oxford just a few weeks before his twenty-fifth birthday, glad to leave dull, drab Bolton. 'I feel very happy and yet very lonely', he wrote, suddenly nostalgic, to Clara. 'It is extraordinary with me, but I rarely appreciate anything at the time. It is in retrospect that I begin to glorify it, and now I am already beginning to regret that the times we had spent together in Bolton are, at least temporarily, at an end. I know I have not been particularly pleasant or obliging when I was at home. I regret it. Perhaps I have been a little spoilt.' But spoiling William was what gave Clara greatest pleasure. 'My love and prayers are always with you darling son', she wrote back. 'You know I love you dearly, dearly and when I have provoked you, believe me, it has been from want of comprehension not want of heart. Another kiss. Your everloving Mother.'

Oxford was immediately entrancing, congenial and romantic, 'vague and loose' after the disciplines of army life. Gerhardie particularly admired 'the unassuming attitude of the dons'. The town was quiet and calm—hansom cabs for hire, meandering cattle and clergymen on bicycles the only traffic hazards. 'I really think it is going to do me an awful lot of good, as I am already loosing a good deal of my natural modesty, and am rapidly becoming conceited. When you see me next I daresay you will not recognise me.' At his own matriculation he was amused by the long Latin oration delivered by the Vice-Chancellor —'so much "Italiano"—out of a Verdi libretto—*"Donne e mobile"* sort of stunt'. Worcester, with its beautiful gardens, he thought unquestionably the best of all the colleges—superior to Pembroke, 'a rotten place' with 'no baths', and Queen's, 'a nasty place' full of 'men who come from the north and who talk in a thick northern accent: "We man from Bradford coom oop here to pick oop all the prizes", and that sort of thing!' Gerhardie, 'so proud to be, at last, a member of the great ancient noble University', enthusiastically described the curiously spartan college conditions (muddling his dates somewhat):

The baths are very good but you have to cross the quad, to get there, which most people find a somewhat chilly performance in the winter. But it was like that in the VII century and they found it unnecessary to alter it ever since.

It was, I am told, exactly as it is to-day 1600 years ago; the hardship was by way of helping the monks who lived in these rooms to expiate their sins; and nothing was ever altered since for historical reasons. An American undergraduate at Worcester who was shown round these ancient buildings and was told how very old they were, remarked very wisely, 'Then why the dickens don't you pull them down and build new ones?'

'I quite agree with the Americans', responded Charles.

In the immediate post-war years Oxford was exceptionally crowded, with several generations of war veterans whose military service had exempted them from entrance examinations, as well as the normal intake. Gerhardie was offered rooms to himself in lodgings, but preferred to remain in college and share. John Rothenstein, son of the painter William Rothenstein had come up from Bedales to read History—History, along with Law, Theology, and Classical Mods and Greats, being apparently one of the very few 'acceptable' subjects. ('English Literature was for women and foreigners', declared Evelyn Waugh. 'There was said to be a laboratory somewhere beyond Keble, but I never met anyone who dabbled there.'[4]) Gerhardie and Rothenstein had a bedroom each, and a large, shared sitting-room in the Queen Anne wing of the college; but William soon found his flat-mate lamentably 'indolent and lazy, casual, careless and slovenly in his habits, so that all the *practical* side of our ménage falls upon me, who, as you know, abounds in energy of that kind!' He set about improving the appearance of the sitting-room himself, hanging framed photographs around the walls (the St Petersburg house, the British Military Mission officers, and members of his family), covered a glass-topped table with green crinkly paper, and placed an amber alabaster pyramid, souvenir from Cairo, on the mantelpiece. Rothenstein, he hoped, would provide some of his father's paintings.

As freshmen they both received scores of invitations ('mostly from old women'). Gerhardie resolved to get up early, visited chapel, and though no sportsman, even went rowing in his first week, but quickly lapsed back into his preferred erratic schedule. The Musical Club claimed his attention regularly, the Anglo-Russian Society once or twice. Union debates he found entertaining: Lord Birkenhead was 'a bully of genius', Asquith 'very very old, but still speaks very well', and as for Churchill— 'I think he is insane.' At an address given by the young Prince of Wales (the future Edward VIII), Gerhardie was surprised to find that he delivered himself 'extraordinarily well . . . clearly and without any trace of affectation whatsoever . . . Altogether he is very popular and has a very distinct personality of his own which I did not believe until I saw him and heard him speak.'

Oxford itself was 'the most conservative place in England, and servants here are about as good and servile as they were in Russia before the liberation of the serfs':

My Scout [an ex-guardsman who had served with Lord Kitchener at Khartoum] thanks me for anything I happen to tell him, whereon I thank him, and then he thanks me back. He knocks at my bedroom door in the morning (about 12.30 or so) and says, 'Thank you, sir. It's 12.30, thank you.' 'Thank you,' I reply, to which he answers, 'Thank you, sir.' Then we thank each other for half-an-hour or so, when I begin to consider the possibility of getting up.

In the sitting-room, however, the scout would flap his duster four times, once at each of the three chairs and once at the mantelpiece, then retire slamming the door. Rothenstein was amused by 'the recurrent fits of agitation, near madness almost, of Gerhardi, due to suspicion that his scout day by day was stealing his marmalade spoonful by spoonful'.[5] Gerhardie found his own dementia inspirational:

> Whether I eat marmalade or not,
> It sinks daily in the pot.

Though fresh from Siberia, he was astonished at the severity of the English weather, and even more at the 'curious habit here of walking down the streets all winter with nothing on except a muffler—I suppose to defy the weather. They used to do it 600 years ago, when it was warmer; and no one hardly ever wears an overcoat.' Miserably cold and damp, Oxford was 'decidedly the most unhealthy place in England', and all the dons, he told his parents, suffered from gout and rheumatism. When he lit the fire a roaring draught almost put it out again, and despite Lloyd George's appeal for economy in coal he was heaping it on. But he was picking up English ways, and soon learned the national method of making tea: 'It's quite easy. I'll teach you how to do it when I get home. You pore some water into the kettle, put it on the fire; then when the water begins to boil you pore it into the tea-pot, throw in two spoons of tea-leaves, give it one good shake—then you pore the tea into the cup and after that, of course it's simple—you pore it *down*—by way of the mouth and throat!'

Oxford during the 1920s was well populated with celebrities and future celebrities, W. B. Yeats, John Masefield, Robert Bridges, and T. E. Lawrence amongst them. Although in his memoirs Gerhardie records contemporaries who subsequently achieved fame—Beverley Nichols, Richard Hughes, Edmund Blunden, Lord Longford, Robert Graves, Evelyn Waugh ('Some of them I did not meet when we were at Oxford, and others I have not met at all'), he had almost no friends in his first year. After many weeks he had only visited Victor Cazalet, who was living in great style at Cranstons, a private hotel for undergraduates.

Rothenstein, by contrast, led a busy social life and his autobiography describes all kinds of individuals, often eccentric, effeminate, and *outré*. But Gerhardie, older than most, no longer desired to cultivate his former pose of deliberate individuality. 'It cannot be said that you have reached a stage of maturity until you have ceased to regard yourself as a personality', he later wrote. 'At Petrograd I still imagined I cut a certain figure, but by the end of Intervention I lost all interest in myself as a personality; and by the time I went to Oxford I turned the corner. It was for that reason that the little airs and graces, the little conceits of the undergraduates irritated me then, whilst I might have been impressed by them before, and condoned them afterwards.'[6] Constitutionally not hearty, he had learned in the army that it was safest to remain inconspicuous and avoid 'the wrath of the collective spirit' by adopting a cheery 'Hello-feeling-fit-eh?' attitude. Some years later he came across a young tutor who remarked heartily that they were both Worcester men: 'I could not think what to say except that the men there, in my time at least, were rather dull on the whole: which brought forth from him: "I like dull men".'[7]

Whenever Rothenstein entertained friends, Gerhardie would emerge from his bedroom, remain for a brief introduction, and immediately disappear again. 'But for the most part, I was as lonely at Oxford as elsewhere. I sat in my lighted College rooms and watched the pinnacles, the spires and towers gradually dissolve in the gathering gloom. And sometimes—often—it rained.'[8] Gerhardie was reclusive, Rothenstein later insisted, because of his naturally nervous disposition, and not on account of social or cultural differences. Rothenstein's own friends, far from being exclusive, 'were disposed to welcome from outside those who were able to contribute intellect, wit, good looks or any other quality conducive to the enhancement of life'[9]—which remark rather confirms what it claims to deny, especially when Rothenstein lists those many classes of people who were beyond the pale: individuals who worked too hard, athletes, and 'cads' who wore hair oil and took women of the town for drives in their racing cars. Being acceptable in English society was altogether precarious, especially when, like Gerhardie, one was so unfamiliar with it all. His speech was a source of trouble. St Petersburg English was unique, a dialect enriched with strange idioms translated from the French, and it was quite impossible for an Anglo-Russian to anglicize foreign words, such as *chauffeur* or *garage* (a gross affectation to English ears). He himself spoke with a foreign intonation, his stresses all over the place, in such a rapid and garbled manner that he was frequently incomprehensible, and was still prone to mispronunciation. His tutor advised him to speak more slowly: 'I rejoined that if I talked quickly it was because I did not wish to take up too much of the time of so eminent a scholar. He replied that by talking too rapidly I often failed to convey my meaning clearly, and in the repetition which ensued, wasted more of his time than if I had spoken slowly.'[10]

Even Rothenstein, from a prominent English family, had his 'imagined idyll of life beneath the dreaming spires' 'violently shattered' within a few weeks of arriving: 'Oxford was full of men who had been taught and who had practised violence during the preceding years of war, who had forgotten the disciplines of school and who experienced recurrent moments of fierce exaltation which arose from the realization that their ordeal was over and they had come out of it alive.'[11] Evelyn Waugh later described how an intoxicated colonial burst into his room and belligerently demanded what he 'did' for the college. 'I drink for it', replied Waugh, and the colonial was hastily removed by his friends before any damage was done.[12] Drunken violence was common, especially after a boat club or athletics success, when unpopular members of the college (socialists and other eccentrics) were hunted, roughly debagged, and, very often, their furniture and belongings thrown out of the window and ignited. Gerhardie had to be careful to remain aloof from Russian politics—'Henry Esbheornargist' meanwhile was reproached for the doings of the Bolsheviks: 'His name, they thought in England, must be Bolshevik. No *nationality* would ever claim it.'

Despite affected indifference, in the social climate of 1920 Gerhardie could not help but be sensitive to the fact that his family, impoverished expatriates living in dingy accommodation in a northern town, now held an ambivalent position in a minutely graded caste system. His war service entitled him to State financial aid which, despite his pecuniary hardship, he proudly declined—and later regretted this 'squeamishness'. He wore clothes that had been mended and re-mended, and shortly after arriving at Oxford wrote to assure his mother that the items of cutlery and linen that she had bought for him were 'as good as anybody's'. He was also discomfited by his singular situation as double expatriate, belonging neither to England nor to Russia. Gerhardie later wrote to Rosie advising her against bringing up children between two worlds, because 'by mixing up cultures children grow up to be neither fish nor flesh and don't fit in anywhere in the end'.

Though quiet and shy in company, alone with his room-mate Gerhardie was a different man. Rothenstein, who nicknamed him 'Baron' ('based on my imperfectly established descent from Baron Girardi auf Castell zu Weyerburg und Limpurg, of the Holy Roman Empire),[13] has described their year together:

We got along harmoniously enough, although there were times when I resented the midday emergence into our common sitting-room of this tall, nervously pacing being with the pale flat face, the high veined forehead, the pale protruding eyes, the sensual mouth, red as though made up, whom sleep had charged with desire for aggressive argument, about politics or literature, but more often about sex or religion, which I regarded as private matters. This view of them he ridiculed, forced me to declare myself, assailed any conclusions I had reached, and in general, by his unkind and disillusioned probing, compelled me, as no one had before, to think clearly and independently. My subsequent gratitude far out-weighed the exasperation which his procedures sometimes provoked: it was, in fact, largely through my intimacy with him that I began to be intellectually mature. Association with Gerhardie was a rigorous discipline, for he talked almost continuously and scarcely ever went out.[14]

'Rothenstein is a very nice fellow indeed and likes me very much', wrote William. 'His father who is a great artist also likes me almost as much as I like myself. We get on very well together and he doesn't bother me in the least.'

It seemed to Rothenstein that Gerhardie worked incessantly—within a week of arriving he had 'bagged the best table' in the sitting-room, hired a typewriter, and was typing the novel begun in Siberia. But he was painfully indecisive about whether or not to take the one-year course specially adapted for war service candidates. He was keen to apply himself to 'the most important work of acquiring a "style" in English'. 'If I take the shorter course I feel I will regret it all my life. Yet if I take the longer course when there is a shorter course that I could take, I feel, that equally I will regret it. So there are only two courses open: either that there should be no shortened course—or commit suicide!—(or go mad).' But the daunting prospect of phonetics, Old English grammar, and Icelandic ('with all respect for the Old Icelanders, who may have been quite charming people, I refuse to exhaust my energy in studying their language which I am satisfied is dead and over!') decided him against the longer. He also enrolled in the Faculty of Music, a 'most dreadfully difficult course', and when he finally gave up his teacher informed him that on the whole music would not suffer from the loss. Some of the English lectures were 'remarkably good'; his tutor, David Nichol Smith, an authority on Pope and Swift, eventually succeeded Sir Walter Raleigh as Merton Professor of English Literature. John Middleton Murry delivered a lecture on the work of the little-known writer Anton Chekhov, and mentioned the work of his own wife, Katherine Mansfield. Shortly afterwards Gerhardie wrote to tell her how much he admired 'Daughters of the Late Colonel', the story of two elderly spinsters left alone and forlorn after the death of their father.

She, encouraged by his sensitive and appreciative letter, replied, explaining in some detail the distress caused by readers and critics having misunderstood the story. 'They thought it was "cruel"; they thought I was "sneering" at Jug and Constantia, or they thought it was "drab". And in the last paragraph I was "poking fun at the poor old things . . ." You will understand, therefore, how I prize your wonderfully generous letter, telling me my attempt was not in vain.'

But Gerhardie gave little time to his studies and soon the novel was complete, though untitled. He invited suggestions from Rothenstein.

'X,' said Rothenstein.

'Too morbid.'

'Y,' suggested Rothenstein.

'Too cheery.'

'W,' said Rothenstein.

'Dull.'

Until at last Rothenstein, defeated, cried 'Hell—I give up. Call it futility', and stomped off.

'Futility!'

'It has turned out well, and, I think, *is* an uncommon book', he wrote to his parents, 'but my natural modesty, you will observe, forbids me to say that it is a work of the *purest* genius.'

In April 1921 the literary agents Curtis Brown agreed to handle *Futility* and Gerhardie paid a successful visit to their London office: 'I saw the agents. There was a very pretty girl in the reception office, with beautiful silk-stockinged legs, but I suppose you will think that this is irrelevant. I was told again that they thought the book was "rattling good stuff", etc., but that it had no plot.' They also stressed that in order to make it worth their while he should agree to place his future work with them as well. A second copy of the novel Gerhardie reserved for sending to publishers direct. Whilst waiting to hear he bought a portable Corona typewriter and began work on his second novel, later published as *The Polyglots*, using much of the material discarded from *Futility*. He wrote in tiny loose-leaf binders no more than two inches high: random observations, notes, and story plots: 'A dying man called out for sun and air and they could not make out whether he perhaps meant he wanted his son and heir.' Again: 'Use as comparison the fate of the man who stooped to pick up a piece of silver paper in the street to send to a hospital, was run over by a motor car, and was sent along with the silver paper.' He had also composed a one-act play, *Died of His Own Accord*, a competent and very funny sketch of the last vain efforts of an old man 'in an advanced stage of decomposition' to become articulate, before dropping dead. The dialogue is hardly more explicit than a series of curious noises, yet Gerhardie's presentation of his characters is successfully poised between humorous sympathy and grotesque disgust.

Aside from his own literary work, Gerhardie's chief preoccupation at Oxford was women. In this he was apparently atypical. Rothenstein described the Oxford climate at that time as one in which 'women were remote, improbable creatures', with 'amorous relations between undergraduates and women outside the University . . . unusual' and always 'discreetly consummated'.[15] Undergraduettes seemed to live in purdah, which was hardly surprising when the university proctors retained the right to expel beyond the university limits any independent woman whom they considered to be a temptation. Some lecturers refused to teach women, and if they turned up to a lecture either shouted obscenities or had them removed bodily by a college porter. Even as late as 1926 the Union passed a motion that 'Women's Colleges should be levelled to the ground' ('Nothing sinister', explained Beverley Nichols cheerfully, 'Just that we didn't want women around too much').[16] Gerhardie wanted them around very much. 'They are frightfully strict here about women', he lamented to his parents. 'One is not allowed to go to any dances or even speak to them. . . . What have I done to be confined to this monastery?' Even so he succeeded with a number of town girls, and later bemused Rothenstein with details—far from 'discreet'—of all aspects of his sexual preferences. One afternoon Rothenstein returned to find a respectable-looking, neatly furred young woman seated in the sitting-room awaiting Gerhardie. When, after half an hour he had failed to turn up, she turned politely to Rothenstein: 'Would you like to go to bed with me?' He politely declined.

But, in spite of these casual diversions, Gerhardie's greatest love was a young Irish nurse Terese Hennessy whom he had accosted while strolling down Westbourne Grove two years before. 'That charming little imp Terry', as Clara called her, worked at the Tooting Bec Hospital in South London. Now she and William resumed their brief affair, taking weekend trips to Colchester and Holyhead, he coyly referring to her in his letters home as 'my "wife"'. All his life he kept her photograph and a bundle of mementoes—notes scribbled on train tickets, pressed flowers, and (a painful reminder) bills from *Madame Claire*, where he had purchased for her a champagne georgette ball dress (£3. 19*s*. 6*d*.), three pairs of stockings, and a pair of silk gloves (10*s*.) to set off her 'amber locks'. She was an exuberant letter writer.

Alexander Darling Prince of Angels,

 Are you delighted to be back in Oxford? It must be perfect now, flowers etc. in full bloom. I do want to come and see you. But what can I do. if I run away my father will run after me. I am not very busy and I am not flirting hope you are the same, Princie. I was disapp. when you did not send me the little bead bag. If you really wanted to see me Love finds a way. Your weak excuse 'Broke' I absolutely ignore. Back of my hand to you 6 Times. Goodbye Fairie boy, your Sadie (new name)

He delighted in her unsophisticated spontaneity, her recklessness: 'What a dreadful person I am!' she used to exclaim, and soon after writing to him ran away from home. But she was a sore trial on account of her extravagance. Gerhardie, deep in his second novel, renamed her Sylvia and cast her as the heroine:

Sylvia was studying the menu, and the enormous head waiter bent over her chair. And I looked at him with dark hatred. Among other things, Sylvia wanted chicken. There were two kinds of chicken. A whole chicken cost 500 roubles. A wing, 100 roubles. The rate of exchange, be it remembered, at that time was only 200 roubles to £1 sterling. The enormous head waiter strongly recommended the whole chicken. 'Straight from Paris in an aeroplane,' he said. I felt cold in the feet.

 Sylvia hesitated dangerously. 'I don't think I want as much as a whole chicken. I'll have a wing,' she uttered at last. I breathed freely.

 'But the wing is larger than the chicken, madam,' said the fiend. I longed to ask him to explain that curious mathematical perversion, but a latent sense of gallantry deterred me. I felt like clubbing him. But civilization suffered me to go on suffering in silence. '*Go away*,' I whispered inwardly. '*Oh, go away!*' But I sat still, resigned. Only my left eyelid began to twitch a little nervously.

 'All right,' she said. 'I'll have the whole chicken, then.'

 Five hundred roubles! £2 10s, for a solitary chicken! My dead grandfather raised his bushy eyebrows.[17]

When Gerhardie revealed to Terry that he was writing a book about her she replied, 'Darling, I'm not interested. I'm not interested, darling.' Unabashed he reflected that 'a woman does not fully exercise our spirit unless she be attractive enough for us to desire her and so stupid that her ways must seem to us inscrutable'.[18] And then he went on to talk about Matthew Arnold, Oscar Wilde, Lord Byron . . .

 'Oh, darling, let us talk of something else.'

 'But I thought you liked—literature?'

 'Well, darling, I *listened*—for your sake. But you are so long, you've never finished . . . I like something more—fruity.'

'One day darling,' she concluded, 'you will be a great author, and I shall read your story in the *Daily Mail*.' A year or so later she caused him bitter anguish by emigrating to Australia, where she shortly married a prosperous man. When *The Polyglots* eventually appeared, Gerhardie sent her a copy—and received no reply.

The rest of his spare time was devoted to the family, who in turn supplied him with a steady stream of socks, collars, handkerchiefs, warm underclothing, apples and sundry laxatives, a sponge, a lemon cheesecake, and a waistcoat with 'a delightful way of dropping hair, as though it were some live thing—a gentleman going bald'. William always insisted on the strictest accounts being kept for these items so that he might not be a financial burden.

And he found himself a new dentist to take up where Goldberg had left off—but this time a former bayonet instructor. He was a small rotund man with a strong resemblance to Hugh Walpole, who spoke in a flowery and pompous manner. He had wanted to be a writer but became a dentist instead and despised his profession, looking into people's mouths with contempt. Gerhardie suggested that he write in his spare time. 'Indeed not!' he riposted. 'The atmosphere is profoundly uncongenial. Were I a doctor I would see life, death, human tragedy . . . But teeth! Where is the poetry, the romance in teeth?'

At Christmas Clara, anxious about her scattered family, urged William off to see Daisy in Paris. France and everything French was always a source of mirth to Gerhardie, who wrote home that the hotel manageress when asked about a bath 'seemed to be staggered at this demand without precedent', and had to send out for a mechanic to set the heating machinery in motion. 'And the legendary excitability of Frenchmen! It does not fail to astonish you however often you cross over! I have not in all these years yet entered a French brasserie without a waiter running up to me with a face lit with excited enquiry and shooting a questioning "Monsieur?" at me, as if wondering for what nefarious purpose I could have wished to occupy a table in his restaurant.'[19] His imaginative grasp of the language was, by his own report, haphazard. 'I slide over technicalities of grammar, I mix up cases and tenses, but on top of it all I put on a sort of dare-devil *Parisian* twist and make up for occasional inaccuracies by a really blinding speed . . . *Enfin! Enfin! Sacrebleu!*'[20]

Daisy, well, happy, and enjoying her independence, was very 'excitened' to see her brother, and welcomed him to the handsome panelled and painted room she shared with another girl. She had grown, he noticed, very handsome—tall and dark with a beguilingly deep voice, her hair fashionably cropped and waved. After unpacking the presents he had brought—a fan, a green jumper, silk stockings, and plenty of food from Clara—they all three dashed off to a dance. 'We went to another dance last night, and we are going to yet another dance this afternoon and then to-night we are, of course, going to a dance as well as to-morrow afternoon *and* night; and next week I daresay, for a change, we shall go to some other dance.'

Rosie, however, was not happy in her new life. In the immediate post-Revolution chaos in Russia the cold and starvation continued, and so many of her friends had died. Leonya's brother, an artist, survived by moving to the country, where food was less scarce, and drawing portraits of the peasants in exchange for meals. When conditions in Petrograd —now renamed Leningrad—deteriorated still further he sent for his sister-in-law to join him. Rosie and her daughter Tamara spent days on freezing railway stations waiting for a carriage into which they could squeeze themselves. At Christmas, with the help of a loyal ex-servant, she made a plum pudding out of Charles and Clara's wedding cake, thirty years old, and for fuel she went out to break up abandoned barges on the river. The Gerhardis in England used all William's diplomatic, military, and journalistic contacts to get food or clothes through until November 1920, when the Post Office told Clara they were no longer accepting parcels for Russia. 'All this rot makes ones blood boil', responded Charles testily. 'That is the result of England putting up with a rotten govt, everything seems topsy turvy in this miserable country though it once upon a time used to be a civilized and great one, *sic transit gloria mundi.*'

William maintained an attitude of reserved approval towards the new regime, praised Wells for his outspoken support of the Bolsheviks, and argued with his sister against supporting further counter-revolutions:

I am frightened of Dolly. She will probably bully me for my reactionary views. I am glad nothing has come of the 'Revolution' in Russia. All these revolutions will lead nowhere. The Russian peasants and workpeople are a lot of ignorant louts who don't know what is good for them, and want a strong and ruthless minority, like the Bolshevik authorities, to keep them in hand. The old regime would have been good enough so far as ruthlessness goes, only the old regime were out for themselves, while the Bolsheviks are out for the good of the people. That is, in fact, the main difference between the two regimes. I am sorry if Dolly does not agree with me; but I stand for *law* and *order* and can have no sympathy with her wild revolutionary ideas tending to overthrow the remnants of authority that exist in Russia today. I suppose I am too conservative for Dolly's liking, but then we can't all be revolutionaries, you know.

He had hoped to visit Rosie during the summer vacation, in order to see for himself conditions under the new regime and perhaps to write a book, but family finances were so low that no money could be spared. Clara's capital had dwindled to less than £100, and profits from the shop were more erratic than ever. 'Well lovie, if the customers won't come to me I must go to them', sighed Clara, and undaunted she set off on foot early each morning carrying samples from house to house, sometimes covering more than ten miles a day. 'I have been going round to see the great of the land as far as Bolton is concerned', she told William. 'I must acknowledge that they have all received me well and treated me as a lady. Some have invited me to tea and last but not least have either bought something or given me orders.' Tormented by the idea of Clara having to work, he implored her: 'You must, dear Mama, absolutely give up all idea of business. It is altogether too much for you to have all this worry of earning a livelihood on your shoulders at your age. You have done wonderfully and no one is *prouder* of you than I am, but you mustn't do it any more . . . I couldn't bear the idea of you trudging on your feet and selling things to strangers.'

Charles, whose taste for gambling had been sharpened by his disability, sent off to Gamages for a mini roulette wheel and set about devising a 'system'. After some preliminary testing this appeared to be foolproof. The greater his successes, the more obsessed he became with the idea that it could provide a systematic means of livelihood in Monte Carlo. Clara voiced her doubts. 'Defeatist', yelled Charles. Clara, brainwashed, 'began to think that a reasonable and sustained income, if played for with system and caution and loyal perseverance by half a dozen members of the family, including my aged and infirm aunt, was perhaps within the scope of happiness humanly realizable'. It fell to William, and William's money, to try out the new system. The début was planned with military precision. Charles issued his son with elaborate instructions as to platforms, hotels, and routes round the town, and devised a secret code so that the successful results could be wired back without detection by the State. He even suggested that as money was now no object William might as well travel by aeroplane.

'I cannot take any journey, however short, for granted; it is always a marvel and cavernous with dark dangers.'[21] William arrived at Victoria

Station uncharacteristically early and dashed out to buy some food; the train left without him. 'I remonstrated, but in vain. The train would not come back.' Arriving at Dover by a later train, he found that the occupants of the early train had each taken a kindly interest in the coat, stick, and suitcase deposited in their compartment, and had handed them in at three different places. At last he reached Paris where Daisy told him she thought the gambling scheme a lot of nonsense. He resumed his journey:

From Paris southward the journey was beastly hot, and the compartment crowded with women young and old, and I indulged in what Rothenstein described as a bit of 'calf-work.' Curious things these Frenchwomen. They talked unblushingly about their corsets and underwear and as they settled for the night they did strange things with their hands beneath their blouses; their waists increased in size accordingly, and they looked flabby and unattractive. But when morning came they all bucked up, powder-boxes and the like appeared on the scene, complexions, hair, all was remedied again; scent was poured on galore; and not a thought of washing! Water was not even thought of!

Gerhardie took an instant dislike to Monte Carlo, scornful of its 'indecent' luxury, 'the luxury of a water-closet', so that even Blackpool seemed to have more character. But when darkness fell he softened a little: 'Monte Carlo at night black and gold. Vulgar. And yet . . . And yet . . .' He booked into a cheap hotel, hot and cross and pessimistic, weak from loss of blood to the mosquitoes, and wrote a letter home complaining of 'an infernal old man' who talked English with an 'infernal' foreign accent and kept insisting that he was an Englishman. 'The proprietor, or manager, of this hotel has a strange custom of coming up to everyone at dinner while they eat, and bowing ceremoniously and saying something kind about the weather. He came up to me and said something about my *appetit*, to which I replied that it came '*en mangeant*'—and he behaved as though he was struck by the fine originality of the remark.' When Gerhardie requested coffee the head waiter looked at him as though he were not quite sure whether it was 'a human being or some other animal' he was dealing with, and explained that coffee was no simple matter, that it had to be made. Three-quarters of an hour later he brought it in a pretentious contrivance of a boiler, and upset it all over Gerhardie's lap.

'No disabled people here', wrote William. He thought it ominous, and began to lose heart at the reality of Charles negotiating the great staircases to reach the gaming tables. There were, however, a great many Russians all looking as if they lived considerably above their income. Watching them he began to despise the reckless way in which people gambled their money away: 'It just makes one sick. I could picture to myself Papa sitting there years ago and telling the croupier to go faster, as the rate at which he poured out his wealth did not seem adequate to him! . . . Of all vices this is the silliest!' And, somewhere, Charles's calculations had gone awry. 'Every system based on doubling gets you in the end (and as for me here, it always got me straight away).' Within the shortest possible time Gerhardie lost four hundred francs and was left with only just enough to get home. He reported back sadly and reluctantly that, 'I know it is a pity; it is a thousand pities: but what can we do? Evidently God does not love us. I am sorry for myself as I had great hopes of solving our financial problem in this utopian manner —but unfortunately it is utopian!' In Bolton again, all the family offered their money to make up his loss. 'It was all my fault,' said Charles, tears rolling down his face. 'I forgot to account for the change in altitude.'

Now in a worse financial plight than ever, William made his own plans for the family. He would not, as he had intended, remain a second year at Oxford, but find a job himself—a post on the League of Nations in Russia or Poland, or as a newspaper correspondent, from which he would be in a position to send home as much of his salary as possible. He was optimistic about this because earlier that year he had received 'another of those parchment things from the War Office', signed by Winston Churchill and recording His Majesty's high appreciation of distinguished services in the field, as well as the Czech War Cross and, best of all, an OBE. 'I am jolly glad, because it is a pretty high order—next but one to a knighthood, and although I have certainly done nothing to deserve it there are others who have had it and have done less. . . . I will now get into next year's *Who's Who*!' The university careers officer would, he felt, be very impressed, and he went off in expectant spirits to the interview. After filling in the necessary forms he proudly mentioned his decoration. 'Damn bad luck!' said the man. 'You go and do your best for them and they go and insult you in this manner. Of course, you were in the Army and they got you there; they knew you couldn't refuse. But it's a damned shame. Damn bad luck!'

Clara, however, was adamant that her son should not leave Oxford. So he returned for a second year, fired with enthusiasm for a new venture: 'literary prostitution'. Two months later *The Amazing Honeymoon* by 'Basil M. D'Azyll' was born. In order to judge 'the limits to which one may go in immorality, as regards pleasing an Anglo-Saxon public', he had first read Elinor Glyn's *Three Weeks*, which had sold several million copies since its publication in 1907. Having scanned such passages as:

'My God! it is you who are maddening me!' he cried, his voice hoarse with emotion. 'Do you think I am a statue, or a table, or chair—or inanimate like that tiger there? I am *not*, I tell you!' and he seized her in his arms, raining kisses upon her which, whatever they lacked in subtlety, made up for in their passion and strength. 'Some day some man will kill you, I suppose, but I shall be your lover—first!'

William came to the conclusion that the immorality was barely hinted at, 'but the sloppy sentimentality, the dullness, and ineptitude' were not only stupendous but maddeningly difficult to imitate. The following 'sexual' passage of Mr D'Azyll's is almost absurdly evasive:

Through the parted curtain of the open window the full moon looked in at them. The night was still. . . . In the palpitating hush she could hear the magic rustle of silk linen, the hollow sound of press-studs; she could feel the sweet torture of existence super-charged with expectation, the floods of life bursting through the walls of paradise into rapturous rivers of delight. And it seemed as though the moon envied them their happiness, these two human beings in the throws of life, carrying the ecstacy in growing volume to the apotheosis of consummation.

A mildly comic 'thriller' with sexual overtones, *The Amazing Honeymoon* is the story of a man who, after a brain operation, finds that he 'remembers' the future and thereby attempts to avoid certain disasters. There is something almost philosophical about the treatment of time, free will, and memory, not at all suitable for a 'popular' book. 'It is the rottenest and most idiotic thing I've ever read', Gerhardie declared, and 'particularly suited for the screen.' 'NOT to be published on ANY ACCOUNT, after my death. TOO ROTTEN! WAG Sept 1923', he later scrawled across it, but now dispatched it to Curtis Brown with instructions to tone down or spice up the more 'lurid' parts, as he considered appropriate. 'If my novels don't go I'll drown myself in the Worcester College pond. If, on the other hand, they begin to go very well, I'll be turning out drivel galore.'

The novel's completion fired the family with fresh hopes. William planned to settle his parents in a modest way in the South of France, or perhaps on a farm in the South of England, where they would be warm and comfortable and where his father could be relieved of some of the stultifying tedium of his wheelchair-ridden life. Clara echoed his mood of optimism, urging 'just a little more patience and that beautiful silver

lining the poet speaks of will illuminate the cloud and disperse the ill
fortune that has been hanging over us for so many years'.

Pending this, however, William was obliged to make drastic econom-
ies. He could save on fuel because his new rooms were heated by the
kitchen below.

> Also towards six o'clock or so there is generally a very strong smell of cabbage,
> which helps to feed me, in a way. I have cut down my breakfast to porridge,
> coffee, toast and butter; and my lunch to bread and cheese and butter and
> marmalade. I have also cut out tea. If the cabbage smell is at all strong I may
> consider other economies. I might, for instance, cut out dinner three times a
> week and live on the cabbage smell alone; but the difficulty is to know
> beforehand on what days the smell is going to be sufficiently strong to keep you
> satisfied. Of course, when it is strong you can go on smelling to your heart's
> content—it costs you nothing. But some days the odour is only very faint, and
> then I pull my belt up one hole.

He was relieved when Clara sent a birthday parcel of cakes, fruit, and
mincemeats—'I've been eating the apples galore and now there is a
battle of the Somme in my inside.' Altogether less reclusive than
formerly, for the first time he began to stress his idiosyncratic Anglo-
Russian origins: 'My retired life gave me a cetain literary reputation, and
friends of mine would bring their friends to my rooms, intrigued by the
rumour that I subscribed to some utterly new view of life and literature.'
'Everybody', he wrote to Clara, 'is falling in love with Daisy's photo.
Scores of proposals by earls. That ought to please you!!' He found the
English ceaselessly entertaining. (How did the new scout, recently wed,
find marriage? 'Everything correct, sir.') Sometimes now he even
ventured to tea parties where 'you had a sensation as if you were
watching a stage play, so exactly like actors in a society play did they look
and talk. The sustained insincerity of the whole thing seemed somehow
incredible.'[22] And then he jotted in his notebook: 'I meet two lords at R's
rooms. The endeavour on everybody's part to convey their indifference
to them is conspicuous. They are nice, well-groomed boys who do not
spit on the floor—and that is the consummative effect of their existence.' Apart from tennis, Gerhardie took only an ironical delight in
English sports, especially during Eights Week on the river when,
'arriving at the riverside just in time for the finish, I would dash in front
of the other men of my college, exhausted by their long run, and cheer
voluptuously: "Worcester! Worcester!"'[23] The college had done particularly well that year and threw a celebratory eight-course Bump
Supper. 'I was horribly drunk at the end. I have never been so drunk in

my life—not since in Siberia. I must have drunk close on 20 glasses of champagne.' Accustomed to neither sport nor alcohol, he got damp and soggy watching the bonfire, was put to bed by a friend, and woke up dreadfully sick all over his coat and dressing-gown.

Rothenstein, now lodging elsewhere and rather missing William's expansive conversations, often stopped by.

In spite of his mainly British ancestry, Gerhardi had the characteristic Russian urge to talk constantly about his fundamental beliefs and the most intimate aspects of his personal conduct. But his talk had nothing of the characteristic Russian idealism and largeness; it was as though conversations from Tolstoy, Turgenev and Dostoievski were parodied by some cynical member of the Goncourt circle. But Gerhardi carried his cynicism gaily; few people I have ever known have an acuter sense of the absurd, of the difference between the realities of life and the obscuring cant.[24]

His own small circle of friends included John Strachey, Edward Sackville-West, and Raymond Bantock, son of the composer Granville Bantock who arrived one day with Sibelius who was wrapped up in a thick fur coat, and took Gerhardie for a walk round the Oxford colleges: 'Sibelius talks a little Russian but very badly, just like a Finn, and gets mixed up a little and brings in other languages to his rescue.'

Strachey was at that time co-editor with David Cecil of the *Oxford Fortnightly Review*, an undergraduate magazine subsidized by Conservative party headquarters which published three stories by Gerhardie: 'Felony', 'Tact', and 'The Proposal'. A fourth, 'Of Hypocrisy', appeared in the *Oxford Outlook*, a new literary magazine founded by Beverley Nichols and L. P. Hartley in order to 'reflect the new spirit of the university after the War'.[25] The choice of journals was entirely incidental. Gerhardie was not a Conservative and he was not much concerned with the post-war university spirit. All the stories in some measure confront the question of class in England, displaying Gerhardie's characteristic concern with the subtlety of individual sensibilities.

Christmas 1921 was an elaborate family occasion: Dolly, her husband Lot, 2-year-old Nora, and 4-year-old Harry had all moved into Bradford Street whilst searching for a house of their own. Clara was keen to set eyes on Daisy, who had just announced her engagement to a young French naval officer. 'So now you know how my heart is aching', she wrote to her son. 'My baby girl is thinking of shouldering matrimony and who knows but what you may drop a bomb on me one day too.' People marry, William pointed out, because of the bad example their parents set them. And, to crown Clara's excitement, Rosie and Tamara had at last been granted permission to leave Russia.

William was immediately captivated by 7-year-old Tamara, who spoke vigorously and frequently of the 'Rush-ya' she had left, whilst bouncing round and round his chair. William asked after the Bolsheviks. 'Bolsheviks? What's it means Bolshevik?' she said, shrugging her little shouders. 'Only lot of dirty mens in the street.' When Rosie married she had converted to the Russian Orthodox religion, and now hung up a lighted icon in her daughter's room. 'Is the halo fastened to God's chin with an elastic?' asked Tamara. She gurgled on about all her friends, her sister and her uncle and her grandmama and her papa. 'Ah! and I have left in Rush-ya my little kitchen—such a beauty thing—and plates my grandmama given me, lots and lots of plates and cups—such a lovely! Ah! such-such pity! Such, such *such*-such pity!' And because she was a little bored and lonely at first: '*Play* with me; oh *play* with me!' William played with her. He took her on a shopping expedition to Woolworth's, where to her joy she found that nothing cost more than sixpence. He bought her a little writing-pad and pen, and a Christmas stocking full of presents. ('For a child coming from a Communist country she seemed to display an extraordinary sense of property.') And he made her a central character in his new novel, the vivacious Natasha of *The Polyglots*.

Tamara soon joined forces with Harry and Nora so that the three of them would run screaming all over the house, out into the garden to pester little Aunt Sissie, back to hinder Clara in the kitchen, then upstairs to the attic where they surprised William at his desk kissing Terry's photograph and murmuring to it. They promptly tied him up. He remained beautifully patient throughout, and began to incorporate all the children into the novel. But he could get little work done at home. 'A big family in a small house', he jotted in his diary. 'The activity is all directed towards getting clean . . . in which process they all get dirty again.' Nora repeated everything Harry said, which was exhausting because Harry persistently asked questions:

'Where is God? Is He everywhere?'
'I suppose so.'
'Is He in this bottle?'
'I suppose so.'
'With the nose lotion?'
'Well, yes.'
'But how has He got in with the cork on?'

'He was there, I suppose, before the bottle was made.'
'But how it is He hasn't got drowned?'
'He can exist anywhere, I suppose.'
'But I can't see Him,' said Harry peering through the murky yellow liquid.
'Nor can I,' I confessed, 'as yet.'

Tamara's English was so curious that soon there was a whole houseful of little polyglots, as the children developed a tongue of their own—lots of 'vish!—bish!' and tortured words, each deliberately twisting sounds in their own language as if to be helpful to the other. They returned, ecstatic, from the cinema one afternoon. 'Oh, what a lovely! Mary Pickford', squeaked Tamara. 'Oh, what a beauty boy little Lord Fountainpen! with long beauty hair like that. Oh, and so sad—I so cried! Oh, how I cried all the time! Oh, how beauty! Oh! Oh!'[26]

Sometimes Rosie's spirits flagged as she thought longingly of Russia and Leonya, at which William would cheer her up by teaching her to foxtrot up and down the wide landing while he whistled the tune. Dolly and William argued heatedly about politics and literature, Dolly in her deep, rather foreign voice, William shrill and caustic when angry. Clara, bossy, anxious to have the last word, argued with everyone. When, one day, William complained of Clara to Charles, he, 'looking so good and mild and honest,' replied simply 'What would I have done without her?' Day after day he sat in the midst of the chaos beside the fire in a cane chair that creaked with every movement. He smoked heavily, and on a cane table in front of him lay a heap of glass cigarette holders which, painstakingly, Sissie cleaned for him every day. The children did not help his temper. Victor visited with his new baby who was left in her cot beside Charles, until she began to cry. 'Damnation hell', yelled Charles, changed in the nick of time to 'Hello little one', as her mother entered the room.

Whenever 'the ominous envelope' containing the oft-rejected manuscript of *Futility* dropped through the letter box, Clara would bring it to William with a look of the utmost commiseration, which irritated him immensely. Far from causing him depression, such rejections filled him with 'a strange, sinister exhilaration'. None the less, with this ever-increasing band of dependants he was impatient to publish, especially as *The Amazing Honeymoon* was being rejected by all and sundry. But as Curtis Brown had begun to lose interest in *Futility*, the only alternative was boldly to seek the help of the already famous. Gerhardie wrote a letter full of insincere flattery to Hugh Walpole, then at the height of his popularity. Walpole declined to help. Arnold Bennett also declined, but more politely. Then, four months after his original letter, Gerhardie remembered Katherine Mansfield. She replied at once, 'honoured' by his request for help and advice. 'First of all—immediately—I think your novel is awfully good. I congratulate you. It is a living book. What I mean by that is, it is warm; one can put it down and it goes on breathing.' She wrote at length and in detail with great warmth and spontaneity, regretting only the limitations of the letter. The novel 'ought to be more squeezed and pressed and moulded into shape and wrung out', but apart from that she advised him to publish it 'more or less as it stands'.

Katherine Mansfield could be generous and kind—she had encouraged both Dorothy Brett and Richard Murry in their work—and the link with Gerhardie clearly came at a very opportune moment for her. Then 33 years old, she was alone, ill, obliged to spend her time in pensions abroad, conscious of Murry's infidelity and lack of understanding, and suffering grave doubts about the quality of her work. 'I live in Switzerland because I have consumption', she wrote. 'But I am not an invalid. Consumption doesn't belong to me. It is a horrid stray dog who has persisted in following me for four years, so I am trying to lose him among these mountains.' Establishing a correspondence with Gerhardie gave her a degree of companionship, sympathetic discussion, and a sense of purpose. She was particularly sensitive to the fact that her poor health had occasioned a loss of what she valued above everything else—her independence. In writing to Gerhardie she discovered casual male companionship, something she had long sought, and which her first husband George Bowden identified as 'being a bachelor along with us'.[27] 'I hope you will write to me . . . Its not easy to talk man to man at a distance,' she told William. His interest provided her with an incentive to keep working at this difficult period. 'I can only repay you by trying not to fail you in the future. And this believe me I shall do.'

Within a week Mansfield had found a publisher for *Futility*. Richard Cobden Sanderson, who ran a small independent firm, visited Gerhardie in February 1922 to discuss the novel, 'So you see how the publishers are *running after me*!!!!' he wrote home, stressing that Cobden Sanderson had rejected over 1,000 novels the previous year. 'He is an awfully nice man himself . . . and doesn't even *try* to pretend that he doesn't think the book is good.' William now began to correct and revise *Futility*, with the assistance of Elizabeth Rendell, an Oxford don to whom he had been introduced ('I spend two hours daily with that woman—going through the novel . . . among other things . . .'). Following Mansfield's advice, he removed many Russian words which, though effective, she felt would 'put people off', and compressed the book slightly. He had given up English Literature and was now reading for a degree in Russian, chiefly because it enabled him to devote more time to his own work. Throughout the spring he closeted himself in his rooms, drinking Bovril, 'Working like h—ll. Hair growing like blazes.' By Eights Week *Futility* was printed and Gerhardie so busy with the proofs that he declined Mansfield's suggestion of an introduction to Lady Ottoline Morrell, adding in his letter home: 'So you see to what "high" society I aspire! But I think I am going to stand out for the Queen herself. The *Queen* or nobody!'

He kept on writing to Katherine. Her long, vibrant, and thoughtfully worded letters to Gerhardie suggest a spontaneous intimacy between them. Her interest provided the first suggestion of the flirtatious, seductive role that Gerhardie the writer was to play with his readers— both in the novels themselves and in subsequent correspondence. His is a deliberate awareness of the invisible reader, of the role of writer as absent presence, even seducer, working through his fiction both as voice and as (implied) physical presence. She sent a photo and he responded with one (she thought he looked 'musical'). She wished they could meet. Gerhardie, as with all the writers with whom he was to correspond, read her stories and wrote in detail about them, so much so that she was overcome with guilt at not keeping up with his replies, adding, 'You always sound so gay'. She was particularly pleased when he understood that 'The Garden Party' was an attempt to convey 'the diversity of life and how we try to fit in everything—Death included'. They talked of Chekhov: 'People on the whole understand Tchekov very little. They persist in looking at him from a certain angle and he's a man that won't stand that kind of gaze. One must get round him—see him, feel him as a whole.' She wrote at length of her stories, her fears about her lasting reputation as a writer, her plans for the future: 'You know—if I may speak in confidence I shall not be "fashionable" for long. They will find me out; they will be disgusted; they will shiver in dismay. I like such awfully unfashionable things, and people.' 'Please do not think of me as a kind of boa-constrictor who sits here gorged and silent after having devoured your two delightful letters, without so much as a "thank you". If gratitude were the size and shape to go into a pillar box the postman would have staggered to your door days ago. But I've not been able to send anything more tangible. I have been and I am ill.'

She wrote about her illness. A Russian doctor was treating her tuberculosis with X-rays, mysterious but promising she thought, and 'at present I am full of wandering blue rays like a deep sea fish . . . But *if* it all comes true it means one will be invisible once more—no more being offered chairs and given arms at night. . . . Well people don't realise the joy of being invisible, its almost the greatest joy of all.' Gerhardie, still further enraptured by this mysterious, disembodied relationship, intimate and distant, later wrote to Clara: 'What a marvellous woman she was, head and shoulders above Murry. Murry is awfully intelligent, of course, and there is nothing he doesn't know about literature; but he has no wings. So he must flop *parterre*. What treasures there are in her letters!'

Meanwhile it was growing increasingly clear that the family would never return to Russia. But England seemed impossible too. 'Business is just as lively as ever, that is—nothing doing', wrote Clara cheerily. 'Still everybody is waiting for a revival and we are carrying on. I hope lovie, you are well and getting a little more rest after that awful "swat".' The shop assistant was discovered to have not only pilfered items of stock, but actually crept into Clara's room with a pair of scissors and cut a strip off her mink. And Charles continued to play the stock market: 'Papa has made a good bit and he received £3 the other day for some Mexican spec: and at once wrote up for a bottle of liqueur which cost him a £1. Well poor fellow he has very few pleasures but he is now indulging in 2 small glasses a day and does enjoy them.'

William looked for more reliable ways of making money. A book on Chekhov would, he thought, do well and as soon as *Futility* was off his hands he registered for a B.Litt. in Russian. In June, having revised hardly at all ('after my old habit . . . I believe in leaving things to the very last'), *Willelmus A. Gerhardi* took his examination *In schola literarum modernarum*. In the same month *Futility* was published.

Futility: a Novel on Russian Themes is not only Gerhardie's first, but arguably his finest, novel. Published in 1922, the year of two of the greatest Modernist works, *Ulysses* and *The Waste Land*, Gerhardie's alignments with mainstream English Modernism are, however, quite independent of direct influences. Though Gerhardie, like Pound, Eliot, and so many great writers of the period, was both an exile and a polyglot, there is no indication that he was then aware of the activities of the English avant-garde. A further distinction of the book, published 30 years before Beckett's *Waiting for Godot*, lies in its suggestions of the absurd—the characters suffer from a constant inability to communicate; repetitive utterances and protracted silences create an overwhelming sense of aimlessness, of perpetual waiting; tragic situations vacillate on the brink of the ridiculous.

It is the story of Andrei, a young English officer stationed in Russia during the Revolution and Intervention, his encounters with the Bursanov family, and his love for their beguiling but infuriating daughter, Nina. Against a background of momentous historical change the Bursanovs remain curiously and comically wrapped up in themselves and their family foibles. Nina's father, Nikolai Vasilievich, waits vainly for an improvement in his dwindling fortunes, watched by his steadily increasing dependants: his common-law wife Fanny, his legal wife Magda, Magda's ex-lover Mosei, and her new love Čečedek, Zina, the girl Nikolai hopes to marry, together with all *her* dependants, 'innumerable aunts and uncles, sisters-in-law, second cousins, and such-like relatives, and of course a collection of giggling flappers practising the piano; two ancient grandfathers—the oldest things in veterans— who had outlived their welcome, whose deaths, in fact, were looked forward to with undisguised impatience and freely discussed at meals'.

To Andrei (unquestionably a semi-transparent mask for Gerhardie despite his epigraph, 'The "I" of this book is not me'), they are all charming though ludicrous, 'enduring this unsatisfactory present because they believe that this present was not really *life* at all: that *life* was somewhere in the future; that *this* was but a temporary and transitory stage to be spent in patient waiting'. 'But do you silly people realize how utterly laughable you all are?' he exclaims exasperated. '"Oh, my God! Can't you see yourselves?" (I could not see myself.) "But can't you see that you have been lifted out of Chehov? . . . Oh, what would he not have given to see you and use you."' For the novel as a whole achieves the Chekhovian poise, characterized by Andrei as existing 'on the line of demarcation between comedy and tragedy—in a kind of No Man's Land'.

If Gerhardie's early play *The Haunting Roubles* was a (seemingly impossible) attempt to 'amalgamate different dramatic forms—comic, dramatic, social, farcical, tragic, intellectual, realistic, romantic', then *Futility* is the achievement of this, and more besides. Gerhardie's tenderness and pathos towards his characters indicates that this is a novel concerned with the intricacies of individuals. We follow Andrei's precarious romantic involvement with Nina to its brilliant and bathetic conclusion. *Futility* is also a novel about history: to the European post-war responses of baffled loss and disillusion, Gerhardie adds his own unique experiences of the Russian Revolutionary upheavals. There is not only comedy and tragedy, but all the nuances and extremes therein: the Bursanovs and their elusive gold mines are funny, then ridiculous, futile, absurd. It is *Futility's* characteristic quality of controlled repetition that keeps one's feeling for the Bursanovs everchanging and alive. A situation that is at one point tragic and futile may later become, as the tragic theme insists on coming up again and again, melodramatic and then farcical; and then, as one settles into the comfortable belief that one is, after all, reading farce, the cruel insistence of the recurring theme draws the Bursanovs once again into the region of tragedy and pathos. Take, for example, Fanny Ivanova's very uncomfortable situation: with the war in full swing she is, as a German by birth, in danger of being deported. She cannot save herself by marrying Nikolai, whom she loves and with whom she has lived for the past thirty years, because Nikolai's wife Magda won't divorce him; when at last Magda consents (because, like Nikolai, she plans to marry not the person she has been living with but a second love) Nikolai, free at last, falls for Zina, so that Fanny must wed Eberheim, old and dying of cancer but a man and willing. Andrei, listening with sympathetic dismay to Fanny's outpourings of misery and tears, is startled to realize that they have been overheard.

'Fanny Ivanovna,' I cried, 'that man has heard everything you've said.'
'Oh *Kniaz*!' she said with undisguised contempt. 'He's heard it all before.'
I felt that this startling news rather took the gilt off the confession. I had flattered myself on being the first, in fact the only one.
'He's heard it many times,' said Fanny Ivanovna. 'Every now and then I feel that I absolutely must confess it all to *somebody* . . . no matter who it is.'
'I thought,' I said a little reproachfully, 'that you had told nobody, Fanny Ivanovna.'
'Andrei Andreiech!' she cried in her tone of appeal to my sense of justice, 'I haven't spoken of it to anyone for more than two weeks . . .'

And the revelation that Fanny plays out her tragedy repeatedly relocates it as farce, melodrama.

To a large extent the novel is about Andrei, the narrator's attempts to write a novel: and the form of *Futility* is as a consequence circular, for the conclusion of the book

I looked out upon the sea for a sign of the steamer. It had completely vanished. I peered at the horizon to see if I could spot the smoke from its two funnels. But there was none.

leads directly back into the opening line:

And then it struck me that the only thing to do was to fit all this into a book. It is the classic way of treating life. . . .

Andrei's encounters with the Bursanovs, the substance of *Futility*, become the substance of *his* novel. The *Cantos* of Ezra Pound also begin with a conjunction, 'And then went down to the ship', plunging the reader epically into the middle of his subject-matter, placing us in cultural history. Gerhardie's 'And then it struck me . . .' throws emphasis not upon cultural history but upon the narrator himself: Struck who? What struck him? When was then? What is 'all this'? Together with the enigmatic epigraph, 'The "I" of this book is not me', this presents the reader with an enlivening assortment of questions about identity and perception before reaching even the end of the first paragraph. It is something of a relief to learn of Gerhardie's later remark that 'A real book cannot be read: it can only be re-read.' And to Edith Wharton: 'No one goes by his first impressions in music; so why should he in literature?'

For Gerhardie, the 'ordered, neat' approach of what he calls 'the older novelists' gives but a poor sense of human experience. They report life 'not as it was really lived, but as they thought it *should* be lived' according to 'accepted forms and standards and conventions'.[28] In *Futility's* first paragraph, he denies the false comfort of traditional story-telling orientations of name, time, and place. With this approach the 'I' begins—and for a long time remains—elusive, unplaceable. For the character of Andrei, an (albeit Russianized) Englishman, is skilfully used by Gerhardie (the Anglo-Russian) to manipulate our shifting sympathies towards the other (mainly Russian) characters. Later on in the novel, Andrei, exasperated by the indecision and recurrent foibles of his hosts, imagines how the family and their hangers-on ought to be organized. He sits at his desk and draws up a list of 'dramatis personae', writing their names in two columns before drawing arrows and circles in an endeavour to suggest the most useful pairings ('I began by mating Nina with myself. This was easy enough: it was obvious. I consented to make Baron Wunderhausen a present of Sonia. That was done'). 'I wanted to help, to be a friend,' says Andrei. 'Anyhow it was my first experience of "intervention".' He wants, in short, to turn from the farcical and Chekhovian to something tidy, orientated, well-designed, and unnatural. Foolishly he tries to explain his plan to Nina. She is at first affronted and outraged by his interference, then bitterly mocks his naïve presumption until he eventually retorts that it is she who is 'making a farce of it'.

Andrei's narratorial 'intervention' reminds us that the narrator's role is, precisely, to *intervene* between the author and his characters, and between the characters and the reader. But the domestic intervention scene attains maximum brilliance at the moment when the reader realizes that he or she has been doing, surreptitiously, what Andrei has done openly. The complication of the domestic intrigues is designed to stir our imaginations for plot, and then the novel's plotless plot catches us plotting. Intervention is, after all, also the condition of reading, it is our relation to the material of reading; and for a moment we see that the 'I' of this book is us. When Nina ridicules him, our identification with Andrei is withdrawn again; but as the Bursanovs' own catastrophic life develops ever further one feels again the need to adjust and rethink; and it becomes clear that Andrei's plan, if only it could in some way turn from a pipe-dream to a reality, is not as unreasonable as the family's scorn made us feel. These shifting relations of sympathy, hesitant terms of the positioning of the author, are characteristic of *Futility*, and mirrored in Andrei's linguistic displacements: 'For I happen to belong to that elusive class of people knowing several languages who, when challenged in one tongue, find it convenient to assure you that their knowledge is all in another.'

Futility is quietly revolutionary, as Gerhardie knew, in its challenge to the reader. The depth and unusual quality of the challenge is indicated by contemporary responses. In a letter to his parents, Gerhardie recounts a meeting with the agents who were trying to place the book:

the silly asses seem to have overlooked the fact that the plot of my book is nothing more or less than a recognition of the fact that there is no plot in real life! The 'crisis' in my book, which takes place at the beginning and does not 'explode', but is allowed to lapse and so dwindles down gradually into a kind of diminuendo until at the end the people find that their position is essentially the same— and that nothing has happened. That is a new departure and is in itself a plot.

This plot about the disappointed hopes of plot is quite explicit in *Futility*. The phrasing of the letter echoes the words of a conversation between Andrei and Fanny Ivanovna:

'How long ago it seems,' she said at last. 'To think how long ago! . . . and we are still the same. Nothing has changed . . . nothing . . . We felt that the crisis could not last. We waited for an explosion. But it never came. The crisis still dragged on: it lapsed into a perpetual crisis; but the edges blunted. And nothing happened . . .

'When I was very young,' I said, 'I thought that life must have a plot, like a novel. But life is most unlike a novel; more ludicrous than a novel. Perhaps it is a good thing that it is. I don't want to be a novel. I don't want to be a story or a plot. I want to live my life as a life, not as a story.'

As the story circles to its conclusion Andrei is forced to realize that his own life—his great ambition to win Nina, to write a novel—has in essence been no less delusory than the hopes the Bursanovs do so much to maintain. As a writer, he feels that he has not lived, because he was waiting to write a novel—not even recording events instead of living, but rather *waiting* to record:

This novel was to be my goal in life, and then later on the novel was to follow my *real* life, a life of augmented splendour and achievement. Pending that achievement, there was, of course, that other life, essentially out of focus with the novel, not really life at all, a transitory, irritating phase not meriting attention.

And it leads, of course, back to the ultimately satisfactory ending of Andrei *writing* the novel—'And then it struck me that the only thing to do was to fit all this into a book . . .' Yet Andrei's elusiveness is also *Futility*'s. The book is pervaded by Gerhardie's preoccupation with the ineffability of experience, but its intricate draughtsmanship and formal ingenuity make it something other than a merely evasive work. It is a novel *about* elusiveness; about art's experience of the ineffable.

7

AUSTRIA
June 1922–April 1925

And there is this anomaly for which Fate must account as it can: there is he who is dead and better off but yet unable to enjoy the sense of his advantage; and here am I abandoned to a fretful and foredoomed existence which I would not willingly forgo.[1]

Futility was an immediate, almost unanimous, success. A 'wonderful' book, wrote Gerhardie's idol H. G. Wells;[2] 'the best book of the year' said Rebecca West.[3] 'His performance is, without exaggeration, astonishing', enthused the *Times Literary Supplement*, praising in particular Gerhardie's presentation of tragedy and comedy, of reality and absurdity; his 'extraordinary individual merit' which 'can narrate all these painful and horrible complications down to Fanny's husband of convenience so inconveniently slow in dying of cancer, with humour and yet without levity, with life and convincing truth and yet without solemnity.'[4] The *London Mercury*, calling it a farce, added: 'But when was there ever a farce which left one with so strong a sense of having been, not in fairyland, but in real, if unfamiliar, life?'[5] Most flattering of all, Gerhardie was hailed as the 'English Chekhov'. Chekhov, however, still suffered from being labelled 'essentially Russian'; of interest but no great relevance to the pragmatic English. And, in a similar vein, a number of reviewers failed to perceive Gerhardie's irony, appreciating *Futility* not for its universal qualities, but merely as a picture of Russia. Others wondered uneasily if it was a 'parody' or not. The *Daily Telegraph* even went so far as to describe *Futility* as 'more valuable still for its revelation of the spirit to which must be attributed Russia's present position of national hopelessness'.[6] John Middleton Murry praised *Futility* highly, but surprisingly also took the narrow view that it illustrated 'most admirably . . . the fantastic little microcosm' of Russian life and the 'Russian spirit'.[7] Even Chekhov's translator Constance Garnett found it 'very fresh and clever', 'very amusing', and 'hardly an exaggerated picture of the class from which the Russian refugees all over Europe are drawn'.[8]

The critical success of *Futility*, though necessarily falling short of William's childhood dreams, lifted his spirits considerably. In particular, his mother and father were enthusiastic about the book ('To my dearest Mama and Papa—this masterpiece from their masterpiece': inscribed in their copy) and Charles, looking at an accumulation of almost one hundred press-cuttings, remarked (albeit mistakenly) that while it had taken Dickens forty years to establish himself, his son had done so in one. Michael Sadleir, J. C. Squire (editor of the *London Mercury*), Aylmer Maude, Elizabeth Russell, and Arnold Bax all wrote to convey their appreciation of *Futility*. Unbeknown to William, Edith Sitwell, Bertrand Russell, Lord Asquith, William Rothenstein, and Lytton Strachey were also reading avidly. He was immediately fêted with interest from editors, publishers, and photographers; Paul Morand asked if he might translate the book into French, and *Futility* narrowly missed the Hawthornden Prize for that year, which went instead to David Garnett's metamorphosic fable *Lady Into Fox*. While the Moscow Arts Players toured the United States, the American publishers contrived to sell copies of *Futility* in the theatres during the Russian performance of Chekhov's *Three Sisters*, with the result that many of the audience believed that the Chekhov was merely a dramatized version of Gerhardie.

In October William received another letter, misspelling his name, but full of admiration for

> the best thing that I've read about Russia since *Oblomoff*. . . . I should not venture to thrust this praise upon you if I admired your work only as an interpretation of Russia. It is because I feel in it so many of the qualities of the novelist born that I want to cheer you on to the next. . . . You not only make your people live, but move and grow—and that's the very devil to achieve.

It was signed 'Edith Wharton'. The name was not familiar and Gerhardie, envisaging himself once again in the role of literary seducer, gaily imagined 'a lovely flapper polishing off her French at a Paris finishing school', until in the nick of time he discovered his mistake—for unlike the young, good-looking, and *outré* Katherine Mansfield, Wharton was 60 years old, an established, rather conservative, and very dignified literary figure. A Cambridge don seeing her off on a long train journey had handed her *Futility*; she opened it reluctantly, but read on with growing zeal, because 'it made the journey seem as short as though I had been piloted by Amy'.[9]

Wharton, an acolyte of Henry James and friend of Proust, was an exacting critic who confessed herself 'so bored by all novels except the superlatives'.[10] As a satirical master of social nuance, *Futility*'s delicate modulations and sensibilities had greatly appealed to her. Gerhardie hastily borrowed two of her books from the library ('she has a kind of *glazed, formally genial* way of writing', he later commented[11]) and replied to her letter, taking care to make the Miss or Mrs look ambiguous. He was, he said, immensely elated, and in regard to her wish to cheer him on to the next 'such a letter would make a dead man write books'. Furthermore, although it was 'about two years, I think' since he had read *The Age of Innocence*, he thought it a really marvellous book. Wharton, delighted by the 'flattering epithets', valued his praise as greatly as he did hers, for she suffered from the misapprehension that there existed between her work and that of the younger writers an unbridgeable gulf. She feared being regarded as 'a deplorable example of what people used to read in the Dark Ages before the *tranche de vie* had been rediscovered . . . My very letter-paper blushes as I thank a novelist of your generation for his praise.'

Their subsequent correspondence is marked by an almost syco-phantic banter on Gerhardie's part (unsurprising given Wharton's reputation), and a pleasant, though sedate interest on Wharton's. She sent him a signed copy of her latest book and a photograph of herself. Her elaborate praise prompted him to ask—with awkward familiarity, and rhetoric such as 'Is it very shameless? . . . Are you very angry?'—if he might make use of her letter for publicity purposes. Quite unchar-acteristically she agreed—'I shall be too proud to have called attention publicly to a work that has so delighted me'—and also supplied a short preface for the forthcoming US edition of the novel. 'I could murder someone in sheer exultation', wrote Gerhardie when he received news of this. 'When I told an American undergraduate at Oxford of your preface he nearly fainted—from envy.' Then Wharton took up the book again: 'I've just re-read "Futility" and it's so *very* much better than anything else that's been done in England in years that I don't care how loud I am heard to shout it!'[12] And shout it she did. 'He has', she wrote,

enough of the true novelist's 'objectivity' to focus the two so utterly alien races to whom he belongs almost equally . . . to sympathise with both, and to depict them for us *as they see each other*, with the play of their mutual reactions illuminating and animating them all. . . . . Mr Gerhardi's novel is extremely modern; but it has bulk and form, a recognisable orbit, and that promise of more to come which one always feels latent in the beginnings of the born novelist.[13]

The only blot on the landscape was General Knox, now retired from the army and working as a tea merchant, who had read *Futility*, recognized himself, and 'cursed it heartily, saying it was "rotten" and that he could not understand how I could write such "*damned non-sense*!"' William, studiedly impervious, insisted that he was 'tickled to death' by Knox's reaction, but none the less made it up nine years later with an adulatory account of Knox in his memoirs.

Meanwhile William continued to entertain Katherine Mansfield. 'Don't change Mr Gerhardi. Go on writing like that', she wrote after receiving and reading a printed copy of *Futility*. 'I mean with that freshness and warmth and suppleness, with that warm emotional tone and not that dreadful glaze of "intellectuality" which is like a curse upon so many English writers. . . . You sound so free in your writing. Perhaps that is as important as anything. I don't know why so many of our good authors should be in chains, but there it is—a dreadful clanking sounds through their books, and they can never run away, never take a leap, never risk anything . . .' And then she went on to talk of other things. 'You write the most delightful letters', she told him. 'I'm so glad we are friends.' They both looked forward to meeting when she visited London in August, but Gerhardie caught flu and could not keep the appoint-ment. Katherine, disappointed, sent him some lemon tea. 'It tastes so good when one is in bed—this tea, I mean. It always makes me feel even a little bit drunk—well, perhaps drunk is not quite the word. But the idea, even, of *the short story* after a cup or two seems almost too good to be true, and I pledge it in a third cup as one pledges one's love . . .' Yet before the flu was over and the third cup had had time to take effect, she was obliged to return to France once more, deeply regretting having missed him. 'Perhaps we shall not meet until you are very old. Perhaps your favourite grandson will wheel you to my hotel room (I'm doomed to hotels) and instead of laughing, as we should now, a faint light airy chuckle will pass from bath chair to bath chair . . . Goodbye. Are you quite well again? The weather is simply heavenly here.'

Shortly afterwards, in quest of the health and peace of mind that seemed always to elude her, Mansfield entered Gurdjieff's Institute for the Harmonious Development of Man at Fontainebleau. Early in the new year John Middleton Murry visited her. After a pleasant, sedate day together Katherine rose to return to her room and ran ahead, carelessly like a healthy person. At the top of the stairs she began to cough, blood came spurting from her mouth. The doctors bundled her, still fully conscious, on to her bed; and like this she died.

'We were so close, why weren't we closer', wrote William, in tiny letters on a square of paper, then crumpled it up. He sat staring at the strange photographs the newspapers printed; 'not my Katherine'. And to Wharton: 'I feel that I know her so well . . . I have never heard her voice, never seen her . . . If I had seen her even once before she died I would have been able to settle down to the thought of her death better. But to have known her so well . . . by letter!' Five years later he wrote to Middleton Murry after reading a published selection of Katherine's correspondence. 'What letters! What a woman! You are quite right: most of them are equal to her best work. And she stands revealed in them, tender and tragic, wise, fragrant, true: an acquisition "for ever"', adding wistfully: 'And how she loved you, *how* she loved you!'

Anton Chehov: A Critical Study was published by Richard Cobden Sanderson in 1923, 'but don't read it. It isn't much good', he told Wharton untruthfully, 'and it's deadly serious, or tries to be. And anyhow, I've had enough of it.'[14] It was the first full-length book on Chekhov (who had died in 1904) in any language except Russian, and it also represents an explication of Gerhardie's own views on literature. The study is centred on a concept of 'the ineffable' which, because of its significance for all Gerhardie's work, deserves close attention. For it is, Gerhardie argues, this 'ineffable' quality that permits the novel to do what philosophy cannot: that is, to hold apparently irreconcilable propositions, aspects, interpretations, and attitudes in a significant relationship. 'Truth', he writes, 'is an enemy of definition', hence the philosopher, the advocate of definition, is at a distinct disadvantage compared to the writer. The philosopher, constrained by the love of logic and a distaste for intuition, cannot do as the artist can—he cannot jump from one road of thought to another, and always runs the great risk of finding himself irredeemably walking along the wrong path. But a 'writer, like a painter, or a composer, can reach out towards truth, and capture it for a few moments, by sitting on the cross-roads'. In his own copy of Beckett's *Proust*, Gerhardie marked the following: 'We are reminded of Schopenhauer's definition of the artistic procedure as "the contemplation of the world independently of the principle of reason".'

The most striking effects in all Gerhardie's novels come from exactly the profound and disorientating juxtapositions that this image of divergent roads entails. Thus, when (in a later article) Gerhardie writes: 'we can only truly live in the imagination; which is the realm of reality, while the immediately tangible things are fraught with disillusionment and disappointment',[15] what might seem like an aesthete's justification of literature as fantasy and wish-fulfilment, is tempered by the sense of the disadvantages of such a predicament. As in *Futility*, Gerhardie's characters are often portrayed as being at the *mercy* of their illusions, which relationship is further suggested by his notion that 'the very stuff of literature, is the appreciation that mortal life, perhaps all life, is lived in a world of illusion'. It is 'the very stuff of literature' not only because one of literature's subjects is humanity's subjection to illusion but that literature works through the very mode it analyses, art *is* illusion.

As it is in Gerhardie's novels, so it was with Chekhov; for Chekhov's is the art 'of creating convincing illusions of the life that is'. Gerhardie praises his work as an art of the combination of elements that outside art would be contradictions:

the material sense of reality, *plus* all the romantic illusions and dreams, *plus* all the sneaking, private, half-conscious perceptions, suspicions, sensations that go side by side with the 'official', barren life of fact. It is the wanton incompatibility of the reality of life with our romantic, smoother private visions of what life ought to be, and that, together, makes our life seem what it is, with its makeshifts, self-deception, contradiction, and emotional misunderstanding of individual and mutual sensibilities, which has seized him, and, because he saw beauty in it, has made him a creative artist.

One begins to see Gerhardie's preoccupation with the significance of the ampersand—all-encompassing, infinite—as precisely the sign of the ineffable: 'as the Biblical "And" at the beginning of chapters and verses in the Gospels by way of continuing the narration'.[16] Throughout his novels Gerhardie's awareness of musical forms serves a similar function: the rendering of experience on levels other than the purely rational, comparable to T. S. Eliot's notion that 'the poet is occupied with frontiers of consciousness beyond which words fail, though meanings still exist.'[17] 'Only music', wrote George Steiner, 'can achieve that total fusion of form and content, of means and meaning, which all art strives for.'[18] Of his later novel, *The Polyglots*, Gerhardie wrote that 'the event-plot' of the book is deliberately concealed beneath the surface because real life, in its confused diffusion, is full of loose ends: to present a novel with a rigid structure and strict plot is all very well for a story, but destructive to a fact. It is the harmonious orchestration of contrary aspects of life that Gerhardie considers to be Chekhov's greatest achievement. With this 'orchestration' in mind, his own novels take the thought even further and perpetually play on the reader's expectation of contrived plot, while seeing beauty in the endless deferral and frustration of these expectations. Likewise most of Gerhardie's examples from Chekhov are passages whose very inconclusiveness sets up expectations of a fulfilment that is never reached.

Gerhardie's first chapter has points of similarity with Virginia Woolf's essay 'Modern Fiction' (1919), in which she laments the 'materialist' approach of Bennett, Wells, and Galsworthy, using the metaphors of the 'luminous halo' and 'semi-transparent envelope' for the 'life' she argues eludes them. She concludes that ' "The proper stuff of fiction" does not exist; everything is the proper stuff of fiction, every feeling, every thought; every quality of brain and spirit is drawn upon; no perception comes amiss.'[19] Gerhardie refers simply to 'the older novelists', yet both writers make essentially the same point: they are anti-'materialist', opposed to the need 'to provide a plot, to provide comedy, tragedy, love interest, and an air of probability'. 'I want the sensibility of an imaginative man', he later wrote. 'Not his imagination.'[20]

Gerhardie admires Chekhov for the complementary way in which tragedy and comedy work together, as inseparable as the individual notes of a symphony which achieve their full effect by juxtaposition with those around them: 'the humour in his plays was designed to throw the tragedy into relief'. Similarly Gerhardie's novels regularly throw the reader into the relief of laughter, by maintaining an agile poise between tragic individual isolation, and comic social self-mockery: by seeing the self from outside. 'What', he asks, 'is that in us which laughs, that will not stand solemnities, that will not be impressed by life? What portent is that safety-valve, that constant rise from certain fact into uncertain sublimation? Is that not the real God from which we cannot tire?'[21]

Such ambivalence operates also on a smaller scale, at the level of the individual sentence, where tone holds a fine balance. This is particularly true of Gerhardie's first-person narrators (in *Futility*, *The Polyglots*, *Resurrection*) where the reader's attitude towards them is continually undergoing revaluation, and shifting between irony and sympathy— an intention expressed in the following letter from Gerhardie to an American publisher:

Must I explain . . . that it is not my characters who are 'futile,' but that it is my angle of vision of 50% sympathy and 50% humorous insight which, applied to a Henry Ford, would not make him any more commendable a creature either in my hands or in the eyes of God?[22]

Gerhardie believed that more than with other European languages, 'the knowledge of Russian is an indispensable equipment for the would-be critic of Russian literature'.[23] He lamented the impossibility of adequate translation of 'polysyllabic Russian lyricism into monosyllabic English', and pointed out that in the attempt to translate idiomatic Russian humour, 'a good 60 to 70% evaporates on your hands'.[24] This, together with the loss of tonal subtlety in translation, he considered to have helped create Chekhov's English reputation for quintessentially Russian gloom. Chekhov's farces in particular 'misfire' in translation. To Edith Wharton he wrote more specifically that 'the chief difficulty is that the Russian language contains so much superfluous stuff compared with any Western language. That is why Tolstoy can afford to be ponderously simple in his philosophical works; the lack of substance in it is not noticed till it is translated'. So the unhappy Russian translator must choose between two equally inadequate alternatives: 'of summarizing the essence of a Russian sentence in his own words and so losing the melodic strain of the original sentence, or of rendering in clumsy English something that in the original Russian passes unnoticed, or sometimes adds emphasis and power'.

The travesties of translation provided an important rationale for writing the study. He feared Chekhov might remain too long misunderstood in the West. And so *Anton Chehov*, in an attempt to right the misconceptions and offer to the English reader the same sense of the 'ineffable' in Chekhov's works that is communicated to the Russian, rather than progressing from point to point, encircles its themes, discussing plays and stories with little system, and making frequent references to long quotes from Chekhov. Despite *Anton Chehov*'s salutary emphases, its meandering nature is less acceptable in criticism than in fiction. Reviewers almost unanimously found it a valuable study, but Richard Hughes voiced a common observation in calling Gerhardie's intellect 'sensitive rather than analytical'.[25] *Futility* mastered these critical problems by translating them into literature, and as such represents the best of Gerhardie's Chekhov criticism. Proust's notion of the writer as translator is thus used twofold in *Futility*—it is a translation of 'the self', and of Chekhov:

the essential, the only true book, though in the ordinary sense of the word it does not have to be 'invented' by a great writer—for it exists already in each one of us—has to be translated by him. The function and the task of a writer are those of a translator.[26]

Gerhardie longed to leave damp, dull Bolton, and was already looking nostalgically back to his 'idyllic' days at Worcester College. 'It's only at

Oxford that I ever could work', he wrote to Rothenstein from the 'aristocratic surroundings' of the Baronial Castle in Bradford Street.

How I miss it—the playing fields (have we beaten Oriel?), the rough and bracing athletic life that I used to lead at Worcester. I play soccer in my dreams, I live through that glorious moment when I scored that goal, do you remember? (We were playing Hertford and I was goal-keeper.) Oh, for a round of hockey. (I hope a 'round' is the correct technical expression.) . . . How is your hair? I suppose by now you have gone bald. My own hair, on the contrary, is flourishing. Such a mop! It begins just above the brows, it's all curly, too, and I look the poet that I am. In order to harmonise my personal appearance with my books, which are all of the good, clean-limbed variety, I have conceived a way of drawing in my lips when I am being photographed, the result being a kind of hardy, sea-wolf, Admiral Jellicoe expression, like this . . .[27]

Yet before he could move on and out of the Lancashire suburbs, Gerhardie had to plan for his parents' future. Richard Hughes and four friends had recently visited Vienna and, because of the extraordinarily favourable exchange rate, lived 'like millionaires'. John Rothenstein, John Strachey, and Eddie Sackville-West had found it a dying city but alive with music. So Gerhardie suggested a move to Austria. Clara, who was finding England 'a very terrible country for rheumatism and no wonder', agreed at once, and put the house up for sale. After much vacillation and heart-searching Rosie decided to return to Leningrad. She loved and deeply missed Russia and Leonya had written begging her to rejoin him. But she left England with a terrible last vision of her father, sitting before the fire, his head buried in his hands and shaking with sobs at her departure.

In June 1923 William set off to Austria alone. Within a few days, interrupting his purpose only to 'make love' in German to a girl in the cinema, he settled at the Villa Edelweiss, a classic Tyrolean wood chalet, remote and lofty amongst the mountains in Mühlau, a few minutes walk from Innsbruck. He wrote enthusiastically to his parents of the turbulent River Inn and the bridges that crossed it, the nearby English church and little wayside calvary, and the Russian-style stoves which once lit burned all day. 'You see also the finiculair (damn this word—how on earth is it spelt!) going up to the mountain and all around are pine-trees, birches, roses, beautiful villas in lanes lined with foliage.' And how to describe the atmosphere?—it was a jewel, it was Oxford, it was Peking at night with lanterns shining between the trees. No motors, only horse-carriages, the streets so quiet you could cross with your eyes closed—ideal for wheeling Papa around. And withal it was not in the least bit dull, with museums, cinemas, the Old Imperial Palace, and Goethe's *Faust* at the stagehouse. And at the villa itself—

in the winter, if we like, dinner can be served for us in a little drawing-room (with a piano) which we can have to ourselves, without any extra charge. *Breakwast—ja da gibt es ein caffe (oder the) mit viel Milch, and zwei Brötchen mit Butter.* This is brought to your room, where you have a special table covered by a white (slightly mended in places) table-cloth. The maid, a very nice girl but with an ugly nose, alas! (I have no luck) puts it on the table and says '*Bitte schön*,' and you say '*Danke schön*,' and she says, '*Ja, danke schön.*' Then she asks you when *der Herr will dass ich sein Zimmer mach?* This is rather a blow to the Herr, as the Herr, as you know, does not like to commit himself. However, der Herr can always go out on the Balcon, where I am now, typing . . . The lunch is very good—*Suppe, nicht-wahr? eine Fleischspeise, mit Kartofflen, jawohl*, lots and lots of vegetables, some tart or something, strawberries, water to drink. (Beer is extra.) Then till 7 or half-acht you are as hungry as a wolf and feel as if you would like to eat up all the cattle you see on the hills.

The Gerhardis were to occupy three rooms on the middle floor: a large and 'awfully jolly' room with two writing tables which William reserved for himself, a second double room, and a single room for Aunt Sissie. It was altogether a reasonably comfortable, but impersonal way of living. They could not go near the kitchen. Hot water was brought by the maid, and they must contrive to do their own laundry in the little sink, and their drying by suspending a string across the balcony. William longed to buy his parents 'some decent looking rags—those you had in the yard at Bolton won't do at all, as one couldn't for shame expose them in front of the servants, to say nothing of their being seen from outside'. He advised them to pack Charles's white flannel suit and old panama hat, and begged them not to forget his own rosewater 'lotion for the nose'. 'I am sure you will enjoy all the rest and the comfort you'll get here—which no one deserves more than you do. And if the journey and the preparations are a bit hard, you should think of the heavenly time you will have when you get here. Why, Oxford is not a patch on it!'

Charles, Clara, and Sissie arrived in July. Here amidst the 'hazy, dreamy consciousness' of the mountain scenery so vividly described in *Jazz and Jasper* they settled into a gentle routine. William and Charles were now 'accustomed to treat each other like gentlemen'. Charles liked to be wheeled to inns and beer gardens in the surrounding hills, populated with accordion-playing peasants in Tyrolean *lederhosen*, gaily plumed hats, and puffing at long curved pipes; the women wore delightfully tight-waisted coloured dirndls. Pushing Charles's wheelchair up the steep hill home again was such an effort that at great expense they ordered an elaborate mechanical support for his paralysed leg to help him walk. But Charles, truculent and impatient, refused to give it a fair trial. 'Throw it out of the window', he muttered crossly.

In Innsbruck the Gerhardis would gather around the bandstand for hours at a time, and it was here that William's most popular story, 'The Big Drum', was conceived. 'Most popular', because according to his agent it had a 'clear and definite message'. It is a brief parable about Otto, a big-drum player. His brass band is parading through an Austrian town while, amongst the appreciative crowd, Otto's fiancée watches wistfully. Otto, hands at his sides, is not playing; he seems reluctant—he cannot, will not deign to blare out his love as his band members all do. 'And as she watched him she felt a pang of pity for herself; wedded to him, she would be forgotten, while life, indifferent, strode by . . . And the music brought this out acutely.' But suddenly the music changes. At once Otto is the centre of emotion, not only her's but all the spectators'. The crowd is captured, roused, enraptured by Otto's drum. 'Otto, as never before, whacked the big drum, whacked it in excitement, in a frenzy, in transcending exaltation. Thundering bangs! And now she knew—what she couldn't have dreamed—she knew it by his face. Otto was a hero.'

The inhabitants of the Villa Edelweiss were an intriguing mixture of curiosities, and Gerhardie sat at meals pen in hand taking surreptitious notes. There was an elderly aristocratic spinster who always wore lilac, had a shrill, scandalized way of speaking, was violently pro-Bolshevik, 'and, I think, a little insane'. A famous English society beauty 'well past her prime' sat arguing hour upon unintelligible hour with a fabulous Russian princess and a fat old Swiss shopkeeper who slept with a fresh woman each night, and when asked by Gerhardie how he liked her invariably replied: '*Prima Qualität*'. 'He often "orders" women for my use—as though it were cabs! But compared with him I am fastidious, and I have turned down every one of his "orders".'[28] The local society was almost fanatically punctilious about social calls. Gerhardie was invited by a woman to tea, and the very next morning, while he sat in his portable bath, 'the lady's husband was already knocking at my bedroom door. I explained I was in my bath. The baron stressed the fact that he was returning my call. A desultory conversation took place through the keyhole, I explaining I could not that moment admit him; he evidently offended.' The moment he was dressed William 'dashed to the baron's house to return his call, but found he was out. Late that night he came tearing up the hill, to return my call, only having seen my card, he explained, ten minutes before on his return from an excursion in the hills, dog tired.'[29]

In January 1923 Edith Wharton, pointing out that she was now only a few miles distant, invited Gerhardie to visit her in France. She had recently made a great deal of money from her novels—*Glimpses of the Moon* (1922) alone earned £60,000—and had bought St Claire Château, an old convent with views over the rooftops of Hyères and down on to the Mediterranean, where she lived an elegant, reclusive life almost as if from another epoch. Gerhardie prepared for the journey and, not wanting to waste money on the railway restaurant car, he asked the pension to make him some sandwiches. Wharton sent her chauffeur to meet him at Toulon station. When they arrived at the Château it was late and dark, and as Wharton was already in bed she welcomed him from her window. Gerhardie was shown to his room by a servant. The sandwiches, enormous slices of heavy Austrian bread, had still not been eaten. Reflecting that 'an immaculate butler would be sure to survey them with critical thoughtfulness, I threw them where they belonged and pulled the plug'. Early next morning there were noises and anxious faces. Plumbers were at work, some unknown person, the butler said, having thrown bread down the lavatory which had swelled and blocked the pipe. 'When a few hours later I advanced to meet Mrs Wharton in the garden we both smiled unconvincingly. If the truth must be told each thought, as we shook hands, of the bread in the lavatory.'[30] Coming from Siberia, she later told friends, Gerhardie was obviously worried that there might be a shortage of food in her house.

Wharton's routine was the same whoever was staying: she would write in the morning, then appear at noon to play hostess, impeccably dressed with gloves, parasol, and hat. She could be intimidating—social delicacy was as open to her scrutiny in reality as in fiction—and she had a tendency to sit so bolt upright that she looked as though she had swallowed an umbrella. Gerhardie, who spent the first day admiring her grounds, came upon a board she had nailed to a tree: PRIVATE PROPERTY NO TRESPASSERS, and just for good measure, POSITIVELY NO ADMITTANCE, striking a discordant note amidst the idylls of nature. He returned to the rose garden forthwith, and spent the rest of the afternoon snipping buds.

All through, she wore a detestable cloche hat concealing all but her worst features. When I came down in the evening there was a woman in the drawing-room with yellowish hair whom I thought I had not seen before.

We sat there waiting, as I thought, for our hostess. Presently we went in to dinner and I found myself sitting by the side of the woman to whom I had not been introduced, because of the absence of our hostess, I supposed. It seemed odd to me we should not have waited for our hostess, and after the soup I said to the woman at my side: 'But where is Mrs Wharton?'

She looked at me with sad, inquiring thoughtfulness and said—very pertinently, as it seems to me now: 'I am Mrs Wharton.'

'Oh,' I said, 'are you Mrs Wharton?'

She looked at me as if she thought I couldn't be all there. 'Of course I am,' she said. 'Oh . . . good evening,' I said.[31]

Wharton thought Gerhardie 'more like a troll than a human being',[32] though she took the greatest delight in his company and curious conversation. They talked at length of Proust. He attempted to change her opinion of Chekhov after she confessed that she had once read a badly translated tale—'something about a poodle'—and never wanted to read anything else. In misspelling Gerhardie's name she had begun as she meant to go on. Was it pronounced with a soft or a hard 'g'? she asked him. A soft—very well, Mr Gerard-y. William gently corrected her. Right you are, Mr Gherhardie. William expostulated. Wharton was adamant: a soft 'g' and no 'h' or an 'h' and a hard 'g'; he could not possibly have it both ways. Gerhardie in turn had trouble with Wharton's butler Favre, whom he understood to be called Father, and so addressed him. Father, he confided to Wharton, seemed rather 'pessimistic'. Father retaliated by intimidating Gerhardie with his scornful disdain of the visitor's unpressed trousers. None the less, when William left Wharton urged him to visit again.

In the autumn of 1924 Sissie returned to England and Charles and Clara moved to smaller rooms a few miles away in the village of Andras. William, who wished to be alone in order to finish his latest novel, *The Polyglots*, moved first to a pension at nearby Ambras, then to Vienna. Well fed and 'content' he drifted between Bohemian poets and exiled Russian aristocrats.

In Vienna dogs, he noted with relief, were all muzzled so that 'you can walk along with your mind at rest and perfectly sure that no creature of the canine tribe will grip you by the ankles'. The constant need to tip was disheartening, but at least in the lavatories it was written plainly on the door of each establishment: '*Pissplatz frei*', and men only had to pay 'in special cases'. There were many other delights, as he was only too happy to recount in letters: an enchanting woman in the park covered in fleas—'Even as I sit beside her, you can see them jumping over to me—jump! jump! jump!'; and in the pension an alluring Hungarian girl, exquisitely curvaceous, with fair locks and dark eyes and brows 'and a really exquisite figure—like this'

Soon after arriving Gerhardie inserted an advertisement in the local paper:

Foreigner wishes to meet young lady: aim, marriage.

His aim was no such thing, but he received several nicely written replies: from Ottilie, 24 years old, 'very pretty', with blue eyes and blonde hair, who lived in a large house with her parents; from Anna-Maria, young, slim, and tall with brown happy eyes, keen on sport and gymnastics, but without money or possessions, and currently working as a governess in Vienna; and from the uncle of Selina, a 'healthy', elegant young woman with a good figure, though no photographs were available. But he cast them all up for Renée, a Viennese watchmaker's daughter, extremely enticing in the style of Pola Negri and with whom he fell 'rather painfully' in love. When his 'rubber goods' failed and Renée became pregnant Gerhardie made speedy arrangements. 'As I don't want to be guilty of the sin of bringing another Willy into this idiot world, we had to despatch him back to his forefathers—at an early stage! And now all is beautifully settled', he wrote to his parents. 'No doubt, you will be astonished. I am chiefly known to you as a creator on another plain as well. But the fact proves my astounding versatility.' The production of children did not interest Gerhardie—too noisy, too time-consuming, too dirty—but the anxiety, the 'glorious uncertainty' of an infatuation was usually productive of good fiction. 'My love affair has exhausted me—but the result of it is the story I am finishing.'

'Tristan und Isolde', Gerhardie's finest short story, embodies his childhood preoccupations with love and death, ecstasy and oblivion. It tells of the love affair between an American visiting Austria and a Jewish girl (based upon Renée) whom, despite his infatuation, he considers his social and cultural inferior. The story is confined to their brief relationship, which is characterized by the operatic metaphor. With little in common except mutual desire, they meet on an imaginative middle-ground, changing their names to Tristan and Isolde, viewing themselves as characters from fiction. Events are minimal. Gerhardie's literary analogy of Wagner's masterpiece evokes inarticulate, irrational tides of love and passion, the perpetual ebb and flow of their emotions towards each other. He craves her and is disgusted by her, sometimes alternately, sometimes simultaneously. She, realizing this, meets his advances, holds back, reconsiders, succumbs. As the story progresses, their individual desires and intentions are revealed and concealed and manipulated. Neither particularly *likes* the other: he is transfixed by rapture, she by romance and the prospect of marriage. The finale of longing and uncertainty revolves around the young man's tentative proposal of marriage: he writes '?' on a cigarette box, dreading both her acceptance and her refusal. In an agony of indecision she writes only '!'. Like Wagner's long-deferred, final cadence, resolution comes almost imperceptibly, subdued into gesture: 'She shook her head.' Their dilemma is resolved—but the only relief comes from oblivion: 'He did not know what he had done, why he had done it, or what had been done to him. He only knew that he wanted to go home, cover himself with the black flag—and die.'

Whilst in Vienna Gerhardie also worked on a play, *Perfectly Scandalous*, based upon the Villa Edelweiss and its inhabitants; some articles —'Mr Lawrence and the Wreck of the Love-Service', 'Goethe's Critical Credo', and 'Schnitzler's *Fräulein Else*', all published in *The Adelphi*[33]; and some short stories: 'The Vanity Case', 'about a middle-aged American who falls in love with a girl in Salzburg, whose vanity-bag must needs convince him in the end that he has nothing more to hope from her, and is rewarded by the unsought heavy friendship of her literary father—a bag of vanity',[34] and 'A Bad End'—'an étude on the black notes'—the fictional tale of manslaughter and a hanging, written in order to show 'the terrible discrepancy which exists between human suffering and legal automata which causes it'.[35] Gerhardie was a committed abolitionist and in 1922 had written to the newspapers to protest against the execution of Edith Thompson and Percy Bywaters for the murder of Thompson's husband. He later sent the story to Horatio Bottomley, a vigorous anti-hanging campaigner.

But most important of all, within a few weeks of arriving in Vienna *The Polyglots* was completed. Cobden Sanderson thought it 'a novel of considerable subtlety and importance', and offered a £50 advance, to the irritation of Gerhardie who had hoped to sign up with a better publisher. The dream of a home of study and rest in the South of France now seemed tantalizingly close to fulfilment. Clara, waiting for her copy of *The Polyglots*, began *Futility* again, 'and really every time I read it with more and more interest. It really is a fine book. Vassinka dear, you are *really* great to have written that book.' Charles expressed himself more reservedly on his son's twenty-ninth birthday:

Dear Willy

Many happy returns of your birthday, may you enjoy good health and prosperity for many years to come and brilliant success in your litterary career and all the success *Polyglots* deserves.

We miss you very much and hope you will soon return for a few weeks holidays, it will be so nice to have your good company again.

How do you like Vienna? Do you find the women pretty and graceful? and the city a fine one? I hope so.

Mama keeps well and her successful perrucue makes her look young and smart. Nothing new here. Mrs Stecher is as nice to us as usual but it is very dull above all without you looking in occasionally.

Well I really have no more news to give you so much to my regret I must close. Your everloving papa.

But William, in the depression that invariably follows completion, remembered how on his eleventh birthday he had felt ashamed of his age: 'Nothing done—no promise shown, and already eleven', and then at 21 he had felt proud of being a captain and independent. Once again he felt ashamed to be so old and with so little achieved, and he imagined that perhaps after three-score years and ten he might be relieved of this compunction and consider as a gift whatever would then be left of life.

In Andras, meanwhile, Clara was having an increasingly difficult time with Charles, now 60 and growing weaker. He had become incontinent, and washing him was 'a real nightmare' because he was too heavy for her to lift. She had to clean up when he was sick, and when one morning he choked on a piece of bread at breakfast Clara—always very descriptive in her letters to William—had to put first her fingers down his throat, then a soft piece of rubber to dislodge the blockage. He was perpetually cold, so that she was obliged to light the stove herself at 7.00 a.m.

because the maid did not arrive in time. But she must have been a woman of great strength and courage, for she always also wrote cheerfully of the beautiful snow, the skiing and yodelling, and the glorious winter weather which enabled them to eat their Quaker Oats supper outside on the balcony. Charles's old obsession with punctuality had not left him, though he had nothing to do, and he still regularly pulled out his watch as if to make sure not to miss a daily event of years before. William paid them a visit and watched him reading *Anton Chehov* to himself, 'angrily munching and swallowing as he always did through restlessness'. Clara read aloud passages from the manuscript of *The Polyglots*. Charles sat silent, now and again declaring that a passage was 'instructive', and when, at a sad part, tears filled Clara's eyes Charles said: 'Don't cry. It's not real. It's only a book. Willy has invented it.' Then William left for Vienna again: 'Well, good-bye', he said, handing his father a little money. '*Bon voyage*', replied Charles.

On 12 January Clara turned 56, and William, enclosing his traditional gift of one guinea, wrote to wish her 'above all 'ealth, happiness, etc., etc. and *a quite unusually long life*, and that when at last you die I should die at the same time and that neither should outlive each other and be transferred together into the realm of Bô Yin Râ!!' He was confident that her next birthday would be spent 'upon a sunny terrace overlooking the blue Mediterranean, and that as many members of the family, big and small, will participate in the chocolate-drinking as may be practicable'. Although, as she put it, her first birthday without a 'chick' present, it was a cheery day for Clara—a dance to the pension gramophone, a special note from Charles in the dining-room, and a dozen family letters, even one from Victor, 'but only just a few words of Congratulations and good wishes. . . . I did so long for a proper letter from him but he is not like my Vassinka and does not spoil me with letters'. She happily anticipated her thirty-sixth wedding anniversary in April.

A few days later William, about to keep an appointment with a young woman in Vienna, received a telephone call from his mother. She had gone to make Charles a cup of tea, talking to him all the while, but after a moment he ceased to answer. She called him 'Karlusha', a pet name not used since they were young, but he lay silent. Unconscious now for several hours, the doctor had given up hope. William caught a train for the twelve-hour night journey to Innsbruck, alternately crying with despair and filled with hope for a miraculous recovery. At midday the train arrived. Walking up the hill to the pension he resolved to devote much attention to Charles in the future, when a car came swiftly down, the snow flying, and pulled up beside him. In the back sat Clara, quiet and exhausted from grief, heavily draped in black crape. Charles had died at 1.00 a.m. Clara had watched over him, stroked his head and whispered, 'Karlusha, Willy is coming! Willy is coming!'

They drove to Innsbruck to make the funeral arrangements. The undertaker, who spoke impersonally of '*Die Leiche*' ('It—the body who overnight was he—my father') unfolded a cemetery map and, attempting to sell them a three-berth plot, involuntarily cast a glance up as if determining their meterage. They decided on cremation, 'altogether a much more satisfactory and aesthetic performance than burial in the wet ground'. At nightfall they returned to the pension. 'I went quickly to the bed on which my father lay, his head thrown back on a pillow; a napkin covered his face, and that suggested two thoughts in succession: that he could not breathe with the napkin over his face, and that he no longer needed to.' Clara gently lifted the napkin: 'You see, he looks quite nice' she said. 'My father's brow looked austere and composed; his eyes were closed, the mouth slightly open: but not a breath came, and the stillness seemed uncanny.'[36] As with the bodies from the massacres in Russia, so it was now with Charles: 'What was once a human being is now an object—like a stone, or a stick.' The proprietors of the pension were frightened of a corpse in the house, so the next day he was quickly placed in a coffin and taken away.

My mother, who, for the last nine years, had had him on her hands, and until this moment had been preoccupied with his removal, now, having followed the men with the coffin downstairs, did not seem to realise, as they drove away so quickly, that he was already off her hands, there, speeding away as he had always wished in life, by himself! Now as she saw him vanish quickly downhill in charge of strange men, for the first time it came to her, the loneliness of her position. Left standing there, wan and hatless, under the freezing porch, she began to sob.[37]

William and Clara threw Charles's false teeth into a ditch with a faint little stream in a thicket, expecting the Alpine water to carry them away, but they lay where they had dropped. 'God grant him rest', said Clara and sighed. 'Rest!' she repeated doubtfully. 'Does he want it? Why, he was restless from so much rest. The poor fellow wanted a little excitement.'[38] A few friends attended a service in the mortuary conducted perforce by a Lutheran pastor in German, a language Charles detested. The coffin went unaccompanied to Munich for cremation.

'In old novels grief is treated as a one-melody emotion. In real life this is not so.'[39] Gerhardie's shifting thoughts at this time are vividly chronicled in his *Memoirs*; 'My Father's Death' is the longest, most poignant section of the book. First numb shock, veering to distracted thoughts of his mistress, wishing the whole terrible business was over—then pain and grief; now squeezing his 'pretty maid' and trading on her sympathy; now a tragi-comic consciousness of the absurdity of it all ('A corpse stroked by a relative lifts itself and shouts: "How dare you!"', he jotted as an idea for a short story). Above all is the overriding sense of disbelief that what has once been a presence, seen, heard, felt, is now intangible, nothing more than an idea.

Clara left Austria for Marseilles, to be close to Daisy. The wretched circumstances of Charles's last years made his death particularly painful, and Gerhardie wrote at length to try to lessen her distress:

I know it's not easy to forget Papa—*nor is it necessary*—and it is sad to think of him gone, vanished, irrecoverable. . . . But regret is a useless waste of emotion. All people are so constituted that they can only enjoy and appreciate *in retrospect*. . . . Unless one knew beforehand the exact date of one's relatives' deaths—when one could time and appropriately accelerate one's kindness towards the particular candidate—one cannot do more than act normally and equally to all, since, for all one knows, one may be the first to die oneself! . . . As for poor dear Papa, whose memory we all treasure and cannot forget, think what it would be to him if he had to wake from the merciful sleep which, at last, was a lasting one—didn't he always want to take sleeping draughts at night and kill his time during the day?—think what it would be to him if he had to wake to the daily routine of injections and shaving and waiting and nothing to look forward to for it. After all when one is tired out, sleep is a boon, and once asleep, few people would bargain for the privilege of waking up again, even at the best of times.

But William, enveloped by guilty unease, 'haunted' by Charles's 'meekness and resignation', was, like his mother, not easily consolable: 'Only later, perhaps three months after he had been burnt to ashes, one bleak Sunday when I was alone in the Vienna *pension*, did the full force of our loss strike me. He had been so quiet, passive. Yesterday he was there, now he was not.'[40]

On a more pedestrian level Gerhardie was also beset with the practical problem of Charles's remains. 'If I had asked my father what I was to do with the urn, he would have said, "Throw it away"',[41] he reflected. The cemetery was, of course, the consecrated and conventional place, 'but far away, among a lot of Huns'. The living-room on the other hand was 'homely'. William placed the urn, wrapped in brown paper, on his mantelpiece. 'I think he would prefer being with me, if he knew, or perhaps knows.'

8

WATER IN THE TEAPOT
April 1925–October 1925

O my God, what a strange, comic, gruesome world this is!

'Mostly all old fogies like me living here', wrote Clara from her 'very staid' Marseilles hotel. She had to admit, however, that the town was busy and sophisticated, full of elaborate shops and women fashionably dressed in the latest flesh-coloured stockings. And after the slow and easygoing Austrians 'the French seem very funny and noisy. The speed they talk at outside my door . . . takes all one's eloquence away, there's no keeping up with them.' But it was a lonely place, beset with devilish weather, winds and dusty clouds. Clara penned emotional letters to her son quoting poetry and describing, with tragic stoicism, the sad fate of the family: Jean, while out walking, had been bitten on the leg by a dog, right through his brand-new suit and his underwear; in Bolton Dolly's garage had burned down; and Charles's sister Mary had died slowly and painfully of a tumour of the stomach. 'God seems to be intent on vigorously exterminating the Gerhardi tribe', commented William when he heard.

Clara, in an effort to overcome her gloomy infestivity, vigorously sought out exiled friends from Russia, and paid regular visits to the English church. In the summer she took a small house by the sea, half-way between Marseilles and Toulon, with eucalyptus, mimosa, vines, and fruit trees growing wild all about. Since leaving the navy Daisy's husband Jean had set up in a precarious business as a dealer in Buddhas and now travelled regularly to Paris. Clara, left alone with Daisy, busied herself playing with the new and very heavy baby, whilst lamenting the terrible mosquitoes, the hard work that Daisy had to do (Jean, though devoted, was not good in the house), and above all the difficulty of adjusting to the loss of Charles. 'I am still just as lonely and do miss him so much. Where is he I wonder. Shall I ever be able to settle down again without him. Somehow at Aldrans we seemed as though we should never be separated', she wrote unhappily to William. 'I would so love to take the urn in my arms and press it to me as I used to press his poor frail body, without him I seem to be a cockle shell, whirled about in a mighty sea, no succor. I used to think it was he who depended on me when all the time it was he who was my strength and gave me hope and courage to go on.' 'You must,' she later admonished, 'not quite forget your mummie.'

Gerhardie, tired of Austria and waiting only for the appearance of his new novel, had neither the intention of forgetting Clara (and sent £60 towards the 'National Debt', dentist's bills preventing him from sending more) nor the ability to stop missing Charles. 'I did not think that we would feel his loss as we do. When he was alive, always sighing and waiting, one felt it was cruel for him to be alive, and now one thinks it is hard on him to be dead; his going has left a scar that does not seem to heel as time goes on.' He insisted to Victor that they not reduce the £60 each they had, since the failure of *Madame Claire*, been paying to their parents every year. Clara may only constitute half of what we once had, he argued furiously, but she still constitutes the sum living total of our parentage. And she needs the money.

The Polyglots, dedicated to Edith Wharton, was published in June.[1] The second of Gerhardie's two really great novels, it shares all *Futility*'s humour, delicacy, historical interest, and fictional innovation; but, very much longer than his earlier work, it shows a remarkable development beyond *Futility*, an increased verve, confidence, and dash. The central character, Georges Diabologh, based again upon Gerhardie, is substantial in a way that Andrei was not, and his self-consciously philosophical inclinations serve to convey much of Gerhardie's exhilaration at this period. In Gerhardie's words, Georges is 'a high spirited young man who, in the course of travelling on a military mission to the Far East, discovers his relatives, their children and friends', amidst the post-Intervention chaos. Amongst these characters are the 'delectable nin-compoop' Sylvia-Ninon, whose seduction he pursues to its curious conclusion, his hypochondriacal Aunt Teresa, amorous Uncle Emmanuel, mad Uncle Lucy, and a great many others.

The scope of *The Polyglots* reaches far beyond the confines of the Russian Revolution and Allied Intervention. Viewing the aftermath of war, revolt, and change throughout the world in 1919, Georges, who travels round the entire globe, witnesses a panorama of ludicrous militarism, a no-man's-land between war and peace, defeat and victory, order and ruin, splendour and squalor. America is glimpsed as a country of bizarre contrasts and dubious moral rectitude; England, a land of drizzle. In Russia and the Far East, families of every race and nationality, as well as the military, are struggling to come to terms with the changing politics. *The Polyglots*, as the title implies, is a world of displaced people, both comic and tragic, obliged by historical upheavals to learn new languages, adjust to fresh values. Yet the chaos is universal, inherent, not confined to race, class, or generation. One critic, misled into observing that 'no doubt the half-disgusting, half-lovable hero is a near image of the youth of to-day—youth which speaks a different language, obeys other rules, belongs to another era than those which pre-War adults know',[2] ignored the fact that in *The Polyglots* morals and attitudes are patently independent of generations. Georges is at heart a pacifist, Anatole his cousin and contemporary a militarist; Sylvia slavishly copies Georges and all her elders, be they her parents or the *Daily Mail*; Teresa, of the older generation, has fled from Europe to *avoid* the war, but it is also Teresa who engineers the dubious morality of Sylvia's wedding consummation, and, just to make the situation clear to that disgusted critic, the morals of Georges's Uncle Emmanuel are the worst of the lot.

The world in which the characters find themselves is peopled with individuals characterized by often ludicrous and repetitive behaviour, part Chekhov, part Dickens, and prefiguring Beckett. 'My idea, in writing *The Polyglots*', Gerhardie later explained, 'was to dispense with the artificial props and scaffolding which rely for sense of form on such external divisions as "Part I, Part II", etc., but to achieve a sense of unity organically from within. This I attempted to do by identifying the people in the book each with a *leitmotiv* and re-introducing them again and again through life and marking, either by a slight change, or by the lack of it, by the suggestion that they have grown older but scarcely wiser, the cruel progression of time.'[3] It is a world often bereft of sense. Yet Georges's striving for order and reason lead him into comic misunderstandings with those around him; he is repeatedly having to come to terms with situations that hover between the idiotic and the tragic, so that much of his interest in novel-writing centres on the rationalizing potential of narrative.

Now that I look back on it from the vantage point of many months it is clear to me that Uncle Lucy's life was a crescendo towards madness, culminating, as you will have seen, in this extraordinary suicide in Aunt Teresa's knickers, camisole and boudoir cap. Why did he do it? Well may you ask. Yet the explanation is, perhaps, more simple than we think. It may have been because he knew that he was going mad that Uncle Lucy hanged himself, and hanged himself the way he did in order to do justice to his madness.

With acute awareness of the conventions and expectations of reading, Gerhardie has deliberately created a work from which it is extremely difficult to remain aloof. From the outset the boundaries between reader and author-narrator are unclear: there is perpetual trespass and intervention, drawing the reader out of the complacency of the solitary, protective, reading state, into the 'real' history of the novel and into an awareness that the novel form is not escapism, entertainment, mere print on a page, but the living thoughts of an individual, the result of genuine experience; for Gerhardie himself was as much a victim of these global upheavals as any of his characters, and a great deal of first-hand factual material is used in the book. At the very end the reader is further involved, forced to *feel*, obliged to *act* not only for the characters within the story, and their uncertain future, but for the novelist himself and the living characters behind the fiction:

And the end? you will ask . . . The end? I don't know and don't care. The end depends on what you choose to make it. And I invite the reader to co-operate with me in a spirit of good will to make the end a happy one for all concerned: Buy this book. If you have already bought it, buy it again, and get your brother and mother to buy it. And the end, for Aunt Teresa and Aunt Molly and the Negodyaev family, will be different—very different—from what it might otherwise become. So tell your friends, tell all your friends—my aunt wants you to.

Gerhardie's future, and that of some members of his family, did indeed depend heavily upon the success of *The Polyglots*. Yet it is, of course, not only a personal predicament that is evoked here.

The Polyglots introduces the 'I' as a displaced person, disturbing as much for the reader as for Georges: 'I stood on board the liner halted in midstream and looked upon Japan, my native land. But let me say at once that I am not a Japanese. I am very much a European.' We must ask, what is meant by 'native land'? What is meant by 'European'? The deliberate ambiguity, as well as creating a sense of a world divided, repartitioned by a war, causes us to ask from the start what the narration insistently asks all the way through: Who is this man? How can we *see* him? In describing the Diabologh family origins Teresa presents a ludicrous parody of what Gerhardie was later to offer in *Memoirs of a Polyglot*: hers is a genealogy littered with idiotic, playful detail, and Georges himself remarks that

'Whether what she said was fact or partly fiction I cannot truly vouch'. We are plagued by a fascinating plethora of identities, glimpsed, unsubstantiated: Georges the central character, Georges the narrator; Andrei from *Futility* obviously bears some relation to the central character of the new work and, of course, Gerhardie is related—albeit to an uncertain degree—to them all.

As in *Futility*, Gerhardie's revolutions are not progressive, but cyclical, and history does not necessarily advance forward: 'modernity is illusory'. But unlike the earlier work, the structure of *The Polyglots*, as distinct from the history it describes, is not circular, though all paths lead around its narrator. Is Georges merely a 'symbol', the double of individuals who have become symbols, or is he more substantial than the characters he describes for us? (Major Beastly and Brown 'were not individuals: they were merely samples of a type'.) Georges's unusually robust physical presence is contrasted with the character of Anatole, his cousin who is away in Europe fighting in the trenches, and who we learn has been killed. He has no 'physical' presence, no body, because he is dead (his family receive his clothes, empty) but also because he never 'enters' the novel—he is a presence off-stage. But in another sense he has equal status with Georges, a name in a book where such distinctions are fictions.

And yet, as a novelist Gerhardie exhibits a far stronger connection with his characters than in his earlier work. Georges's falling in love with Sylvia parodies a Pygmalionesque infatuation of the novelist for his own creations. Everything that Georges admires in Sylvia resembles himself—her calves, her fine black brows, her dark hair, her eyelashes—and shortly she is repeating everything he says, having words put into her mouth by him. Even Georges's interest in the child Natasha is as a potential wife created expressly by and for himself. The deliberate narcissism, so integral a part of this novel, incites him to rebel against the limits of the form in which he is constrained, for shortly after saying:

A novel is a cumbersome medium for depicting real people. Now if you were here—or we could meet—I would convey to you the nature of Major Beastly's personality in the twinkling of an eye—by visual representation. Alas, this is not possible.

he tries to attain greater substance by posing before a looking-glass:

Women like me. My blue eyes, which I roll in a becoming way when I talk to them, look well beneath my dark brows—which I daily pencil. My nose is slightly tilted. . . . But what disposes them to me, I think, are my delicate nostrils, which give me a naive, tender, rabbit-like expression, like this—'M'm'—which appeals to them.

Gerhardie persistently calls attention both to the reality behind the novel, and to the fantasy within it. Alluding to the notion of fiction as armchair fantasy, the opening of *The Polyglots* is cast almost entirely in the vocabulary of the dream world, as he arrives 'spellbound' in the 'enchanted island', Japan. Georges mirrors the readers' experiences to some extent by missing out on 'real' life because of a preoccupation with literature and philosophy; he reproaches Sylvia for her impatience to know what will become of them all 'in the end', and finally reaches the limit of his calm, having felt himself imprisoned in the novel for too long: 'I am mortally sick of them', he exclaims, 'of immoral old uncles, insatiable women, Belgian duds, impecunious captains, insane generals, *stink*-making majors, pyramidon-taking aunts! . . . I wanted to *do* things, to live, to work, to build, to shout.' Half-a-dozen pages later the book is brought to a close.

Georges's intervention between the fictional world and the 'real' novel-reader finds further expression in his implied reproofs to our prurient interest in the characters—as when describing Emmanuel's visit to a bath house:

Presently the door opened. Some lithe thing in a black hat and black silk stockings flitted past the keyhole and obscured my view. The black hat came off . . . There was a rustle of crisp garments . . . I do not know how all this strikes you. I am a serious young man, an intellectual, a purist, and disapprove of Uncle Emmanuel's sedate irregularities. A veil over my uncle's doings!

The primary intimacy is, of course, between the reader and the mind of the novelist; the novel is a kind of exhibitionism, all the more intimate for the implied biographical content, but the limits of the relationship have been rarely explored. Gerhardie's debt to Sterne's *Tristram Shandy* (a popular novel in Russia), in investigating what a novel may and may not do, is also, to a smaller degree, evident in Georges's references, which prefigure Gerhardie's later novel *Resurrection*, to his own origins: 'my thoughts', he writes at the very start, 'went back to my birth, twenty-three years before, in the land of the cherry blossoms'. In true Shandy fashion this is followed by a reference yet further backward to his own conception: 'At the Imperial Hotel. An unlooked-for diversion during my people's pleasure trip in the Far East, I fancy.' Later in the novel, when Georges falls ill, we are offered another foretaste of *Resurrection* when Georges appears to hover trance-like above his own body:

I lay in bed, ill, and dreamed into the future, back into the past. Long, peaceful thoughts. In those still twilight hours when you lie on your back and float as if outside and beside life, draw from the deep well of inhibited emotion that dreamy substance which underlies our daily life . . . What is that soul of yours, and is it *you*? My I, as I now came to see, had always been changing, was never the same, never myself, but always looked forward—to what?

It is not accident that Gerhardie acknowledges his ambition to become a *part* of English literature by middle-naming his hero Hamlet: a young foreigner, with the nickname 'Prince', a difficult family, a fancy for ghosts that speak of death, and a propensity to soliloquize. '"I have been so weak", I wailed melodramatically—and really feeling the part. "So miserably weak, so indecisive. I have imbibed this curse of a Hamletian vacillation with the name, I suppose".' In fact he no more than fleetingly resembles the Shakespearian extreme of egotism, introspection, and indecision, and Gerhardie's use suggests Chekhov's ironization of the tendency to tragedy. Georges's perpetual involvement with his thesis, his long soliloquies, recall *The Seagull*: Treplev's elaborate metaphysical speeches in the opening of his play, and Nina's complaint to him: 'It is difficult to act your play . . . There is very little action in your play—nothing but speeches.'[4]

All Gerhardie's novels have tended to defy traditional categories of fiction. Works of satire may contain recognizable truths, but they do not demand a naturalistic identification of reader with the world portrayed, such as Gerhardie creates. Malcolm Bradbury has described, very broadly, two traditions of novelistic comedy: that of characters like Quixote, Walter Shandy, and Mr Pickwick who, although evoking 'identification and sympathy', 'occupy strange and extravagant worlds'.[5] Then, in a different tradition of comedy, Bradbury describes worlds which 'partake of a humane realism, a central balance which destroys extremes and gives the centre its due', naming Jane Austen, E. M. Forster, and Kingsley Amis as examples. Gerhardie's creation in *The Polyglots* (and, apart from *Jazz and Jasper*, which additionally contains elements of pure fantasy, to some extent in all his novels) is a world that is absurd, often extravagantly so, but which is also naturalistic and in which the characters are obliged to make what sense they can of a bizarre universe. For Gerhardie the real *is* the absurd. For some critics Gerhardie's world, like that of Chekhov, remained strange, extravagant and remote, peopled with curious foreign eccentrics and devoid of relevance. Yet Gerhardie's attempt at deliberate inclusion of the reader in his fictional world is as important in regard to understanding his comedy as it is with more serious issues. Georges's looking-glass reflects reality, but it is a looking-glass world. Many of Gerhardie's characters possess curious names which, though they appear to the reader as unreal, function to show that reality *is* absurdity: Major Beastly, Uncle Lucy, Corporal Cripple, the batman who is aptly named Pickup, and Captain Negodyaev whose name 'translated into English would read Captain Scoundrelton or Blackguardson'. Yet Georges's *explanation*, his comments of 'What a passport for a man! . . . yet Captain Negodyaev was meak and servile, humble and very timid', indicates that this is not a world 'morally separate' from our own, in Bradbury's sense. Georges even attributes his uncle's bizarre suicide to having been named Lucy. No character in *Vile Bodies* would comment upon the names of Miles Malpractice, or Margo Metroland, or Mr Outrage; and yet we find that Georges himself bears a name almost equally absurd which, because he is also part of our, the reader's, world, he is obliged to explain as naturally as he is able, whilst remaining fully conscious of its absurdity:

When I, a distant offspring (born in far Japan), was joining up a Highland regiment to fight in the World War . . . the recruiting sergeant looked at [the name Diabologh] and looking at it looked at it again, and as he looked at it he looked—well—puzzled. His face began to ripple, changed into a snigger, developed into a grin, he shook his head—'*Gawddamn*'.

'I have scarcely ever done more in my fiction than transpose or transplant real incidents as supplied by life itself', Gerhardie declared when accused of making up improbable events, 'here and there toning them down to conform to the notion that life is stranger than fiction and fiction, therefore, more sober than life.'

Of all Gerhardie's novels *The Polyglots* generated the most optimism, the greatest promise of success and, ultimately, £1,000: 'It all depends on *The Polys*—on which our destiny depends', he wrote with echoes of Nikolai Vasilievich: 'now it isn't long to wait.' Arnold Bennett praised it highly and Anthony Powell some years later described it as 'an outstanding novel', worthy to be called a 'classic'.[6] But its favour with contemporary critics did not quite match that of *Futility*. Some considered it flippant, others reproached Gerhardie for 'pouring more water into the same teapot'; Gerhardie's very just and modest reply to this silly criticism, 'that no extra water was needed, since it was a large teapot and *Futility* was only one cup', seems a remarkable understatement.[7] Even those who admired the novel ignored its formal innovations, and only

S.P.B. Mais in the *Daily Graphic* indicated an awareness that *The Polyglots* strove 'to probe into the difference between illusion and reality', and compared it to the work of Pirandello.[8]

Complimentary copies were sent to forty distinguished individuals, 'so that they should *talk* about the book in society!! to interest the intelligentsia in it, and the low-brows will then follow along!' After the success of *Futility* Cobden Sanderson began with an impression of 2,000 'which, for him, must seem enormous!' These were soon exhausted: 'Dickie hopes for a new edition in the near future. But Dickie's optimism is another man's pessimism . . . the business evidently, so far from showing signs of pegging out (as I had hoped!) has grown larger.' Once again editors and publishers besieged Gerhardie with letters (Jonathan Cape in particular attempting to buy him out of Cobden Sanderson). In the US it sold in ten days enough to earn $1,000 royalties (£200) and in August appeared on the best-seller lists, though actual sales had only reached about 7,000 (not 'overwhelming').

William wished to send a copy to Rosie, but hesitated lest it get her into trouble, 'though I do not think there is anything the Bolsheviks can object to'. He need not have worried. *The Polyglots* was translated the following year by the Soviet State Press as *Nashestvie Varvarov* or *Invasion of Barbarians*. So Rosie sent *him* a copy. Some sections he had to admit were superior even to the original English, but the whole was 'a poor, clipped bird in the Russian. Many of the best passages are left out altogether, others are so badly done that it makes one blush.'

'Oh, Willy what a Book!!!' exclaimed Clara, lamenting that Charles was not there to share her pride.

I have both wept and laughed over it and only wish I had an audience to read it to. I am simply spellbound by it and feel I must find time to write and tell you how wonderful I find it. I seem to be talking to all those people and feel just one of them. Every word, every action is real to me how ever have you been able to do it and such a thick book, why it is all essence no stupid empty sheets of paper.

Despite Gerhardie's eager anticipation, before the war, of his startling entrance into the London literary scene, his most pressing ambition by this time was to set up a comfortable, independent establishment in an agreeable climate. 'Sick and tired of this hotel and pension life', he made elaborate plans to build with some of his *Polyglots* money a permanent *pied à terre* where all the family could live. France, deep in recession, was still for the most part very cheap, particularly during the then unfashionable summer months in the South. Jean had quietly whispered in a letter of a plot of land for sale, a remarkable bargain: 10,000 square metres planted with olive trees, water and electricity laid on, comfortably remote yet only a twenty-five minute train ride from bustling Bandol and the fashionable casino, and all for about £100. *The Polyglots* continued to sell quite well, and Gerhardie, though not yet rich, expected to be so in the near future. The zeal and fervour that he put into the planning of this house excelled even the most adventurous of his many later schemes. He drew up elaborate plans that would be easily adaptable to architectural improvements in line with his financial improvements, when they happened: a two-storey verandaed building, the second floor as yet unbuilt except for the outside walls and roof; wooden partitions inside could at a later date be removed in order to make larger rooms when the upper storeys were constructed, together with a broad, red-carpeted, stone staircase. The house would at first be furnished with home-made cushions and the simplest square peasant chairs and tables painted in white enamel. A young servant girl would live in and the horses' stable would eventually be turned into servants' quarters. And outside in the garden, Charles. Gerhardie, who disliked the 'rather vulgar, cemetery look that most monuments and crosses have', sent Clara a design for a recumbent tombstone ('a great cross showing behind the trees on a moonlit night would be uncanny and disturbing in our own garden'). He also designed a device for making a 'removable grave' should they decide to leave, but conscious of the fact that 'one hardly wants to make a jack-in-the-box affair of it'.

It was, then, in an atmosphere of serious commitment to a somewhat isolated literary existence that Gerhardie received his first lordly summons: a note from Beaverbrook requesting William (whom he had mistakenly addressed as Paul) to drop by when next in London, as 'I would like to talk over with you some journalistic matters'.

Gerhardie was flattered but sceptical. 'I can't think what the noble lord can possibly want from me, and I have written to him to ask him to put his proposals in writing . . . Perhaps he liked the way I cursed his rival paper the *Daily Mail* in *The Polyglots*, or perhaps he liked the way I cursed Churchill and Birkenhead.' A reply from Beaverbrook refused to be more specific. Gerhardie, not unduly excited but deeming it foolish to miss such an opportunity, agreed to visit London and if necessary write enough journalism to pay his expenses for no longer than a month. 'If the noble lord thinks I can turn out articles for him of the same quality as my books he is mistaken. Literary art, of my quality', he wrote in a letter to his mother, 'is like highly specialized coffee which rich people drink at the end of lunch—coffee made by the coffee machine drop by drop; whole journalistic articles are like coffee poured out simultaneously with the milk by some barmaid behind the counter at a cheap sailor's stall—at 3*d* a cup.'

Before setting off he visited 'the slime baths' at Pystian in Czechoslovakia in order to cure his stiffening joints and general weakness caused, as he believed, by 'creeping arthritis'. Writers were unaccountably entitled to a 40 per cent reduction, but as usual William had a tortured time with 'a positive swarm of waiters and porters and other menials. I have given up the idea of tipping weekly, as I would have to spend the week in calculating what to give each if I did.' After ten days of massage, mud packs, sulphur baths, slime, and gymnastics he began to feel much better—which was ominous because according to all authorities one should feel worse, and only begin to feel better after six months. Clara, uncharacteristically sorry for herself, declined William's offer to buy her a present and pressured him not to be away long: 'I don't think that even a little bead bag would help, the only thing that would be any good is if my *Bübchen* were here to talk to me. Ah, well, perhaps you won't be long now . . . You dear boy always manage to calm my doubts and fears. Here I have nobody to talk to.'

At the start of October Gerhardie left Austria, carrying Charles's urn in his haversack: 'From now on my father, reduced to a few ashes in a zinc receptacle, began to travel furiously all over Europe. He had, poor man, wished to do so when still alive and confined to his chair. Now he covered mile after mile with a vengeance.'[9] At the French frontier an official asked what the haversack contained:

'*Une urne*', he replied.

'*Quoi?*'

'*Une urne.*'

Failing to locate Jean as arranged in Paris, he deposited the urn at the Gare de l'Est, posted the receipt to Clara, and took the boat to England where on arrival in Dover he enjoyed 'a nice cup of English tea at the station and a pork pie. It is v. refreshing after the continental diet!'

9

2/6 A DAY
October 1925–December 1925

I was launched on the shoulders of Katherine Mansfield and Edith Wharton. My third patron is Lord Beaverbrook. My fourth, methinks, should be a Duke, my fifth a Grand Duke, my sixth a King-Emperor, and my seventh the Pope. Unless I thus reach at the Vatican, I will not consider that I have succeeded.

On an afternoon in early October Gerhardie, clad in an old navy-blue overcoat stitched up and mended, a brand new but oddly ill-fitting black suit made inexpensively by a Viennese tailor, and a bowler hat, ascended to the lofty heights of Lord Beaverbrook's office in St Bride Street.

Goblin-like, Beaverbrook rose with outstretched hand to greet him, a middle-sized figure but 'shaped like a pair of scissors with a small upper frame and disproportionately long legs', a wide grin stretching from ear to ear, and a 'strange glint in his pale, wicked eye'. 'What will you have to drink?' he asked, 'Champagne?' At once Gerhardie succumbed to Beaverbrook's 'intoxicating', mishievous charm. 'Lord Beaverbrook, like Mr Lloyd George, has the air of being enormously privileged in meeting someone whom no one else has ever met, or even heard of. He made me feel as if I had indeed heard of myself.'[1]

Beaverbrook began to question Gerhardie minutely about all aspects of his life and work until he was 'overwhelmed by the powerful, if inaccurate, interest he took in your subject'. Gerhardie was a great writer! Beaverbrook would be his patron! He wanted a short story at once, then a novel which was to be serialized at once. And he waved aside as irrelevant William's anxiety that his fiction lacked the necessary suspense. More questions, more promises. In regard to *The Polglots*, Gerhardie later wrote home, Beaverbrook had surpassed his most sanguine expectations.

He can't say enough for it and is going to boom it in his papers, is going to take my next novel as a serial at once, also short stories, articles, or anything I may care to write . . . The fact of the matter is, as I have now discovered, that Lord Beaverbrook (who is only 43 [*sic*]) and at the height of his power and wealth, wants to be *the* man in everything and he is lionizing me because he wants to say afterwards that it was he who discovered me. I don't mind of course. But he has really read my books and thinks the world, of *The Polyglots* especially, and keeps telling everybody: 'I am convinced that W. Gerhardi is our great literary figure'.

When Beaverbrook heard that the *Daily Express* review had been the worst of the lot he then and there ordered a menial to bring up the review and read it aloud, after which he instructed one of his editors to write a praiseworthy piece. The very next day a photograph of Gerhardie, young and naïve, appeared on the front page of the *Express*.

NOVELIST WHO LIVES ON 2/6 A DAY

ran the headline, followed by an outline of Gerhardie's career to date. What was Mr Gerhardie's ambition? 'To live on 5/– a day.'[2]

Lord Beaverbrook had been born Max Aitken, forty-six years before, in Maple, Ontario, whither his father, a Minister of the Church of Scotland, had emigrated in 1864, about the time that the original William Gerhardi had landed in Russia. He was 'a clever restless little boy always up to mischief'[3] and always up to making money: when a soap company offered a bicycle in exchange for a great many soap-wrappers, the young Max borrowed money from a friendly store-keeper, bought a hundredweight of soap, and peddled it from door to door at cost price on condition he received the wrappers, thus acquiring a free bicycle. By his early twenties he was vastly rich. 'Is Max an abbreviation of Maximilian?' enquired Gerhardie. 'Maximultimillion', Beaverbrook replied. In 1910 he arrived in England with his wife Gladys, whence began his career as politician and press baron. For a number of years—amongst a host of other activities—he channelled his energy into vigorous support of the Conservative politician and Prime Minister, Arthur Bonar Law. In 1922 Bonar Law died and Beaverbrook, finding himself suddenly and un-expectedly on the outside of political life, turned his attention back to his newspapers. He already controlled the *Daily* and *Sunday Express*, and in 1924 purchased a very minor paper, *The Evening Standard*, which his relentless inspiration and drive swiftly transformed into the 'quality' evening paper of London. Yet what enchanted Gerhardie was Beaver-brook's singular habit of conducting his business while entertaining his guests 'as if his friends were his real pre-occupation, and business an agreeable irrelevance':[4] such a soothing, stimulating contrast to his own father's wrathful mode of business. He had built *The Evening Standard* into a newspaper without obvious political bias, catering for the educated reader, and in common with many other journals of that time carrying a weekly article or review by a well-known author. Dean Inge presented 'a cultivated nihilism'[5] (which appealed to Gerhardie) and Arnold Bennett ran a very popular column entitled 'Books and Persons' from 1926 until his death in 1931. It was to some extent with the *Standard* in view that Beaverbrook patronized Gerhardie. Beaverbrook was friendly with a number of writers—Rudyard Kipling, H. G. Wells, Somerset Maugham, George Moore, Arnold Bennett—and whilst sailing off Southampton his attention had been drawn to *The Polyglots* by Wells's praise of it. But if, as Gerhardie believed, he had read the book this was unusual, for he was impatient with literature and relied upon synopses compiled by his secretaries who would draw his attention to the more exciting parts. He tried one day to reread *Kidnapped* which he had enjoyed as a child, but soon put it down again, saying 'too many words'.

Throughout his life Beaverbrook inspired the most diverse opinions. His close friend and biographer A. J. P. Taylor found him a dear and loyal confidante. Margot Asquith, when William invited her comment, whispered in his ear, 'Scum of the earth'. Frances Donaldson has recently described Beaverbrook as 'one of the few deliberately wicked men in British history. Others have done more harm but few have done it intentionally',[6] referring specifically to his use and abuse of power through the vehicle of his newspapers. Taylor insisted that Beaverbrook was merely 'mischievous' and perhaps at times 'irresponsible', although even he agreed that, above all 'Beaverbrook loved to make people. Once they were created his interest in them declined.'[7] Gerhardie was ideal material: young, unknown, impressionable, talented, and keenly hoping for success. Perceiving that Beaverbrook liked to astonish, he tactfully adopted the attitude of 'a newly-fledged chicken', and to everything that was pointed out to him he said 'Ah!' He noticed that Beaverbrook treated his staff 'like dogs . . . when he wants his secretary he simply whistles—and she appears. I am glad I am not his subordinate.' But for all this he felt that Beaverbrook was 'possessed of something very like genius'. 'There was a kind of rudimentariness bordering on inspired idiocy about his pronouncements, and yet a fundamental and instinctive fairness which recognised truth where and when presented to him', a 'courageous spontaneous honesty, applied as soon as perceived.'[8] He was a man of enormous energy and enthusiasm, restless and spontaneous. Like Gerhardie, he could never be entirely serious, even in the most solemn moments. 'Wherever Beaverbrook was, there were always shouts of laughter.'9

Beaverbrook was immensely taken with Gerhardie. The sophistication that Rothenstein described was of a very unorthodox nature, for Gerhardie's unusual upbringing and education had both privileged and hindered him. Though nervous and highly strung he could be extremely amusing, a brilliant conversationalist, but he also displayed a naïve, child-like (occasionally child*ish*) manner, and his scepticism was partnered by tremendous enthusiasms. Much of his immense charm, even in old age, rested in these contrasts, and in his great naturalness. He was polite and kind, but without pretension; he never behaved as he felt he *ought* to behave. 'William is one of the most truthful men I have ever met', said Beaverbrook. What also attracted Beaverbrook and Gerhardie to each other was the mutual recognition that they were both outsiders in England; neither quite belonged. Both, despite a taste for society, tended to be solitary individuals. They thought they could help each other—Beaverbrook had money and the power of mass communication, Gerhardie the promise of a great writer and a photogenic personality.

In a state of delirium Gerhardie left Beaverbrook's office—but only for a few hours. They were to meet for dinner that evening, and lunch the next day, for dinner the following day, and the day after and the day after ... Thus began a new life for Gerhardie, as Beaverbrook 'lavish with his praise and assiduous in his friendships'10 fêted him with all his characteristic restless enthusiasm. 'I will provide the champagne, and you the conversation', Beaverbrook announced. 'You will provide both', replied Gerhardie, and covered page after page of letters to his mother describing the hectic round of social engagements, the perpetual company of his new patron. He told her of Stornoway House, Beaverbrook's London residence overlooking St James's Palace, 'the most exclusive club in London', as Wells had called it, which, with its vast white, marble staircase 'beats even ours at Petrograd into a cocked hat!' He found that Beaverbrook had the disconcerting habit of asking people whom he was introducing what they thought of each other, 'a method of introduction more agreeable to the introducer than to the introduced' —and in the first two weeks alone, was so presented to Bertrand Russell, the Aga Khan, Maurice Baring, Admiral Beatty, John Middleton Murry, Margaret Kennedy (to whose recent success *The Constant Nymph*, *The Polyglots* had been compared), Beaverbrook's gossip columnist, the charming and portly spendthrift Irish baronet Valentine Castlerosse, and a host of others.

For all Beaverbrook's wealth and power there was a pleasing informality about his gatherings. When Gerhardie telephoned to ask his advice on 'a romantic impasse', he was told to come along at half past ten. Presuming that he would find Beaverbrook alone, William was then invited to tell his troubles to Lloyd George and a party of guests. Later Lloyd George mumbled that he had enjoyed a book of his 'about Vladivostok. I can't remember the title.' And, just to vary the tone, the following evening William was entertained by a party of young lords and chorus girls at The Vineyard (another of Beaverbrook's houses, where he went 'to swing a loose leg') in Fulham. Late in the evening Gerhardie walked into an upstairs bedroom to find Beaverbrook busily engaged with two women.

In the course of numerous conversations Gerhardie had revealed his boyhood admiration for H. G. Wells. And shortly Beaverbrook 'with his usual air of being able to produce any rabbit you liked out of his hat',[11] produced Wells. He, however, failed to catch the name and passed on, and only after his wife had nudged him did he respond, 'What? What do I hear? Gerhardi? The very man I always wanted to meet! Wonderful books—you're v. young to write them.' Going into dinner Wells then urged Gerhardie to precede him through a doorway: 'I am yesterday, but you're tomorrow.' He invited Gerhardie to his country house for the weekend. Gerhardie, of course, missed the train, upset Wells's luncheon plans, forgot his black tie, and excused himself from playing a jolly English ball game that Wells had invented. One day Wells told him that he had a double chin. Gerhardie said nothing but thought 'that's because he's so tiny. Were he my size he wouldn't see it.'

In turn Wells introduced him to Arnold Bennett. Gerhardie was astonished by Bennett's appearance, 'a greyhaired, morose man who one moment looked as if he had been struck by a fit of apoplexy and would not recover; the next moment came to life with a twinkle'. After a dinner party at Bennett's house, the host insisted on coming down with his guests and making sure a separate taxi was called for everyone. 'Very courteous, I thought, but awkward for anyone who can't afford to pay for the taxi at the other end.' As they took leave of each other Bennett announced, 'I am pleased with you.' 'Why?' thought Gerhardie to himself. 'Because I had behaved at table? Not spoiled the carpet, not smashed the furniture?' Later Beaverbrook telephoned Bennett and asked what he had thought of his new find. 'Excellent talker' was his reply. Some months later Bennett, suffering from neuralgia, sat up all night unable to sleep and read *The Polyglots*: 'This work is too long, lacks shape, and has a few short passages of merely silly jocosity, but as a whole it is individual, original, comical, touching, and full of flavour', he noted in his diary.[12] And then there was Shaw. Bernard Shaw, William noticed, had a very red nose 'which belied a little the good things we hear said about his diet', but he praised Gerhardie lavishly:

'If you're English,' he said, 'you're a genius, but if you're Russian . . . well, then, of course . . .'
'I am English,' I interjected . . .[13]

Sartorially Gerhardie was ill-equipped for his new life. Bruce Lockhart remembered seeing him in an old and shabby suit with very baggy trousers. Having at last abandoned the Russian dinner jacket, he had ordered a curious new Innsbruckian model, but he noticed that in London dinner jackets appeared to be completely out of fashion, and that the smart set now wore tails. And on the rare occasions when Gerhardie procured tails, Beaverbrook contrived to turn up in a dinner jacket. He was shortly obliged to buy an opera hat, a new coat, and white gloves. 'Altogether the only people who do not admire me very greatly seem to be these servants of the rich!' And how he hated butlers. 'They will take your hat from you with a reverence which suggests a tender regard for your hat and the utmost contempt for your person.'[14]

At a literary tea party Gerhardie observed another 'curiously untidy person in a morning coat, which bore evidence that he had put it on under protest.'[15] The figure turned: it was D. H. Lawrence, who 'at once conveyed to me his disapproval of nearly everybody else in the room, and this, coupled with his jolly sort of approval of my *Polyglots* and a lot of advice as to what I should avoid as a writer, all proffered in the most cheerful way, surprised me agreeably, since I had imagined Lawrence to be a disgruntled individual.'[16] William was invited to tea the following day and stayed for eight hours, talking at great length and in spite of many differences of opinion. As for *The Polyglots*, Lawrence admired Gerhardie's 'absolutely original humour' but warned him to 'eschew sentiment like poison', and inquired why he showed such a fear of death.[17] Georges and Sylvia had reminded Frieda Lawrence of Birkin and Ursula in *Women In Love*, though Gerhardie explained that he had conceived them as Chaucer's Troilus and Criseyde. Frieda thought how much Katherine Mansfield would have 'adored' Gerhardie, though she kept suggestively quiet when William pressed for an explanation. Lawrence's 'ebullient naturalness' was infectious, he had a glint about the eyes 'which denotes a kind of gaiety of spirit, the real name for which must be genius, and which intoxicates one',[18] though Gerhardie was less enthusiastic when Lawrence urged him to go abroad with them. He was also a fine host, carrying in the dishes in a thoroughly domestic fashion with all the pride of a first-class chef in his unmatched creations. Lawrence's father, a Nottinghamshire miner, had recently sent a cutting from the *Daily Express* about a novelist called Gerhardi who had been living on 2s. 6d. a day compared with whom, he pointed out, his son David was not doing at all badly.

They talked too of Lawrence's work, which Gerhardie admired in spite of what he saw as lack of humour, lack of subtlety, and needless repetition. 'Lawrence all his life never got off the subject of "relationships". As tiresome as though one never got off the railway.' Lawrence gave Gerhardie a letter of introduction to an American magazine, and most vehemently of all he urged Gerhardie to beware of Beaverbrook: 'He hates you', Lawrence warned, with dark passion.

'I don't say he hates you personally . . . But these men, they're like vampires. When they see an immortal soul they hate it instinctively.' His eyes gleamed. 'With a terrible black hatred, and instinctively try to annihilate what is immortal in you.'

At which remark Mrs Lawrence trembled with rage and expressed her agreement with some violence. . . . D. H. Lawrence, wincing at this display of superfluous emotion, said quietly: 'Not so much intensity, Frieda.'

Mrs Lawrence, perhaps living up to the elemental naturalness of her husband's heroines, replied: 'If I want to be intense I'll be intense, and you go to hell!'

'I'm ashamed of you, Frieda', he said. Whereupon Frieda's hatred for Lord Beaverbrook transformed itself into hatred for her husband, and was soon a spent cartridge.[19]

But the advice was disregarded, and Beaverbrook continued to monopolize Gerhardie. They dined together, supped together, visited night-clubs together (usually with a large entourage), so that he went to bed 'half dead' at five or six every morning. On a typical evening Gerhardie, after dining elsewhere, would hurry to join Beaverbrook's party at the theatre, after which they would drive around London dropping off all the other guests one by one, then drive to Stornoway House to pick up two servants before another hour's drive to his country house Cherkley where they would sit up talking till the early hours. Not only did Beaverbrook permit Gerhardie unannounced access to his office, to his private interviews, and to meetings with his editors (which greatly irritated them), but he habitually dressed and undressed in his friend's company, wandering about in his underpants and suspenders. 'I simply can't get away from him', Gerhardie wrote in mid-November after six weeks. 'Even when he was ill in bed with a heart attack he asked me to come and see him and we dined together in his bedroom—chicken, champagne, etc!—and spoke till midnight.'

He had lately grown solicitous of his protégé's domestic welfare. 'I'm very fond of you', he announced one day. 'Why aren't you married?' 'Because', replied Gerhardie, 'I am afraid that a girl might wish to marry me for my genius, not for myself, and I'd find out too late.' 'You're too modest', said Beaverbrook, waving his hand. 'Now, there is the daughter of a friend of mine who is—that's neither here nor there—a millionaire. If you married her you would make me very happy. And you'd be able to sit back and write masterpieces at your leisure.' So Beaverbrook gave a dinner party for Gerhardie, inviting fifty guests. But the two took an instant dislike to each other; everybody at the dinner party seemed more eligible and more desirable. Gerhardie remained single.

William, nocturnal by inclination, found Beaverbrook the most stimulating—if exhausting—companion:

I still think Lord Beaverbrook is incomparable. He cannot be shocked, he is uncontaminated by moral indignation, and is open to argument at any hour of the day or night on any subject in the world. I have myself, at two o'clock in the morning, when everyone was fagged out and longed to go home, opened a conversation concerning the illusory nature of time, and Lord Beaverbrook, who was helping himself to a whisky and soda in the corner of the room, swiftly turned round, took up the question and argued ably till half-past three.[20]

It was not only Beaverbrook he had to cope with, but a perpetual round of engagements from every possible quarter: editors, politicians, literati, and society hostesses. 'I am torn to bits by appointments and invitations, people even send their motor-car for me in order to get me to lunch and dine with them', he wrote to Clara. He soon had to abandon answering the scores of unsolicited letters he received, and once offended Beaverbrook by failing to turn up to a dinner.

In the very midst of all this Clara, Daisy, and Daisy's husband suddenly started to send urgent telegrams about the urn. It was wrong, they felt, that Charles should sit in a station cloakroom; but Jean—who frequently passed through Paris—found the receptacle too distasteful to collect himself. William, infuriated beyond words by their insistence that *he* should go, damned their Catholic squeamishness and insisted that he was suffering from a sore throat, neuralgia, and toothache, and that every minute of his time was taken up with business appointments. More telegrams arrived from the family ('The longer you tarry the more sinister the outlook'). He retorted furiously that it was time 'to act reasonably and not lavish money on a man's ashes which they begrudged him when he was alive', and reminded them that Chekhov's coffin had arrived in Moscow in a goods van marked 'Fresh Oysters'.

He had, meanwhile, begun *Jazz and Jasper*, a satirical fantasy chronicling the relationship between a press baron, Lord Ottercove, and a young writer, Frank Dickin. It is a fine evocation not only of the fast-moving, media-dominated, post-war world, but of the diverse power of Beaverbrook/Ottercove upon those around him. Frank Dickin, like Gerhardie both entranced and intimidated, reflects:

To be alone with a man who has wrecked more than one Ministry, and register his sigh cumulative of a strenuous day's work, to feel the contact of power! By no means a negligible experience. Frank felt he would like to incite Lord Ottercove to further action. But what action? Something big, something shattering, something gigantic. Wreck the Celestial Empire? Imbue the Fascisti with Socialist sense?[21]

Beaverbrook was immensely pleased to be the hero of the novel and not only proved 'a willing sitter' but lent his own fervent imagination towards bettering the plot. Whilst Gerhardie was an intriguing conversationalist, Beaverbrook excelled as a story-teller, embellishing the narrative and embellishing history, piling on suspense and drama, mesmerizing his listeners. He 'exulted in stories of contrast and reversal of fortune drawn from real life, which he related with a kind of mock-tense air of highly coloured drama which should satisfy, he judged, the general high taste in story-telling. He always ended with a sort of half shy, half menacing, "Grand story, isn't it?".'[22] Theological language came readily to Beaverbrook, who as a child had spent many hours in his father's church listening to sermons and parables. 'He knew the Bible from cover to cover and backwards: indeed, he could, at a pinch, recite it by heart under an anaesthetic.'[23]

'Well, we must bring your personality before the public', says Ottercove to Frank in *Jazz and Jasper*. 'I am sure that if your personality is brought before the public, the public will begin to get curious about your personality and begin to want to buy your books.'[24] In this way Beaverbrook encouraged Gerhardie to believe that success could be instantly obtained. He was not, primarily, interested in his work, but in the effect of his work upon the public—Gerhardie as a literary figure, a personality, a challenge. Beaverbrook's patronage justified Gerhardie's nurtured self-esteem, for despite the egocentricity so familar to his own family, he was unassertive, even diffident. To some he was 'almost pathetically shy'. Beaverbrook was fond of telling the story of the first meeting with Wells, and an article written for his own newspaper which relates it ended: 'I never saw such an alteration made in a man by a single evening . . . I have to convey the impression of innocence, of youth, suddenly convinced that it was of importance.'[25] Not forceful himself, Gerhardie responded when others showered attention on to him and thrust him into the limelight. Three years previously he had written to Edith Wharton: 'Praise is a curious thing. When I am praised I blush, and feel "It's too much, too much!" But I have a good digestion for it, and the next moment I already feel that I could do with more . . . I like it—it's new to me.'[26]

Much of the praise that Gerhardie received at this time was extravagant and indiscriminate. In a sense he was well aware of this ('at that time everyone called me a genius'), as his shrewd and ironic portrayal of Frank in *Jazz and Jasper* suggests. Dancing with Lady Beaverbrook one evening Gerhardie said to her: "What a charming man your husband is"—just to get her to say, "He says you're a genius."

"Yes," she replied, "he's a genius."

"How? What? Yes, of course," I agreed.'[27]

His humorously immodest letters to his mother were simply the most effective way of convincing her of his ability and value, now publicly acknowledged: 'You will probably think I've grown intolerably conceited, but I have to tell you how I have been received . . . But pl. don't think of sending this letter on to any one', he insisted. Clara responded with alacrity: 'I say and I repeat you are wonderful! Oh my Vassinka I am so so proud of you and you are such a big big comfort to me. I kiss and hug you again and again.' Gerhardie perpetually sought to demonstrate his worth to members of his family. In old age he wrote: 'At the fag-end of your life you don't care much what you say or what is said about you. One has shot one's bolt and it is too late, one's loving parents who might have taken some pride in commendation, long since departed, to take much pleasure in praise or hurt or blame.'[28] The constant use of devalued terms like 'genius'—in vogue throughout the 1920s—proved an encouragement to morale, but a professional distraction.

In *Jazz and Jasper*, Ottercove allows Frank to draw upon his bank account without limit. The reality was less philanthropic. Beaverbrook agreed to begin paying the £250 advance for the British serial rights of the forthcoming novel in weekly instalments of £12. Gerhardie, uneasy about living on this money when so little had been written, also found it difficult to interpret Beaverbrook's insistence that he should 'look to him in money matters'. Frank, tempted by Ottercove's immense wealth, yet scrupulously anxious not to overstep the mark, reflects that 'He would sooner assassinate his old grandmother for the meagre contents of her purse than overdraw Lord Ottercove's account',[29] and decides at length to clarify his position:

He was as much pained by the thought of exceeding Lord Ottercove's generosity . . . as he was by the possibility of erring quite needlessly on the side of financial timidity and reluctance to use his good fortune. There was no kind of security in this arrangement, and suddenly he felt he couldn't stand it. It was already in his throat. 'I want to ask you to—'

'I've had a man in here just now playing'—Lord Ottercove pointed at the piano—'Rimsky-Korsakoff. That lovely bit from his opera. Oh, what's the name? It's on my lips—'

I want to ask you to turn off that financial arrangement', Frank said. 'It's too upsetting. I—'

Lord Ottercove had pressed the bell button.

'Stop that banking arrangement Mr Dickin has with me,' he said, as Mrs Hannibal entered the room.

Frank gasped.

Mrs Hannibal made a shorthand note of it and retired.

'It's on my lips,' said Lord Ottercove. 'I know the opera well. Lord! now what *is* the name?' He pulled out his watch and looked up at Frank.[30]

On arrival in England Gerhardie, after staying three nights with his Smolensk cousins, had taken lodgings at 34 Glazbury Road, West Kensington, where he was paying 30s. a week for a moderately comfortable bed and breakfast (bath 2d. extra). He described to Clara eating 'now at an ABC shop, now in the smartest restaurant with Lord B., now at a Mayfair house, now at a penny stall in the street'. Both amused and discomfited by the contrasts in his fortunes and anxious to secure his future, he again urged his mother to buy the land in France, and sent her a cheque for £174. 9s. 7d.

Clara, still at the Hotel Guillon in Marseilles and impatient with living out of a suitcase, had been busy investigating the possibility of building a house, perusing pamphlets that advertised a '*cottage algérien type B à 6 pieces*' for £350 paid over 15 years. She, too, had been to the Pystian slime baths: 'I am feeling well and strong and do so long to get going with a home.' If she was dismayed by Beaverbrook's overbearing influence and suspicious of her son's sudden change of fortune she did not show it, and wrote: 'It is all so wonderful that I sometimes think it is a dream', betraying anxiety only about his welfare—that he aired his bed, did not put on damp clothes, kept his stomach in order, and didn't work too hard and 'get a breakdown'.

In fact Gerhardie was under considerable strain. Instead of being encouraged by the pressure, as he had hoped, he found it impossible to work when Beaverbrook repeatedly asked how much had been written and when he might read it. 'That feeling of dependence is the worst thing of all while one is at work on a novel . . . because hitherto I was not committed to any time or any person.' Curtis Brown, 'a very cool, sane man', who took an intelligent interest in his client's career, was worried by the influence of Beaverbrook and sceptical of its outcome because, as he pointed out, *The Polyglots* was not a 'best seller' type of book. He was quite right. Beaverbrook's attention certainly made Gerhardie a success: but social, not financial. To some extent Gerhardie blamed Cobden Sanderson ('such a fool') who, at the height of the publicity, failed to meet the demand, and then suddenly shut up shop altogether after a death in the family. 'So now for a whole week no bookseller can get any of my books simply because Dickie's father-in-law had given up the ghost!!' Gerhardie exclaimed, exasperated.

With the advent of winter he was finding England 'miserably miserably wet and cold and damp and rotten. I can't work—except in the sunshine.' Beaverbrook urged him to come to Vienna and Italy and even offered a voluptuous young divorcée as a lure. Gerhardie wavered—and left England alone.

10

A MOST UNPLEASANT SORT OF LUNATIC
December 1925–June 1927

There are two ways of being disappointed: getting what you want, and not getting it.[1]

Thankful to escape, Gerhardie arrived in Marseilles in time to spend Christmas with Clara, Daisy, and Jean. William had expected Daisy's husband Jean to be a stage Frenchman, all gesticulation, and was surprised and a little disappointed to find him quiet and sedate. A little too sedate: for Jean, the affair of the urn not forgotten, met him at the station dressed in black and very sombre, 'a sort of silent reproach to me!' Daisy, proud and doting, fussed over her spouse, served him first at mealtimes (always the largest portion), and with monotonous predictability sided with him in arguments. 'Few things irritate one more', wrote William 'than the spectacle of a devoted wife, when one happens not to be the husband.'[2] They constantly borrowed money, repaid only grudgingly, and were quick to ask favours: as William had met the Aga Khan he could surely persuade him to buy a Buddha or two. They also evolved an elaborate plot in which William, disguised as an art collector with cane, monocle, and pointed beard, was to spy on Jean's business partners in New Bond Street. But as for their new baby, here William relented: 'Jean-Jacques is too sweet for words and has already more hair on his head than his Uncle.' Jean-Jacques, as soon as he had learned to talk, said: '*Grandmère est marié avec oncle Willy.*'

The plot of land, however, never materialized, and instead Gerhardie rented La Saharienne, a cottage complete with orchard and stables at Pont du Suve, near Toulon. At £18 per year it was considerably more picturesque than comfortable, but also 'the first roof which I could call my own'. Clara was appropriately wary, pointing out that it was little more than a pigsty. William, enthusiastic for the simple life, saw in it infinite 'possibilities'.

Winter was less than romantic. They began by painting the rooms white and yellow, and employed the village carpenter to knock together some basic furniture. They attempted to stop the roof leaking, and to raise the temperature above freezing, but little could be done about the creeping wet, the muddy red soil, and the damp. Mould grew everywhere. The front door refused to stay shut. Beyond the garden was a narrow railway track full of tins and other rubbish; every couple of hours 'a tiny tea-kettle of a locomotive puffed along, trailing in its wake a string of under-sized coaches, and gave a piercing whistle each time it passed the house at the bend, lurching perilously over the curve.'[3]

Then there were Gerhardie's exasperating relations with the French peasants. His 13-year-old maid Elise was only a little less sullen and unreliable than 18-year-old Suzanne who suffered from perennial toothache and who, when Gerhardie offered to take her to the dentist, replied, 'I'd rather die'. A grimy milkmaid underwent an arduous journey to the cottage every day but dragged the milk away again if there was nobody to pay immediately. They were beset by the attentions of Emile, a half-witted young farmhand who stared vacantly, and in response to whatever inanity was uttered replied heavily: '*Je comprends*' ('And it seemed appropriate that he should say it, since he understood always with an effort').[4] Their immediate neighbours were a prolific family who practised Adventist rites with a vengeance, banging out loud hymns on a broken piano in anticipation of the Judgement Day. And they dreaded the weekend visits of their landlord 'the Captain', an enormous burly figure, overflowingly genial and suspicious, with a loud voice and a very loud gramophone. His wife, a small woman who walked always on high heels, borrowed Gerhardie's primus stove several times a day to cook her husband gargantuan meals of cockles, mussels, snails, and other such unpalatables. The Captain pressed upon Gerhardie quantities of his own invented aperitif, then dragged him off fishing to ensnare ingredients for his next bouillabaisse.

Occasionally there would be a pleasant, though brief, encounter with a local girl. For the rest—solitude, but punctuated rather too frequently by the need to feed the hens, collect the eggs, kindle the fire, draw water from the well, and haggle with the local shopkeepers. 'I don't know what I look', Gerhardie later wrote in regard to his nationality. 'I only know that I am an Englishman in Russia, an Anglo-Russian in England; and only in France where an Englishman is a congenital imbecile to be rooked at will am I fully an Englishman.'[5] His diet shrank to little more than fruit and milk.

Hyères and other fashionable towns of the Riviera were only a few miles along the coast. Gerhardie became a frequent visitor at Edith Wharton's Château St Claire, 'a sort of intellectual lighthouse in the distance', and purchased a trap and harness and Zaza, an elderly malnourished horse, to convey him there. But he was never able to make Zaza share his enthusiasm for these excursions, and it was often necessary to walk backwards in front of the horse to lure the beast on with a carrot. In *Pending Heaven*, which includes a fictional account of this year in France, the hero Max Fisher goes to the stable the day after Zaza has arrived:

The horse could not rise in the morning. Max ran for Emile, thinking the horse's last hour had come. Emile came, but could not lift it. He went to fetch Etienne—a filthy Italian peasant who had emptied their drains in the winter and seemed not to have washed since then—and with the help of the men and Mme Etienne Max lifted the horse to its feet. After that Etienne and his wife came every morning to enquire whether the horse needed lifting in case Monsieur Fishaire intended to use it that day.[6]

Occasionally Gerhardie would arrive at Wharton's astride the skinny animal, always at a gallop because trotting was dreadfully precarious, and when walking Zaza was likely suddenly to lie down. Stories filtered back to the drawing-rooms of London of Gerhardie riding around the south of France like the White Knight, a typewriter dangling from his left hand. Wharton, anxious lest the horse devour her immaculate garden, advised him to buy a Citroën instead.

Through Edith Wharton, Gerhardie gained acquaintance with a number of French naval families who impressed him favourably with their literary proclivities, so absent in the English navy ('While we call our battleships *Vindictive*, if not *Malignant*, they call theirs *Voltaire*, *Pascal* and, if I may anticipate, *Marcel Proust*'[7]). Gerhardie was invited on board a battleship, where an admiral asked what he had written. '*Des jolies choses*', replied the captain's wife, after which Gerhardie received a royal reception. He kept in touch with Beaverbrook. 'I don't know whether I had ever told you how grateful I am for the wonderful time you gave me in London', he wrote. 'It was so much more than I could have expected and it was done with so light, so pleasant a touch that I can never forget it. May I say, quite sincerely, that I was deeply touched by your whole attitude to me, and cannot get over it even now; and as for the dinners, dances, luncheons, supper-parties, even there I have learned. I have learned the relative inferiority of the food in an ABC shop.'[8] Whenever

Beaverbrook and his entourage chanced to be in the area Gerhardie would drop all work and spend the day in fast motor cars and picnicking on champagne before Beaverbrook abruptly vanished again.

Gerhardie stayed as Beaverbrook's guest at the Negresco Hotel in Nice at an outlandish £10 a night and tried to interest him in a 'stupendous' new scheme: they would collaborate in writing a musical comedy. Gerhardie had a good plot and quite a few good melodies, although 'my musical education is sadly inadequate. But I could overcome this by humming them into a recording phonograph . . . and we could get some old hack to set them down in writing and orchestrate the thing.'[9] Beaverbrook preferred to discuss the Immaculate Conception at the Casino at Monte Carlo with Lord Rothermere. 'In England we have plenty of everything except brains', Rothermere told Gerhardie. 'Let me have your address.'[10] Gerhardie detected that Edith Wharton was slightly jealous when he went to stay with Beaverbrook and his friends. He later told how, foolishly wishing to impress her, he had said: 'Would you like to meet them?' She, who had learned how to impress people without showing it, countered with: 'Well, I don't mind if they come here to lunch. But that does not mean I want to *go on* seeing them *always*.'

Lord Rothermere invited Gerhardie to Cap Martin, where he lived in the most opulent surroundings. But despite his millions Rothermere was beset with earache and unable to get back to London because the trains were booked up for weeks ahead ('for his own sense of the ridiculous prevented him from buying a train'). 'A sudden feeling of the futility of wealth came over me. . . . Arrived back at my little Toulon cottage with the well and its rusty chain off the wheel, I did not resent my poverty.'

Throughout the year Gerhardie worked on *Jazz and Jasper*. Curtis Brown was immensely thankful that William had escaped from London, and admitted that Gerhardie's relations with Beaverbrook had made him very nervous: 'It seemed so incongruous that you should be "taken in hand" as it were.' Yet his relief was premature. Gerhardie began well—'the Muse is visiting me every morning'—but soon felt constrained by the pressure, both moral and financial, to produce something suitable for serialization. The events he was attempting to incorporate were simply too close. 'I can only write in retrospect, when the irrelevant has filtered through.' He was also having trouble with the plot, which had originally been placed in the future until Wharton said she thought it gave the book an air of unreality. At which William went home and promptly tore up the manuscript. 'This novel, owing to my trying to please Beaverbrook, was the most difficult of all to write', he later admitted. Like the hero of *Pending Heaven* he suffered from 'this curious blight on all creative activity: a tendency to dream rather than do'.

Gratefully he would clutch at the first excuse to postpone the work which he knew was the one thing in life that could have made him happy. . . . There was a deep, universal reason why he could not content himself with the present. By an implacable spiritual law, his imagination—which was the receptive faculty—could only focus that which was absent. It was as if Nature, in perfectly good faith, had meant to provide the race with rosy spectacles, but by an oversight had sent us, readers of the book of life, a pair of field-glasses. The far-away things accordingly seemed clear in focus, but the book of life before him so blurred as to be well-nigh illegible.[11]

He looked wistfully back at his life in London, which now appeared as a lost idyll. Beaverbrook continued to keep in touch in his curiously abrupt manner, enquiring ceaselessly as to the progress of the serial. Gerhardie's responses betray his genuine awe of the man:

if you wanted you could easily gather round you all the bright young spirits of the age and reflect them through your organs—though to what purpose I don't know! Still, a sort of central illumination attracting everything into its orbit by its blinding glare! Quite seriously, there is about you something quite apart from your position as a 'General of the Press', a personal magnetism, a sort of suspended genius, seething and boiling over, so to speak, which seems to attract all the original minds. . . . This looks as if I wanted a drink from you.[12]

With the arrival of summer, life at La Saharienne improved—but not very much. The sunshine also brought dust storms and mosquitoes, and he was beset with fruit, one moment hard and inedible, the next dropping in squashy heaps around his feet. Recalling the romance of his Austrian love affair, Gerhardie invited Renée, the watchmaker's daughter from Vienna, to visit him. She proved not only unromantic but 'a considerable bitch'. The French, who had not forgotten the war, eyed these two German speakers with suspicion.

Whilst in France Gerhardie received from Alec Waugh a copy of an anthology, *Georgian Stories 1925*, and an invitation to contribute to the 1926 edition. His attention was drawn, not to the work of Huxley or Forster, but to a story by a little-known author, Hugh Kingsmill, entitled *WJ*. Gerhardie wrote to Waugh asking who this brilliant writer could be. Waugh passed the letter on to Kingsmill, who replied enclosing a copy of

The Dawn's Delay, a collection of short novels in which *WJ* had originally appeared. In another of these, *The End of the World*, a character named Polmont so captivated Gerhardie that he speculated on the pleasure of conversing with this enchanting fictional individual and promptly wrote to Kingsmill inviting him to visit.

Kingsmill accepted, and shortly afterwards a taxi drew up at Clara's cottage and a bulky figure emerged. He was rather middle-aged, with a curious downward-sloping nose which ended in a point some way below his nostrils, untidy, with his short hair half-brushed, and he walked with a lurching gait.

He was at once cynical, nerve-wracked, jittery, casual in the extreme, peppering in my mother's presence his disjointed speech with pithy Saxon adverbs of the more unprintable variety about his '—— father'. He was distracted, green of countenance, with suspiciously septic teeth, narrow-eyed, and avoided looking you in the face.[13]

Kingsmill threw himself into a deck-chair on the red-tiled terrace and swore again about his father. Clara, who had first spotted the excellence of his story, now looked with dismay as though to say, 'Is this the face that set us wondering who the unknown author of that enchanting piece may be?' 'He looked such a red, fat-faced farmer and my Vassinka so slim and lovely and such a contrast.' Yet, to Gerhardie's joy, he found that Kingsmill was exactly like Polmont, and now greeted his host with enthusiastic exclamations, striding capaciously ahead in the summer sun:

We boarded an open tram, the clanking familiarity of which palled on me. But I noticed that Kingsmill sat beside me with a wondrous smile; and when an Italian peasant passed us in his donkey-cart Hugh murmured beatifically, and when, screeching, we curved into Toulon past a slatternly old woman who was hanging out her washing Hugh, like Polmont, waved his hand to her, and when she smiled he said these folk of the Midi were hard to beat for sheer excellence of human nature.[14]

The single day of Kingsmill's invigorating company is recounted in the first chapter of *Pending Heaven*. At this time Kingsmill (whose real name was Hugh Kingsmill Lunn) had published only one other novel, *The Will to Love* (1919), and though exactly six years to the day older than Gerhardie his career as a writer had hardly begun. He had been educated at Harrow and Oxford, and after the outbreak of war joined the army in a regiment of cyclists. But only a few weeks after being posted to France he was captured by a group of German soldiers and marched off, quoting Heine at the top of his voice 'possibly in an endeavour to make his peaceful intentions quite clear to them'.[15] Whilst Gerhardie was enduring the rigours of barrack life in York, Kingsmill was happily acclimatizing himself to Karlsruhe prison camp, where he spent the following twenty-one months writing and reading and conversing in an amiable way with his fellow inmates.

Kingsmill was no stranger to family troubles. 'Friends', he used to say, 'are God's apology for relations.' He had been raised in, and later revolted against, an atmosphere of stern, even gloomy Methodism. His father, Sir Henry Lunn, had founded Lunn's Tourist Agency, originally with the task of arranging personally conducted tours for clergymen. For many years Kingsmill, along with his brothers Brian and Arnold Lunn, held a highly paid, low-responsibility job with his father's firm, mostly in Switzerland, for which he earned the astonishingly high salary of £2,000 a year ('About this time, too, the various Lunn offices throughout Europe appear to have become suddenly staffed with a number of his personal friends').[16] Like Gerhardie, Kingsmill never got on with his father, who considered him a great disappointment. In 1915 he made an unsuitable marriage to 'a woman of simple, rather puritanical, tastes who disapproved strongly of her husband's literary activities'.[17] Unsympathetic Eileen Lunn may have been, but Kingsmill's two biographers, Richard Ingrams and Michael Holroyd, both acknowledge his immaturity with women. Ingrams considered that 'he was incapable of a natural relationship with a woman. If women didn't attract him, he ignored them. If they did, he fell hopelessly in love, becoming in the process as idolatrous and sentimental as a schoolboy.'[18]

The picture that emerges is that of a man who has never quite grown up, irresponsible with money, impractical, erratic, and with a disconcerting habit of disappearing quite suddenly without telling where or why. Yet for all this Kingsmill was clearly a man of superior wit and ebullient charm. When Hesketh Pearson met him, 'the first thing that struck him was his laughter. He had a natural exuberance about him which some people found overpowering and even offensive. But to others like Pearson it was irresistible.'[19] 'I have never been so stimulated by any company', wrote Alec Waugh. 'He is like the sun shining on you. You become happy. The present is rich. The future radiant. You talk well. . . . He envelops you with warmth and friendliness',[20] and Edwin Muir spoke of his 'rich spontaneous genius'.[21] For Gerhardie, with his passion for animated conversation, Kingsmill was to have 'a marvellously vitalizing effect. . . . Beside him no other man seems to have any life in him. At least, I find that, intellectually, all the other men I know are like dead fish.'

Towards evening of that first day as Gerhardie and Kingsmill dined on a Mediterranean quay with sailors lurching past, they were joined by a close friend of Kingsmill's, John Holms. Gerhardie and Holms had already met, briefly, some weeks previously at La Saharienne. Exceptionally talkative that day, Holms had greatly enchanted Gerhardie. Clara, seeing Holms sitting on the terrace stroking his little red beard, was reminded of the student Trofimov in *The Cherry Orchard*. He stayed the night, and the next day they breakfasted on grapes from the orchard. Then Holms took up his hat, his cane, and his rucksack and departed.

Although (or perhaps because) he spoke but seldom, Holms had the quality of drawing divergent opinions from everybody who met him. 'Holms gave me a greater feeling of genius than any other man I have met, and I think must have been one of the most remarkable men of his time, or indeed of any time', wrote Edwin Muir, an opinion shared by Kingsmill.[22] Osbert Sitwell met him at a party and thought him extremely intelligent, whilst Hesketh Pearson described him as 'an inarticulate ass'. Holms had literary ambitions, yet he had published only one story and was never seen to write. Nicknamed Oxo on account of his 'erstwhile ruddy chubbiness', he never became as close to Gerhardie as Kingsmill was to both of them, but appeared in several of William's novels as the character Bonzo.

Holms filled the void between his potential self-development and his lack of practical achievement with an air of insincerity and bluff, suggesting an impenetrable sagacity not capable of being confined within the laws of language . . . For it was as easy to romanticize upon his hidden and unknown qualities as it was to satirize his superficiality and inertia.[23]

Here Michael Holroyd has pinpointed exactly the qualities that so intrigued Gerhardie and that led him to consider Holms as the nucleus of a fictional character: elusive oscillation between the promise of ineffable significance and the empty and ridiculous. He was a true Henry Esbheornargist figure. Alec Waugh's description of Holms as 'the negative, uncreating artist, who is always going to write a book, but never does'[24] suggests not only Gerhardie's early preoccupations and fears but also his (uncomfortable) awareness of the gulf between aesthetic sensibilities and their adequate artistic expression, a theme to be most fully expounded in *Pending Heaven*. Gerhardie defended Holms as 'inarticulate through undue fastidiousness', and in Holms's obituary, entitled 'Portrait of an Unknown Man', wrote:

The genius of the untried raises the question whether anything said can really compete with everything unsaid. The greatest practising artist is only out to please himself—'self-expression' he calls it.[25]

Holms, two or three years younger than Gerhardie, had been born in India and educated at Rugby and Sandhurst. Like Gerhardie, he was exceptionally devoted to his mother, and like Kingsmill was constantly at odds with his father, a former Governor-General of the United Provinces of India now living in retirement in Cheltenham. He had enlisted young and, so the story went, had been awarded the Military Cross for killing four Germans whom he had inadvertently disturbed whilst they were breakfasting under a tree. After six months on the Somme he was taken prisoner and spent the last two years of the war at Karlsruhe, in the company of Hugh Kingsmill and Alec Waugh.

He and Kingsmill were both self-centred, unsatisfied men of literary vocation, lacking self-confidence; they provided an important function for each other. Holroyd describes how, in return for sympathy towards Holms's depressive tendencies, Kingsmill 'demanded from Holms an unstinted appreciation of his own novels which he could find nowhere else . . . and the criticisms he gave . . . were composed of a mixture of sound and imaginative perception, interspersed with hyperboles of praise'.[26] Over the following decade the growing friendship between Kingsmill and Gerhardie provided increasingly the same kind of moral and professional support.

The day after Kingsmill's arrival in Toulon Gerhardie called at his hotel, anticipating further pleasant conversation. But, true to form, Kingsmill had departed quite suddenly leaving no address. Shortly afterwards, Clara, too, left to spend the summer in Bolton with Dolly and Sissie, and Gerhardie removed to the coast.

Rebecca West was also enjoying a youthful literary vogue. After a brief correspondence Gerhardie joined her at her hotel for a few weeks' holiday. Pension Josse, between Antibes and Juan les Pins, was then occupied mostly by English professional people enjoying the cheap summer rates. Scott and Zelda Fitzgerald were staying nearby, and in the harbour at Antibes was an old fisherman who had once built a boat for Maupassant. An American publisher at the pension paid regular visits to Isadora Duncan in Nice, in an attempt to persuade her to write her autobiography, just a few months before her untimely death.

Rebecca West was working on *Sunflower*, a novel about Beaverbrook with whom she had had a brief and very unhappy love affair.

Beaverbrook did not want to be the subject of West's novel; when he heard of it he made his annoyance quite plain and the book was abandoned.[27] Gerhardie found her 'a witty woman' with 'a beautiful cooing voice', so that 'the first day o two we were very pleased and charmed with each other, but towards the end got thoroughly bored with one another.'[28] West was more than bored by Gerhardie, she thought him 'a most unpleasant sort of lunatic, who had come over because he thought he ought to have a love affair with me because of our literary eminence, but on seeing me decided I was too sarcastic and too old' (she was 33).[29]

Another resident, Yvonne Kapp, wife of the artist Edmund Kapp, remembered that Gerhardie had been regarded as a curious individual, almost a figure of fun, as he stalked the beach at Juan les Pins in a dark three-piece suit and panama hat. He surprised everyone by remarking in an insistent and somewhat affected manner: 'I shall never *speak* to anyone who doesn't like *The Constant Nymph*.' And they laughed when William, not realizing that Beaverbrook signed his letters 'Beaverbrook' because of his title, simply signed 'Gerhardi'. Rebecca's twelve-year-old son Anthony compounded his mother's view of Gerhardie by reporting that he had seen him in the office at midnight checking out the residents' bills—in fact nothing more than harmless curiosity in someone who habitually roamed about in the dark. When Beaverbrook arrived in Antibes he invited Gerhardie to tea at his hotel. Gerhardie, very nervous, asked Edmund Kapp to accompany him. When they returned Yvonne was surprised to find that over tea with Gerhardie and Beaverbrook her husband had lost his beard.

Yvonne Kapp found William conceited, odd, dotty, and rather laughable, not someone to be taken seriously, but she considered in retrospect that the rest of the guests had been less than kind to him. Gerhardie invited the Kapp's young nanny out with him one evening. Anthony West, taking his supper early, was surprised to find he had company: Gerhardie had requested a 6 o'clock meal with the child so as not to have to provide dinner for the nanny—'He resented from the bottom of his purse the clumsy convention which requires that before two people can meet one must contribute to the other's bodily sustenance, to the profit of unscrupulous restauranteurs and the detriment of his personal budget.'[30] Then he became acquainted with a very young girl called Chloe and on a moonlit night seduced her on a tombstone 'in the hearing of the dead'.

In the autumn Gerhardie returned to La Saharienne and Clara

rented a small house five minutes' walk away. It gave Clara great satisfaction to watch over her son as he sat at his desk writing; 'really these creations are not easy to give birth to and are attended with many pangs in spite of your prolific genius'. But they could live neither with nor without each other. 'I have no thought, no feeling that I cannot share with my mother', wrote William. 'She is like a second conscience to me, her eyes like a glass reflecting my own image.'[31] But the truth was not always palatable, and Clara was not only nervy and brittle, but also bossy. She could not keep quiet and she always made her feelings known. William reflected that in the old days she was 'very self-possessed and far from excitable, a trait she developed in old age with the dwindling of responsibilities—a kind of sleeplessness by day'.[32] She was especially anxious and fussy whilst travelling, and one of her particularly annoying habits was to regularly rearrange the furniture. They would express 'a constant and irritating solicitude as to the other's welfare'. William noticed that in the presence of her excitement he usually felt 'reproach-fully calm'; whereas when he got excited his mother's calm dignity seemed to 'reprove' him. Like Clara, William's own eagerness and excitement often turned into nervous over-excitability. Few but his family saw Gerhardie in a rage: all his aloofness would vanish as he grew almost childishly hysterical and shrill, hurling abuse liberally, dragging up old grievances from the past, something Charles, for all his horrible tempers, had never done. 'No one knows better than I that half or more of the *terrible things* you say, when you are in a passion, you do not mean', wrote Clara who had noticed 'a strain of cruelty' in her son. Such quarrels usually culminated in an exchange of this kind:

> 'My house, it's my house!'
> 'Your house would be better with *your* living in another.'
> 'In that case, please leave my house.'

Which one of them would do, only to come back again in the morning. Eventually, tired of the cold and the wet, Gerhardie crossed alone to North Africa.

In England Ernest Benn issued Gerhardie's only published play, *Perfectly Scandalous or The Immorality Lady: A Comedy in Three Acts.*[33] Set in a Tyrolean pension with the heroine based upon the 'mad pro-bolshevik Englishwoman', Gerhardie described it as 'rather in the Chehovian tradition',[34] and further specified that 'the first act is a farce, the second a comedy, and the third a tragedy', 'the theme being the puerility of most human differences and preoccupations and the comedy of everyday relationships'.[35] At a time when theatre audiences were accustomed to farces by Ben Travers or the social comedies of Noël Coward, the play certainly encompasses unfamiliar ideas. Scene One opens climactically with pistol shots, and decelerates towards the eventual tragi-comic death in Scene Three of the heroine. The characters, both in appearance and in the medley of noises they utter, waver between the real and the ridiculous. An afterword informs us:

The state of the theatre, as we all know, is low: not as low as before the war; yet low. Ever anxious to oblige the managers, I have prepared an alternative, low-brow, and perhaps more pleasing ending.

The heroine, instead of dying, leaps up and executes a wild dance to Chopin's Waltz (Op. 64, No. 2).

Curtis Brown, on receiving the typescript, had called it 'a wonderfully vivid presentation of us worms wriggling about vaguely in the cosmic mud', but lamented its unsaleability to 'materialistic' theatre managers, begging Gerhardie to 'please humour our present childish yearning for things like plot-story—and educate us up more slowly? The present play is so far in front of us that maybe we can't get anyone to do more than say "How wonderful", without putting up any cash.' And indeed many critics were flummoxed by its curious innovations; others welcomed its originality as 'the work of a dramatist with vision',[36] and the *Daily Telegraph* described it (not unkindly) as a 'nonsense' play in the manner of Lear or Carroll.[37] But its publication caused some trouble for Gerhardie, who had caricatured Jackie Lys, the Provost of Worcester College. Lys was more than a little annoyed. Unfortunately Gerhardie had, for one reason or another, neglected to actually take his degree, which by 1930 could no longer be postponed. As he was permitted to take it in absence only if he had very persuasive reasons for remaining abroad, he asked a friend in Geneva to post a letter for him, because 'the ordeal of sitting down to tea with [Lys] and his outraged wife was more than I could face, and I would have postponed taking the degrees till they were dead'. In order to make his stay in Geneva seem imperative he suggested that he was engaged 'on a work ridiculing Labour Ministers —Socialism being unpopular at Worcester College'.[38]

In 1935, again attempting to get the play performed, Gerhardie sent *Perfectly Scandalous* to J. B. Priestley; Priestley replied that he thought the comedy very good indeed but that it seemed by then to date a little. 'It belongs essentially to the Nineteen-twenties, and not the 'thirties. This may not matter in 1960, but it matters now.' As it happened, *Perfectly Scandalous* was not performed until 1947.

   Gerhardie arrived in Algiers in January 1927, after exactly a year in France. He checked into an inexpensive hotel, where two notices caught his eye:

Dogs. Any food consumed by dogs will have to be paid by him

The second instructed:

Prière de bien vouloir veiller à la fermeture des robinets du lavabo après usage.

'Note the word *veiller.* It means watch. It means that in the night you must not sleep but *watch* that the taps don't go off somehow and cause disaster.' A letter from Clara, hovering ambiguously between candour and self-pity, described having spent her birthday 'all alone, the very first one in all my life'. But she had gone for a long walk, happy at having received so many family letters. She returned William's £1 present and offered instead to lend him money, warning: 'Do be careful of the Arabs in every guise. Black or white.' The Arabs that Gerhardie found most invidious were the little shoe-cleaning boys: 'If you sat down in a cafe or only slackened your pace, one of these numerous urchins had already got hold of your feet and was polishing them. A display of feet, however casual, they interpreted as an invitation.'[39] Then there were those who insisted on conducting him to the *Chat Noir* night-club, adding enticingly, 'They're Parisians there and they do everything.' This annoyed Gerhardie who in coming south had especially hoped to procure dark-skinned girls; he later summarized his experience of Algerian brothels as 'negligible'.

   Believing that Algeria should be seen 'swiftly, kaleidoscopically', he visited the Kasbah, the native quarter, the Great Mosque, and the Ruisseau des Singes, a brook where whole families of monkeys came down from the trees to greet him. From Algiers he took a nine-day motor-coach trip south to Bou-Saada and to Biskra, 'a fashionable oasis visited by Europeans and Americans', where he rented an idyllic Arabic house surrounding a small courtyard with a fountain in the middle. Here there was even less to occupy him: the market-place, the Ouled Nails native dancing display, a visit on horseback to the dunes, more Ouled Nails. After two weeks he felt that he knew the faces of the camels.

   And it was in an Algerian hotel room that at a quarter to five one quiet afternoon, he found the material for his most curious story. Bent over the basin washing his face, he suddenly became aware that a ghost stood beside him, watching his activity with 'unearthly detachment':

He looked—how shall I say?—as if Algiers was as good a place for him as another; as if, indeed, he had never left our world, but was no longer in need of its amenities. We had taken the trouble to put him in a coffin and conduct him with a degree of lugubrious pomp and solemnity to the cemetery. Liveried men in cocked hats and looking like field-marshals out of a workhouse had walked funereally two each side of the hearse; and he, the hero of it all, had never even got into the coffin.

The ghost neither moved nor spoke. Impressed by the calm repose, Gerhardie, in a sudden existential vision, saw that it was he himself who was the ghost, still trapped in a strange world, awaiting release.

If others did not shrink at my approach it was because they were ghosts too and we lived in a ghost world. But the Being who had dreamt me looked on with tolerant detachment—tolerant because always he could say: 'enough'. And as at the end of a tedious and squalid dream one is about to cease being the dream to become once more the dreamer who can dream of other, better things as well, so I felt that presently the trance would pass, the dream would end, the chill and ghostly world would open out into another. The mist would rise, and I would cease to be a ghostly dream and become the dreamer who has dreamt us all.

Meanwhile, for heaven knows how long, I was a ghost . . . I saw myself an ill-used man, a novelist producing sterling work in the world of ghost critics, ghost newspapers, ghost women, ghost love; inadequately read, inadequately paid, inadequately loved.[40]

He finished washing and walked out into the streets, where 'ghosts crowded the pavements, drove past in motor-cars, sat in the cafés, danced in lugubrious halls, staring with uncomprehending eyes out of mortal sockets'.

Gerhardie posed for some photographs in Bou-Saada, looking dapper but curious in the same three-piece dark suit and panama hat, surrounded by camels and colourful local merchants. On a visit to Algiers he made a tour of 'the houses of ill-fame for which Algiers is ill-famed, but my instinct for self preservation', he explained to Beaverbrook, 'causes me, in this place, to multiply precautions so that I feel I might be in a padded overcoat'.[41] Instead he stood watching the native girls in the market-place until one in particular caught his eye. He approached her pretending to have lost his way and she, who had seemed remote and aloof, suddenly smiled warmly. He suggested that she come to live with him, and engaged her as his servant and mistress.

Khandra, an alluring Arab girl, *café au lait* as she described herself, had been married at the age of 11 and had run away from her husband four years later, since when she had been in service.

To run away (*se sauver*), to 'escape' from your husband was regarded in the nature of having successfully avoided military service, a recognised but irksome obligation not to be compared with the fun and glory of domestic service in a European home.[42]

She could neither read nor write but she cooked well, and was sweet-natured and compliant. When Gerhardie asked how old she was she replied: 'Don't know. Twenty, what do you think?' They lived agreeably together in Biskra, visited regularly by Khandra's girlfriends who were, it seems, equally compliant. He continued with *Jazz and Jasper*, sent articles to London periodically, and signed his name 600 times for a limited edition of his play, a feat which Clara sympathetically compared to the Prince of Wales having to shake hands all day long.

After six months the solitude began to pall. He had grown tired of the heat and desert, the perpetual wandering about and meeting people only to part again. *Jazz and Jasper* was finished and, believing it would help his work to settle amongst English-speaking people and build up 'a sort of literary coterie', Gerhardie decided to settle permanently in London and wrote advising Clara to do the same. To add to his discomfort Beaverbrook had recently written warning him that he was in danger of being forgotten: 'I must tell you that neither for good nor evil are you being talked of by men and women over at the present time.' Then, having convinced him of his own obscurity, Beaverbrook set about trying to amend it, and enclosed with the letter an article written by himself, entitled *The Future of Gerhardi*? It would, he promised, give him 'great publicity', which would 'make them talk', but Gerhardie was perfectly free to reject it if he liked. The article praised him in a manner more suited to a Hollywood actor, concluding dramatically: 'And yet I tremble for his future. One view is that he is simply written out . . . that *The Polyglots* is only a piece of autobiography . . . I reject this opinion . . . There is genius here.' Beaverbrook's accompanying letter stated: 'if the gloomy view is true it cannot do you any harm. On the other hand, if the optimistic alternative is the correct one, it will do you a lot of good.'

This sensationalism, though publicity of a kind, and probably well intended, had a damaging all-or-nothing quality about it, the implication that if Gerhardie did not continue to be a dazzling success then he was a complete failure—quite inappropriate to a serious writer, who may build a reputation gradually. But, with so many dependants Gerhardie was impatient to do what Wharton, Wells, and Bennett had done: earn a serious literary reputation *and* make a great deal of money. To Clara he admitted (reluctantly?) the article was 'jolly good publicity' and agreed to its publication. To Beaverbrook he wrote: 'It's stupendous! I embrace it in its entirety. It excited me so that I couldn't sleep all night—"excited" in the English sense of course. In French, "excited" means sexually excited, and that . . . it fails to do.'[43] Financially speaking Gerhardie *had* been unlucky. A letter from Curtis Brown indicates the gulf between his outstanding literary reputation and the paucity of his earnings: 'Well, don't lose faith in us. I don't believe anyone else would have worked so unremittingly for so little financial reward just out of sheer admiration.'

In March, William wrote to Clara of his intention to visit her in Toulon on the way to London, bringing with him Khandra who would do '*all* the work and cooking'. Clara was not taken with this idea, and pointed out the folly and expense of such a scheme, the problems and responsibilities should she become pregnant or should he tire of her. 'As for having her here', she reminded him, 'that is also not convenient for you are quite aware as to my feelings of living in the same house with your mistress. . . . Let me better help you to settle something in England. Are not there plenty of nice English girls (white and not black).' And so Khandra went back into domestic service. The evening before he sailed she helped him to pack and she told him that for a time she would feel sad at his leaving, but not seeing him would soon forget him. The next day he stood on the deck of the ship looking out to where she waited on the quay, perfectly still and not waving. The ship pulled out. 'It grew chilly and dim. I could not forget the figure of Khandra standing there modestly behind the barrels.'[44]

He arrived in Toulon alone. In June, after eighteen months away, Beaverbrook's yacht picked him up and sailed back to England.

11

LONDON
June 1927–April 1928

'I am Lord Ottercove and I cannot deny it.'
(Beaverbrook to reporters in New York)

Almost as soon as he returned to England, Gerhardie was caught up with Rosie's troubles. British mistrust of Soviet Russia was undiminished. In May 1927, two hundred police raided the London offices of Arcos, the Soviet trading organization, in search of evidence against the Communists. None was found, but diplomatic relations were broken off and in Russia everybody with English connections became vulnerable. In the six years since her return Rosie, homesick for England, had frequented the remnants of the British colony and become friendly with the English consul and his wife. She and Leonya had also attended luncheon parties as the guest of Lady Muriel Paget, an Englishwoman who organized a number of relief organizations for both Britons and Russians throughout the country. Now Leonya was thrown into prison on a trumped-up charge of espionage, pending possible execution. Rosie, heavily pregnant, was left without money; 10-year-old Tamara fell ill with appendicitis; in giving birth to the baby Rosie developed puerperal fever; the child was found to have cerebral palsy.

Though William persistently complained about his family—'that pose of "relations are nothing to me"', as Clara called it—he would go to enormous lengths when they were in trouble. At once he set about writing letters to influential Socialists and Communists—John Strachey, who since leaving Oxford had become a Communist and frequently visited Russia; Fenner Brockway, Chairman of the Independent Labour Party; Rakovsky, the Soviet Ambassador in Paris, and many more. He exhorted them to use their influence in Moscow, explaining that his sister Mrs Misernuik was married to a man of the utmost insignificance in the Ministry of Bees. 'Such was his insignificance that, though not a member of the Communist Party, he continued in the same department for bee culture throughout two revolutions.' Arthur Cook, secretary of the Miners' Federation, kindly supplied Gerhardie with a personal letter of introduction to Rakovsky, but took a placid, not to say naïve, view of events: 'I am sure you will realise there is a very difficult situation in Russia and they will not punish anyone without cause.'

Next Gerhardie contacted all branches of the family advising them to write, in Russian, on Leonya's behalf, and to underline the fact that Rosie and all her relatives were 'really far more Russian than English, having been born and brought up in Russia and having a lively sympathy for the country of their birth', and that he himself had written two 'powerful satires on the anti-Bolshevik campaign'. The family remained in a state of nervous uncertainty regarding the fate of Leonya; William confided to Edith Wharton his sudden fear that the various interventions might, paradoxically, irritate the authorities into executing him. Wharton was, of course, a sympathetic audience. 'Such an accumulation of suffering must be a feast even for the Bolsheviks', she wrote. 'Have you noticed, by the way, that while the humanitarian world (or its *soi-disant* spokesmen) have—whether rightly or wrongly—raised a world outcry over the supposed mis-trial of Sacco and Vanzetti, not one protest has been made public as to the murder without trial at present going on in Russia?' At length, after three months in prison, Leonya was released, 'very ill and nervous but happy to be alive'.

In June Ernest Benn issued *Pretty Creatures*, a volume containing Gerhardie's five short stories written in Austria. Wishing to dedicate them to his patron, William wrote to enquire which of two options was acceptable: 'In the absence of Napoleon Buonaparte to William Maxwell Baron Beaverbrook' or simply 'To Lord Beaverbrook'. The former, replied Beaverbrook promptly. And William, who always took the greatest care over the appearance of his books, was immensely annoyed by a variety of printer's errors and returned the proofs annotated thus: 'Will the printer pl. refrain from using his own judgement. I don't care for his improvements.' Further on: 'The printer even seems intent on improving foreign words by misspelling them!' And again: '*Note*: why can't the stupid printer keep to my version? This is really scandallous [*sic*] printing.'

Gerhardie was a gifted short-story writer, and the genre well displays the delicacy of his language and his Chekhovian attention to nuance— all five stories, 'Tristan und Isolde', 'The Big Drum', 'A Bad End', 'In the Wood', and 'The Vanity Bag', achieve their greatest effects through tone and mood and, like his Oxford publications, through 'emotional misunderstanding of individual and mutual sensibilities'.

'In the Wood' implicates literature and story-telling with sexual desire and expectation. A group of Russians in a boarding-house are seated at dinner one evening. Lieutenant Barahmeiev, an ex-hussar, is attempting to seduce Vera Solomonovna, the handsome wife of his landlord. To assist his seduction Barahmeiev recounts an incident from his past: he was seated amongst a group of people 'discussing something—literature I think, and then, quite relevantly, we switched off on to love'. Beside him a beautiful girl, Zina, was 'vehement in her denunciation of everything relating to the attraction between the sexes', but later consented to take an evening stroll with the young Barahmeiev. Suddenly Zina removed her clothes and stood before him naked in the moonlight. At this crucial point in his story Barahmeiev stops, to the frustration of his eager listeners:

'Well?' we said. 'Go on.'
'That's all,' said the Lieutenant.
'But what happened afterwards?' asked Vera Solomonovna.
'Nothing happened.'
'But *how?*' she said in a tone as though she had been wronged.
'Well, that's all there is to tell.'
'But—it's no proper story even.'
'I can't help that,' he answered almost angrily. 'This is what happened, and this is where it ended. I can't falsify the facts to suit your taste. We don't, my dear Vera Solomonovna, live our lives to provide plots for stories.'

Curtis Brown had admired the stories, but worried that they were too difficult for the average reader and suggested that it would help if the author were to write an introduction pointing out 'how engagingly popular these stories really are if one doesn't insist on reading them "through a glass darkly"'. In spite of his fears (and fortunately no such introduction was forthcoming) *Pretty Creatures* was a popular collection. Some reviewers, insensitive to their subtlety, considered them insubstantial and 'plotless', but the reaction of the *Daily Express* was extreme and atypical, when it accused Gerhardie of making the world and its inhabitants 'stupid and ludicrous. He jeers at them all.'[1] Yet it is an interesting review because so closely resembling critical reactions to Katherine Mansfield's 'Daughters of the Late Colonel', which she had discussed in her first letter to Gerhardie, adding: 'It's almost terrifying to be so misunderstood.'

Exhaustive attempts to sell the stories individually to magazines in America failed. When Gerhardie, doubting his agent's perseverance, wrote to suggest that he had not bothered, Curtis Brown retorted that the very idea gave him heart failure and caused him to utter a nightmarish scream in the office. They were, he said, simply too advanced for American readers.

Gerhardie was renting a one-room flat in Soho, green inside with a roof garden and flowerpots, in a house once occupied by Karl Marx. The massive amount of extra work engendered by Rosie and the Russians led him to buy a new typewriter and engage a secretary, an attractive young redhead whom he selected out of a long line of applicants. He encouraged her by explaining that they must work extremely hard in order to produce enough money to pay even her minimal salary, and he quickly seduced her. 'She is the most passionate woman (having been separated from her husband) that I have ever known, and spends the whole day with me in taking down dictation or typing her shorthand, as she says that no other man has ever given her such pleasure', he explained to Clara. 'If anybody calls too suddenly I disappear into the cupboard which has a door like that of a room (so that I pretend that all the other rooms, such as the ballroom, are behind that door), and she calls to me in a voice as if I were far away: "Mr Gerhardi has gone upstairs into the ballroom and will be back in a few moments", which gives me time to adjust my clothes in the cupboard before I come out to greet the visitor. Her name is Mrs Hotstuff, or rather Hardstaff.' He also contacted Kingsmill who, since their meeting in France, had fallen passionately in love with a very young woman named Gladys, and had impetuously relinquished his wife and child. After an acrimonious exchange of letters with his father, Kingsmill found himself suddenly without a job—after which Gladys relinquished *him* and returned to her rich guardian.

By early October Gerhardie had taken a lease on a self-contained maisonette in Sinclair Road, West Kensington at 3½ guineas per week, and invited Kingsmill to share it—'It promises to be a perfect menage', he wrote optimistically to Wharton. He found Kingsmill a very pleasant companion, 'the first man whose mind exhilarated my mind and exercised it to the full', and together they spent many hours in conversation; 'Not bad, old man! Not *bad!*' was Kingsmill's highest term of praise, uttered always with hoarse vigour. Gerhardie was particularly sympathetic to Kingsmill's contempt for what he termed 'Dawnism', the 'heralding the dawn of a new world':

An excited anticipation that some form of collective action is about to solve all the troubles of the individual is an intermittent but apparently incurable malady of mankind.

Kingsmill strode into the room one morning announcing: 'Where there is vision the people perish. I admit,' he hastened to add, 'they perish also where there is no vision. Either way, in fact, their situation appears to be damnably awkward.'[2] This appealed not only to Gerhardie's hatred of abstractions but to his wry sense of the humorous tragedy of existence. And in more personal matters they had a lot in common. Kingsmill was, on the whole, an immensely cheerful person, exuding good will and zest. 'I am optimistic about everything I cannot control,' he once remarked. 'And as I can control practically nothing I am optimistic about practically everything.'[3] They both loved music, so that Kingsmill took the greatest delight in Gerhardie's (rather limited) rendition of Wagner's *Tristan* on the piano. Clara's initial dislike of him was now aggravated by jealousy, for she wrote to her son: 'I *was* glad to get even a hurried note from you this morning as out of sight, looks a little like, out of mind and makes me think you do not love me as you used to.' Kingsmill, reading and advising on the manuscript of *Jazz and Jasper*, was also usurping her role as critic: 'Tell me something of your work dear when you write again,' she prompted William. 'I feel quite out of it.'

Though invigorating, Kingsmill was also a risky companion. Apart from unusually powerful lungs ('All the Lunns have resonant voices, said to be the result of rounding up tourists'),[4] he was a man whom, as Gerhardie put it, nature never intended to live in a confined space:

Hugh Kingsmill usually broke something or set something on fire in mere inadvertency, and when I proffered the mildest objection would exclaim in the voice of a·man outraged in his deepest feelings, 'Damn it all, you're the host!' identifying the vocation of a host with that of a martyr. But this did not prevent him from being as sensitive as Beethoven on the artistic side.[5]

William, on the other hand, was particularly careful with his possessions, and rather fussy in the house. *Pending Heaven* contains a faithful account of their life together at Sinclair Road:

He [Kingsmill] now appeared to Victor [Gerhardie] a curiously clumsy fellow—not on the best terms with crockery. A man who might sit down on a gramophone record and say, jovially, 'Sorry, old man. Nothing lasts for ever,' and, reading discomfiture on Victor's face, in augmented tones of irritation: 'I said: *sorry*. I can't go on saying it.' (As though the main thing about it all was his, Max's, sorrow, and Max was vexed with him, Victor, for his failure to sympathize with him.) Irritated, Max would lean back with a jerk and break the back of the chair. By Jove,' with a laugh, 'I *am* sorry this time! But your things *are* brittle, there's no doubt about it. However, enough of this! Let's talk of other things.' A difficult man to keep house with.[6]

And, to crown Gerhardie's growing anxiety, within a couple of weeks Kingsmill had also seduced the red-haired secretary. Gerhardie was speechless with rage. But Kingsmill, in his chivalrous and entirely impractical manner, invited the secretary to move in permanently, which she did, bringing her 3-year-old daughter. Like Gerhardie, Kingsmill was a great lover of children and in many ways not unchildlike himself. The little girl, 'as noisy as three Noras', constantly besieged the adults, hurling poached eggs and boiled carrots across the dining-room, solicitously cleaning out their inkwells, until Kingsmill pointed out that the arrival of her one-and-a-half-year-old brother would be bound to deflect her attention ('children playing together were models of composure'). The little boy arrived. Naturally, they simply made double the noise and trouble, in the process exasperating their mother who now became irritable, exhausted, and reluctant to work.

They had to engage a nurse for the children. In the meantime the maid left without giving notice, and the landlady complained of the noise of typing, small footsteps, and raucous piano-playing, and that they were 'wearing out' the light switches. The phone rang constantly and there was a steady stream of tradespeople at the door demanding money—all this in the space of two weeks. As a prisoner of war Kingsmill had acquired the useful habit of working in public. He had sat in Karlsruhe happily writing with the combined noise of singing, chatting, wrestling, and ping-pong tournaments in the background. Gerhardie, who had not had the benefit of a POW camp training, was driven almost to distraction. Kingsmill still kept to his old habit of disappearing suddenly and without warning, and even kept his hat and coat up in his bedroom instead of in the hallway, so that he might the more swiftly abscond.

Then Kingsmill, deeply infatuated, became insanely jealous of Gerhardie's relations with the secretary, and after several days of gathering gloom a spirited quarrel at last erupted, and he demanded that she choose between them. A woman who knew the two suitors took a rather less romantic view of the situation: keeping in mind that the secretary was poor, overworked, and only slept with Gerhardie to hold her job, she was not surprised that 'Mrs Hotstuff' opted for Kingsmill. He and the secretary departed in a taxi with one child, the nurse, and a lot of suitcases, whilst Gerhardie remained in the flat with the new maid, who was also a cook and who was taking the remaining child home with her every night. He remarked to his mother that Kingsmill, having just left his own wife and child, was now saddled with more dependants, no visible income, and only £100 in the bank. Kingsmill's mother, in turn, hated Gerhardie, thinking that the secretary's children were really his, now unjustly supported by her own son after being abandoned by their father.

At last a reconciliation of sorts was accomplished and Kingsmill returned plus one child and minus the secretary, but was almost invariably out. In *Pending Heaven* Victor reflects upon the situation:

The *ménage à trois* had contracted to that of one man who lived with two children and a cook. He was suddenly aware of being a man with a family—two infants who called incessantly: 'Uncle Victor! Look! Look!' and brought him things, for the most part his own, to examine, which they left on the floor or took away to the kitchen, and who desired to be lifted to the window to see a big dog in the street. After lunch he took them for walks . . . And if he took hold of their hands they cried bitterly, and if he left them alone they made at once for the traffic.[7]

Quite apart from diversions such as these, Kingsmill, who had lived all his life in financial comfort, found it well-nigh impossible to adjust to poverty. He frequently borrowed money and was perpetually in debt, often to Gerhardie who could ill afford it.

Hugh Kingsmill was an honourable man. He would never do a needy person down. But if he borrowed money from you, he hesitated to return it unless he was satisfied that (a) you needed it and (b) deserved it. Since he made himself the sole judge of (a) and (b), his sitting in judgement on your money had the effect of infuriating you; after which he no longer, he said, felt friendly to you, and any previous arrangement he had contemplated for liquidating his debt in the fullness of time was now null and void. And you were back in the ignominious position of having to coax and wheedle him into parting with your own money.[8]

In order to keep solvent himself, Gerhardie had been working hard at journalism, and by the end of the year was regularly supplying articles and reviews to a wide variety of publications, earning anything from £4 to £12 a time. Desmond MacCarthy, editor of the *New Statesman*, offered him a job as drama critic ('it would be a pleasure to have such a colleague as you'), but he warned that a large proportion of plays were of no importance. Gerhardie, anxious to learn stagecraft before commencing a new 'commercial' play, agreed. His enthusiasm was short-lived. The plays and the money were so bad that within a few months he considered it financially preferable to continue with his own work. In the meantime royalties from his books had trickled down to almost nothing, but there were occasional sums of money for reprints (£50 for the fifth edition of *Futility*) and foreign rights (£15 for the Czech option on *Futility*). Clara, canny with money, opened a bank account in France into which William could pay his American earnings and avoid English tax. Thus he maintained a reasonably comfortable income, and invested £50 in an electric dictaphone.

Free from the tribulations of a secretary, Gerhardie simply lay on the sofa and spoke into his new machine. He had sought permission to dedicate *Jazz and Jasper* to H. G. Wells and received a warm response: 'A dedication from you is an honour to be desired. Thank you for it . . . Good wishes and all the respect the old can pay the young.'[9] Yet Gerhardie's mood was subdued, as though the exciting prospects of only a short while ago had dwindled into routine. And Beaverbrook, who insisted that *Jazz and Jasper* was 'brilliant', after weeks of suspense and skilful evasion of the issue, at last declined to serialize the book. He gave no reason, and in fact *Jazz and Jasper* would probably have done well in instalments, but he did pay the promised £250.

Gerhardie was busy with several new works: one was to become his fourth published novel, *Pending Heaven*; another is the forty-page typescript fragment *Ladies Prefer Bounders*, taking its title from Anita Loos's highly popular *Gentlemen Prefer Blondes* (1926), and purporting to be the confessions of a man—by name William Gerhardi—whose major preoccupation is women. Though the narrative begins by skilfully exploiting the sense of intimacy between reader and writer, which is here both literary and sexual, it eventually lapses into a sense that he is transcribing, uncritically, his own experience. Increasingly this was Gerhardie's difficulty. In order to produce his finest work he needed time to digest his experiences. Acute financial pressures made this impossible. A new and only mildly interesting comic play *Lord Brute*, written with commercial success in view, concerns the attempts of a group of individuals to certify as insane a megalomaniacal millionaire and thus acquire his fortune. Another and far better idea for a play involving Gerhardie's more outlandish imagination was, regrettably, never developed:

A liner sinks; but the life in the ship goes on as before. A steward swims up with a tray and serves tea. Passengers swim up to return a book borrowed from the library. Then fish, large and small, look in through the portholes. Finally they come in and take charge of the ship and grow more and more human-like; and the crew and passengers become fish-like, swim away.

Arnold Bennett introduced Gerhardie to the concert pianist Harriet Cohen, 'a wild, wild creature', not unlike a silent-film heroine with finely drawn, arched, rather tragic sloping eyebrows. Gerhardie particularly admired her black hair and long neck, and her literary taste, for she praised *Futility*. He also loved to hear her play: the first time alone together she performed *Tristan und Isolde* and the music of Chopin for six hours without cease. The second time, with Clara present, they laughed all evening, and Harriet played surrounded by strongly scented white lilies and wearing only a chiffon slip.

She found him an 'affectionate, sarcastic and rather formidable character'; her letters during their brief love affair show an appealing recklessness. But it was an acrimonious relationship. He painted an unkind portrait of her in *Pending Heaven* as Helen Sapphire, a fey, girlish harp player over-eager for applause—one he admitted was exaggerated and malicious but refused to alter. Professional jealousy was his chief motivation, for Harriet not only had a successful career, but was courted by Beaverbrook, Shaw, Arnold Bax, and many others. Gerhardie preferred his women to be more compliant, less prone to outshine him, and he was particularly irritated by her consciousness of her own popularity.

Though co-tenants still, Gerhardie and Kingsmill were no longer on speaking terms but, like Nikolai Vasilievich's feuding family on the journey to Omsk in *Futility*, communicated by a series of notes. The cook was preoccupied with the children, and William experimented briefly with a new fasting diet involving only orange juice, which he had seen advertised as a cure for gout, rheumatism, kidney trouble, and piles. Then, as Christmas approached, the cook gave notice, taking the children with her. Before she went, solicitous for her employer's well-being, she purchased Gerhardie six eggs to last him over the holiday. He awoke on Christmas morning miserably cold and forlorn and lay propped up in bed reading, swathed in rugs and blankets. Suddenly Kingsmill, whom he had not seen for a while, appeared round the door and cheerfully informed him that he had eaten *his* three eggs and offered, as a gesture of seasonal goodwill, to cook the remaining three eggs for his friend. William was speechless: 'a peace offering of his own eggs—No! as well might Lear, about to brace the storm, accept from his daughter's hands the loan of a mackintosh.'[10] A reconciliation did not take place. Hastily Kingsmill departed for the South of France with the secretary, who had first skilfully inveigled him into buying her a new set of clothes. Clara was irritated to distraction by his uncanny knack of doing well for himself: 'It makes me wild to think that such rotters as Hugh Lunn can carry on as they do and then fall onto their feet as he has. Fate is terribly unjust, who could admire such a man or compare him with you.'

Imagining the idyllic life pursued by Kingsmill and the secretary in the South of France with John Holms and his new love Peggy Guggenheim, Gerhardie longed to go abroad himself but felt tied by his job of drama critic, by the imminent arrival of the *Jazz and Jasper* proofs, and by the need to attend to the publicity. A Christmas parcel containing a decanter and twelve glasses arrived from Victor, and Clara sent a green and yellow handkerchief. Cold, dispirited, and lonely (for even Beaverbrook was abroad), he moved in with friends for two days over the holiday.

Clara, too, had been having a trying time attempting to remove from her cottage in Toulon after a catalogue of trials: faulty chimneys, broken pumps, virulent weather, troublesome neighbours. She attempted—unsuccessfully—to sell the trap and harness, so that for many years to come they recur as a sort of comic leitmotiv in her letters to William ('trap still unsold'). Some of their belongings, including William's papers and books, were packed up, others sold. 'One has, considering the shortness of life, to make financial sacrifices for comfort, or one is simply sacrificing years of one's life for nothing', he advised her and insisted she take 10 per cent for herself on all the sales. Then she and some stray pieces of furniture moved in with Daisy, who worried that the ceilings, already weakened by the weight of several hundred Buddhas, would cave in. Moreover, Clara had to act in a cloak-and-dagger manner because her presence was to be kept secret from Daisy's mother-in-law. Clara was growing homesick and wished to settle in England again, despite the bad weather: 'say what you like but one's "ain folks" or rather "ain countree" draws one'. She continued to visit old friends, make trips to the theatre and opera, and keep William informed of all the family tribulations.

In the new year Gerhardie removed—alone—to a furnished flat above a fruit-and-flower shop off Baker Street. It was small but compact: a sitting-room and two bedrooms, electrically heated bathroom, and 'labour-saving' kitchen, and at 3½ guineas a week 'quite cheap'. But he was beginning to find living in a flat 'dingy, cramped and uncomfortable', and was irritated by complaints about the noise of music or typing. He consoled himself, as usual, with speculation of a brighter future: 'If [*Jazz and Jasper*] is a best-seller I shall buy a house in

London and then you will come and live with me, won't you?' he wrote to his mother, suggesting a 'fine, lofty' abode in the Cromwell Road where Rosie, Leonya, 'and all the lot of them' might live. He also decided to risk another secretary and engaged Patricia E. E. E. Rosenstiehl, 15 years old and 'such a wise, sweet-tempered girl'. She was tall and slender with a round face and curly fair hair, and though he found her 'quite pretty' he apparently made no attempt to seduce her—or at least to record such a seduction. Her father, a professional chef from Alsace who worked on liners, had taken to England, married in Cambridge, and settled with his wife in Dulwich, whence Patricia, their only child, fresh from secretarial college, came every day to her employer's flat.

In April Duckworth published Gerhardie's third novel, *Jazz and Jasper*, after Richard Cobden Sanderson had at last been persuaded that it was in the author's interests to relinquish the rights.[11] As testimony to Gerhardie's popularity the dust jacket was simply an unusually large full-facial photograph of himself. There is a considerable amount of confusion about the title: Gerhardie wished to call it *Doom*, but this was deemed too gloomy and not adopted until the 1974 edition. In the meantime the book appeared in 1947 as *My Sinful Earth*. The first American edition of 1928 bore yet another title, *Eva's Apples*, because the American publishers, Duffield, insisted that the word 'jazz' had been 'worn threadbare' across the Atlantic.

At first glance *Jazz and Jasper* has little in common with *Futility* or *The Polyglots*, being a momentous scientific fantasy of the 1920s, and culminating in the disintegration of the world through an atomic chain reaction. As for the title, 'jazz' encompasses the indulgent Twenties era, while 'jasper' refers to the apocalyptic vision of Revelations. With the character of Frank Dickin, Gerhardie makes his closest author–hero identification to date, and one that, by 1928, would have been discernible by contemporary readers. Shortly after the novel opens, Frank, summoned by the powerful newspaper owner Lord Ottercove, begins to read aloud his novel *Pale Primroses*, a narrative of the complex relations of a family of Russian refugees. For the first time Gerhardie is publicly satirizing himself: we quickly recognize a parody of his own novel style—meanderingly plotless, with a succession of bizarre expatriates and their hangers-on, the novelist hero who writes always in immediate retrospect of his own experiences—to which Ottercove responds:

'Still, what attracted me—and that is chiefly why I wrote to you—are the people in your book. So real. It seemed to me I knew them.'

'Well, I do try to make them living. I think it is up to a novelist—'
'I don't mean that. I think I know the family you describe.'

It is disorientatingly and characteristically difficult to judge *who* is the object of the comedy—Frank for copying too 'frankly' from real life, or Ottercove for responding in this literal-minded manner to a work of literature. When later Frank modestly deprecates *Pale Primroses*, Ottercove agrees enthusiastically: '"Damn poor stuff . . . That's why I am interested in it. . . . Any fool can sell a good novel. But it takes genius to sell a poor book."' He promptly publicizes it as 'the rottenest book of the century', and Frank becomes a social, if not financial, success. The difficulty of determining who is the fool, Ottercove or Frank, brings to mind Gerhardie's rejection of comic labels:

Critics feel uneasy when a writer is not solemn. Who is he laughing *at*? who *with*? . . . The much-vaunted distinction between laughing with and laughing at your characters has always seemed to me unreal, because if you are laughing *with* your characters you must be laughing with them *at* some other characters.[12]

Ottercove frequently proves himself unable to distinguish between life and literature—though again it is not clear whether it is he or Frank who is at fault:

'Come and sit in this chair and read me your manuscript. Now then.'
'It is difficult to relate these things in their proper sequence. Some things stand out, others fade; that is all.'
'Are you talking now or reading?' asked Lord Ottercove.

Jazz and Jasper is a sophisticated meshing of factual and fictional, written and experienced, real and imaginative, literature and pulp. Because of the novel within the novel, and the fact that the book is to some extent a *roman à clef*, whole chains of identifications and inter-actions reveal themselves: William Gerhardie as Frank Dickin leads to the comparison of characters in Gerhardie's novel with those in Frank's work; and so a general comparison of all these characters with their 'originals' in real life, such as Beaverbrook, and, once again, Gerhardie; and thus back to the reader, who is himself real life and potential novel material. The situation is further complicated by Frank's eventual inclusion of Ottercove in his latest novel, the novel that we are reading and Frank is simultaneously writing—a fictional reversal of Gerhardie's (real-life) desire for inclusion in Beaverbrook's newspapers. Ottercove's potency—and Frank's vulnerability—obliquely reveal themselves in Ottercove's almost casual habit of trumping Frank, even in the realm of creative imagination, for it is an essential part of the nature of Ottercove that he believes that journalism ' "is philosophy. Life is a dream, according to my philosophy, a dream of illusions. And this faculty of creating illusions in a world of appearances is, I claim, the function of the journalist." ' Gerhardie's novels, of course, also gain their effects to a great extent through an awareness of the illusory aspects of novel reading. *Jazz and Jasper*, while commenting on the power of the press to encourage illusion and fantasy, falls itself into the category of fantasy fiction.[13] It is both fantasy fiction, and a satirical comment on the current popularity of fantasy fiction. And though Ottercove appears as a diabolical plotter, manipulating history through the written word, he is introduced to the reader as Frank's *god* when, in the first few pages, the theistic references are spelled out: on his way to meet Ottercove Frank sees the commissionaire as 'ever-jealous . . . like Peter, of his guardianship of the access of God'; the lift takes him 'up and up . . . higher and higher' to a lofty region where he is escorted by a page who is 'altogether removed from the race of mere lift boys'; as they ascend 'the last golden ladder to heaven', Frank is divested of his 'cruder clothes of the street'; the page knocks 'reverently' at Ottercove's door, and Frank is at last shown into a celestially 'radiant space of yellow and blue'. Ottercove's powers are truly vast, and such remarks as 'I will not have humanity let down' come readily to his lips. 'Lord O' and 'O Lord' become almost interchangeable: Frank's girlfriend Eva (based upon Terry) innocently writes of Ottercove using a capital for the pronoun 'He', and Ottercove himself, carried away by his own gifts as a preacher, quotes Revelations to a large crowd, as if they were his own words:

'. . . descending out of heaven from God, having the glory of God: and her light was like unto a stone most precious, even'—Lord Ottercove stopped as if seeking the *mot juste*—'like a jasper stone,' he said, 'clear as crystal.'

Ottercove's divinity is ultimately ensured: when at the end of the book Eva gives birth, the child is deemed to be not Frank's but Ottercove's and named Adam, first of the new, post-Apocalypse race.

Gerhardie's portrait of Ottercove, like Beaverbrook's influence upon Gerhardie, perpetually resists categorization as 'benevolent' or 'malevolent'. Arnold Bennett, Beaverbrook's closest friend in the later 1920s, found that Ottercove was presented 'with profound subtlety, and with a ruthlessness which yet somehow shows both appreciation and affection'.[14] The 'subtlety' consists in Gerhardie's deliberate blend of flattery and mockery, a perceptive literary representation of

Beaverbrook's peculiar omnipotence and its effects. Frank invites Ottercove to dinner in his studio flat. In answer to an anxious enquiry over what he would like to eat (Beaverbrook 'fussed over his diet'[15]) Ottercove requests a boiled egg. He arrives and is duly presented with the egg, which he politely and gravely consumes. But on the way out he mutters to himself 'A joke's a joke', and orders his chauffeur to drive at once to a night-club where he may be properly fed. The awesome almightiness of Beaverbrook/Ottercove generates the question 'How literally should one respond to such a person?'; it also creates oscillation between different categories of comic worlds, from the plausible to the absurd and back again. The book skilfully and disorientatingly defies literary categories and expectations—many critics were put out by the fact that, for example, almost half-way through an apparently natural-istic novel, Ottercove's motor-car takes to the air and flies.

Both Frank's novel and Gerhardie's maintain close ties with the contemporary world. Ottercove admits of *Pale Primroses*, whose charac-ters have the same names as the people upon whom, in Frank's world, they are based, that 'but for the names my serial editor might have easily passed it over'. It is a comment which satirizes not only the prurience of the newspaper-reading public, but the contemporary popularity of the *roman à clef* (the one having, perhaps, fostered the other). In *Jazz and Jasper*, topical characters and news items, clear to 1920s readers, are still recognizable: The Prime Minister Stanley Baldwin 'a country squire, who had been persuaded to shoulder the burden of government much against his inclination', 'a confirmed dog lover' with a 'wait and see' policy; a comic travesty of the Fundamentalist versus Evolutionist issue in America in 1925; a 'march through London by the Unemployed', heralding the General Strike of 1926; Arnold Bennett, depicted as Vernon Sprott, 'the foreman of British fiction, proud of purse and dexterous with the pen', author of *The New Babylon Hotel and Restaurant* (he signed his next letter to Gerhardie 'Sprott'). Beaverbrook's gossip-columnist, Valentine Castlerosse, appears as the scientist Lord de Jones, not making or breaking *individual* lives but those of the entire world. H. G. Wells appears as himself, as do Bernard Shaw, Lord Birkenhead, and others. Less specifically, there is fear of Bolshevism, increasing struggles of labour versus capital, allusions to the comparatively recent science of relativity, to contemporary eugenics debates (the problems of the New World and how it is to be populated), as well as all the trappings of the 'Jazz Age' made popular by Arlen, Waugh, Coward, and Fitzgerald. The novel raises questions of individual responsibility and influence, drawing on the rise of the press empires of Northcliffe, Rothermere, and Beaverbrook, and the newly formed BBC, domain of Lord Reith. It also suggests contemporary politics such as Mussolini's Fascism and the totalitarianism of Lenin and Stalin. The prophetic plot of Frank's book *Pale Primroses*, the novel within the novel, draws our attention to the prophetic potential of *Jazz and Jasper*. To modern readers the most powerful example is the devastation caused by one man's horrible dream, de Jones's disintegration of the atom and development of a new race, with its foretaste both of Hitler and of the atomic bomb.

Gerhardie's introduction by Beaverbrook into the society of the 1920s, where he met not only writers but politicians, scientists, and a wide range of public figures, was also his first real contact with sophisticated contemporary thought. Aside from his two (rather solitary) years at Oxford, his life had been spent abroad or in the army, and somewhat removed from the sense of hope, opportunity, and optimism of the 1920s that has been described by so many—A. J. P. Taylor calls the period 1925–9 'The Years of Gold' and cites as an example of the general mood the *Today and Tomorrow* series begun in 1924 which 'depicted the endless improvement of everything: science, morals, humour, and man himself. Utopia was not something to be striven for: it would arrive automatically. The old order, in Marx's phrase though not for his reasons, would simply "wither away".'[16] David Garnett believed, during the twenties, that 'the forces of intelligence and enlightenment were winning',[17] whilst Wells wrote optimistically about scientific advance. Gerhardie's reluctance to subscribe to such views demonstrates not so much pessimism, as profound scepticism of such radical notions of change and progress. His highly parodic religious material, in juxtaposition with the scientific sophistication, simply stresses his sense of the inherent sameness of the generations. Although Gerhardie's sympathies had long lain in this direction, *Jazz and Jasper* developed under the influence of Kingsmill's 'Dawnism', and as such represents an early example of a popular category of literature, the anti-Utopian (*Brave New World* was not published until 1932). In the novel, Gerhardie is clearly sceptical of idealism—though not all the reasons for idealism are shown to be misguided:

Of course there had been misery, tribulation, hate, lies, sordid hours, and moments of pain. But there had been other moments. He remembered how fourteen of his friends had volunteered to be bled to save his mother's life.

Like Gerhardie, Frank enthusiastically participates in the gaiety of the 1920s but is also subject to presentiments of its transience. In this respect *Jazz and Jasper* is also proleptic of a shift in literary sensibility: from the optimism of the 'golden years' to what Samuel Hynes has termed 'an apocalyptic vision of approaching destruction and the end of civilization'.[18]

And yet, in Gerhardie's fiction at least, there *is* a post-Apocalypse world, and everyday life (of a kind) reasserts itself almost immediately. In both moral and literary terms, *Jazz and Jasper*, like *Futility* and *The Polyglots*, speaks of 'revolution' as a period of immense and dramatic change that lapses back into futility and inaction. The plotlessness of the early chapters of the novel, aimless and meandering as the lives of Frank and Eva (or of the Bursanovs in *Futility* or the Vanderflints in *The Polyglots*), begins to gather momentum after the meeting with Ottercove. Once the disintegration of the world gets under way, events happen rapidly and the narrative becomes swift and terse. Ottercove, shouting from the rooftops 'Faster! faster! faster!' pre-dates Agatha Runcible's identical cry in Evelyn Waugh's *Vile Bodies*, published two years later —*Jazz and Jasper* was always Waugh's favourite Gerhardie novel.

With the subsidence of the Apocalypse, Gerhardie's survivors are left on a silent, empty piece of the earth. The 'plot', too, loses momentum and Gerhardie's familiar style reasserts itself, just as the new world begins to repeat the old. It is Frank, the peaceable artist, aimless and uncommitted, who (almost inadvertently) anticipates the next conflict:

He ambled on and, when he was well out of sight, dashed across to the archducal Schloss and hoisted his striped shirt, for want of a flag, according to the rules of the old world. And according to the rules of the old world, he looked about for something with which to defend the newly acquired possession, and felt that in doing so he was also performing an act of loyalty to the old world so ignominiously done in overnight. He waited for Lord de Jones to attack him with bombs and shrapnel and machine guns. . . . It was odd, this feeling of proprietorship, in the face of all this dissolution. And yet he told himself again and again that this castle . . . was his and his alone.

The apocalyptic 'evil suspense' has evaporated, along with the fictional 'evil suspense'—as Gerhardie himself frequently termed it. Utopia is shown to be as futile as novel plotting, notions of radical new worlds as obsolete as the notion that fiction must needs be sensational.

Arnold Bennett read *Jazz and Jasper* and at once, in his *Evening Standard* column, announced Gerhardie's 'wild and brilliant originality', his 'genius', bracketing him with Lawrence as an English novelist 'who counts'. But Bennett had trouble digesting modernistic tendencies and had recently complained of Virginia Woolf's lack of 'logical construction', her 'dissipated' interest. Thus, unsurprisingly, he criticized the 'mechanics of the narration' in *Jazz and Jasper*, and the lack of organization, concluding: 'Gerhardi has all the gifts of a major novelist except, apparently, the gift of marshalling and controlling his gifts.' Bennett also felt that the 'interminable promiscuities' of the book were not typical of life.[19] H. G. Wells, something of a Casanova himself, took a different view:

I like it. It's as true to life as *The Forsyte Saga* or *Sense and Sensibility* but because it does the Jazz side of life it will be called Extravaganza. Disconnected people like your Ottercove are as real as Soames Forsyte and very few novels have the courage to state the normal promiscuity of mankind . . . as well as you do. I don't greatly admire the wind-up, but you had to get out of the jazz somehow and what has no purpose has no climax of its own. I like Bennett and Beaverbrook as stars in the sky. In fact I like most of it and have been greatly amused. Go on. I approve of you myself.

And I wear my dedication with pride and satisfaction.[20]

Edith Wharton disliked the novel. Rebecca West wrote warmly: 'I think it is very wonderful of you to have kept a real effect of lightness and gaiety and dream-like insubstantiality all through a long book. I read it with the greatest possible amusement.' Less eminent critics were also divided. Almost all appreciated Ottercove, but many were irritated by the levity of the book and considered that Gerhardie's talents had been squandered. Others admitted defeat: 'The worst of some of these modern writers is that they make us more ordinary men feel not only out of date but dead and buried.'[21]

12

DIGRESSION ON WOMEN
April 1928–October 1929

All lost men and women. Lost. Some more luxuriously lost than others, but all, all lost. Lost and damned. No escape![1]

'But Oh, how the invitations flood in!' Publishers wanted him to do this, sign that, appear here and visit there. Harpers tried to lure him away from Duffield with £100. Society once again clamoured for him. Despite the mixed reviews, *Jazz and Jasper* was selling better than either of his previous books and it considerably strengthened Gerhardie's reputation as a vividly inspired, outlandish young man, 'The Darling of Mayfair' in Arnold Bennett's words, 'The Pet of the Intelligentsia'. 'I think', William mused, 'I am justly desired.'

His letters and diaries over the next two or three years record meetings with scores of celebrities: writers, artists, politicians, musicians, businessmen, and all the famous society hostesses. When Wharton extended another invitation to Hyères, he politely declined. London didn't seem so bad after all; in fact he now liked it more than any other place in the world. 'I am so happy and comfortable here in my flat with a population of nine million to choose from for companionship. I can't think why I ever went to live at Pont-du-Suve. But in retrospect even that nightmare of a place seems to bristle with qualities. Of course, I have a hankering after Morocco.'

Gerhardie was an excellent, if often unpunctual, guest. Arriving late for dinner with Arnold Bennett one evening he explained that 'to avoid being late, I had specially gone to set my watch by Selfridge's chronometer, which operation deflected my journey so that if indeed I was late it was in the good cause of being on time'.[2] Unaccustomed to alcohol, William was easily inebriated, his nervousness receded, and he—where others 'gave but stintingly of themselves'—threw himself into whatever the conversation with exhausting wholeheartedness, evolving into 'long labyrinthine thoughts' (Kingsmill described his English as 'brilliant but uncertain') before surprising everyone by coming suddenly back to the point. So much so that he returned home believing the host owed him yet another meal for his dedication to the evening. He was particularly scornful of Beverley Nichols's conversation; his 'coy asides' addressed to old ladies ('Flowers are the permanent things'), and depressed by the man's amazing capacity to please everybody.

Aldous Huxley, William thought, resembled an undertaker on stilts, so professionally serious as to be comic. Michael Arlen was like a Hollywood actor, whilst Somerset Maugham just looked wicked. Lytton Strachey, a great admirer of his novels, which he read aloud with Dora Carrington, told Gerhardie that he found *The Polyglots* particularly amusing 'in the Dickens-Dostoievsky-Douglas style'.[3] Many evenings Gerhardie spent at the theatre, the opera, at balls and dances. At Cecil Beaton's cocktail party he fell for a handsome débutante, Lady Bridget Poulett, but she did not return his love. He attended a 'table turning' party, where a girl sitting next to him fell suddenly screaming to the floor, having seen the ghost of her dead lover. Gerhardie added to the growing chaos by pretending that he felt someone touch his face as if with a bladder.

He dined with Lord Beaverbrook, Lord and Lady Weymouth, Lady Louis Mountbatten, and Lord Castlerosse, 'all lords, you see, except my common self'. He continued to associate with Beaverbrook, but at a weekend in the country with Lloyd George and Pola Negri, Gerhardie noticed with regret how his old patron had altered. 'There was a sort of absent gleam in his eye—not as if he were not there, but as if his guests were mere shadows—coupled with an extraordinary volubility. Beaverbrook now usurped more than the lion's, more than three lions' share of the conversation. . . . But there was an air of "What I say, goes" about his utterances which robbed them of their former charm.'[4] Later, at a weekend at Cherkley with Harriet Cohen, the outstanding event of the evening was when the Lord raised himself from his dining chair and 'began to declaim from a Book of the Old Testament. . . . He chanted the whole Book: it was an awesome and moving occasion.'[5]

Gerhardie, ever amorous, became passionately involved with an Italian countess, Yvonne Franchetti, and also with her younger sister. Yvonne, the daughter of an English mother and an aristocratic Italian father, 21 years old, exquisitely dressed, a great society success, was, according to Gerhardie, even more irresponsible than the impish nurse Terry with whom he had consorted at Oxford. He told her that he loved her so much that if she gave herself to him he would die, and then asked her to help him commit suicide. He also got on well with her cuckolded—and unfaithful—husband Luigino, one of whose own lovers had recently been pursued by *her* husband and shot before his very eyes. When Yvonne returned to Italy Gerhardie suffered terribly. She departed by train and he, attending a lunch beforehand, was driven swiftly to Victoria Station by Lady Louis Mountbatten wearing a straw hat and green velvet dress in a racy Hispano-Suiza; soon, his misery forgotten, he was having a love affair with her instead.

One evening a Rolls-Royce drew up outside Gerhardie's flat and a shabby-mackintoshed and grubby-trousered man stepped out. It was John Holms, in a borrowed motor, come to take Gerhardie on a drive round London while the immaculate chauffeur regarded his two passengers with faint distaste. Over the next few months Holms would ring Gerhardie up about once a week with a welcome dinner invitation: excellent food (one evening a ginger and salmon soufflé), plentiful wine, and always the impression that Holms was the most remarkable man in the room ('yet the other men in the room, listening to him, were hard put to it to decide in precisely what way he was remarkable').[6] Gerhardie soon realized that Holms had been unusually talkative when they met in France and that normally he was silent, 'all tentative suggestion, nuance, insinuation, himself almost tapering away into innuendo'.[7] He still had not written a line. Kingsmill asked whether he now intended to begin. 'Life is difficult', murmured Holms.[8]

Still vain about his appearance, Gerhardie presented a curious picture to many. Tall and fair with dark, pencilled eyebrows, he had lately adopted the Edwardian habit—also practised by T. S. Eliot—of powdering his face white. He thought himself immensely handsome. He was also proud of his aristocratic feet, and 'another outstandingly elegant feature of mine is a behind which is flat at the sides, like a horse'.[9] Considerably smartened since his first shabby appearance in Beaverbrook's office, Gerhardie had taken to wearing blue to further enhance his pallor. 'You always wear blue suits?' a friend asked him.

'Always.'
'You mean you never wear anything else?'
'Never.'
'How many blue suits have you got?'
'One.'

He wrote to tell Clara that he had ordered some new shirts of his own design, 'which, to say the least of it, look pretty b____y. They certainly attract attention—but of the wrong kind.' When out he was never without a hat and gloves, partly from convention but also because the gloves protected him from contact with unsavoury elements, for his fastidiousness did not lessen as he grew older. He was never without a clean handkerchief with which to wipe door handles before touching them, and though exquisitely polite and always ready to extend his hand in an introduction, he ensured it was the briefest contact. Even his own sister Dolly noticed that he grew agitated at the thought that she might have wiped her hands on his towel; and when Clara returned some clothes she had mended, she vigorously stressed that 'no *one has even seen or tried on, never even worn, your dressing gown*'. Even so, knowing what a 'fusspot' he was, she had '*washed it again* and with a special solution which has made the cloth lovely'. His pet hates, he told an interviewer, were dogs that fouled pavements and women with moulting fur coats that dropped hairs on his clothes if he sat with them. He once remarked that he put the lowest possible interpretation upon the word 'gentleman', as someone who cleans his nails, does not soil your books, is reasonably clean, has a tolerably good breath, and does not cough and splutter at you in the course of conversation, 'in a word, a being whose society can be enjoyed without physical disgust'.

Ethel Mannin's interest in Gerhardie was aroused when a friend of hers insisted that they would make a marvellous pair to show round New York together. She too had had a youthful success as a novelist, though her books were a good deal more popular than Gerhardie's. She greatly admired *Futility* but was annoyed by the author's patronizing attitude towards women. The night they eventually met, Mannin dressed in a silver and white gown with 'milk-white pellucid lillies'. But they found they had little in common, and regarded each other fixedly across the dinner table 'with the cold stare of curiosity rather than the warm light of interest'.[10] Mannin said that she thought that all women were natural-born masochists; Gerhardie retorted that one might as well say that all mice were masochists and all cats sadists. Mannin said perhaps they were, and thought to herself: 'You with your pale baby face and your stone-cold blue eyes, you're a sadist.'[11] Gerhardie circulated the port in the wrong direction. At the end of the evening the host, anxious to help things along, put them in a taxi together. Mannin denied feeling cold, but Gerhardie put his arm round her, nevertheless. He found her 'almost indecently silly', but her conversation over dinner had caught his interest. 'So you're a masochist?' he asked. 'Not particularly', she replied. Then they went up to his flat to see an advance copy of *Jazz and Jasper*, after which their respective accounts differ. According to Mannin, Gerhardie attempted to seduce her: 'We quarreled quite bitterly, and Gerhardi wound up by referring to himself as a man of genius and me as the meanest woman he had ever met.'[12] The only thing they seem to agree upon is that seduction did not, after all, take place.

Some years later Gerhardie commanded a chapter to himself in Mannin's memoirs as 'Another Study in Superiority Complex' (the first was Osbert Sitwell). Shortly after its publication they met at a party. 'Will you ever speak to me again?' she asked him. 'Only through my solicitor . . . to discuss damages', replied Gerhardie. 'Shall we fix it at—er—£3,000?'[13] Then he responded in *his* autobiography:

She accuses me in truth of cherishing unliterary designs on her during her brief visit to my flat. Miss Mannin was clad in a heavy overcoat. All I said indeed, with a grave old-world courtesy, was: 'Madame, I have a few minutes which it pleases me to place at your disposal. Pray divest yourself of your overcoat.' Miss Mannin, however, failed lamentably to rise to the occasion. I may say she behaved most extraordinarily—she refused. But she has had her punishment. The offer was not repeated.[14]

Mannin was only one of scores: Gerhardie's desire for conquests bordered on the obsessive. Yet his preoccupation with hygiene appears never to have curbed, though it may have modified the details of, his sexual appetite. Like the hero of *Jazz and Jasper*, he often reflected how little he was disturbed by most misfortunes, 'but that every woman whom he looked at twice did not immediately yield herself to him was something he found hard to bear, harder to forgive'. He dreamed of possessing all the comely women in the world 'in a sort of cumulative, consummative kiss'.[15] His ideal woman was, he declared, slender and blue-eyed with dark, cropped hair ('I often wonder why fair girls with blue eyes do not all dye their hair jet black. It is the obvious way to enhance their looks by fifty per cent').[16] She must also be a good swimmer and dancer, and drive him about in a large car smilingly; and, he might have added, be very, very young. He could scarcely meet an attractive woman without attempting to seduce her. If, at a dinner party, he was placed too far away to speak, he wrote on his place card: 'What is your telephone number?' and slid it across. 'We were always so afraid to go in a taxi with him', recalled one anonymous old lady who in the 1950s bumped into a friend of Gerhardie's in the tea-shop of the British Museum. She would have been even more alarmed had she known of his private fantasy of sex in a taxi, specifically between the Marble Arch and Paddington Station. 'The *crescendo* of ecstasy has to be timed and superintended according to the progress of the drive—streets have to be watched. The climax falls in with the moment when the taxi pulls up. A porter opens the door and staggers back, unspeakably shocked. X cries out cheerfully: "No, thank you, don't want a porter!"'

Gerhardie's sexual fantasies did not stop at taxis. His library contained, amongst other more lurid works, the writings of the Marquis de Sade and *A History of the Rod* by the Revd Wm. M. Cooper, describing flagellation practices from ancient times to the present (Chapter XLIII, 'On the Whipping of Young Ladies'). At Oxford he had described in great detail to John Rothenstein his preference for a girl to lie naked on her back with her legs right up towards her face, so that he might beat her thighs and buttocks. 'Are you making love a lot?' Yvonne de Franchetti wrote to ask him. 'How many girls have you beaten on the striped sofa of your sitting-room?' Whether Harriet Cohen was a willing participant in Gerhardie's desires or not, she found the experience unpalatable:

I'm sorry I cried last night—there is a black bruise this morning—sinister on such a place . . . that explains why. I know you didn't mean to hurt like that. All forgotten and forgiven.

Of course I know men have to do queer things when they are 'en rut' as French novelists keep on explaining—personally, I like *love*.

Yet another precarious female friendship was soon to be established. One day in 1928, Gerhardie was sitting on the top of a bus on his way to the Gargoyle Club. Close by sat a young woman, reading *Futility*. Looking up, she recognized the author from his portrait on the book jacket, but hesitated to approach until they both rose to get off at the same stop. Then she accosted him, showed him *Futility*, and revealed that by coincidence she too was on her way to the Gargoyle (Gerhardie was, she remembered, rather vague about whether he was actually a member). This was exactly the sort of contact that most enchanted him. Dorothy Cowan was young—though she could have been even younger —good-looking, and above all highly appreciative of his books. They dined together, met again, dined again, met once more, and so forth.

Dorothy, intelligent, well-read, and emancipated, was rather different from most of Gerhardie's women friends, and they spent many hours discussing the intricacies of literature. She invited him to listen to Bach, Liszt, and Chopin on her wobbly gramophone, and took him to meet Jacob Epstein at the Café Royal. He evangelically introduced her to the little-known Chekhov, and encouraged her to write herself. She found his conversation full of charm and intuitive perception, and he himself rather sensitively good-looking and dapper. But she also noticed that he was vain, insecure, and touchy about himself, and for this reason sometimes rather difficult to talk to. One day when she visited she remarked on the fact that he had put up her photograph. He, blushing, replied: 'I'm much fonder of you than you give me credit for.' 'You've only one love', she retorted. 'Yourself.'

Dorothy often spent the afternoon in his flat. Quite often on these occasions the doorbell would ring and a woman, or sometimes a girl, appear. Gerhardie and the caller would disappear into the bedroom for forty minutes or so, then he would show her out, whilst Dorothy sat there the while. Many of these were women Gerhardie accosted in restaurants or in the street. He often overtook girls in the park on their way home from work, or picked up women in tea-shops, which (to his amusement) shocked a friend who told him he ought to sleep with women in society, and offered to introduce him to some. But Gerhardie was well at ease with lower-class women, partly because their lack of sophistication, and in particular lack of the pretence of sophistication, appealed to him, but also because of the sense of security that liaisons completely outside his usual circle afforded him. One girl, from Woolworth's, received money from Gerhardie so that she could pretend to her husband she was working overtime. He was particularly angered, he claimed, by the fashion of rich society girls taking jobs for the fun of it and robbing others of employment.

His experience of love was generally an intense—often painful— infatuation that totally absorbed him ('I love women, but I do not like them. . . . I find most of them damned annoying'). As a subject it intrigued him: he was especially familiar with the love affairs of Goethe, Stendhal, and other writers he admired. Above all it was identified with the elusive and ungraspable: 'Only love, never actual, was foreshadow- ing something real to come through a long series of anticipations.'[17] Sex, on the other hand, was tangible and finite, and in order to produce 'a deeply satisfying flavour, must be nurtured in the dark recesses of our natures. It is through the keeping apart of the sexes that this desire brews and passes through all the difficult stages till, like old wine, it is there to be enjoyed.'[18] He thought Lawrence a brilliant novelist, but deplored his open attitude to sex, and whilst recommending *Lady Chatterley's Lover* to Edith Wharton warned of the 'over-done' erotic passages, 'so unattractively presented that it would make the fiercest voluptary feel chaste'.

Gerhardie always considered that his most sexually ecstatic moment had come unexpectedly and mysteriously at a dance when 'desire was overtaken by a surprising and almost simultaneous fulfilment'. He caught sight of a girl who so answered to his 'inmost dreams' that he was torn between longing and apprehension. She, however, had no such inhibitions. She spoke to him, danced with him, and led him into the garden where 'we, as if by some mutual signal, forgot everything, ourselves and our separateness'.[19] They never met again. The wicked Eleanora of his childhood fairy-tale created in him the most intense *imaginative* rapture, one that he searched in vain to recapture, and was partly the reason why he always encouraged literary contacts with young female admirers, urging them to send photographs so that in writing he might visualize them. 'I am delighted to hear some good-looking young women appreciate my book', he wrote to Clara. 'If they are *really* good-looking, and *really* young, I would not mind their paying me a visit when they come to London.' One such was Miss Schitt, very pleasant and attractive although her face 'looked as if she had lain three weeks in her coffin'.

The anecdotes about admiring and admired women run on and on: 'Salome Stubbs (Mrs)' wrote to say that she found her 'Maestro' 'wonderfully fascinating, your mouth especially attracts me, its delicate sensuality and the depth of sadness in your fine eyes! . . . Your slender fingers haunt me in my slumber, I awake to find my body hot remembering your dream caresses. . . . My thoughts of you are sins of the deepest dye, but I really can't help myself.' She enclosed a drawing of herself naked, and suggested a meeting: 'I beg you not to put this letter aside as written by a young and giddy girl. I am 28 years of age. . . . From One who worships from afar.'

Miss Catherine Haughley, a young journalist from Michigan, wrote 'exhilarating' and later rather intimate letters which she exhorted him to destroy, enclosing photographs which puzzled Gerhardie because in some she appeared stunningly seductive, while in others '*ganz ordinär*'. Likewise she sometimes alluded to her colossal fortune, at other times hinted at dire poverty ('but always an unfailing admiration for my works!'[20]). He was intrigued with the idea that she had apparently fallen in love with him as the regular 100 per cent English-officer type, and responded with titillating details of his love affair with Yvonne. He and Miss Haughley became engaged, until she eventually metamorphosed into Comfort of *Pending Heaven* and ran off with Max Fisher.

Gerhardie's seductions did not go unnoticed by the press. Beverley

Nichols, at that time a young journalist eager for a name, described the importance to the British public of a 'label': 'It seems that there are a certain number of niches in the contemporary temple of Fame, and that unless you fit into one of these niches you will never be recognised.'[21] The Sitwells, he pointed out, occupied the 'Chelsea de Luxe' niche. The publisher, Gollancz, reminded Curtis Brown that for publicity purposes reviewers liked personal details about the authors, 'particularly gossip' and 'any sort of social or personal item round which a story can be written'.[22] Gradually but inexorably Gerhardie's public image was shaping itself, an image that Beaverbrook's frantic publicity of 1925 had helped to mould: 'Polyglot, educated, cynical, indiscreet and erratic, Gerhardi typifies the age', wrote one American newspaper.[23] From this time on William Gerhardie was always more famous than his books.

Gerhardie, convinced by Beaverbrook that publicity was all-important, at first did nothing to discourage such attention. Throughout the late 1920s he was constantly in the news: 'Brilliant Novelist', 'Handsome Mr William Gerhardi'—such epithets were encouraged by his particularly youthful appearance and the fact that, by going late to Oxford, he was mistakenly identified with a younger generation of undergraduates and writers. The image was, for a time, a comparatively lucrative one: he received, for example, 30 guineas for an Epilogue to *The Technique of the Love Affair*, by 'A Gentlewoman', and an unspecified fee for promoting a new brand of cigarettes (Gerhardie did not smoke, but he thought the habit rather glamorous):

It is true: there is no other quite like it. 'WIX' ensures complete relaxation of the nerves and projects your mind into a state of well-being unknown since the Fall of Man. All men, even more all women, should smoke 'Wix'.[24]

The years 1927–9 were his most prolific for journalistic output. A minority were serious articles—'Turning Over New Leaves', on pessimism and literature,[25] 'The Elders, Ourselves and Our Critics',[26]—or semi-serious: 'National Charm',[27] 'The Mind of the Russian'.[28] The great majority were flippant and often highly humorous: 'What Women Have Taught Me',[29] 'Snobs'[30]—but even these were too ironic, insufficiently anecdotal, to catch on in the popular press. 'Why I Am Not a Best-Seller'[31] begins:

For no reason at all. But the question was posed and I must answer it. I blame neither the Church, nor the State, nor the Law.

His best journalism was often (as editors complained) too 'philo-sophical', his humour too 'subtle' and elusive for the mass market. His worst was dull and sententious.

Though Gerhardie viewed these small writings as money to buy time for larger works, as something of an outsider (neither Russian nor English, 'fish nor flesh') he none the less took almost perverse delight in living up to the role that had been pushed upon him—not-quite English eccentric egocentric. Gerhardie was gently, mockingly iconoclastic. Conceit was un-English: with his parents' early scorn for his abilities uncomfortably present at the back of his mind he made constant, slightly mocking, reference to his own brilliance. Politeness was essential to the English: Gerhardie, exquisitely polite, none the less imagined that it might be helpful if hosts would charmingly articulate their private views when making introductions:

> 'Mr Harold Smith, a fine fellow but a rotten friend.'
> 'Mr Jacob, shady.'
> 'Mrs Glass, unpleasant.'
> 'Mr Shepherd, financier, and suspected of double-dealing.'[32]

Snobbery was essentially English, the curse of Fleet Street in particular: he caused considerable confusion at a smart soirée by encouraging the maids to take an active interest in the conversation, and pointed out how distinctly original it would be if butlers could be trained to silently respond with a 'sad, witty, flat, stupid, daring, weighty, moribund or humorous' expression. He applauded the way 'Little boys when they are first old enough to be taught to take off their hats in greeting often take them off continuously and promiscuously to dustmen and family friends. That's the right attitude and they shouldn't be *laughed* out of it.' He was more than pleased when the working-class Ramsay MacDonald was elected Prime Minister, and his scepticism about the notion of a 'gentleman' is typical: 'The original gentleness implicit in a gentleman consisted in a faculty to delegate the necessary churlishness incumbent in his privileges to others, and for the rest expressing himself in genial and endearing amiability. A gentleman was gentle, was expected to be gentle, because he could afford it.'[33]

A judge who sends a criminal to the gallows can do so without raising his voice. A graceful movement of the hand, the clerk removes a piece of black cloth from his lordship's wig, and the implication that the sordid business has been carried as far as gentleness can carry it is perfectly understood: the rest is for a specialist in murder—not quite a gentleman.

He found the English endearing, reasonable, humorous, but quite unnecessarily prudish: 'I get very tired indeed of hearing my novels described as "immoral", all because I let my characters have a good time with each other and emerge none the worse for it in the end.'[34] And as supposed animal-lovers the English were grossly hypocritical. Dogs they pampered silly while foxes and deer (so much cleaner and less irksome) had their insides torn out. They eulogized over the island's bird life—robins, thrushes, woodpeckers, and herons, but not it seemed pheasants, partridges, and grouse. Hunting he abhorred because of the brutality, but also through 'a real reluctance to risk my neck; for I cannot forget that I have a head at the end of it. It is a different matter for the hunting type of man, whose head, by the look of it, is merely a projection of the neck.' After a heated discussion with an English friend on the subject of bullfighting, he jotted scornfully in his notebooks:

James thought that bull-fighting was cruel to the horse. Not a word about the bull. Because there was just a chance of the bull doing in the man it was not cruelty! As though the bull had signed on a contract, entered on an agreement.

That so many of Gerhardie's articles concerned women was largely a sign of the times. In 1927 women under the age of 30 were at last granted the vote; they were earning money as never before, and Fleet Street was not slow to tap this rapidly expanding market. Beverley Nichols (he of the razing women's colleges to the ground) pointed out that almost all popular journalism during the 1920s seemed to revolve around the question what women might and might not do. Should women bant? Should women sunbathe? Should women put perfume on their Pekinese? Should women make up in public? Should women exist? 'Rivers of ink and mountains of newsprint have vanished in the service of these wan discussions.'[35] Most of the journalists were, of course, men.

Gerhardie could be as offensively outspoken as any of them. 'Wives Who Love Too Much' is a particularly unpleasant example:

A wife who fondly believes that she is 'everything' to her husband cannot realise what a mug he must be to be content with so little. On the other hand, her presumption must be colossal if she imagines that she alone incorporates for him all that is worth while in the rich and varied realm of the 'Eternal Feminine'. Such egotism carries its own penalty. For the vanity of women who presume that they are all-sufficient to their husbands tires men, and they neglect their wives for other women, thereby hitting their vanity; the punishment, it will be observed, fitting the crime.[36]

My Papa and Mama at Nice

1. Charles and Clara Gerhardi

2. Daisy and William in the ballroom of the St Petersburg house

3. William with Clara, at the time of writing *The Polyglots*

4. Leonya Misernuik with Tamara in the St Petersburg ballroom

5. Victor Gerhardi

6. Rosie and Tamara

7. William with his dictaphone working on *Pending Heaven*, 1929

8. Patsy Rosenstiehl

9. Frances Champion with her mother and father

10. William with Margaret Penn and
Oliver Stonor in Devon, summer 1939

11. Vera Boys (Dinah in *Of Mortal Love*)

And so on. Such 'candour' was, he argued, in keeping with his general iconoclasm, his studied sensationalism. In this case it is, of course, a very shallow sensationalism. On the subject of class, bloodsports, or morality his witty acerbity is employed in a genuine attempt to shock or shame, to beat against a treasured bastion of English life so loudly and humorously that he could scarcely be ignored. On the subject of women he was simply reinforcing commonly held prejudices. The only novelty was his ironic unselfconscious insistence, his language not his beliefs. He regularly trotted out the old clichés—women were vain, silly, empty-headed, scheming, and so forth, which sentiments also sadly served to belittle parts of an otherwise exceptionally fine autobiography.

None the less, Gerhardie's published views on women deserve more than to be dismissed as simple bigotry of a period, for they are the result of a complicated personal prejudice: his utterances clearly waver between affectation and phobia. And in the context of the age as a whole he comes out comparatively well—he recognizes the tyrannies of marriage, the unfair insistence upon chastity, seeing women as 'individuals at a disadvantage resorting to subterfuge and ingenuities to gain their ends'. 'Time is against women. And prestige is against women. And this being so, women are against women. Which all contributes to the advantage of man.'[37] Such conciliatory sentiments appear not only in his public, but sometimes also in his private work, and even though lightly voiced they suggest a genuine, if vague, sympathy with women's lot. There is a sense of a man with a deeply rooted sense of unease, who cannot quite conceal his perceptive mind.

In another example Gerhardie envisaged a time 'when the indecent custom of differentiating between married and unmarried women by the use of such labels as "Mrs" or "Miss" will fall into disuse, thereby lifting an undeserved stigma from spinsterhood'. Unfortunately his analysis from then on is cleverly phrased rather than intelligently developed: 'the difference in the attitude of men and women towards matrimony, however out-of-date and ridiculous, remains to this day a difference of prestige—desired by women and disdained by men.'[38] In 'Let Women Rule the World', he goes on to suggest that increased financial, political, and moral power for women will inevitably lead to intellectual independence and, ultimately, quite likely a better world. It is a solution he would probably (unlike most of his contemporaries) genuinely have appreciated. But there is a sense that such titles are used to titillate other men by suggesting that this famous author has betrayed his sex, and the tone, though mocking men's arrogance, is crudely patronizing (and moreover prurient) of women's solution—he proposes a modern-day Lysistrata:

Now, I say, let women have a chance to show what they can do. . . . I should like to see them, sobered by the spectacle of man's mistaken philosophy, apply themselves forthwith to reducing drastically the population of the world. It is a noble end, and man will claim that he has substantially contributed towards it by waging war whenever the number of humanity became uncomfortably large.[39]

Gerhardie often received letters from women readers—housewives, shop assistants, secretaries—letters he was happy to read and in fact went out of his way to encourage. These writers, feeling their way to adequate expression of their interests, sometimes display a clumsy style and a crude sentimentality. But what is basically a lack of education Gerhardie was all too ready to dismiss as a lack of intelligence—a failing that is far less frequent in these communications than his scorn would lead one to believe. Dorothy Cowan, who suffered from no such disadvantages, conjures a shrewd picture of Gerhardie's public image at that time, in a letter written in response to one of his articles:

You make silly women long for your 'blood'; whilst the mere sprinkling of educated women mentioned in your article, dismiss you as a youthful egoist whose attitude to our sex is as much a pose as it is an intellectual ??? theory. They cease to take you seriously when they discover you suffer from a bias which does not let you remember that the emancipation (so-called) of women is but a recent event. . . . My dear, do stop this preening yourself as the 'pet of the intelligentsia', this making a virtue out of your failure to write a best-seller; this milk and water aestheticism which makes you like to imagine yourself some superior being waiting for inspiration to give to the world a highly original work. A capacity for indefatigable work has always been a distinguishing characteristic of genius. Do conserve your energy for work befitting an artist and an intellectual; and do stop dribbling it away on pot-boiler articles which give the vulgar press armaments to prolong and intensify this battle of the sexes which is as degrading as battles between nations.

Robert Bruce Lockhart, who since leaving Russia had worked as a journalist and now moved in Beaverbrook's circle, also considered that Gerhardie's involvement with the press was harming him, and noted in his diary: 'Saw Humbert Wolfe. . . . He says Gerhardie is being ruined by Beaverbrook or rather is killing himself.' Four years later, however, Gerhardie advised Lockhart to leave Fleet Street and write books. 'The press, you know, that leaves a smell.'[40] And indeed, after a meeting with Beaverbrook in 1929, he wrote to Clara that though 'I am very fond of old B,' his offer to give William all the journalism he wanted '—meaning well of course', was misplaced; it was a kind suggestion that actually meant 'dancing attendance on him, like Castlerosse, eating out of his hand and writing on his own lines at lower prices than Curtis Brown gets even out of Beaverbrook's editors! Frequent journalism', he continued, 'lowers the prestige (and the prices) of a novelist and should only be indulged in from time to time—at a high price and conspicuously advertised.'

Clara meanwhile had had her usual dose of troubles. Rosie, ill, distressed, and fading, had written to her mother in France with heart-rending accounts of her troubles in Russia since Leonya's release from prison. Immediately, Clara made up her mind to visit her daughter—and though Finland and Victor were in some ways no closer to Rosie than France, she hoped, if only by virtue of her relentless courage, at least to secure her daughter a more comfortable situation. She hastily left the pension, returned to England, picking up on the way Charles's urn which was at last interred in the Wadsworth family grave in Bacup, and then hurried on to Finland to stay with her recalcitrant son in his comfortable house. Victor, with status in the small English colony and plenty of Russian servants of 'the old school' who had fled with the Revolution, reminded Clara of the past. 'Somehow I begin to think that old life out there never really existed', she mused. At a visit to the theatre Clara met up with old friends from pre-Revolution days. Then, leaning forward in her seat, she gave a shriek: the woman in front was wearing the very earings that Charles had had made for her, and which she had been obliged to leave behind in Russia.

But the pleasant atmosphere could not and did not last. Clara soon noticed a lack of the home spirit and camaraderie that she so enjoyed when staying with Dolly or William. Finland after a while seemed a dull country, and Victor preoccupied with kroner, dollars, and power, happy only with his horses. 'Poor V.,' sighed his mother, 'he is much to be pitied I suppose he cannot help himself but he is the greatest kill-joy I ever came across.' In spite of all his business success Victor appeared to her to derive little happiness from life. Seemingly conscious of his own lack of fulfilment, he indulged his habit of running down members of the family, and now berated his mother for past injustices. 'I think I have never met anyone so bitter and biting as him', observed Clara in great distress to William, who tried to calm her by pointing out that it was characteristic of Victor always to blame others for his failure to get the best out of life. Added to which the combination of Clara and Victor was always volatile: Victor had something of his father's temper, Clara her own spirit, and both were fearfully stubborn. One morning Victor was reading his newspaper at the breakfast table, whilst Clara insistently tried to talk to him.

VICTOR (*sternly*): I don't like conversation at breakfast.
CLARA (*doggedly*): Too bad. I do.

To add to Clara's troubles, she was having the usual difficulty obtaining permission to enter Russia, and in December Victor told his brother, not without some satisfaction, 'You will doubtless be surprised to hear that your friends the bolchiviks have forbidden your principal parent entry into their paradise.' Undaunted, Clara pressed on, and was at length granted a thirty-day permit for Leningrad. In February she crossed the frontier and was 'practically undressed' by suspicious officials, thoroughly examined, and some of her belongings—a subversive toothbrush and a Trotskyist book about flowers—withheld. The Misernuiks came to meet her at the Finland Station. Six years had passed since they had last met. Despite the freezing February weather Rosie, who had spent the previous seven weeks in hospital, was barely clad, in a threadbare gown; Tamara had on a thin cotton frock and two pairs of thin cotton stockings, worn over each other to hide the holes; her shoes were without soles and her toes were sticking out. Leonya wore an old coat of his father's, far too small, a cotton waistcoat and trousers, and an old black sweater. 'God knows', wrote Clara after distributing a large bundle of clothes, 'whether there is another little group of so thoroughly worn out and ailing mortals.'

The family was fortunate enough to occupy three rooms with a shared kitchen and bathroom. Clara admitted that the house was warm, but found the food terrible: 'water called tea, with milk and bread without butter' for breakfast; then between 4 and 5 p.m. a horrible mockery of a soup and either the beef from it or some black macaronis; and at 9 p.m. weak tea with dry bread. Everyone in Russia seemed demoralized: there was no woollen material to be obtained, no eggs, no butter, though Clara had arranged for the old Nanny Liebe, now a midwife in Reval, to send the occasional furtive supply of butter to Rosie in times of crisis. There was no flour, grain, or salt in the villages so that the peasants flocked to the towns 'looking hungry and defiant'. The black bread ration of ½ lb. per person had to be queued for, often as long as three hours. 'Petrograd is a dead city compared with former days and the people look dirty and destitute and mostly ragged,' said Clara. 'There is one thing I can honestly proclaim which is that the worst in England is better than the best in Russia.'

Yet Rosie was fatalistically cheerful, preoccupied with her baby Galina, and Leonya ('such a dear good fellow') now employed in the Agricultural Museum. Rosie, as far as was possible, followed William's career with the greatest interest and pride, and she questioned Clara closely about him and asked for a photograph. They read aloud *Jazz and Jasper*: 'then we come to some beautiful part full of deep and beautiful meaning and we stop to wonder and ponder over it.' Clara, nostalgic for her old life, one day took a walk along Vibourg Quay. The surroundings had all changed, with vistas of space where many familiar buildings had once been. But the old house was still standing.

My mother approached it. It had not, for many years, received its annual coat of paint which, in my childhood, had made it look so gay as we returned to it every autumn after summer at the seaside. Yet it looked fairly respectable. It had been turned into a museum and some public offices, and there was a brass plate on its walls. My mother hesitated. Then she caught sight of her curtains—the ballroom curtains. A heavy feeling overcame her, and she hurried away.[41]

When her visa expired Clara, determined to help Rosie escape from Russia, returned to Finland, and to 'a most awful burst up' with Victor who refused to show any sympathy for his sister's condition, insisted her illness was sham, and began again to harangue Clara for past injustices. 'Victor is perfectly inhuman', she wrote to William. 'All these months Victor has torn nearly every member of the family limb from limb beginning with poor Papa.' Clara found herself 'chastised in public for my husband and children'. 'It is not that I do not love him, I do. But I cannot understand him, he is such a stranger and does not want to seem to love me.' William, who always had the deepest sympathy for Rosie, wrote to Victor:

I am quite sure there has never been anything the matter with Rosie and that she has cajoled the hospital to conspire with her into maintaining the bluff of her illness merely to annoy her brother in Helsingfors so as to provide him with an excuse for venting his bitterness against the world, Grandpapa, Aunt Mary and Papa having all passed beyond the reach of criticism and there being only Rosie, Lenja and Edmond left on the list. I think that this pent-up steam in you, if you did not dissipate it on your less fortunate relations, would run a turbine engine and propel a fair-sized ship across the seas.... And I suggest to you that it might be well to give Rosie and Lenja a rest and take up Edmond again for a bit, or better still Lloyd George or President Coolidge or the Perpetual Secretary of the Royal Geographical Society.

Conditions with Victor deteriorated to such an extent that Clara removed to a pension where she continued her struggle alone. But the problems seemed insurmountable. If Rosie came to England how would they meet the medical bills for her and her handicapped baby? And if she was ill, how could she work and support herself? Over the past years she had suffered all kinds of as yet undiagnosed illness, with fainting fits, heart trouble, and fatigue, and had entered an excellent Military Hospital because the doctors were particularly interested in her case. Leonya spoke only Russian and a little French and had no chance of earning a living in England. Even were he to obtain a permit the Russian authorities might pounce on his parents after he had left. To crown it all, she found half the inhabitants of her pension fit for the circus, the other half for the lunatic asylum. William acknowledged the difficulties but urged that they none the less continue to work hard to get a permit for Rosie. At last, in August, a temporary exit visa was granted. Rosie, Tamara, and Galina crossed the border into Finland.

Rosie went at once to a Finnish clinic, and Galina to a children's hospital where Clara visited them daily. William wrote urging them to defect and come to England, whence he would gladly pay their travelling expenses. 'Tamara's schooling is a small thing compared with the chances which Western Europe offers against those of Russia.' It was an impossible dream: 'I simply have not the strength to risk starting life afresh and counting on my own capacity for working', wrote Rosie, whose medical treatment, free in Russia, was already costing the family a fortune. And, were she to defect, Leonya would be liable for all manner of reprisals. But she decided it was best to let Tamara go. Rosie and Galina returned to Leningrad. Tamara and her grandmother sailed to England. 'God preserve us from any Bolshevism', said Clara. 'And I say this piously after what I saw in that unhappy land which is devastated by this new religion, for to the Soviets, *this is their religion.*'

Hugh Kingsmill had also been having a difficult time abroad, exchanging acrimonious letters with his father and attempting to support himself by writing. In 1928 his biography of Matthew Arnold was generously reviewed by Gerhardie, who found it 'extremely good but a little hard as if written with a carving knife'. He was not the only critic to observe Kingsmill's curious malevolence towards his subject. When he later mentioned this Kingsmill replied, 'After all, you must not forget I have had a hard year'.

From mid-1929, after Kingsmill's return from the Continent (where incidentally he had fallen out with John Holms), he and Gerhardie met and corresponded quite regularly, 'refreshed by intermittent short-termed quarrels'.[42] As before, Kingsmill could be very trying. He was easily offended, so that in conversation with him one had to avoid touching on so many aversions of his that few subjects remained for discussion. When anyone got annoyed with him, or showed anything short of good nature, he simply grabbed his hat and was off, muttering, 'You are full of resentment.' He was rather stingy, and imagined that everybody but himself had money. Confronted one evening in London by a ragged woman with a sickly babe in arms Kingsmill stepped quickly aside and indicated Gerhardie: 'Here's a rich man for you—he'll unfork.' And his personal habits were as tiresome as his niggardliness. 'He generally, rather peremptorily and always unilaterally, appointed the time of our meeting, usually in ambiguous places. You would turn up at the Tower of London when he meant under the tower of the Alliance Perpetual Building Society in Baker Street; or at the entrance into Regent's Park, which has several entrances.'[43]

But in spite of their many differences, this was to Gerhardie un-questionably a valuable friendship. The selfishness of friends who are yet affectionate is an enduring theme in his works. Kingsmill later appeared in several of his novels as the portly Max Fisher, a man who 'though he never drank, exuded a constant exhilaration distilled by his unaided high spirits. The pressure from within was so great and the jet of wit so high and powerful that one understood why Max Fisher needed no recourse to alcohol, and one rather feared to think what might happen to him if he did have recourse to it.'[44] Kingsmill-the-sober did not, however, share Gerhardie's taste for high society. 'I really think you ought to live out of London a bit, and not waste your time on Ethel Mannin and all that sort of rot', he told his friend. 'But my good advice only annoys you, damn you.' He himself had dined with Beaverbrook only once—'and once too often, from what I infer', said Gerhardie.

Undoubtedly Kingsmill was beneficial to Gerhardie's state of mind. Unfortunately he exerted a questionable influence upon Gerhardie's work. He was well read and well informed, but he had a number of debilitating prejudices and suffered as a fundamentally conservative character from 'a failure to conform with the spirit of the age'.[45] Anthony Powell thought him a brilliant talker but considered that he was in revolt against Victorianism, yet remained a Victorian himself in the complacency of his judgements. He was exceptionally familiar with Shakespeare, Johnson, Wordsworth, Tennyson, Dickens, and a few more whom he knew almost by heart, but turned a scornful blind eye to many others and, especially, though he admired Gerhardie greatly, pooh-poohed the Modernists. His anthology of English literature, *High Hill of the Muses*, is an unremarkable compilation, except that the final section omits Lawrence, Joyce, and Eliot because he considered their work 'largely spurious and enjoying a transitory reputation by their oddity rather than residue of merit, and having no root's in man's immortal estate'.[46] He regarded all writers as strictly subjective and would hardly listen to a discussion of Hamlet that did not accept him as an exact projection of Shakespeare at that time. It was by applying his literary conservatism to Gerhardie's work that he consistently encouraged all that was worst in it, and ignored or discouraged Gerhardie's really original contributions to literature.

In principle, both Kingsmill and Gerhardie, like Nabokov, rejected the social, political, and moral emphases of literature and subscribed to the view that art should rather concern itself with the lure of what Gerhardie termed 'the ineffable'. In practice, Kingsmill's mystical sense was very much stronger than Gerhardie's, more unquestioning, and often highly sentimental. Where Kingsmill presupposes the existence of a world beyond our own, and concerns himself with its evocation, Gerhardie probes man's imagination and perception of such a world. Kingsmill's attitude to literature resembled his attitude to women: he was attracted to evocative beauty and romance, but paid little heed to the larger context, or to the intellect within the sentiment. His criticisms of Gerhardie's work often consisted of a list of numbers—lines selected out of context that had appealed to him for their emotional effect, their pathos, or lyricism. He rarely considered any given novel as a whole, or the extent to which it was an original contribution to contemporary literature—a serious impediment to appreciating the work of a writer who stressed the importance of cumulative effect, the 'tiny trigger-movement releasing enormous forces'. Alec Waugh, who wondered why Gerhardie had been so impressed by *WJ*, speculated as to whether as a writer Kingsmill had 'the complementary defects of his qualities as a conversationalist so that he visualized books in terms of *mots* and repartees; writing in terms of sentences and paragraphs instead of chapters building to a final chapter? Did he express himself so completely in conversation that only a pallid residue was left to him at his desk?'[47]

Kingsmill's work has attracted a loyal body of admirers, of whom Gerhardie himself was the keenest. None the less, he was greatly Gerhardie's inferior. Anthony Powell considered that although his journalism was composed with care his books failed to do justice to him as wit or critic. Gerhardie was conscious of the fact that many thought his own literary enthusiasm for Kingsmill's work was biased by friendship, whereas the truth of the matter, he claimed, was that 'my literary enthusiasm for him has inveigled me into a precarious friendship'. To some extent, however, there were emotional reasons for Gerhardie's support. Kingsmill was also a great devotee of Gerhardie. When, in 1941, Gerhardie wrote: 'I find it impossible (except in the cases of people I love) to be entirely unaffected by adverse judgement of my books in my benevolence towards theirs',[48] not only was he considerably understating (he could be vitriolic), but the inverse was also true: he praised those who praised him. As Gerhardie grew increasingly sensitive to criticism, his own critical judgements grew increasingly biased.

There was no intrinsic reason why such aloofness should have harmed Gerhardie, yet 1928–9 was a particularly crucial period for his work. After the originality and quality of his two Russian novels he had, with *Jazz and Jasper*, significantly but not altogether successfully altered course. At exactly the moment when he could most have benefited from serious literary exchange with his distinguished Modernist contemporaries, he turned towards the mutual praise of Kingsmill and his circle. Gerhardie disliked competition. In Kingsmill he found a companion whom he could believe was a potential genius, yet who was far less successful than himself. This literary isolation contributed not only to the impoverishment of his work but (unjustly) to his eventual critical neglect.

William had spoken very warmly of Kingsmill to Dorothy Cowan, and lent her *The Dawn's Delay*. She wrote to tell Gerhardie how much the book had impressed her, and asked him to pass on her note to Kingsmill. Dorothy and Kingsmill met. And fell in love. Gerhardie cursed Kingsmill for absconding with a *second* woman. For weeks on end his reproaches veered wildly between sulky petulence and vicious tirade. When Dorothy wrote to thank Gerhardie for having brought her into contact with Kingsmill, he replied enclosing the following invoice:

> 1 Hugh (Kingsmill) Lunn,
> complete with boots,
> deliverable at domicile
> P.O.D.
> Discount on Cash

'My pleasantry was not received in the spirit in which it was sent, and was judged to be in bad taste even by Kingsmill who, on his own, would have roared with laughter but, in circumstances of romance, echoed his girlfriend's censure.'[49] Dorothy now found herself caught in the middle of a vindictive tangle of emotions; Kingsmill, also jealous and possessive, tried to forbid her to see Gerhardie. Relations between the three now varied, sometimes strained and sometimes outrightly vindictive: Dorothy thought Gerhardie's rages like the uncontrolled tantrums of a child; 'semi-mad', his face contorted, he would literally spit with fury, and yet physically he was completely non-violent—'I think he would have allowed himself to be kicked to death in a fight'. To add to it all, Kingsmill was also professionally jealous of Dorothy. When she had finished her first novel she asked him to look at it. For two months he said nothing. When finally she mentioned it he simply remarked, 'I left it on the underground'.

As the year wore on Gerhardie became increasingly obsessed with the effect of *Pending Heaven* upon his future: 'Never have I had greater hopes', he wrote to Clara. 'My whole future depends on it.' As each chapter was finished he sent them to Kingsmill who, failing to perceive that they were inferior to *Futility* and *The Polyglots*, was almost invariably enthusiastic, and whose influence upon the book is evident. Gerhardie had also entered the novel for a fiction competition sponsored by Jonathan Cape which carried, in addition to the promise of great publicity, a first prize of £1,000 advance and a further discretionary Special Award for any outstanding runner-up. Of six hundred novels submitted anonymously, the judges, Sheila Kaye-Smith, Frank Swinnerton, and Hugh Walpole, had chosen *Pending Heaven* as one of six finalists. And as soon as the novel was off his hands he took up a publisher's suggestion to write an autobiography, having first made sure of favourable terms.

Then Gerhardie received an invitation to lecture in America. In recent years lecture tours of the United States had become something of a vogue. Beverley Nichols, Rebecca West, John Cowper Powys, and (as one American lady put it) 'Mr Wedgwood (of china fame)' had all been successfully received, though Bertrand Russell had been boycotted because of his controversial book *Marriage and Morals*. Gerhardie had long regretted that he was not better known across the Atlantic—Curtis Brown described his following as 'eclectic' and concentrated in New York, Boston, and Philadelphia.

The tour would be beneficial in every way, especially since the invitation had come from Lee Keedick, a well-established tour manager. Keedick advised Gerhardie to wait until after publication of *Pending Heaven*. Gerhardie, rather unreasonably, argued for January 1930 until Keedick reluctantly deferred, agreeing to pay his fare and expenses and to split the profits. 'I shall soon, I think, be rich', Gerhardie wrote to Clara, and began again to look to the future: this time he envisaged not only a large London mansion but a native house in Biskra, and 'a small harem'. He wrote to the Home Office to enquire if, by changing to the Mohammedan religion and marrying native Algerian women according to native law, he would be entitled to bring into England 'my four wives (and if not all the four, one at a time)'. Also whether he would be subject to local divorce laws or to English ones. When I am rich I think I will become a Mahometan', he wrote to Clara, 'and have several wives, who won't bother me as they will have little to say—and you will be the head of the house that way and won't need to fear anybody interfering with your authority in the house. Do you like the idea?' Clara would remain in London, with Rosie occupying the top floor of the house. Leonya would run the Biskra estate, 'look after the Arabs, superintend the building of outhouses, garden etc.'[50] William would spend the winter in Africa, bringing with him Dolly, Lot, Harry and Nora, Daisy, Jean, and Jean-Jacques in a perpetual family musical chairs.

In the meantime, anxious to avoid the English winter, he was arranging an Algerian holiday before the start of the lecture tour. He had already contacted his Arab guide and dispatched postcards to his friends: 'Mr Gerhardi, owing to cessation of earning power, has given up his flat at 5 Paddington Street, W.1. for good and, like old Tolstoy, has taken to the road.'[51] Though still impoverished he calculated that the total cost would not exceed his expenses in England, and planned it to coincide with surrender of the lease on his present flat. On 3 October he moved from Paddington Street to the Strand Palace Hotel, not smart but 'at any rate very clean and efficiently run on modern lines and the rooms are fitted up in a bright thoroughly up to date manner'. The 'extraordinarily loyal and competent and honest' Miss Rosenstiehl helped with the removal and arranged storage of his belongings. But on the day he was to set off for his African retreat Gerhardie had a toothache and so postponed his departure until the morrow. The same day he received a letter from Valentine Castlerosse, who was languishing in a Baden Baden sanatorium:

6th September 1929

Dear Gerhardi

I am going to arrange your life—You are going to be the great writer of the world, the ½ world and the double world.

You are going to India—

You are going to be employed by the most beautiful, lovely and extraordinarily intelligent Princess—A reigning Princess—A widow—A wow!

You will fall in love with her—You will be happy. You will be inspired—Your genius will blossom—Her name is Indira! that is her first name.

I have arranged that you shall have a post in her state—You will even be paid—

You must fly with her to India on the 26th from Paris in the meanwhile you must come to Paris—to the Ritz Hotel and report to me—All your expenses will be paid. All your troubles are over—Dawn is breaking!

I arrive Paris next Sunday night—be there on Monday.

This isn't a dream—it's true—It means love laughter and just Heaven—
But it is a secret.

What are you expected to do? Why—just to give expression to what is in you and here is a lovely, beautiful, adorable, supple, clever woman to be your patron.

The Arabian nights are over—The Indian nights are starting.

THIS IS SERIOUS.

as ever
Castlerosse

P.S. I have told HER that Wells and Shaw say that you are a genius.

P.S. Read Haggard's SHE and then you will know something of what's coming.

Gerhardie responded with alacrity. 'The stuffing is out of European courts nowadays and there's not a writer in our days who would seek his fortune at any of the few remaining royal palaces. But the splendour of India is unrivalled', he wrote to Clara, imagining 'hosts of servants and slaves!' It was a project that was bound to appeal, since it promised to fête him as much as an individual personality as it did as a writer: 'You know, I always had a presentiment that something like that would happen to me. Of course, apart from anything else, the publicity of it afterwards will be invaluable. Byron's reputation was largely the result of such romantic travel', and he envisaged the Maharani bestowing upon him a house or palace to which Clara and all the family would be invited, as well as Kingsmill and other friends, establishing 'a really intellectual court'.

He immediately arranged with Curtis Brown to write a series of articles on India, and passed the next few days spending the money that

he had borrowed for the Algerian trip 'on rigging myself up to the Ritz
Hotel standard—in order to produce a tolerable impression on her
Highness!' This included a fashionable mauve hat, and some safari
clothes. Daisy wrote at once urging her brother to be sure to buy plenty
of Buddhas while he was there. Clara advised him to rest, and to use a
quarter-pound of senna pods infused in water for his stomach. 'Do not
get carried away by the feminine beauties that will surround you', she
warned, nor go into any 'lonely and dangerous places. Run no risks you
are too precious to me.' And she added: '*Your brain* is hyper sensitive and
will not stand trifling with like an ordinary one.'

Gerhardie missed his 11.20 train from Victoria. With time to kill, he
and Miss Rosenstiehl took a leisurely walk through St James's Park and
procured a map of India at the Indian State Railways office in the
Haymarket. Then they strolled to Trafalgar Square and spread the
map out over a lion, before Gerhardie departed for India and Miss
Rosenstiehl returned home to Dulwich.

13

INDIA AND AMERICA
October 1929–March 1930

Attention, a strange land. Sexual excitement invariably roused by every new city, leading me forward to explore it.[1]

Douglas Fairbanks, Mary Pickford, William Gerhardie, and the Maharani of Cooch Behar dined together in Paris. Castlerosse introduced William to the Princess: 'Well, here he is! What do you think of him?' ('She told me she couldn't be more interested.') And 'What do you think of *her*?' 'I told her I couldn't be more charmed . . . and with such complimentary feelings we are starting on Saturday.'

Cooch Behar, Gerhardie now learned, was a small but ancient Indian state at the Himalayan foothills. In the nineteenth century the Maharani's father, a distant relative to the then-reigning maharajah deposed for misrule, had been plucked, illiterate, at the age of 12 from a small jungle village, to govern Baroda, one of the largest states of princely India. He became one of the most enlightened rulers in Indian history, and an associate of Gandhi. He brought his daughter up to be cultivated, a fine linguist, and (she claimed) the first Indian princess to graduate from a college. In certain respects, however, he was still a traditional Hindu: at 18 the Princess was betrothed to an elderly, rather conservative maharajah of equal rank. She found the man a bore. The terribly sophisticated younger brother of the Maharaja of Cooch Behar, with a reputation for wild and unorthodox behaviour, was a much more interesting prospect. In defiance of family and tradition, she married him instead. Three weeks later he succeeded as ruler of Cooch Behar, and nine years after that he died of drink. His young widow stepped in as Regent.

Gerhardie was lodged at the Hotel Chambord, 'not unpleasantly decorated (to harmonise with the taste of those used to dilapidated furniture in ancient castles and old ruins with moats)'. But the Maharani was a socialite even more indefatigable than Beaverbrook, with an insatiable taste for 'dancings' (five or six a night), and sometimes so blotto that friends had to hold her up. Increasingly bored and exhausted, Gerhardie followed in her wake: 'We've had a perfectly maddening time—going to bed at 6 and 7, rushed from place to place . . . I am quite ill with champagne fumes', he wrote to Clara. 'How I *detest* nightclubs. I am both spiritually and physically constipated and have a sickly feeling in both regions.' In the space of a few days they lunched, dined, and partied with Michael Arlen, Edith Wharton, André Maurois, Rudolph Valentino, and all the 'smart young set' of Paris. He found the Hollywood crowd a 'poor lot': Mary Pickford told long and very boring stories and Rudolph Valentino was a dreadful snob. At the weekend the Maharani flew to England to spend yet more money at Harrods, and add to the several hundred pairs of shoes she already possessed. She asked Gerhardie if he had a message for her lover Lord Molleneux. 'Yes,' he replied. 'Mutual dislike.'

Gerhardie meanwhile found himself in the familiar position of having 'about £10 in the world (and even that borrowed)'. To complete his forebodings Kingsmill wrote and amiably pointed out that 'this adventure of yours doesn't seem to promise a new world to you, does it? One hardly leaves for Elysium with Castlerosse and Mary Pickford waving handkerchiefs from the platform. However, there's sure to be material for a book in it.' But most inauspicious of all, Gerhardie learned that the novel competition had been won by Miss Muriel Harris with *The Seventh Gate* and the discretionary Special Award had been withheld by the panel on the grounds that there was no other book of 'outstanding merit'. The disappointment was all the worse that the news came at the start of the Indian trip when he found himself once again in the company of the very rich. Had he been able to approach India with the guarantee of good sales ahead he would leave in a happier frame of mind. 'I usually take literary reverses very lightly', he wrote to Clara, 'as you know yourself, when publisher after publisher turned down my *Futility* and I did not take it in the least tragically. But this time I was so *sure* of it (thinking that no one else could have written a novel like *Pending Heaven*) that I was literally staggered. I had also wanted to send poor Rosie some money out of my winnings—I had made up my mind to send her £20 at once. I suppose this is the penalty one has to pay for being artistically and intellectually in advance of one's time.' Almost penniless, his only hope of immediate cash was to persuade the publishers into releasing some of the £500 advance on his autobiography, and in addition the US lecture tour now became a definite fixture.

The Maharani had arranged to travel home by air—a route only recently established—in the flying-boat *City of Alexandria*.[2] From embarkation in France they flew short distances, frequently stopping for fuel: Basle, Genoa, then on to Rome—'Who killed who here?' demanded the Princess. Because of the low altitude it was a voyage of great beauty; on the way to Corfu and Athens an enormous black eagle passed beneath them, and looking down Gerhardie saw the islets of Greece spread out like a map below. Less romantically, in Naples news reached them that their sister craft, the *City of Rome*, had just foundered in the Gulf of Genoa and all on board had drowned. 'All the less probable that we too should crash', reasoned Gerhardie staunchly to himself. At Mersa Matruh the plane stopped to refuel, and on take-off a buoy bobbed up out of the water and ripped off a strut. Rigidly composed, the passengers transferred to the *City of Athens*.

Gerhardie, whose fear and distrust of flying had been little alleviated, though by now slightly exhausted, at last leaned back to savour the take-off. The plane sped through the water, rose gracefully into the air, and promptly came down with a loud and heavy bump. '"Nothing unusual", I thought. "These fellows know what they are up to."' But instead of rising again the craft was rushing headlong towards the natural rock breakwaters. In an instant the pilot (a ginger-haired young man, William remembered) decided to stop the engines. Unquestionably this saved their lives: the plane first appeared to dive, then leaped into the air and landed with a crash upon the rocks, which ripped open the undercarriage. Sea water gushed in, flooding the passengers to waist level.

It became clear to me that it was most important that I should not perish. But sheer good manners kept me in check: I stood still and deferred, through no love of my fellow creatures, but dislike of panic and the fear of showing fear, to several passengers. I climbed on top of the machine, quietly, the excitement in me subduing my movements. I felt as you do when praised, that you would like to excel yourself. Nobody praised me; they were preoccupied with themselves. But I had merited my own approbation for behaving with composure. At the slightest encouragement I might have sacrificed my life; for of such emotion heroes are made. Or my nerves might have betrayed me. I don't know. Clearly, it would have been touch and go.[3]

Perched precariously on the roof of the plane Gerhardie was in time to save the Princess and her coat when the latter caught in the propeller. Then he sat down to await the rescue boats, carelessly crossed his legs, and was struck by the central propeller which split his heel to the bone in two places, while only denting the shoe. At length, with much fluster and ceremony the Governor of Alexandria conducted him to hospital. The foot was stitched up with horse-hair 'while the Maharani, soaking wet, set beside me, puffing at a cigarette, and smiling to herself at the thrills which life provides, unasked'.[4]

Unruffled, the Princess flew on to India. To Gerhardie's great relief a mistake in the bookings prevented him from joining her and he made his way alone by train to 'watery, wicked, secretive, obscurely lighted' Port Said. On board the P. & O. liner he arranged for his suits and linen to be washed and pressed, then cabled a sensational story to the *Sunday Express*[5] which emerged with the headlines:

PRINCESS CAUGHT BY PROPELLER

FAMOUS AUTHOR BESIDE HER IN 'PLANE CRASH

'NEARLY MINCED'

He was, in spite of all, still looking forward to the trip, and wrote to tell Clara that he and the Maharani were already intimate friends though he had not yet seduced her ('It is difficult in an aeroplane!'). But after nine days of monotonous sailing—the stifling heat, injured ankle which prevented him from dancing, and boring companions—he again grew pessimistic and arrived in Bombay thoroughly uncomfortable.

For two days and nights he travelled by train in dust and sweltering heat, talking to an engineer from Stoke-on-Trent. At his side, Goethe, Chekhov, and Proust, 'always with me. I always imagine what they would do in the same situation. Sometimes I get very sick of them. Sometimes they cheer me. Always they are at my side. We form deeper friendships with the spirit of great men who, in their books, have given us of their best than in contact with personal friends with whom we exchange egotisms.'[6] In Calcutta Gerhardie, trailing the Viceroy by a mere ten minutes, stepped out of the train on to a regal red carpet. A Rolls-Royce lined with white silk (this detail at the Maharani's behest) conveyed him to a hotel before he began the journey northwards on the morrow.

Bamboo-and-thatch houses perched on stilts, the roofs covered with great scarlet plumes of hibiscus, rose out of the jungle to greet Gerhardie as the train puffed into Cooch Behar state, with here and there a green snake visible in the undergrowth. Broad, red, gravel roads lined with palm trees heralded the town itself, with small white temples and cool, green, temple pools. No larger than Sussex, the ancient state was poor and unsophisticated—only an occasional bicycle or motor passed by. But a network of rivers and marshes, heavy grasses and reed jungle had made it superb hunting country. *Thirty-seven Years of Big Game Shooting in Cooch Behar* by the previous Maharajah is its outstanding literary remnant, for this ruler, whose statue stood in the town square, had spent an ample portion of his reign tracking bison, sambar, tigers, leopards, rhinoceros, antelope, wild pig, and—on one occasion—a fourteen-stone python.

The palace was long, elaborate, and centrally domed, built in the 1870s by an English architect and seemingly twice as large as Buckingham Palace. Wide verandas stretched on each side, looking on to the numerous small lakes resplendent with colourful water birds and fireflies, a rose garden with a marble mausoleum, and on a clear day a view to the snow-capped Himalayas. The whole was surrounded by jungle. Jackals that cried in the night sometimes crept into the palace itself. When Gerhardie first walked into the Maharani's room he was suddenly enveloped by the fairy-tale of his youth, the child who is nursed by bears. 'Apparently there was nothing like this palace in the whole of the jungle kingdom which I had traversed. Nothing but a few shackles dispersed over the dim and lonely land. And suddenly mirrors, halls, chandeliers, and the sadness which the little girl must have felt in the immense underground palace. Indians were another race, like bears.'[7] He was given a vault-like suite of rooms next to Indira's. Indian palaces, he soon discovered, were a curious combination of splendour and shabbiness. ('You behold, from a distance, a palace which looks as if it were out of the Arabian Nights. You inspect the interior, and find a really ghastly combination of colours and furniture.') For several days he was quite alone (the Princess having inexplicably disappeared) but for an army of servants—five hundred altogether, each assigned a specific function, including a state band of forty musicians who played each night before dinner. His personal valet, Islam, a gaunt, consumptive, barefoot, bearded man who coughed incessantly, insisted on doing up all William's buttons and was never out of earshot. Islam's grasp of English was rudimentary—he used the word 'open' for both open and close, and 'leave' for both leave and arrive: they had trouble planning expeditions. A car and a chauffeur were placed at Gerhardie's disposal, along with 'another enormous man with a hell of a turban on his head' who brought everything with great pomp and solemnity. Night in Cooch Behar fell quickly to the sound of temple bells and the smell of incense. He strolled into the drawing-room to try the piano: a servant rushed forward to switch on the enormous chandelier and promptly fused the whole electric system. So William sat down by the light of a candle and played 'my poor one and only *Tristan*!'

'My new experiences have stimulated me, put new life into me', he wrote to Clara in his first week. But after the return of the Maharani the touring began. 'Oh, the nuisance of sight-seeing', lamented Gerhardie who hated this as much as he had hated his childhood shopping trips when he had noticed only two things, 'fatigue in my own limbs and tedium at what I saw around me'. People constantly plucked at his elbow, exhorting him to take notice of this and that and something else, and when he visited the local university dressed in *kurta* and *lungi*, with a stout pair of English brogues on his feet, all the students giggled. Gerhardie told the Maharani that he missed his secretary: immediately she ordered him a complete staff of office clerks who stood by ready to take dictation, but they could not hear what he said because of the constant noise of the electric fans. On a trip to Mysore in the south the sight-seeing gave way to socializing and Gerhardie mixed with rajas and maharajas, begums and princesses, and even the Viceroy came at last to meet the man who had trodden on his red carpet. But the endless formality was enervating, the British embarrassing, and the atmosphere not unlike that of Russia on the eve of revolution.

Then came the big-game hunting, a spectacle which he particularly dreaded; it was not only offensive but downright dangerous. The party set off at daybreak mounted on elephants who carried them deep into the jungle to a model camp 'looking like a small city of canvas by night'. Across the River Kapini native beaters, tapping and yelling, started to round up wild elephants. By the third day forty animals were roped in a stockade, and Gerhardie watched 'the big tusker, leader of the herd, and his subsequent humiliation as he rolled in the mud and sobbed with anger before his own cows, till his spirit was broken and he was dragged along by four tame elephants, exhausted and looking a little ashamed, and tied to a tree, henceforth a prisoner, perhaps for a hundred years to come.'[8] A fine leopard was tracked and eventually surrounded: 'she (for it was a lady) showed no fight at all but hid herself under a bush, and only her eyes glared and she growled diffidently, as if not sure of herself. Then came several shots. She died quietly.'[9]

Contrary to all expectation there was a complete dearth of women. Almond eyes followed him from behind screens and yashmaks, always out of reach. And as for the promised mystery and romance of the Princess herself—Gerhardie's provocative silence on this point suggests that if he did as Castlerosse had predicted and fell in love with her, she did not fall in love with him. Added to all these disappointments, he was never alone, yet at the same time found himself nowhere the centre of attention, always one amongst many. It was impossible to take his daily walk without either melting in the heat, sinking into a marsh, or being eaten by a tiger. He hated the incessant demands for money, the dirt, the damp enervating heat, and the insects—'lots of little green mosquitos who, of an evening when the lights were lit in the palace, fell scorched on your face, down your neck, into the soup: there was no end to them. This depressed me exceedingly and I wished I had not come to India.'[10]

After less than five weeks Gerhardie departed, ignoring Castlerosse's pleas to remain and establish a cinema production unit. He sailed on an Italian ship to Venice—fifteen days of rapturous eating with Anglo-Indian colonels. 'At table I was silent. Nobody knew who I was. I had not told them. Because if I had, they still wouldn't have known. So silence, in the circumstances, was, I judged, the more dignified course.'[11] On Christmas Day all the English and Americans on board joined together to sing hymns and carols. Then he saw Venice for the first time. Enveloped in its mystique he forgot the country he had just left, and recaptured instead the beauty of St Petersburg and the river Neva and the great granite quays. But dusk fell and the enchantment vanished. 'Venice seemed venal, black, shabby, threadbare. I marvelled that a great number of adults should have nothing better to do than to offer to conduct you to the Venetian glass factory. At the hotel I stayed—no one but an old crow. A solitary dinner, and then to my solitary bed. The dark blue wallpaper shuts me in, and behind the shuttered window laps the heavy water. Hush, I am in Venice, and then . . . I am asleep.'[12]

Back in England with just three weeks to prepare for the American tour, Gerhardie ordered himself a new suit, and from the bed-sitting room of a private hotel in Westbourne Terrace began dictating his lectures to Miss Rosenstiehl. He dreaded the approaching ordeal, never before having made so much as an after-dinner speech: 'I'm *very nervous* about lecturing and so sick of travelling that the idea makes me ill!', he wrote to Clara, who shortly joined him. The Indian trip had quite upset him. Now he nursed a deep fear that 'the nervous strain of lecturing in strange towns at the end of a long train journey may wreck my rather sensitive organism . . . Unless I am alone at least 6 hours a day I am (spiritually) ill, and unless I can walk at least half that time, I get very restless.' With *Pending Heaven* still unpublished there were, as Keedick had predicted, only half-a-dozen American bookings. To complete his sense of foreboding the Wall Street stock market had crashed only weeks before, so that he approached a country depressed and in turmoil.

Gerhardie sailed from Southampton on 23 January 1930, travelling rather less lavishly than twelve years before. Yet he later vividly recalled the Atlantic crossing and a cold and solitary night walk amongst the snow-bound wooden houses of Halifax where they had stopped for a few hours, 'all snow and bitter wind and darkness'. Canada in the morning evoked winter in Finland, driving in the snow. 'In the evening a lamp on the table. Reading, writing. It is the things we ignore which make our life . . . The impression of Halifax, unforeseen and fortuitous, is life; the object in my mind which took me to America is a phantom.'[13]

Stepping off the boat in New York he was greeted with a barrage of flash-bulbs. 'I have arrived in order to give the continent of America an opportunity of entertaining me', he announced to reporters who anxiously awaited the outrageous Anglo-Russian eccentric. The *New York Evening Journal* had recently featured a moralistic article on the basis of his opinions on 'The Attractive Woman': alongside a large photograph of Gerhardie, who 'interests all girls, because he is so handsome as to be almost beautiful', it purported to be shocked by his preference for sophisticated French girls driving large cars smilingly, and piously asserted,

We want a girl to be GOOD, SIMPLE, HONEST, FOND OF CHILDREN, and anxious to have a good many of them.

If she can wear a little white muslin dress coming to her ankles, a blue sash around her waist, a far-away look in her eyes, believe in the goodness of human nature and respond, with pity, to misfortune, she suits US.[14]

He had been advised to have some suitably inane and witty answers up his sleeve. Thus, when asked at a publicity interview for his opinions on American women, he paused as if for thought, then replied: 'It is my considered opinion that the American women are all different, but there is one point in which they're all alike' (another pause) 'and that is in their uniform desire to be different.'[15] The next day headlines appeared all over America: 'Gerhardie says of American Women all Different while all Alike' ('There were hints that I had sized up the American woman; also hints that I had already overstayed my welcome'). But those who conducted private interviews found him very different. The 'fair-haired, blue-eyed Englishman with a ready smile that would bring tears to the eyes of a toothpaste press sales manager' sat on a table, legs crossed, swinging his watch chain reflectively and creating a distinct impression of shy, nervous charm, not nearly as 'cocky' as he was rumoured to be.[16]

The Women's Club in which he was to speak first did not appeal— 'appalling examples of feminine mass-eagerness for cultural perfection swallowed in tabloid form', as he later described such organizations, suggesting they be disbanded at once. But contempt made his introduction no easier. He had much to live up to, for the lecture brochures now shuffled by an expectant audience displayed a romantic photograph of the 'Brilliant English Novelist and Literary Critic'. Whilst making a great deal of his early and sudden success (patronage by Wells, Beaverbrook, and Wharton) they heralded him as 'an entirely new type of novelist and one having a deep understanding of modern life'. Gerhardie apparently possessed a 'remarkable personality' and had spoken 'audaciously' in public many times; he could talk seriously when the occasion required it, yet—let it be noted—he also possessed 'a deep sense of humour'. Hot and limp, he stood to face his listeners as he had decades earlier when called upon to play a piano solo before a large audience including his mother and father. Now, acutely conscious of the need for wit, he adopted an opening used by G. K. Chesterton in Sweden who, seeing the great height of the platform from which he was to speak, expressed the view that 'were he to fall from the platform he would create a deeper impression by his fall than by his lecture'. Despite the fact that Chesterton was a good deal more bulky than Gerhardie, this proved successful at first,

till I came to a place where, after first making sure that Mr Chesterton had not lectured there, I discovered at the last moment that neither was there a platform to lend force to my opening words. It was too late to jeopardize my opening, and I said how glad I was there was no platform, for were there a platform, and were I to fall off it, I might make a deeper impression by my fall than by my lecture. There was no laughter. But worst of all were those places where the platform was no higher than four inches. My opening sentence did not carry conviction on these occasions.[17]

Then on to the lecture itself. 'The "Message" of the New Generation' had seemed, when he wrote it, to be entertaining, comic, and ironic. But painfully shy on the podium, William's voice seemed to disappear ('you cannot spend your first eighteen years in Russia without getting the habit of keeping the chin down, which stifles the windpipe'),[18] added to which was his tendency to talk at incredible speed. He nervously shuffled his notes around, only to abruptly interrupt the torrent mid-sentence while lost between one page and the next.

At Oxford he had noticed how English flippancy shocked the visiting American and Canadian debaters. Now he found his audiences endowed with 'a quite hopelessly under-developed sense of irony', and endured embarrassing silences when they 'abstained' from laughing in the appropriate places. 'I went through agony', he confessed to Clara.

In Virginia, Gerhardie was chaperoned by Miss Florence S. Peple, a middle-aged admirer who showed him the sights of Richmond whilst describing her love for a young Anglo-Russian. So engrossed was she in her narrative that she ran her motor-car into a parked tram and injured Gerhardie's knee. Unperturbed, she finished her story, pulled out a snapshot of 'my long lost Wally', and only afterwards noticed the damage to her car and passenger. Gerhardie remained exquisitely polite. He lectured that evening on 'Love and Literature', proposing that if Stendhal's mistress had loved him she should have yielded to him—at which several women rose and left the auditorium. Miss Peple later kindly wrote to reassure him, however, that he was 'much liked personally and the more intelligent persons thoroughly appreciated much that you said.'[19]

In Ottawa, Gerhardie paced the freezing streets in a thin overcoat, past a blazing theatre ('a wild hope rose in my breast that it was my theatre . . .'). A bookshop displayed an enormous portrait of a carefree young man—'I gave it a sick glance. It was myself, young, happy, taken before I had ever heard of the ordeal of lecturing.'[20] When later he learned that only forty seats had been sold, and most of those to the Governor General and his retinue, he eagerly suggested that it might be insulting to Lord Willingdon to proceed with such an empty hall. Lord Willingdon agreed and instead they dined together and talked agreeably of India. In Montreal Gerhardie spoke, with the help of half a bottle of champagne, quite successfully to eight hundred people. When, later, he pointed this out as an example of a *popular* lecture, Keedick reminded him that yes, as far as it went, which was scarcely half an hour, and that the remaining thirty minutes were occupied by the chairman's skilful manipulation of questions.

Rhode Island was a different matter. At the British Empire Club he addressed an audience of 'elderly self-satisfied business men', teetotal at that, who found him a poor contrast to the poised, fluent Beverley Nichols. Years later Gerhardie recalled the ghastly moment when, 'after fumbling along for awhile and stopping out of sheer honest shame, I suddenly felt it was very cruel, very unjust of these red-faced men in ill-fitting clothes to recline in their chairs and puff at their cigars (why could I not recline and listen, too?) while I had to stand and apparently speak, and I felt I wanted to cry'.[21] 'Love and Literature' was not to their taste, and they demanded he speak instead on the Boy Scout Movement. Gerhardie could not oblige. The audience demanded their money back. 'It is open to them to regard me as a complete village idiot, as it is up to me to doubt their intellectual capacity to absorb an original point of view', William retorted in an acrimonious correspondence with Keedick. And he pointed out that his subject was not (as they claimed) 'beneath their notice' but clearly 'above their intelligence'. 'My lecture trip proved disappointing—to the audience',[22] he later confessed, and resolved never, under any circumstances, to speak in public again.

In February 1930, *Pending Heaven*, 'Dedicated affectionately to my mother', was published in England.[23] 'A fantastic, semi-symbolical, loosely written narrative in which the characters are a pack of lunatics with farmyard morals', according to the *Liverpool Post*,[24] Gerhardie himself described his work as 'a novel about two men treading the donkey-round of paradise deferred, their literary friendship strained to breaking-point by rivalry in love.'[25]

It is the story of a frustrating and comic search for fulfilment, both bodily and spiritual; but it is also an attempt to address the question of how one can find adequate expression for those sensations which constitute one's unique self. The two central characters, ostensibly portrayals of Kingsmill and Gerhardie, are Max Fisher and Victor Thurbon. But it is a curious manipulation of identities. In the early pages, both physically and biographically Max is Kingsmill and Victor, Gerhardie. Yet within a few chapters the identities appear to switch. Instead of, as in real life, Victor/Gerhardie occupying the house in France, bargaining with the horse dealer, and conducting love affairs, it is Max/Kingsmill who does so, and becomes the central character for the rest of the book, which is to a great extent the narrative of Gerhardie's own life in immediate retrospect.

The discontinuity between what is perpetually *promised* and what is fulfilled leads Max to imagine himself 'immersed in a life curiously strange, as if hiding something tremulously real under the heat and burden of the day'. When they go for a walk they pass an old man reading his newspaper in the fading sunlight of a public park, 'and that too struck them as beautiful and somehow significant'. In vain Max and Victor seek a correlation between the world they inhabit and the sensibilities that this world inspires. They are perpetually disappointed:

In London, things struck Max not so much as commentaries on, as illustrations of, the life of the soul. If he saw anything, whatever it was, he was no longer surprised, but said: 'Hm! It just shows you—' Though what it was precisely it showed he would have been hard put to it to express in any of Europe's leading languages familiar to him.

And yet Max and Victor, 'with the facility for invoking images which is the privilege of the literary man', are the best qualified to dispose of such discord. Ostensibly they are portrayed as writers in accord with (in the words of Isaiah Berlin)

the characteristically romantic notion that poets and painters may understand the spirit of their age more profoundly and express it in a more vivid and lasting manner than academic historians . . . because artists tend to have a greater degree of sensibility . . . [are] more responsive to, and conscious of, inchoate, half-understood factors which operate beneath the surface in a given milieu.[26]

But it becomes increasingly clear to the reader that Max's and Victor's self-conscious pursuit of a vocation displaces the question of their actual creations. An alternative view reveals itself, one which is closer to an Absurd sense of the artist as egocentric, futile, and essentially comic. Max is described as having 'a forehead, eyes, and nose like Shakespeare's', though he is portly and red-faced. Victor has 'said that he had noticed about his own face a resemblance to a dozen eminent men of letters: something of Shakespeare and of H. G. Wells, of Tchehov, Shaw and Byron and Goethe and Oscar Wilde. Yes, and of Dickens and Hardy. And withal, of Mussolini and Napoleon I.' They constantly see themselves as *other* literary figures, never themselves. More often than not their sensibility *obscures* their vision, just as in *The Polyglots* Georges's obsession with literature causes him to ignore the desires of those around him, and in *Futility* Andrei's preoccupation with his own proposed novel results in him losing Nina. The more Max searches for happiness, fulfilment, and a means of elucidating his own potential, the greater seems the rift between the present state of 'pending', and the deferred 'heaven'. Victor, undergoing similar difficulties, purchases a dictaphone, hoping that this will facilitate the expression of his thoughts. However, we later find that

The dictaphone had proved successful, but did not entirely obviate effort and difficulties of composition, for Victor found that inspired thoughts flocked to him in great droves while he was striding on the lawns of Regent's Park, but they sat small and reluctant round the skirting of his room when he reclined on his sofa and courted the dictaphone. Much might still be invented to assist expression before he was quite equal to his potent self.

Ultimately the unsatisfactoriness even of Gerhardie's literary projection is implied, and Victor thinks 'how stupid it was that Max, sitting opposite, did not know what he, Victor, thought: that for all the richness of emotion and experiences which was his he must seem to Max a thin and trivial individual'.

After untold complications—bloody-minded horses, diabolical neighbours, accumulated mistresses—the book ends with Max's death from influenza. It is very much a surrender: having, he feels, failed to pin down anything from the tantalizing flux of experience, he ceases to exist. Yet during his final illness Max experiences 'an inspired vision, seen in delirium, of the indestructible essences streaming forth from the broken images of life'. 'I tried to show', Gerhardie later explained, 'by the analogy of the delirium at the end, that the composition of life's texture was no less inconsequent than that of a dream, and was of passing significance compared with the immortal essences of things which achieved their own harmonies as in a symphony.' In his Introduction to the 1971 edition of *Pending Heaven*, Michael Holroyd has written of the novel: 'through the imaginative use of symbol and metaphor it expresses complicated things very simply and lucidly.' Yet the simplicity is deceptive. For it is the very point of *Pending Heaven* to express the impossibility of expression, the fact that experience eludes the reductiveness of language. The 'broken images' do not capture life, nor can they capture the novel:

He had been hoodwinked, taken in by the multifarious aspect of things, and had believed that souls were like small coin. There had been too many mirrors about reflecting the Soul and he had believed that each mirror contained its own soul. But now, seizing a hatchet, he smashed all the mirrors, and behold! they reflected no soul.

The essence of both life and the novel lies in their totality, their flux, irreducible to symbol and metaphor, which remain incomplete and misleading approximations.

'The tale is extremely funny', wrote Arnold Bennett in the *Evening Standard*.[27] 'It is bitter, capricious, occasionally incoherent, and without any feeling for the existence of organised society. But extremely funny it is, and extremely original. No sentence in it can be foreseen. The man has genius.' *Pending Heaven* is unquestionably amongst the most entertaining and comic of Gerhardie's novels. But for all its sophisticated range of ideas, as the story of a literary quest it betrays as well as portrays the author's lack of direction at this period. 'There is insufficient objectivity, insufficient dramatization, too much the sense that what we are being given is a thinly disguised transcript from life'[28]—Walter Allen's complaint (of Gerhardie's later works in general) has here some justification, although Allen, a keen admirer, was not the first to ignore the finer distinctions of Gerhardie's 'autobiographical' novels. *Futility*, *The Polyglots*, and *Jazz and Jasper* were no less 'intimate' than *Pending Heaven*, but their agile, responsive tone, and the fact that they were carefully integrated into a historical framework, puts them above such criticism. Even Kingsmill, who adored *Pending Heaven*, considered that the character of Helen (Harriet Cohen) was 'taken too directly and too freshly from experience . . . She is not digested.' Edith Wharton, who had disliked *Jazz and Jasper* and *The Polyglots*, had, however, no such objections and praised it wholeheartedly as 'a jewel'.

Altogether the book elicited a number of interesting reviews. 'Many people write of disillusionment and its trail of bitterness in the grand style', opined the *New York Herald Tribune*. 'Few can take off their rose-coloured spectacles, stare human folly in the face and then treat it lightly, without rancor.'[29] The *Glasgow Evening Times* considered the sexual comedy to represent 'an art which has not been common in English literature, and only once was perfect in the plays of Congreve',[30] and the *Times Literary Supplement* saw *Pending Heaven* as continuing 'the pure tradition of English nonsense lavishly, perhaps oversexing it, but giving it a salutary touch of the exotic and the intellectual'.[31] Some claimed that the novel was too ultra-modern to comment upon, others that Gerhardie had (again) squandered his talents, and regretted 'his continued attachment to the post-war philosophy . . . that the only meaning to be discovered in life is that it has no meaning'.[32] This was a criticism that he found particularly unjust, until a friend reassured him: 'don't you see that you are not attacked for writing about "futility"— Russian futility that is—but for suggesting . . . that futility is to be found in England? For one thing . . . the English play games.'[33] Several weeks later, *Time and Tide* pointed out: 'The people who deplore Mr Gerhardi and all his works have found a new name for him. The name is "un-English" and it is the very last word in opprobrium.'[34]

After the 'nerve-racking catastrophe' of lecturing was over, Gerhardie settled down for a couple of weeks to enjoy himself in New York, and to try to sell his stories and articles. He gave a fifteen-minute radio interview, but found that in America broadcasting involved so many things to trip over—cables, ropes, microphones, and even mice. Instead of the calm of the English studio, where he was under the agreeable impression that he was talking to himself, American technicians constantly 'tested' his voice, while a pianist nearby kept his hands poised over the keyboard lest Gerhardie faint, falter, or fall short of his allotted time.

Cecil Beaton gave several cocktail parties and introduced Gerhardie to publishers and editors, one of whom instantly 'grew pale, stammered, and shuffled away in quick, small, mincing steps'. The philanthropic millionaire Otto Khan presented him to Dorothy Parker ('rather like Rebecca West—a bewildered animal'). At Mrs Cornelius Vanderbilt's mansion he ran into Lady Louis Mountbatten and discovered that their love affair had 'all fizzled out'. One morning Gerhardie looked into the office of a New York publisher and learned of D. H. Lawrence's death from tuberculosis. Greatly affected he stood by while the publisher, note-book and pencil in hand, 'addressed in insistent whispers the deceased author's agent: "Is there anything? A completed book? No? Any unfinished manuscripts that could be issued as a novel?"'[35]

Gerhardie's disillusion with America was complete. Repelled by 'the pervasive air of sentimentality', the high-mindedness, and what he saw as lack of individualism, he told friends that he had found it the most snobbish country in the world, a sorry parody of Europe. 'You Americans are the most charming women in the world', he later wrote to a young admirer. 'But what sad dogs you are, artistically. What an inferior, simulacrum race! You take everything at its face value. You cannot distinguish between prestige values and real values.'[36]

The chaos of New York was such that he hardly got to know a soul and in spite of all found himself 'bored and lonely and a little helpless'. Nobody suitable to wed had presented themselves, except for one exceptionally rich woman who hinted that she would be willing, 'But she is at least 38, growing flabby, has a most difficult disposition—in a word, is "not my cup of tea!"' Then, the night before he sailed, Gerhardie visited the opera. Beside him in the box sat a young widow, 'really beautiful and very shy and sensitive'. The very next morning before catching the boat he telephoned her and proposed marriage. He arrived in England a betrothed man. When friends expressed doubt or surprise at this curious method of engagement Gerhardie pointed out that it was 'love by intuition', embracing his most cherished values: 'The full scenario of her story is still shrouded in mystery; but her face, her voice, her manner towards me have outlined the synopsis, so to speak, of her past and given a probable indication of the kind of ecstasy I may expect in the future. My nerves are braced; my soul on tip toe. I am *expectantly* happy.'[37]

14

MARRIAGE?
March 1930–June 1931

*. . . and it became clear that we had really never stepped off . . . the edge of
our magic past.*[1]

'I could appreciate your cheque to cover the balance of my expenses
better', Gerhardie wrote to Keedick, who had demanded (unsuccessfully) that they split the loss incurred by the tour, 'if it had not been
accompanied by a letter containing some thinly veiled insults. Your
opinion of me is of interest as illustrating the working of your mind—but
there its interest to me ends.'

Not one of his old articles was sold, and with a single exception
American editors had refused to commit themselves to any new work;
after several weeks *Pending Heaven* had sold only 3,000 copies in the
United States and 2,000 in England, leaving the publishers with a loss
of, respectively, £250 and £125. 'The reviews (with very few exceptions)
have been quite incredibly *stupid*', wrote Gerhardie, adding ominously,
'I shall deal with the critics in my autobiography.' Exhausted and
irritable, he warned Clara that if they met they would be bound to
quarrel. Anxious for solitude, and time to think out his memoirs,
William set sail for North Africa.

Throughout the crossing, cold and wet and windy, he remained aloof.
'We might have died, this assorted bunch of us, from so different lands
and fates we came and with so different pasts, who had nothing in
common but the time of passing over.'[2] But his general air of helpless-
ness when travelling invariably drew fellow passengers, eager to assist,
and he was befriended by his cabin companion. Herr Himmler was a
shy, nervous man, but a staunch Nazi supporter and back home in
Germany, he insisted, a veritable Mussolini. He listened eagerly to
Gerhardie's conjugal plans, and when the ship docked helped him to
purchase some fine-quality flea powder.

Tunisia proved an exquisite contrast to America. At Hammamet, 'an enchanting little place by the sea-shore', there was not a porter or taxi in sight, but a tiny Arab boy dragged his suitcases and deposited them first in a ditch and then on to his donkey cart. After about a mile of travelling, Gerhardie seated alone upon the luggage, a terrible hailstorm burst upon them, at which precise moment their donkey was deflected from the path of duty by another (female) donkey and after that would hardly budge—'*C'est parce que maintenant il est triste*', the child explained. Drenched, they arrived at the hotel, and when at last the rain stopped, 'I walked in solitude between dripping lilac bushes, to the sea. . . . And suddenly there came a whistle, as I stood there, and a train went past. Where? To Sousse, to Gabès . . . to the desert. Why was I so happy? I knew. It brought back my childhood; the railway whistle recalled another blown by the train that I longed to carry me away from school, from drudgery, from town, from St Petersburg to the sea-shore.'[3]

Day after day he wandered aimlessly about, savouring the isolation. 'Wherever I went I had to take myself with me: enough, it would seem, to damn any holiday,'[4] A half-built Arab house in Gabès with an idyllic plot of land attracted his attention, but first of all doubts about his impending marriage had to be settled. He hoped Josephine would agree to a quiet wedding, and thus avoid 'the vulgarity of public weddings' which, even as a guest, he abominated. 'I either write circuitously via the Cape of Good Hope that I cannot attend the wedding unless they can see their way to postpone the date till my return, or, more generally, ignore it and, on meeting the bride or bride-groom, reproach them for having failed me with their invitation, and on their assuring me that they remember having sent it, express scepticism, stressing that letters do not get lost in the post, "at least not one in a thousand", shaking an accusing forefinger at them, while looking straight into their eyes.'[5] A register-office affair would dispense with the 'ghoulish bridesmaids, peeping strangers, ready-made congratulations, "Roneo" smiles!', the 'brutal extortion of presents', and the conscious dramatization and suspense of the bridal night.[6] There was so far no way of telling if Josephine would fall into the 'odious' tendency of writers' wives to praise and echo their husbands in public. And of course the prospect of monogamy was not inspiring. 'As I have never given my Algerian desert love project a fair trial', he explained to Clara, 'this is the very time to do it, so that by the time we meet in May I shall feel quite certain whether marriage, or a life *à la* Mahommed, is *my* cup of tea.' But, for all his extravagant hopes, the search for concubines proved fruitless. Hour upon hour of tramping desert paths in the wake of gesticulating guides proved only that the promised women were too old, too dirty, too expensive, or too invisible. At last, weary of the heat and the Arabs, he sailed back to England.

Reluctant to take a flat until his plans with Josephine were settled, William retired to a coffin-shaped room in a Westbourne Terrace hotel: 'It is, you will see, run on modern lines: all the single beds at midnight become double and issue with loud groans. A delightful place.' From here, with Miss Rosenstiehl's enthusiastic approval, he announced his forthcoming marriage to Josephine Kaufman. In their brief hours together in the opera box Gerhardie had ascertained that Josephine was the widow of the 'Ever-ready Razor King' who had died two years previously, leaving her with a little boy, a little girl, and two million dollars.

How seriously Gerhardie planned to cast aside his 'Mohammedan' life for love or for money is hard to determine. 'The idea that I might have to go slow where other women are concerned is too disheartening for a man of my versatility', he wrote worriedly to Clara in a letter affirming his love for Josephine. There is no sense that he envisaged married life as anything remotely realistic. Like Kingsmill he compartmentalized his relationships with women, who existed, invidiously, as two-dimensional symbols: maids, housekeepers, objects of inspiration, but rarely as individuals with sensibilities, and never as individuals who might penetrate his own self. With Clara alone could he even countenance female criticism, and even that invariably drew him into a tantrum. There was also the curious problem of money: 'as I could never think of taking—and I doubt if she will want me to do so—a penny of her money (beyond living with her in her chateau) I might be sacrificing too much of my freedom for mere convenience; and God knows how far love can be trusted in marriage!' But, on the other hand, the fortune might offer him more time in which to write. And he was comforted that in this marriage there would be 'no need to make any' offspring of his own: 'I prefer to play about with my nephews and nieces. When they begin to howl and make a nuisance of themselves and want to go "po-po" and "do their business" and so on, you hand them back to their Mamas, and there your responsibility ends.' With miserable early memories of Charles still vivid in his mind, William had no intention of becoming something so unpalatable as a father himself. Besides, children would deflect attention away from himself—Clara's attention in particular.

Josephine, with a flat in New York, country house, maid, governess, motor car and chauffeur, wished to spend her summers in London and her winters in France. A May marriage seemed ideal. Then she wrote to say she would be motoring round Italy before arriving in England—a friendly letter, but guarded on the subject of the engagement. Three months later she again contacted Gerhardie, who learned with dismay that she had already been in Europe, unbeknownst to him, for six weeks. He thought it a bad omen, but arranged to meet her after his luncheon appointment with Amy Johnson: 'my fate will probably be settled one way or another that day'.

The day arrived and Miss Johnson, triumphant and spectacular for having flown half the earth to Australia in a ludicrously small plane, paraded through cheering streets towards a riotous lunch at the Savoy. The four hundred festive guests included Noël Coward, Alfred Hitchcock, Charles Laughton, Ivor Novello, Malcolm Sargent, the two Waughs, and William Gerhardie ('Rejoice to accept the invitation as a graceful token to a broken heel', he had wired, recalling his own brief aeronautical adventure). 'They roistered; they sang; they revelled', and somebody danced. 'All the splendours of society, and some of literature, were there.' At dinner a few hours later Mrs Kaufmann talked only of whisky sours, white ladies, and monkey glands. The maid persistently hurried in and out of the room preventing any seduction ('which might have advanced matters'). And Josephine couldn't conceal a look of pity on her face when Gerhardie, exaggerating considerably, told her that he earned 'between £1,000 and £2,000 a year', and even offered to pay his share of the dinner ('which I declined with much pride'). She promised to see him two days later, but disappeared instead to inspect a razor factory at Cricklewood. The following day he caught her on the telephone just as she was about to hurry abroad again. 'Another pending heaven gone West!' Gerhardie sighed. 'But I am easily consoled'—and he proceeded to reflect on the fact that she was already 28, had put on weight considerably since their last meeting, and showed every sign of expanding into a stout woman like her sister. 'She even rolls a little from side to side when she walks. And in her coat and hat she wasn't at all so fetching—rather a bulky, matronly type of woman—very "homely". There is something to be said for being a bachelor, still standing on, or falling off, his own feet!'

With the disappearance of Josephine, Gerhardie's fiscal problems loomed large again: his income was on the way down, his commitments very much on the way up. Eight extra shillings a week were needed to cover Tamara's food, two shillings for her pocket money, and sundry other sums to clothe her and pay for urgent dental treatment in order to prevent her teeth 'just crumbling away'. Added to which her passport needed regular renewal at the Soviet Consulate. Victor, who had lost money in the slump, now reduced his share of his mother's allowance, so that William was obliged to make up the difference. 'Truly we are all born to misery!' lamented Clara. 'To what end? is the vital question.'

Tamara had arrived in England knowing almost nothing of the language, for Rosie always spoke to her daughters in Russian. As soon as she and Clara had returned from Russia at the end of 1929, Clara arranged for her granddaughter to attend Blackburn High School whilst lodging with family friends. Then Clara departed for Antibes to spend six months with Daisy, who was pregnant with her second child and plagued by ill health and lack of money. William lent his sister money whenever he could, and often as not never saw it again. 'Don't you think posterity will be very angry with you all for not supporting me, the genius of the family, but neglecting me and exploiting my kind and generous nature?' he wrote when the exchange rate was especially favourable to her. When she ignored his requests he wrote again, not kindly at all.

In July the end of the school year approached, and Clara hurried back to England to look after Tamara, who was settling quite happily into English life and was sufficiently fluent to begin evening classes in shorthand and typing. But Clara found her such a severe strain upon resources that with uncharacteristic despair she wailed to William that her granddaughter would have to return to Russia. The immediate crisis was solved when friends created a vacancy for Tamara, working an office telephone exchange at 21s. a week. Clara still had the problem of where they were to live. Hitherto they had lodged with Dolly, but the house was not big enough and Dolly and Lot, in keeping with the rest of the family, had little money. Since leaving Russia Lot had set up in partnership with his father as 'Automobile and Electrical Engineers', but they lived frugally, and were pleased when William, in response to a request from Clara, parcelled up some of his little-used clothes for Lot.

Clara and Tamara moved into a set of rooms in the house of a doctor's widow, until driven to distraction by the woman's three Pekinese dogs yapping round their ankles. Aunt Sissie had recently written to Clara, 'as one old woman to another', suggesting they live out their remaining years together. Unmarried, Sissie would have liked to have raised a family of her own, but her beauty had been obscured by her giggles and instead she had nursed her parents until their death, then lived from year to year in permanent rotation between four or five relations. Clara, tired of hotels, pensions, and spare rooms, decided she would settle permanently in England ('a fine country and the centre of the world really') in a house of her own.

Number 12 Forton Avenue, four years old and semi-detached in Bolton, with a back view stretching more than twenty miles over fields and the distant towns, was considerably smaller even than Bradford Street. Clara paid £160 deposit after selling jewels, and arranged a £300 mortgage spread over seven years. But though only 'a doll's house', Clara spent innumerable happy hours arranging her possessions, at long last under one roof, and choosing furniture, carpets, china, pots and pans, and (to her embarrassment) 'lots of odds and ends from Wool- worths'. Lot brought a wireless set and Harry helped to lay out the garden. That year William took the unprecedented step of spending Christmas in Bolton.

By the spring of 1931 Gerhardie, envious of his mother's new stability, and with memories of Josephine fading, began to consider more permanent accommodation. After inspecting some seventy apartments, he settled for the lease on Number 19 Rossetti House, an unfurnished fifth-floor flat in Hallam Street, close to the BBC and Regent's Park. The block was three years old and 'about as good a proposition as I could wish. If I were a millionaire I could not want a better one', he wrote to Clara, enclosing a detailed plan and praising the ground-floor marble entrance-hall, the lift and uniformed porter, electric cooking and a new type of patent central-heating pipe, tradesman's lift, polished parquet floors, and modern steel-framed windows—all for £4. 5s. 6d. a week, a most reasonable rent for so central a location. 'Don't take Lunn to live with you now you have a flat and please don't tell him *I* said so', replied Clara.

William had no intention of taking anyone to live with him, for he was growing increasingly reliant upon his secretary Miss Rosenstiehl, 'my little ewe-lamb', 'probably the most honest little girl in the universe', who watched every penny spent, kept the accounts, and knew all about his work. Kingsmill, who nicknamed her Rosie Posie, had noticed her partiality for her employer. 'She is astoundingly, I mean rightly and naturally, loyal to you. A true woman, she measures the universe by its treatment of you.' Clara thought Patsy 'a brick'.

Gerhardie now began the exquisitely pleasurable business of decorat- ing and arranging the flat to his own meticulous taste. The best room he deployed as a joint study and drawing-room, with green silk curtains, matching green leather armchairs, a bright oriental rug upon the wood floor, and a steel filing-cabinet to go with the dictaphone. He thought the green drawing-room walls looked particularly well against the pink carpet, and ordered 'a very superlative and *expensive*!' sofa. The second room he used as his own bed-sitting room, the third as a dining-room, and the fourth as Patsy's study, doubling as a guest room. Then he toured the Caledonian market for bargains: a five-armed chandelier for ten guineas, a walnut oval dining-table for 35s. Horrified by the prospect of others (especially men) using his lavatory, he wrote off to Boots the Chemist to enquire about a disposable paper product he had observed in public lavatories abroad which covered the entire seat. Friends lent him furniture, carpets, and lamp-stands and he asked Clara to make a pile of cushions 'filled with any old stuff, such as bones, stones, rabbit skins and a dead cat or two'. These preparations were not without tribulations, for he was fussy and exacting about his purchases. When some gold-net curtains for the glass on his front door proved to be full of irregularities the manufacturers offered 25 per cent discount; Gerhardie argued for 33 per cent and got it. Two modern-design 'scientific-seating' chairs —'Osbert' for Patsy and 'Big Bertha' for himself—proved less than satisfactory. The retailers wrote a letter demanding payment but received a tart reply: 'So far from your threatening to "place the matter in other hands", I wish you would place the manufacture of your chairs in others hands.'[7]

Once settled he ordered some printed writing paper from a smart shop in Upper Regent Street. The sensitive owner, a specialist in heraldic designs, refused to comply until he had visited the flat in person. He walked from room to room deep in thought, awaiting inspiration—then departed and cut a very fine die of plain upright lettering in deep blue. Years passed. Whenever Patsy returned to re-order stationery, 'she found him progressively more gloomy. Then he began to stamp his feet at the mere irritation which the sight of customers caused his aesthetic sensibilities. Later, Patsy heard, he shouted at his customers, then grew really violent if anybody entered his shop, and, at last was carted, screaming, to a lunatic asylum. The shop's no more.'[8]

The visual arts engaged Gerhardie's interest but little. Although he was attracted by the work of Glyn Philpot, his near neighbour in Hallam Street, he admitted that he had no eye for paintings, and preferred his picture of a kitten tucked up in bed that he had picked up in Vienna. He also had a penchant for gold-framed looking-glasses. But shortly after moving to Rossetti House he agreed to sit for his own portrait. The artist, Margaret Lawson, had wanted to paint him ever since reading *The Polyglots*, but while she painted they argued. He insulted her by saying that women have no conversation. She replied that she could not talk intelligently and paint at the same time, and moreover she was *not* as he claimed 'a nasty hard-boiled feminist'. But where women were concerned Gerhardie could not be objective, and when at last he saw the picture he thought he detected something 'unpleasant' in the face; his friends, he told her, had considered it a 'nasty impression'. This was distinctly fanciful. The portrait is an amateurish but oddly accurate likeness and he hung it in his dining-room. A second young woman painter he rejected after she visited the flat and combed her dandruff all over his armchair. He was better pleased by a sculpted bust completed the same year by the young Countess Bianca de Treuberg, great-granddaughter of Dom Pedro I, the Emperor of Brazil. The bust, Gerhardie thought, did full justice to his good looks and he placed a cast of it in a prominent position in his flat. By which time he had fallen in love with the clean-haired, tactfully compliant Bianca who, unfortunately, was already engaged to Gerhardie's friend the exiled German aristocrat Prince Leopold von Loewenstein Wertheim-Freudenberg ('I do not envy other men's houses and motor-cars, but I have not yet got over envying them their beautiful women').[9] He wondered how best to win her, and decided that 'by stressing the barrier of friendship for Loewenstein which must needs separate us I am about to encourage her to jump the barrier, as well as her own barrier'.[10]

Despite the domestic upheavals, Gerhardie had been busy with his autobiography, sending the manuscript, in instalments, to Hugh Kingsmill. Kingsmill, now married to Dorothy and living in Switzerland in a remote house 'not inelegantly situated and with all medieval conveniences',[11] had recently completed his own war memoirs, *Behind Both Lines*. 'I suppose there is a hush over London', he wrote to a friend when no notice was taken of the book. 'Just look out of the window and make sure, will you? And wire me when the storm breaks, and the mob starts rushing the booksellers.'[12] Whilst Kingsmill's influence upon Gerhardie's fiction was on the whole unhelpful, Kingsmill made some excellent suggestions for the *Memoirs*, correcting lapses into journalese, re-ordering paragraphs, and deleting irrelevancies ('spiritualist seances and other rot of that sort'). But Gerhardie, who eagerly sought Kingsmill's praise, was disgruntled by his forthright approach. And, for all his admiration, Kingsmill could be perspicacious about the role he was required to play in their relationship: 'None the less, all sacrifices must be made in the interests of your genius', he wrote, making light of Gerhardie's displeasure, 'so I beg you to apply yourself with all your faculties to this rare work of yours—to watch your tending to careless phrasing—to cut out all apologies for writing about yourself.'

Memoirs of a Polyglot was published by Duckworth in June 1931, the intended dedication 'To Hugh Kingsmill, A fine writer but a rotten friend' having eventually and inexplicably been abandoned.[13] Humorous, highly entertaining, and sensitive, it ranks, with *Futility* and *The Polyglots*, amongst Gerhardie's best work, sharing with them an exploration of the elusive, undefined, authorial role in literature. An 'Author's Speech' prefaces the work, a flamboyant piece of rhetoric that instantly acknowledges Gerhardie's own public image:

An autobiography at thirty-five is not encouraged? Yet the idea that I should consecrate a book to my life came from a publisher. And the suggestion is irresistible even from a layman. Only think of it: your own, your very own life!

and in so doing establishes a starting-point from which to diverge. Whilst *Pending Heaven* concerned itself with the private complexities of creative self-expression, *Memoirs*, comically sceptical of the claims of autobiography, reveals the futility of a deliberate literary presentation of the self for a public. It is as much about the process of writing an autobiography as it is an account of his life, taking its rationale from Proust's notion that voluntary memory is (in the words of Samuel Beckett) 'of no value as an instrument of evocation'[14]—'We do not recall the spirit of a man by thinking about his spirit', writes Gerhardie 'But we come across a suit, a tie that he has worn, and our heart melts into tears.' To him, autobiography is an inescapably theatrical venture, presupposing an inquisitive, even prurient, audience. The distinctive rhetoric of his 'Speech' is taken up immediately in Chapter One:

Yesterday, at dinner, it suddenly occurred to me what a fine fellow I was. How modest I have been! How good! How unduly unassuming! Arnold Bennett once confided to me that it didn't matter how you wrote: what mattered was whether you were a good fellow. How unerring that man's instinct!

The critics' complaint of egocentricity must have been particularly irritating: it uses a perceptive term in the crudest fashion—to condemn. Gerhardie's work is 'egocentric', for it is about ego, about the problems of representing ego, the position of the self, and the influence of the self and all that surrounds it. The very structure of his work insists that the readers' attitude to this 'egocentricity' is, under Gerhardie's guidance, in constant flux, continual revision, often at Gerhardie's expense. The critics accused him of arrogantly displaying the life of Gerhardie, and yet totally failed to perceive that Gerhardie is indeed presenting an ego, but is uncertain to whom it can accurately be said to belong ('Our "personality", moreover, was even in life only properly discernible by others. The owner was only conscious of a certain always changing combination of feelings as registered by his senses, themselves in process of change').

Wyndham Lewis, in a story narrated by Ford Madox Ford, bursts into Ford's study and dragging him outside, harangues him on the 'impressionistic' techniques practised by Ford, James, and Conrad:

But that isn't what people want. They don't want vicarious experience; they don't want to be educated. They want to be amused . . . By brilliant fellows like me. Letting off brilliant fireworks. Performing like dogs on tightropes. Something to give them the idea they're at a performance. . . . Efface yourself! . . . Bilge![15]

The artist as performer: with a flourish—'Yesterday at dinner . . .'— Gerhardie introduces himself, a contemporary figure in the *middle* of his life, a consciousness in a perpetual process of change, like Proust's notion of the individual as 'the seat of a constant process of decantation . . . from the vessel containing the fluid of future time . . . to the vessel containing the fluid of past time'.[16] Throughout *Memoirs* its author perpetually resists anonymity, insists on an intimacy with his readers, challenges them to respond—to a greater extent even than Georges in *The Polyglots*. The distinction of *Memoirs* is achieved through the manipulative use of tense, a refusal to reduce a record of a life to conventional linear narrative in the manner of history, and an insistence that the essence of great autobiography must be a constant awareness of time. Years later the title of Nabokov's autobiography, *Speak, Memory*, uses much the same effects, juxtaposing the immediacy of 'speak' with all the weight of Nabokov's past, his 'memory'. Similarly, Gerhardie's opening word 'yesterday' makes play upon the metaphorical (that which is long past) and the literal (that which is closest to today). And the work ends by looking forward to his future which, like that of Georges in *The Polyglots*, will be significantly affected by the reader's attitude to the volume which conveys this information. This moment of the reader's engagement will influence Gerhardie's success.

Throughout *Memoirs of a Polyglot* Gerhardie makes use not only of what Desmond MacCarthy termed 'acute spontaneous comment'[17] but deliberately provocative addresses to the reader which, with great control and poise, blatantly take advantage of the *lack* of communication between reader and writer. He strikes a fine balance between observing the proprieties of patrons and literati and transgressing those proprieties. Thus, *Memoirs* often strikes one as a precarious book; there is a sense, when Gerhardie is recounting recent events, for instance, that he is introducing the reader into the company of those he is about to offend. Similarly, complaints about Gerhardie's 'regrettable lapses of taste' in his 'sordid amours' and in the disposal of his father's ashes were criticisms not so much of the deed as of his gall in writing down the deed. The *Glasgow Herald*, in an unusually perceptive review, declared:

There is nobody quite like Mr Gerhardi, and few good British people would wish to be. Mr Gerhardi does no more than quite a lot of others, but he writes about everything—which is simply not done. However, it should be remembered that art and life are not synonymous, nor are society and art, though both have conventions. And Mr Gerhardi is an artist—in an un-British way.[18]

Gerhardie is well aware that books provide a very specialized form of human contact. 'Lecturing was not the same as writing. If a reader does not laugh at your joke it's his affair. If a listener abstains from laughing at your joke, it becomes very much *your* affair.' In staging this point, *Memoirs* tells of a gathering at which Osbert Sitwell enquired, '"William, are you English?" I affirmed the fact, and, in accents more reminiscent of the Neva than the Thames side, began to support my statement by some details from my autobiography. . . . I was already well into the period when my father's father, on landing in Russia, travelled with his family in sleighs from Riga to St Petersburg, wolves pursuing them, when I noticed that Osbert had, probably some time ago, turned to the other side and was conversing with a middle-aged lady of mournful mien.' But what Sitwell found boring on a first hearing, the reader, as Gerhardie is well aware, has already heard *before*, in some detail back in Chapter One. Literature is a more accommodating place in which to meet people: as soon as our feelings are uncomfortably engaged we may shut the book.

The later chapters tell of his entry into a world of the famous and literary, fostering in the reader too a sense of intimacy with these celebrities ('Edith Sitwell . . . shrinks back when you talk to her, as if your voice were too loud'); only the solipsism of the title, 'The Visible World Exists?', reminds us we are actually engaged in a very solitary activity. His accounts of those he meets are irreverently levelling; 'The Author's Speech' grandiosely assures us: 'Nobody who appears here need resent it, since his appearance . . . is a guarantee of my approval, of my opinion that he or she must be preserved—rendered time-proof;

and so far from blaming me, they who walk these pages should rejoice at finding here an immortality not perhaps vouchsafed elsewhere.' Yet they are 'immortalized' chiefly for their trivialities. Gerhardie, in the words of the *Glasgow Herald*, makes 'delightfully suburban figures of these intellectuals':

His memoirs raise the question of reticence in literature—not so much reticence about sexual affairs as about social contacts. The puerilities of the great should be passed over in silence, because a belief in great men is one of the last dear illusions of democracy.

The (characteristically nineteenth-century) notion of the narrator as reliable and morally correct is upturned by Gerhardie, so that our reading becomes a process of puzzlement, outrage, and (perhaps) revaluation. Part IV tells of Gerhardie's entry into the world of the famous and literary; to begin with, this section looks as if it will conform to the more traditional notion of 'memoirs', where the centre of interest lies outside the writer, but instead attention circles almost imperceptibly back to the narrator, whose authority the reader must first determine for himself.

Despite his manifest scepticism of the value of autobiography as a form, Gerhardie acknowledges—albeit ironically—his awareness of its conventions and expectations: 'I must here confess that I am a descendant of *the* Gerhardie', and then he mockingly supplies full details of his pedigree. But, like Tristram Shandy, that over-scrupulous narrator of his own being, Gerhardie is immediately confronted by the problem of where to begin and what to include:

A scrupulous autobiographer feels he must not leave out an account of the places he has lived in. Yet he cannot afford to deal adequately with all the countries he has lived in without causing his book to swell to an unportable size. I am tempted to dismiss certain countries . . . and confine myself to a section containing the names and places I lived in, and having for its text merely the words: 'I been there'. Tunisia: 'I been there,' Paris: 'Also been there: Hotel Chambord.' Venice: 'Hotel Bauer', and so forth. I beg to remind the reader that I have been twice round the world. My autobiography accordingly could be rewritten, were this desirable, on a geographical basis. But would this exhaust the thoroughness of one's treatment, unless, writing of the places I had visited and reluctant to remain superficial in my reports of their scenic aspect, I probed everywhere down to the earth's core, rearranging my material and viewing the whole life from a geological standpoint?

Like Sterne he plays with the empirical limitations of both literature and individual experience. Attempts to describe the valet assigned to him in

India are doomed: 'He looked very like our old Russian coachman, Alexei. But as I have not described Alexei, the comparison is not illuminating.' And once recognized, the problems of autobiography multiply: instead of progressing, he becomes involved in perpetual humorous irrelevancies. The following passage, coming at the end of a long narrative about the Gerhardi relative who was—possibly—Gold-Stick-in-Waiting to George III, turns into a digression, after purporting to avoid one:

My readers may have grown impatient of all this speculative stuff. What is gold-stick to them, anyhow? What is he to me?

There they are wrong. Let me prove it. Supposing George III had been attacked during a state procession: the loyal gold-stick precipitates himself on the miscreant and decapitates him, while another assailant aims a stone at my potential ancestor. The gold-stick is flung from his saddle: they stoop, kneel over him—his heart has stopped beating. And the present book fails to make its appearance in this, or in any other spring list.

In an age notable for its exploration of the role of author in literature, Gerhardie insists that to a great extent it is the expectation of the reader that defines 'fiction' or 'autobiography':

It is difficult to know where to stop when writing of the early impressions of childhood. The danger is that it might prove more fascinating to the writer than the reader. After all, if I digress on the pleasures of my first motor-car will it not irritate the reader who, quite properly, will feel that my emotion cannot compare with his own at the gift of his first locomotive? And where is one to stop?

Once a book is labelled 'autobiography' the author must maintain a socially acceptable balance of informative, but not self-obsessive, narration. In spite of the pleasurable anticipation that 'You may speak of yourself without interruption—an indulgence which would be considered ill-bred anywhere else but in an autobiography', Gerhardie acknowledges such conventions of manners by ironically transgressing them.

The deliberate *avoidance* of an 'artistic shape', the refusal to see life—even one's own—in terms of plot, or an overall unity, in *Memoirs of a Polyglot* reaffirms Gerhardie's appreciation of Chekhov's 'loose-end' rendering of existence. For Gerhardie, the autobiographical problem of how to *convey*, with accuracy, a sense of oneself, is pre-empted by yet another question: that of how to *perceive*, how to extract relevance from, the flux of experience that is oneself. The *Glasgow Herald* grasped Gerhardie's awareness of these questions when it called him a 'will-o'-

the-wisp. He is without substance. He is disembodied sensation darting about over a marsh of prose . . . he refuses to be defined because he admits no standards.'

Chapters One and Two, 'Birth' and 'Childhood', circle perpetually round and round their subject—Gerhardie—exciting interest yet consistently resisting any streamlined interpretation. There are numerous conjectures which serve not only as pointers to possible historical facts, but as an encouragement to the imagination. Gerhardie even admits: 'What I have stated is as nearly true as I myself know or can surmise; and nothing, or next to nothing, follows therefrom.' After narrating some childhood memories and experiences, he concludes:

When I think of my childhood this is how it presents itself to me: There was this, then there was that. Then there was my mother's '*jour*'. Then my father's first motor-car. Not that these things come to me in chronological order. They rise all round me like little jets of water which remind me that just here is an oasis. But what total worth can I extract from my childhood? That depends on the calm of my soul.

Though he concedes (following on a host of childhood memories clamouring for inclusion) that: 'I have to limit myself to such experiences as may be shown to have been productive of some value and significance in respect of my character, such as it is', it is a reluctant concession: he is sceptical of the very notion of 'character', of 'being yourself', believing that there is no single personality, but only a situation analogous to that of 'a serpent changing skins'. But despite his pervasive diffidence about how and indeed whether a genuine autobiography can be written, *Memoirs* gives a full account of Gerhardie's life. And through its candour and humour it effectively expresses his personality as both nervous recluse and outspoken performer.

Memoirs of a Polyglot met with an enthusiastic—and spacious—critical reception. 'Whenever a new book by Mr William Gerhardi is published there sets in a period of Grave Warnings, reminiscent of the Great War. Mr Gerhardi is gravely warned that he is not doing justice to his own talents . . . that he shows no sign of being a Playboy of the Bulldog Breed', wrote Humbert Wolfe. 'Mr Gerhardi thinks aloud. . . . He is prepared to break through the conspiracy of restraint imposed by normal manners.'[19] L. P. Hartley was, however, the only reviewer (apart from the *Glasgow Herald*) to begin to grasp Gerhardie's use of his ego as a conscious literary device: 'an author does not cease to be brilliant, humorous, and delightful just because he is aware of being brilliant, humorous and delightful.'[20]

15

SATAN
June 1931–November 1932

*Perhaps we mustn't be quite real, because that would make us limited
and therefore ultimately dead . . . A being we imagine is alive, pulsating; a
being we know is but another dead rat like you and me, all eaten up by
hound Habit.*[1]

Letters arrived by every post. Prompted by the immediacy of Gerhardie's narrative style, unknown readers told him of their lives. 'I do not
know why I write this, and do not know if it is going to the right
gentleman', wrote one mysterious correspondent. 'Your reading, and
how you went into the Park for thought made it all come back', and she
went on to describe her solitary life, her happy days with her black
cocker spaniel, 'a Gentleman the *only* kind of mail I have ever walked out
with and I am 54 years'. She signed herself only C. May, 'A Servant',
and gave no address for a reply.

Another reader wrote to tell him of her husband, a war veteran of
William's own age and a victim of heart disease, lamenting that although
she enjoyed his novels they were 'alas' far too sad to give someone in her
husband's sorry condition: 'I only know your grim books. If you have
written anything else in a lighter vein please let me know.' A young
cotton worker from Rochdale asked if Gerhardie might read his
manuscript, and received a letter full of detailed and helpful criticism.
Others responded to the *Memoirs*' invitation: 'If there is anything in my
book you don't like, let us meet, let us discuss it, let us thrash it
out together', and suggested all manner of alterations and amendments.
And, most prolific of all, ghosts resurrected themselves from
Gerhardie's past—in Russia, the army, France, Austria. Always dis-
inclined to renew old acquaintances, William made an exception with
Jason Gurney from the Military Mission in Vladivostok, who entertained him at his West End club, Chez Minerva.

Predictably, Gerhardie also succeeded in scandalizing. 'Your bragging about checking your father's ashes in the Paris cloak-room puts you beyond the pale', fumed one incensed reader. Overtly Gerhardie dismissed such responses as the insensitivity of imbeciles (and often replied to just that effect), but he found it disheartening to be regarded as a 'laughing hyena', his pathos and sympathy unperceived. 'Sophistication, cynicism and the like, which still cling to me, I don't know why, have not endeared me to anyone', he wrote in a moment of despair. 'Sobriety, a dogged dullness, goodness and honest stupidity should be stressed as features characteristic of me. Then England will begin to read my books.'[2]

Nevertheless, most reviews had been encouraging and Gerhardie was nursing high hopes of the success of *Memoirs*, but sales quickly slowed down—only 1,850 copies by early August. So many people seemed to have read the book, so few to have bought it. His spirits sank again, a despondency aggravated by the financial worries which the book had been expected to alleviate. Then a hostile review appeared in one of Beaverbrook's papers. Harold Nicolson, whom Gerhardie admired, seemed a victim of 'that poor twisted English insularity that can't even approach a book freshly without invoking comparison with old drivel, "public school", "gentleman" and the like. . . . It is kind of him to say I am *not* a bounder, after putting it into people's heads that I am!'[3] Gerhardie, who always somewhat overestimated the power of the critics, believed his book was easily good enough to sell itself, provided it was not killed at birth, and wrote to Beaverbrook in dismay. Although they had been out of contact for a year or so—Gerhardie had been rude to a Beaverbrook friend—Beaverbrook, pleased with the portrait of himself in *Memoirs*, wrote to heal the breach and invited his former protegé to dinner. 'With a proper rift of offended greatness', Beaverbrook spoke only a couple of words to Gerhardie all evening.[4] And in response to Gerhardie's plea, he wrote blandly back: 'But, I think you should be quite indifferent to criticism anyway. . . . Do not be discouraged by the attacks of critics. Some people unwittingly invite attacks. I do. You do. Go on with your good work. And', he added ominously, 'read the life of Rousseau.'

It was often hard to reconcile Beaverbrook's extravagant protestations of friendship with his reluctance to perform apparently simple favours. Years later Gerhardie conceived the metaphor of Aladdin's lamp to describe their relationship: 'However slyly, however cunningly I rubbed the lamp, this way and that, the genie would not come out to grant my needed wish. To wit, an independence endowed to cultivate my own

Arabian garden', rather than 'wearing out my wits in guessing what everyone else, but I, might wish me to say about a given situation—a form of earning one's daily bread by eating one's own words in print'. Instead, the genie inveigled him into the lamp, where he became a prisoner. According to Taylor, Beaverbrook had an unpleasant habit of 'switching people on and off according to his mood. When he needed someone, no trouble was too great for him. When he turned to something else, his closest friends and even his wife ceased to exist for him.'[5] Full of unfocused good intentions towards acquaintances like Gerhardie, he consistently fostered expectations which he failed to meet, and often broke promises to print articles. If Gerhardie was foolish for continuing to believe Beaverbrook, Beaverbrook was myopic in failing to see that Gerhardie could not afford to ignore these promises. Greatly discomfited at so direct an appeal, Gerhardie none the less wrote again:

My dear Lord Beaverbrook,
   I reflect that you have it in your power to
   (a) serialize my book in your Press or parts of it;
   (b) cause a review to appear in the *Sunday Express*; and
   (c) ask Lord Rothermere to lift the embargo from a misunderstood author who has a weakness for newspaper proprietors.
   At this crucial moment this would make all the difference between success and comparative failure. I reflect that if my perhaps too blatant interest in my own fate on this earth may irritate you to inaction, you could not do more than *not* act on any one, or all, of these three points; in which case the result would not be worse than if I did not write to you at all. Nor would it dim my agreeable memories of you one wit . . . You must contrive to forgive me for bothering you about my own affairs. But it looks as if whatever I wrote, and however I wrote it, I was doomed to appeal to a dishearteningly small public.

And nothing came of it all. William continued to see a good deal of Beaverbrook ('What was the man's diabolical, unbelievable fascination?'). They dined together, partied together, and on one rare and memorable occasion visited the theatre together (Beaverbrook, considerably more egotistical than two years before, now disliked having to keep quiet while others did the talking, and preferred to occupy the centre of the stage himself). But the conversation was no longer of Gerhardie and his potential. 'He found me troublesome in the end', William acknowledged in old age, sympathetic towards his patron over the constant demands of those 'taking it for granted that you have to give them money'.[6] Evelyn Waugh was less concessionary, and remarked that Beaverbrook 'was much disappointed by his failure to promote the success of Gerhardie (who deserved it). I think it made him realise the impotence of the press.'[7]

Beaverbrook had been busy. Literary matters cast aside, he was launching his campaign for Empire Free Trade, something he believed would solve the country's chronic economic ills. With the help of Lord Rothermere he founded the United Empire Party; his campaign quickly became a mission, and in this fervent Empire Crusade he grew more and more to resemble Lord Ottercove: 'Hannibal playing quoits with the world', as Frank Dickin observes. 'Not, I regret to say, because he loves the world, but because he loves playing quoits.'[8] Gerhardie saw Beaverbrook speak at the Paddington Baths in support of the party candidate, 'with a strange mystic look in his eye, raising his arm now and again as he walked up to the platform. The hall was filled with hysterical women. Lord Beaverbrook, after shaking hands with the personages on the platform, immediately began to rage and weep and implore, looking at a distance like a sublime frog. . . . His voice rose and sank, rose and sank, his gestures went out in appeal, in defiance. He staggered back, and, spent, sank into his chair. With eyes that did not see, the eyes of a sleep-walker, he left the platform.'[9] In September 1931, shortly after the formation of the National Government, Britain went off the gold standard; the same evening Gerhardie dined with Beaverbrook and a group of financial experts, and he was amused to observe that they were all 'in a dithering state of panic' and without the remotest idea what had caused the crisis or how they would cope with it. 'The atmosphere was that of wealthy people on the *Titanic*, whose sense of doom was aggravated by what they had to lose in addition to their lives.'[10] On election day a month later, Beaverbrook gave a large party where Gerhardie soon discovered that all the rich people were losing their money fast, 'which is cheering. I went to see Lady Louis Mountbatten the other day, who is selling her Park Lane house, as well as her country house. She can't afford to pay the enormous super tax and says they have always been paupers, anyhow. The Prince of Wales is storing her furniture for her. Which is more than he has done for me.'

And throughout it all Beaverbrook continued to be pleasant. 'I am very fond of my Gerha'di', he announced after picking up the telephone and buying a million pounds worth of shares; but he gave no practical expression to it. What Beaverbrook did give very liberally was advice: on what Gerhardie should do with the money that he did not have, how best to utilize his US earnings, and what sort of books he should write. He also offered publicity as part of a new series he had conceived, entitled 'Splendid Failures'.[11] Clara was furious. 'I find old Beaverbrook a fraud and certainly not the man to be at the head of the B. Government. His word is not sacred. I am glad he did not invite me. I do not want to see his froggie face at all! disgusted!!', and she even considered changing from the *Sunday Express* to the *Sunday Referee*: 'I don't think I will help to fill Beaverbrook's coffers any longer—I'm sure he will feel it don't you think!' But Gerhardie acquiesced to the article, thankful for any limelight.

In truth it must be said that Gerhardie was something of a financial idealist. 'A real writer would rather starve in the streets than do an honest day's work', he rather pompously declared, quoting Shaw. The comfort of his youth led him to treat poverty lightly, not through forbearance so much as foolish faith, as *Memoirs of a Polyglot* eloquently testifies:

The effect of early wealth cannot be taken away, as the Russian Revolution, which took it away, has shown. What you have had you retain, and what you have come down to you are inclined to regard as a period of transition. A cursory study of the cheerful (if sometimes foolish) hopefulness of Russian refugees through-out the world amply bears this out. Though I have not as yet soared high enough above overdraft 'accommodation' anxiety level to take a bird's-eye view of it, the sight of wealth in others leaves me untroubled. A nostalgia for a stately white-marble staircase alone remains with me. But that is all.[12]

Gerhardie could readily have found employment in a variety of (not uninteresting) ways. Good interpreters were in short supply between the wars; both Evelyn Waugh and Graham Greene were considerably inspired by their work as journalists abroad. Very occasionally Gerhardie considered literary translation, but he had little inclination because he believed that ideas 'demand a form and style of expression precisely their own', 'that is why genuine writers, who cherish languages on account of the idiom which reveals a new world to them, cannot be made, except with the utmost reluctance, to express their thoughts in a medium other than which they had made uniquely their own, however fluent they may be in a foreign language'.[13] He once considered entering the diplomatic service, but found, on drawing up a list, that there were eighteen reasons for not doing so (including lack of money—the service required some degree of private means) and only one for: vanity. He often teased Clara by announcing that he had decided to give up writing and take up dirt-track racing, conjuring, or psychoanalysis as a pro-fession, and Clara, 'who apparently can never be sure of the extent of my sanity', invariably took him seriously and worked hard to dissuade him. But William had no intention of being deflected from literature; he thrived on 'glorious uncertainty'—with the proviso that it not last long. The prospect of a regular but modest income had no appeal, a romanticism for which he was prepared to sink to the level of 'Splendid Failure'. And even though it was becoming increasingly clear that a career in literature was far more precarious than he had at first imagined, Gerhardie's enthusiastic optimism about eventual success was almost unbounded. After years of disappointments Patsy wrote to Clara: 'I really do wonder at myself sometimes—that I, such a sober and level-headed person should have so succumbed to your Willy's optimism that I fervently believe in the riches coming to us from Irish Sweepstakes, toothbrushes, plays, books, heiresses, etc!' 'Verily', commented Clara, 'if a policeman's job is a hard one, so is a writer's.'

In later life Gerhardie was rather proud of not having been deflected from his writing, though a misplaced pride it was. Being so short of money, he was constantly having to compromise what he wrote, always keeping in tune to some extent with popular opinion. He no longer had the time to digest his material, to 'filter out the irrelevance, so that only the essential remains'. But, more importantly, his material was growing sparse. Desmond MacCarthy had perceptively warned of Gerhardie's desire to 'put up the Proustian shutters and regard the outside world as existing only for the sake of its reflection in his private *camera obscura*. In Gerhardi artistic detachment has been reinforced by cultural rootlessness. There is, therefore, a danger that he may not care enough about anything except his work, to save that from becoming thin and fantastic.'[14] This was gradually coming true. Gerhardie's best work is a result of involvement with historical events—Vladivostok, for example, was 'an ever-shifting, changing *sense of being alive*'.[15] Yet increasingly Gerhardie cultivated a Proustian reserve. It was an unfortunate result of his early acclaim, the perpetual label of 'genius', that led him to believe that the genius lay primarily in himself, the individual, rather than in the product of the individual. His notebooks and jottings make fine, rather Chekhovian, reading but increasingly they became the *substance* of his work. 'I simply can no longer dispense with a secretary, as my whole process of writing (the keeping of a kind of journal and card-indexing every thought) has developed into a real organization', he wrote when he first appointed Patsy. But the thoughts and observations were now spawned from a far narrower field than previously, and for him London society was a poor substitute. His best books of the 1930s, *Resurrection* and *Of Mortal Love* are fine novels, but they do not do justice to Gerhardie's brilliant early start.

In fact, that very year he had begun work on a critical appreciation of Proust, at the invitation of the publishers Harpers. 'You will find there is a comical jealousy about him', he wrote to Edith Wharton, who had been invited to take over the unfinished portion of Scott-Moncrieff's translation, *Le Temps retrouvé*. '*So* very many people consider themselves the only person authorized to understand Proust, while one would think he did not lack explicitness in his works, and in fact explained himself so well that there is precious little left for commentators.' Wharton declined the invitation, and Gerhardie's book was eventually abandoned, probably because Samuel Beckett's *Proust*, which he much admired, appeared that year.

Reluctantly he pressed on with articles, publishers' reports, and book reviews, praising in particular Phelps Hodges's *Britmis*, a 'lucid, strangely fascinating' account of the Allied Intervention, in which 'travel and adventure in circumstances not to be arranged by a Cook's tour loom largely over every page'.[16] With the really dull fiction he invariably wrote, 'It is by far Miss Smith's best!' because it did not commit him to anything and gave the reader an idea what her worst must be like. But he found it weary work: two days to ponder the subject, three days to actually write it, and the weekend to overcome the ill-effects. When commissioned journalism grew scarce, Gerhardie submitted to the *Express* a list of suggested titles aimed at the popular market: 'Why I am anti-dog'; 'Why I love children'; 'Sons and mothers'; 'What I would do if I were king'; 'Are you a social climber?' But the mood was changing and the press no longer wanted flippant, inconsequential subjects such as these, but material more in keeping with increased political awareness. Even dining with Beaverbrook, where formerly they had danced and drunk champagne, the party tuned in to hear H. G. Wells broadcasting about what he would do if he were dictator. Afterwards Beaverbrook sat in a corner discussing politics with Leslie Hore-Belisha before rushing off to telephone Churchill.

Such political proximity he found entertaining, and many experiences were later incorporated into his ambitious 'biography of the age', *God's Fifth Column*. But as a novelist Gerhardie, like Nabokov, believed that he should remain distant from political issues. 'Literature, though it holds no solution for life, is in the nature of its passion a shedder of light, illuminating the dark labyrinths we tread.'[17] Art had the power to redeem only inasmuch as it could sensitize and improve the scope of the imagination. And imaginative poverty was as regrettable as any other kind of poverty:

When it comes to names, styles and titles, I am all in favour of aristocracy. I don't believe that the 'blood' of an eighth Marquis is any different from that of a chimney sweep, and I am conscious of the circuitous and fortuitous way in which the eighth Marquis succeeded the first. But I feel it adds colour and mental pageantry to life when the butler, having announced a Mr Smith, improves on it with: 'His Majesty the Emperor of Russia'. The effect is aesthetic. . . . it is also artistic because, after the manner of art, a historic name recalls and suggests and sets phantasy into play. If the title fits the person, well and good. If it does not, all the better: the incongruity leads us to appreciate life's contrasts and the essential flux and instability of human values.[18]

Whilst Socialism had appeared a necessary goal for Russia, England, smaller and more literate, required, in his view, a Liberal government. His Liberalism, though sincere, illustrates more his profound aversion to any form of extremism or involvement than his political conviction. It developed eventually into an idealized notion of *laissez-faire* individualism, taking little account of the circumstances of the situation. 'My sympathies have *always* been on the side of the people', Gerhardie told a friend who considered voting Conservative. 'For the people's cause has always proved, retrospectively, to be the right one. To vote conservative at any time, anywhere, is—forgive me—an absurdity and always an anachronism.'[19] He occasionally made a political gesture: in 1932 he wrote to the *News Chronicle* protesting against 'a really scandalous example of public insensibility', the fact that there was still a man undergoing penal servitude for desertion in the Great War.[20] He continued to argue heatedly with Dolly, a fervent admirer of Churchill, and once, under circumstances that are not recorded, he stood up on a soap box and spoke in the park ('I have embraced the cause of the revolution. . . . I have taken up the cause of the unemployed and the extreme Socialists against the National Government'). But these were isolated incidents.

Gerhardie's aloofness extended to the circumstances of his daily life. In love affairs he tended to be civil, but easily irritated by demands made upon him. When a casual affair was beginning to get 'a little out of hand', he wrote, not without irony, 'I don't know what women want. All I want is not to give them any money. Not to take them out. Not to buy them anything. To have them at my beck and call, and not to bother me when I do not require them.'[21] Though capable, in rare moments, of the most forceful emotions, most of the time he retained his 'baffling detachment'. Anthony Powell, who worked at Duckworth's in the 1930s and had a few brief dealings with Gerhardie, remembered that he was perfectly friendly in manner 'but distinctly "foreign" and always wanted everything to be on the chilliest business footing', so that when the director of Duckworth's asked him to luncheon Gerhardie replied, 'Need we eat? Can't we just meet?'[22]

Some people saw this attitude as offensive. Yet it was an offensiveness bred of the desire to be alone rather than to insult. An ex-teacher, saddened by his description of Kensington College in *Memoirs of a Polyglot*, invited him to return now that Mr Bumphill had retired, and to see for himself how different things had become. Gerhardie declined, kindly but firmly: 'I think the only way to get full satisfaction out of life is for each person to live on his own emotions, and not to allow them to be governed by what is less real, such as some assumed sense of obligation not shared by oneself.'[23] Harriet Cohen also found herself on the receiving end of Gerhardie's aloofness. 'You don't *give* much to your fellow human beings, do you?' she wrote. To some extent this was also true in a literal sense: with the exception of Clara, William preferred to be free of the obligation of giving presents, and he always said that he liked to dine at the expense of the rich because 'the notion that hospitality should be returned at all is, on the face of it, absurd—a cruel contradiction in terms. For it thus dissolves into an obligation thoughtlessly contracted and, oh misery! to be repaid.'[24]

He was still in regular contact with Kingsmill who, with Dorothy and two young children to support, was so worried by poverty that he had written to the red-haired secretary and demanded 'under menaces' the return of the money he had spent on her. 'Really he is quite naif—a child', commented Clara. Influenced by *Pending Heaven* he too had tried his hand at an autobiographical account of the years 1927–9, in which Gerhardie was presented 'with flattering emphasis' as a character called Paul Mavatini. This was eventually abandoned and Kingsmill was currently occupied with *The Table of Truth*, a collection of parodies including one modelled on Gerhardie's style, 'I Cross the Rubicon'. The two of them now considered working together, and over the next few years toyed with a number of ideas. BBC debates were currently popular and Kingsmill suggested that they conduct a series: 'That early recognition is good for a writer', 'That marriage is good for a writer', 'That private means are bad for a writer': ('I don't mind which side I take, though, personally, I think private means are devilish good for a writer').

None of these ideas developed, but early in 1931 Gerhardie began collaborating with Kingsmill's younger brother Brian Lunn. Lunn was born in 1893, and his Oxford years had been interrupted by the war. He was posted to Mesopotamia as a second lieutenant in the Black Watch, where he suffered a nervous breakdown, a collapse vividly described in his autobiography *Switchback*. At least twice he tried to kill himself: once he borrowed a raincoat from a passer-by and trudged out to sea but, finding no water (it being low tide), was obliged at last to turn back; on another occasion, after a matrimonial dispute, he made for the window in order to jump out, but hurried back to bed when his wife called him. Like Kingsmill he had spent many years during the 1920s working abroad for his father's tourist agency, and like Kingsmill he was eventually removed from the family business when his marriage collapsed (his wife ran off with a Serbian called Popovitch).

Lunn was lodging in an extremely small room with a divan at the top of a house, 'but Gerhardi, coming in one night when I was in bed, observed that I had only to think myself on wheels in a sleeper and I would be enjoying accommodation which a rajah would not disdain'.[25] Lunn greatly valued Gerhardie's stimulating company; William appreciated Lunn's 'ironic and kindly outlook and temperament'. Gerhardie had recently conceived of what he termed a 'plane' history, a history whose special aim was to present events simultaneously as they occurred in different parts of the world. He suggested that, as it was an ambitious book, they should write it together, splitting the profits half and half. Lunn, £1,000 in debt and anxious to tell his disapproving father that he was at last working, but none the less intimidated by Gerhardie's intellectual arrogance, suggested that he do half the writing and most of the reading for one-third of the profit. Sir Henry Lunn advised Brian to draw up a contract. 'Gerhardi replied that as I had introduced my father into the affair we had better have a general family discussion to which he would invite his mother and his aunt. A few days later I rang him up; he said his hands were soapy, so he could only talk into the telephone, not listen.'[26]

Lunn joined the London Library and began to supply Gerhardie with all kinds of strange anecdotes culled from little-known French and German books, but they had the greatest difficulty in getting the plane idea to work. Gerhardie said they needed a character who had experienced human history as a whole; one afternoon they were walking in Regent's Park, talking of Goethe's *Faust* and the Wandering Jew, and there and then they fixed upon the title *The Memoirs of Satan*, 'a history of mankind presented through the imaginary experience of Satan who, at crucial moments in the lives of famous figures, real and legendary, enters them in turn to enable him to give the inside story in every case'.[27] But the book continued to be troublesome. It took the two of them not half the time (as planned) but double, and more than once William came close to abandoning it altogether. He complained that he could not write until his accommodation was properly furnished. To Lunn's exasperation he took infinite trouble with the arrangements of the flat and 'no woman could have been more painstaking in dealing with shop people. His fastidiousness amounted to morbidity, and as mine is under-developed our relations were not free from friction.'[28] And yet Lunn admitted that no one could have been both so stimulating and encouraging to a novice, and 'but for this collaboration, I could never have embarked upon writing a book by myself'.[29] Sometimes Gerhardie was irritable, due, he later pointed out, to Lunn's mistaken notion that alcohol stimulated his intelligence. Gerhardie worried about Lunn, 'who never baths year in, year out, and wears no pants so that his trousers do the work of pants in perpetuity, and who is a *chronic* drunk and splutters at you in his animation'. The fastidious William also disliked Lunn's alcoholic tendency to grow red in the face and sweaty.

Lunn, occasionally melancholic, shared much of his brother's delightful eccentricity and muddle-headedness. He invented a new pair of wooden water-wings which he hoped to patent and hurried Gerhardie along to the public swimming-pool to try them out. Lunn appeared from the changing-room, a chaotic figure in a vermilion bathing suit, the wings attached to his body by a ludicrously complicated series of rubber bands. Once afloat the whole contraption impeded his movements so much that he could neither sink nor swim, only drift helplessly along. Outside of the swimming-pool Gerhardie found Lunn a helpful though unimaginative co-author, 'a very bright, interesting, clever lad, but with whole strings of links missing unexpectedly here and there. He seems to lack both mental and emotional continuity which is apt to jar on one. And the privilege of being tired, the luxury of being irritated he seems to regard as a Lunn monopoly.'[30] Lunn for his part noticed that Gerhardie's good temper would last for three visits after a useful contribution and then, on the fourth, his mentor became increasingly pained, 'and as the lift clicked its way past the four or five floors to his flat . . . I felt as apprehensive as when I went into form in my early schooldays with scamped homework'.[31] Gerhardie never really put his heart into *Satan* and later annoyed Lunn by speaking of it slightingly as a novel which 'strove to be *consciously* popular'.[32]

When nerves were particularly bad Patsy soothed them, 'her remarkable influence as mediator being due to her goodness of heart and the fact that she inspired absolute confidence in her sense of fairness, which with her sense of humour made it possible for her to be equal friend of both of us without prejudice to her loyalty to Gerhardie, whom she called not "William" like everybody else, but "Genius".'[33] Patsy was, in fact, astonishingly similar to her boss in temperament. Normally shy, nervous, and very mindful of her privacy, in certain company she could transform into the wittiest of entertainers. Like him she was prone to rages of volcanic intensity—although they never quarrelled with each other, only teased. Her knowledge of literature, developed under William's guidance, was formidable, and her literary judgement impeccable. Although, curiously, Patsy nowhere appears as a fictional character in Gerhardie's novels, her invisible presence as stimulus, critic, and sage is boundless.

Gerhardie was still savouring the pleasures of his new flat, not least of which was that he could now accommodate Clara with ease. He continued to pay occasional visits to Bolton, but it was a taxing experience, not only because of the 'mournful soullessness' of the town itself, but the lack of tranquillity within the family. He usually travelled by the cheap night train and arrived in the early hours. Clara always retired to Tamara's tiny room on these occasions. Her own, which William took, was chilly, and smelled of the lace that she had loved to wear in Russia, now old and neatly folded away, and all around were photographs of her 'remarkable family'. The drawing-room too was damp and cold and the fire lighted only one day a week for economy—and still more photographs: the five children dressed in sailor suits, Clara and Charles in Monte Carlo, the family relaxing in their wooden dacha long before the shadow of revolution, William, Daisy, and Dolly on the tennis court, Clara and Rosie in a carriage outside the St Petersburg house. 'I want you to take everything very quietly and to enjoy a thorough rest while you're here, dear', she would say to William, putting him to bed with a hot-water bottle as soon as he arrived. But she could not keep away for long, and kept hurrying in and out to get things she needed from the cupboard and because she had thought of something amusing to tell him.

Clara, who complained that the stairs were killing her, constantly hurried up and down them. Lying abed William heard the sounds of her dragging something heavy upstairs, whereupon she entered the room backwards pulling behind her a large, black, oil stove. Then she would disappear, reappear again, and tell him that a meal would be ready in forty minutes, so he had enough time to get a good sleep first. But knowing he had only forty minutes he could not sleep at all, until thirty minutes had passed when, just as he was dozing off, Clara would enter 'with a very cheerful face, all full of exuberance and loving kindness', exhorting: 'Rise up, bold Jack, and fight again!' Then she would go downstairs again and shortly afterwards call up to Aunt Sissie that it was time to get up. Sissie always replied—'*All-right!*'—in an old, piping, hoarse voice too weak to carry, so that Clara called a second time ('with a slight tone of resentment this time')—'Sissie! I *said* you could get up now!'—and again Sissie answered (this time on a higher note)—'*All-right!*' Up popped Clara again at William's bedside. 'I really must tell you, darling, how glad I am you've come. It is really lovely to have you here. I do love to spoil you. Now you must stay a long time and have a thoroughly good rest. But I mustn't stay talking to you. I must see to the boiler. The bath will be ready for you in another ten minutes. Don't get up yet.'[34] The house was bitterly cold, with linoleum on the floor and only a few rugs. William lay in his bath until he heard the sound of his mother's voice again. So he got out of the warm bath and walked, dripping, to ask what she had called. 'I said, "You have another ten minutes!"'

Clara and Aunt Sissie were excessively punctual—their lives were a fuss of excitement to keep set meals, and their relation one of perpetual telepathic feud: Clara dominant, Sissie surreptitiously attempting to foil her dominance. Though Clara fussed over and cosseted Sissie, she never tired of pointing out that she only took the house to give Auntie a home, and sometimes when Auntie got too much on her nerves a round of visits was suggested, and Auntie wrote off to her Wadsworth nieces to say she was thinking of coming to stay with them. William tried to speak to Sissie when Clara was not there, so as not to rouse his mother's jealousy; whenever he greeted her she replied, 'Well, well—Oh dear, oh dear', with a look 'of helpless irony as if to imply that if she had the managing of this world things would be different'. 'How am I? No, not very well, no. I don't know what I'm doing on this earth. As Grandpa used to say, "It's time to go to my long last home."' He noticed that her white skin had turned yellow, like a shrivelled lemon, and the beautiful, long, carrot-red hair of her girlhood was almost white, but she still curled it every night with curling papers in a Queen Alexandra fashion. She always sat in a miniature straw-plaited chair which almost enveloped her, and laughed in an 'old, quakey way'. One visitor whom she entertained with her tales of her trips around Russia as a girl found her 'a lovely elfish old lady, pure Tchehov'.[35] She made a point of never going to church, having inherited old Wadsworth's notions that all clergymen were bounders, liars, and parasites.

Sissie could not sleep at night and wanted to come down as early as possible in the mornings, an ambition which Clara concentrated all her nervous force to frustrate. Sissie took *Home Chat* magazine, which she then sent on to Rosie in Russia, and the *Daily Mail*, and she knew everything there was to know about the royal family, though her erudition became unreliable farther back than Queen Victoria. She had strong views about the present government: she did not think much of Baldwin, and 'as for MacDonald—"oh! dear me! dear me!" she exclaimed shaking her head and waving her hand in a hopeless gesture'. She longed to help in the kitchen, but Clara for some perverse reason was adamant that she should not, and always managed the cooking herself, though she hated to do so. When William was staying she prepared all the Russian dishes that he had loved as a child: pies stuffed with cabbage, *bitochki* (little meat balls), and Russian pancakes with plenty of jam and honey to satisfy his sweet tooth. She insisted on giving second, third, and fourth helpings, urging, 'eat it while it's hot, you must eat while you are here'.

Looking around Clara's Bolton house William, as he remembered the beautiful dull-green and bronze drawing-room in St Petersburg, thought to himself that she had 'lost her aesthetic orientation'. Clara was proud of having done so well on so little money, but her taste had been too greatly influenced by Dolly's sombre preferences. William painted a portrait of Dolly, as Dinah's sister Katherine, 'fond of everything brown', in *Of Mortal Love*:

Katherine's life was as sober as her colours. Her house was as sober and neat as her person, as her life. She had very little money to spare. Everything was worked out to go a long way. They had a car which absorbed the minimum of petrol and took them long distances. Her family lived in harmony and she was as content with her life as she was content with her family; as content with the national Press and the daily discussion of problems it offered as she was content with the national broadcasting for the variety of entertainment it afforded within the home; and reviewing the equivocal state of the world in general Katherine was content with her country as she was with everything else.[36]

As soon as lunch was over Clara worried about tea. Dolly lived close by and usually visited on Sunday afternoon with her family. Clara had a tendency to show off William which annoyed his sister, who refused to treat him as a favourite. Clara also argued with William. 'You have been and gone, like some bright meteor flashing through the sky', she wrote after a particularly inflammatory visit. 'Only I had wished it less scorching at times.' But despite the disputes Clara was in her element: the older she grew the more family-conscious (even family-obsessed) she became. Once Victor's daughter Christina visited with a young friend; but the child, sent out on an errand, was gone an unusually long time. When concern was expressed Clara looked puzzled and asked, 'What's all the fuss about? She isn't a member of the family.'

Dolly was not the only regular visitor, for Clara was popular in Bolton and known affectionately in Forton Avenue as the 'Old Queen' after Queen Mary. 'I never knew that titles were obtained so easily,' she remarked with pride. She had a prosperous admirer, Mr Waterhouse, who wished to marry her, but Clara felt she was too old to change her ways. Her clever son was even more of a celebrity: even the sales-girl in Boots questioned her closely about the famous writer. Occasionally William would tolerate tea with Clara's friends; he appreciated their attention in the abstract but found it irritating in practice, and never remained in Bolton longer than a few days.

Thankfully back in the peace of his flat, William had always aimed to obviate the effort of life. He dreamed of a machine which in the morning 'insinuated itself into your bed and on a steel arm lifted and lowered you into your tub, where it washed and shaved you, and thrust you expeditiously into your clothes.'[37] With this in mind he had employed Edith, a hefty middle-aged maid-cum-charwoman, who styled herself 'housekeeper'. She would turn up when it pleased her, wake him up, and cook his breakfast. If she was late he stayed in bed with a clear conscience, and if she failed to turn up he failed to get up. Edith was loyal but not very efficient and annoyingly talkative. One morning she came to him beaming—

'Oh,' she cried, 'I asked my hubby' (a policeman), 'Oh,' I asked, 'What do you think of Mr Gerhardie's novels?' 'Rotten,' he said. 'Oh, they are rotten!' All this with a smile of enthusiasm.[38]

Worst of all, she suffered from bad hay-fever each year and sneezed everywhere. Gerhardie wrote a play scenario about just such a woman whose employer, too kind-hearted to give her notice, poisons her.

Clara paid her first visit to Rossetti House in July 1931 after William had gone to infinite pains to make sure her room was warm and perfectly comfortable. She brought a vacuum cleaner and some curiously shaped pyjamas she had made for her son, and spent the following weeks cooking for him, arranging curtains, carpets, and furnishings, and advising on *Satan*. William found her exhausting. Every morning, very early, she strode into his bedroom demanding cheerfully: 'What are we going to do today?' William pointed out that she ought to take advantage of her holiday to stay in bed, but she only replied, 'I am an old woman and I have my habits.' Each day he racked his brains for ways to amuse her. To Clara's great delight they attended a society garden party at which the British Gaumont Film Company had been given permission to make a 'talkie', and they later watched themselves on the screen at a private viewing. He remembered that Victor Cazalet, who had been in Vladivostok, was now an MP. Cazalet duly conducted them both round the House of Commons one afternoon before sitting down to listen to a debate at which Clara, too, was very talkative: she vociferously lamented that she had not been given a programme, then nodded assent throughout the speeches and made elaborate whispers, until William pointed to a notice on the wall saying that visitors were not allowed to make comments. Then at the conclusion of a speech, unable to contain herself any longer, she said aloud, 'Quite right!'

At the theatre she had a maddening habit of explaining what was happening. She had been brought up to be bright and cheerful in company, and the more grand and elaborate the party, soirée, or ball, the more eagerly Clara participated. On such occasions William always wanted to convey to his mother that the event was the grandest, the most impressive and spectacular that London had to offer, whilst simultaneously remaining casually unimpressed himself. She always appeared with a great deal of jewellery, lace, and ornamentation. Rather too much ornamentation, her niece Christina considered, who thought she looked like a Christmas tree. 'You must admit that I looked nice,' Clara said after one particularly grand occasion. 'I noticed Sir James, while talking to me, was all the time looking at my diamond necklace.' Her son then regarded her 'in that quasi-unintelligent way that people have who have been taken aback', so that she continued, rather reproachfully: 'You never told me how I looked. I think I was a credit to you. But one never knows.' William, torn between love, pride, and irritation, invariably ended up losing his temper.

Clara viewed Patsy with approval—'your trusty and valiant helper'— and because she enjoyed 'a really first-rate comical insight into character', she had even grown to like Hugh Kingsmill, 'an irresponsible dear and such a boy'. In fact Clara was quite at ease with all her son's friends and would sit up late at night with them discussing the day. Once she asked an aspiring writer what time he liked to wake up in the mornings, adding, 'I thought you might be a late riser like he is. One can never tell with geniuses.' Her greatest pleasure was to feel herself a part of William's domestic and cultural ménage, 'a member of your circle', able to talk literature with him and not 'vegetate'. She liked to sit and listen, knitting, whilst he dictated to Patsy. Then he would read it back aloud for discussion. Clara's role as ideal reader—sensitive, careful, attentive and deeply appreciative—was perhaps her most valuable asset. 'You know so much and I love to learn from you', she wrote. 'I always look forward to our talks which educate and enlarge my understanding. I fear I go back when I do not see you for some time, my dear clever boy.' And so as soon as she had departed, William, overcome with relief, then grief and nostalgia, sat down to write to her. 'I felt very sad after you had gone off. It was such a short stay. And when I came home and saw your empty bed I felt a lump in my throat. I wished you were still here. That empty bed of yours is a very sad sight. You know I love you *dearly* and couldn't live without you—even though we argue each other's head off when we are together, all about nothing.'

Clara always responded to these letters as soon as she received them, sitting down in Forton Avenue with her spectacles and pen to think out the reply. 'My own sunny boy, my Vassinka', she would address him. 'Now lovie, good bye for the present. I won't send kisses they would be a bit sticky perhaps in this heat but tons of love to you dear.' She continued to cosset him from afar, sending food, clothing, and items from her 'beauty box', mending a shirt after the laundry had returned it 'ripped and torn as if it had been in a bullfight'. Anxious over his habit of sitting up till 4.00 a.m., she recommended rusks with boiling milk, and sent a warm 'coatee' to wear in bed. When she learned that Edgar Wallace had died from flu, all her concern was justified: 'It is *very very* dangerous stepping out of a hot bath, or any bath, onto a cold floor. I do wish you would not risk your health so.'

December came and *Satan* was still troublesome. 'This Christmas finds me in as uncertain a mood as last Christmas and the Christmas before; and anyhow, I hate Christmas.' William spent it alone in Rossetti House, 'working on that damned history', eating the Christmas pudding and the enormous mince pie that Clara sent, and fighting the flu.

One evening in the new year Gerhardie was enjoying the company of some bright young débutantes at a society ball, when he was unexpectedly accosted by an imposing elderly woman who said that she recognized his photograph from his book jacket. This was Lady Muriel Paget who had earlier written to Gerhardie about Rosie's plight in the Soviet Union. Paget now informed him that, according to her agents in Leningrad, Rosie was again in 'dreadful distress'. She earned only a pittance from teaching; Leonya could not find work because of having been in prison, and was suffering from painful sciatica ('Poor fellow, his turn has come', commented Clara. 'I only wonder how he has held out so long'). The family were all practically without shoes, subsisting on gruel made from potatoes and water, and entirely dependent upon parcels from England. Paget had advanced the Misernuiks £3 worth of supplies (which sum she promptly extracted from Gerhardie). To add to their troubles, Rosie's youngest child, 6-year-old Galina, had suffered from diptheria and kidney trouble. Also severely spastic, with little control over her limbs and her head prone to flop, she needed not only medicine but constant attention, and she was easily irritated by the slightest noise, draught, or light. 'If the Lord would only take poor little Galina what a happy release it would be for the poor little thing', sighed Clara.

The next morning William assembled two large parcels of provisions, including £15 in cash, and arranged for Victor to dispatch the necessary medicine from Finland. With Paget's help he succeeded in arranging for Rosie to receive a sack of flour regularly at the expense of the British government, and opened her a credit of £20, the cost of the visa out of Russia. He then sent a letter by diplomatic bag direct to the British Consul in Leningrad, which was delivered by Paget's representative so as to avoid falling into Soviet hands. In this he warmly urged his sister to come to live in England; he promised to pay her expenses, look after her when she arrived, and somehow find her work. He had, he explained, a really big scheme in hand which he hoped would make them all rich shortly. 'My own dearest brotherkins', wrote Rosie when at long last a letter got through. 'You do not know dear how fond of you I am and only wish I had shown you my love when you so needed a little more help and affection. Honestly I never knew what you had to go through when you enlisted as a Private during the war!! Poor boy!' To comfort herself she read and reread his books, composing long letters to the family (breaking into Russian at particularly emotive moments) and enclosing her own poems.

Clara, however, was growing weary of the perpetual calls for help. She had recently spent many months in Antibes nursing Daisy yet again. Daisy's husband, who had never fully recovered his nerves after the war, seemed quite incapable of looking after his wife, and their fortunes were sinking. 'I fear poor Jean will have no socks to pull up soon,' remarked Clara, who could not imagine how they were to take on the responsibility for any more sick and impoverished people. In regard to Rosie, Clara felt it was not a good idea for her to come over. She particularly disapproved of the (now inescapable) fact that if Rosie came she would be parted forever from Leonya. 'Marriage in my day meant "for better for worse" and I believe still, that one should try and play the game.' Moreover, she pointed out, 'Galina is his heart's delight and what he would suffer if she was taken from him I would not care for anyone to go through'.

But William's spirits were buoyant, for *Satan* was drawing to completion and he had succeeded in selling it, without the intervention of an agent, for an advance of £1,000. Cassell's, immensely impressed with the book, thought the idea 'one in a thousand' and, convinced it would be 'a big winner', planned for enormous sales. When Beaverbrook saw the proofs he made his mistress read aloud the Jesus and Noah chapters, and misled Gerhardie into believing he would serialize it in the *Daily Express*. *The Memoirs of Satan* appeared in November 1932, together with a substantial publicity campaign involving fifty plaster copies of Bianca's bust of Gerhardie distributed in bookshops around London, each one surrounded by lurid pictures of Satan. The book itself carried a sinister dust-jacket of Satan in human form seated at his desk in three-quarters face ('He frightens me. I hope he will not alarm the readers').[39]

Yet it failed to attract the slightest attention. Gerhardie, who was accustomed to receive between forty and fifty reviews in the first three weeks, complained that the book was largely ignored. What reviews there were, were not encouraging. Only Kingsmill, more *outré* than ever before, praised it to the skies and compared it favourably with T. S. Eliot's 'sluggish criticism in his *Selected Essays*, a book without one living sentence'.[40] In desperation the authors resorted to devious means, and telephoned Lord Donegall's gossip page in the *Sunday Dispatch* to reveal that they had received sinister death threats. Other readers, they told him, having apparently identified Satan with Gerhardie, were performing black-magic rituals outside Rossetti House. Still no results, so that Lunn ventured into Hyde Park one Sunday and read aloud passages from a soap box, gesticulating appropriately and growing very sweaty in the process. A meagre crowd assembled but soon got bored and drifted away one by one, until only a single tramp remained. *The Memoirs of Satan* earned £192. 6s. 8d. out of its £1,000 advance.

16

RESURRECTION
November 1932–September 1934

It is the things we ignore which make our life ... they are the dead awaiting their resurrection.

'Thirty-seven, and so little achieved. I do not cherish birthdays which remind one that one is growing older', wrote Gerhardie on 21 November 1932 after admitting to Clara that *Satan* had been a 'complete flop'. Yet this moment of despair later formed the opening paragraph of 'the crucial book in my career', *Resurrection*.

In fact the Universal Film Company had found *Satan* 'a magnificent story' and toyed with the idea of allowing Douglas Fairbanks to film it, with the tall, svelte, and suavely sinister Conrad Veidt in the title role. But after considerable vacillation the idea was dropped because of the prohibitive cost of production and censorship problems (the *Evening Standard* had observed of Satan himself that 'most of his active intrusions into human affairs were in order to possess women').[1] Gerhardie received a rather vague offer to go to Hollywood as a script-writer ('I will accept, of course, if there is anything in it, which I doubt'), and he was approached by another, less celebrated, film company who offered to pay £500 for every film story he could produce. But they began by asking to borrow £50, promising to repay £75 at the end of three weeks. Gerhardie retorted that anyone who paid such exorbitant interest could not be financially responsible.

The failure of *Satan* had left him very badly off, and by the end of the year his bank was demanding repayment of a £200 overdraft. A friend who wished William a Merry Christmas and Happy New Year received the reply: 'Now I never issue any congratulations at either season as I find there is precious little in this world for congratulation.'[2] Josephine reappeared briefly, having lost half her money in the Wall Street crash, but still possessed of £10,000 a year. 'She is, however, drunker than ever', William told Clara. 'I haven't seen her sober. She is still playing with the idea of getting married, but after spending one evening in her drunken company I am glad we didn't get married. In fact, we would have been divorced by now.'

Gerhardie's despondency was relieved to some extent by the agreeable contemplation of a house in the country, particularly now that, with the Depression, many large places were for sale cheaply. The lease of Rossetti House was due for renewal and he found himself making less and less use of London society, but impatient with being 'cooked up' in a flat. He envisaged engaging a married couple to housekeep, an odd-job village boy to look after the horse, and buying a motor car for £25 which Patsy would drive, smartly got up in his own military peaked cap. Clara and Sissie could either stay for long periods, or move in permanently.

To reduce the inevitable possibility of friction which arises when people used to having their own way begin to live together, we could make a rule of having meals apart in our own dining rooms, but prepared and served by the same servants, and so we could invite each other to dinner or lunch just as if we lived in different flats. You could keep an eye on the servants, and Patsy as usual would keep the house-keeping accounts. *You would have no expenses*, but instead, in consideration for providing you with food, service and accommodation, your allowance could be reduced, say, by, x and become £50 a year.

But Clara was a good deal more practical, and though she was taken with the idea of tending pansies and rose-bushes and growing their own vegetables, she warned her son against the high running-costs of a large property, and suggested instead that he take a small place in Buckinghamshire, where friends of hers had recently settled. William, annoyed by her criticism and by the suggestion that he should want to live near her Bolton friends, snapped back: 'It is useless to pretend that two such "dictators" as you and I could ever live smoothly in the same house, unless the house were large enough to admit of two separate ménages for such a Hitler–Mussolini combination!'

To a great extent Gerhardie's desire to leave London was influenced by Kingsmill who, in the spring of 1933, after three years abroad, returned to England to live with Dorothy and the children in Hastings, in a converted windmill, roomy and romantic, with views over fields and sea. That year Kingsmill published his biography of Samuel Johnson which, though well received, 'created no outrageous stir and was soon forgotten.'[3] Gerhardie thought it the 'richest and finest' work his friend had produced, probably because Kingsmill's veneration for Johnson softened his usually abrasive approach—Kingsmill's next book, another biography, was notable for the author's 'harassing pursuit of Dickens from page to page.'[4]

Whilst still grappling with *Satan* Gerhardie had formed an agreement with Kingsmill to collaborate on a life of Casanova. The idea appealed to Gerhardie because of his own preoccupation with seduction, and to Kingsmill on account of having written a life of Frank Harris, a self-confessed modern Casanova. Gerhardie planned to exploit his own amatory reputation and include an epilogue entitled 'The Expert Lover' because, as Kingsmill pointed out, 'there is no doubt both the public and the publisher will expect something of this kind from you'. Above all, however, the incentive behind the agreement was financial and the collaboration was intended to save time and effort. Actually it proved not only arduous but occupied both its authors for a long time—throughout 1933 until its publication late in 1934—and it was with the greatest difficulty that *The Casanova Fable*, written for the popular market, found a publisher at all. Cassell's, cautious since the failure of *Satan*, thought it would never sell 'because, whereas Satan is an Englishman, Casanova is a foreigner'. Hutchinson, who considered the book, warned Gerhardie that librarians would jump to the conclusion that Kingsmill had written the book and he had merely put his name to it, and suggested suppressing Kingsmill's name. William delighted in drawing their attention to a press rumour (perhaps fuelled by *Pending Heaven*) that he and Kingsmill were the same person, which he felt added 'a certain piquancy' to the collaboration, but which infuriated Kingsmill. *The Casanova Fable* was eventually published in the autumn of 1934 by Jarrold in a superior edition containing some mildly erotic illustrations. Unfortunately, there had been a glut of Casanova books that year, as well as a West-End play, and it received little attention. It remains an agreeable but unremarkable narrative, and was never published in America.

William became a frequent visitor to Hastings. He and Kingsmill worked well together but the atmosphere was rarely free from tension, partly due to the presence of Dorothy whom Gerhardie had never forgiven for preferring Kingsmill to himself. Kingsmill seemed to inspire jealousy. His breezy, expansive manner made him much in demand amongst his friends—Holms, Hesketh Pearson, Malcolm Muggeridge, Douglas Jarrold, Edwin Muir, Kenneth Hare—who vied for his attention. Gerhardie was irritated by Kingsmill's behaviour when in other people's company—in particular that of John Holms. Holms, though not a humorous man himself, was greatly amused by Gerhardie, but considered him flippant, and once asked Kingsmill what he saw in him. Literary discussions at Hastings were fruitful—up to a point. Participants were always well read within a certain field, but those fields tended not to overlap. Kingsmill and Holms knew Wordsworth very well, but Gerhardie did not, and was impatient 'because they either quoted Wordsworth to each other—on which I did not come in at all—or went off into reminiscences of their German captivity—on which I did not come in either. I had to wait my turn till they touched upon Goethe. Then I promptly insinuated myself and quoted a few magnificent lines here and there to my entire, and their partial, satisfaction.'[5]

Gerhardie usually visited Hastings with his current girl-friend in tow, and was then irritated by Kingsmill's inevitably sentimental attitude towards her.

In the presence of attractive women he was at his dullest, and I felt a faint whiff of ill-will distend from him in my direction, as he questioned them earnestly, with an occasional frown at me to discourage me from participation in the conversation. He would ask them if they preferred spring to autumn, town to country, cold to warm weather, and similar questions. To all their answers he seemed to attach the utmost significance, and volunteered complex reasons for their preferences; whereas it was quite obvious to everyone, including the women themselves, that the superfluity of their answers exposed the stupidity of his questions. A stupidity which was but the base of a rare intelligence, the musk of his perfume.[6]

To add to Gerhardie's exasperation, his hosts insisted on observing the 'conventions' and accommodating him and the woman in separate rooms, so that he had to creep furtively about in the night lest he incur their disapproval.

Gerhardie's latest love, a young married woman named Vera Boys, he had met through mutual friends in a London theatre foyer. He found her exquisitely beautiful, with alabaster skin, sable locks, fine black brows, and blue, blue eyes. Driving home with her in a taxi one wet and desolate November night, he realized how much she resembled his vision of the wicked Eleanora of the fairy-tale. William introduced her proudly to his mother, then when she had left waited for Clara's praise. 'Yes, she's pretty enough. But isn't she *thin!*' said Clara, who was not. 'How she keeps any life together is more than I know. So *thin!* But now isn't she? Isn't she *thin?*' William, enraged, replied that Clara's ideas were out of date, and that by modern standards she would herself be considered decidedly stout. Huffily Clara rose to observe herself in the long looking-glass, remarking that 'as a girl her figure was considered perfect and that most people still marvelled how at sixty she retained her youthful outlines'.[7] At which William laughed aloud, and a spirited quarrel ensued.

Vera had little in the way of intellect but, like Terry, she had considerable charm; she was spontaneously open, vunerable and candid. Her husband, preoccupied with tinkering with his gramophone, seemed to take little interest in his wife, so that she was especially demanding of Gerhardie in her desire for attention: '*Concentrate* on me', she used to say. He described how she would 'urge him not to brood over the past or dream of the future from which she was excluded, and when he indicated that he enjoyed the present . . . she squeezed his middle finger by which she held him tighter as if to indicate that he was not to slip into enjoying the present an inch out of her orbit'.[8] After years of a dull marriage she hoped for excitement and adventure, and particularly longed to appear in the fashionable illustrated society journals. Though less gregarious than formerly, Gerhardie was still something of a celebrity and his photograph regularly appeared in the *Tatler*, the *Illustrated London News*, or the *Bystander*, which last had recently featured 'Beautiful Blondes', an illustrated series of well-known young men including Mr Randolph Churchill and Mr William Gerhardie.

William, anxious that Vera should not also make demands upon his purse, introduced her to Beaverbrook. '"She's very *pretty*", he said, as if with astonishment.' When next they met, Beaverbrook said that he had made a mistake in thinking she was pretty: she was the most beautiful woman in London. But the third time Vera was irritated to hear Beaverbrook say of a pale young female: 'Have you ever seen a more beautiful woman?' An inexpensive weekend could be enjoyed by visiting John Holms and Peggy Guggenheim in their harmonious Devonshire retreat, Hayford Hall (Hangover Hall as it came to be known), with Holms instructing Guggenheim 'daily, hourly, without stinting himself or sparing her, how to spend her money to the best cultural advantage'.[9] They rode ponies every day and lay around drinking in the evenings; Holms had taken so much to the drink that his once-ruddy face had faded to 'a gaunt alcoholized liverish and sallow crome'. The house was luxuriously mysterious, but Gerhardie disliked staying away from his flat for more than a few days at a time and was never entirely comfortable— one day he took a leisurely stroll out on to the moor in his bedroom slippers and sank ankle-deep into the mire.

One quiet evening in March 1933, Gerhardie, alone in Rossetti House, was preparing to attend a ball. With time in hand, he lay down alone on his bed to rest and fell asleep. He awoke with a start—

Because I had stretched out my hand to press the switch of the lamp on the bookshelf over my bed, and instead found myself grasping the void, and myself suspended precariously in mid-air, perhaps on a level with the bookcase . . . I was at that moment fully awake, and so fully conscious that I could not doubt my senses . . . Then my body turned round. And turning, I became aware for the first time of a strange appendage. At the back of me was a coil of light, like a luminous garden hose . . . To my utter astonishment, that broad cable of light at the back of me illumined the face on the pillow, as if attached to the brow of the sleeper. The sleeper was myself, not dead, but breathing peacefully . . . and here was I, outside it, watching it with a thrill of joy and fear.[10]

In this apparently disembodied state Gerhardie, incredulous yet absolutely certain that he was not dreaming, began to move about the flat. ' "Now be scientific," I said, "this is one chance in a million. You must convince yourself so that nothing later will make you think it was merely a dream." '[11] The evidence, strangely inconclusive to the sceptical reader, was, when verified later, some consolation to him: he accurately noted an open window, a curtain drawn in a particular manner, an object precisely positioned, the time on the clock. Throughout all this, Gerhardie observed, his own will apparently held sway over his movements. Then quite suddenly a 'strange power', hitherto present but passive, resumed its lead 'and began to play pranks with me. I was being pushed along like a half-filled balloon. . . . Out I flew through the front door and hovered there in the air, a feeling of extraordinary lightness of heart overtaking me. Now I could fly anywhere, anywhere— to New York, visit a friend, if I liked, and it wouldn't take me a moment.'[12] Fearful and exhilarated, Gerhardie willed himself back above his own sleeping body, then out again through the window only to find himself apparently suspended from a thick brown beam against a white ceiling 'effortlessly, like a bat', with the sound of a typewriter tapping. Eventually, some thirty minutes or so later, he felt himself back in his flat, 'lowered' painfully and yet with utmost precision back into his sleeping body. He opened his eyes, back in the natural world. 'I felt a blow had been dealt to my more poetic ideas of unimaginable life beyond the grave.'[13]

Completely convinced that he had not been deceived, Gerhardie immediately began to incorporate these events into a novel, opening with his despairing words on his thirty-seventh birthday, and using a musical analogy to convey not only the structure of the work, but the delicate ineffability of its significance. The book, 'quite new in conception and technique and the most ambitious novel I have yet attempted . . . is constructed on the lines of a concerto, in which the theme (resurrection) is at first only indicated without commentary; then is elaborated, analysed, and worried out; and is finally taken up again and developed to a passionate and soaring climax in the finale'. Its title, *Resurrection*, was settled early on; thereafter, following the advice of a fascinating recent book, *The Projection of the Astral Body* by Sylvan Muldoon and Hereward Carrington, Gerhardie succeeded in inducing several further projections of varying intensity, once revisiting the brown beam which he now identified as Kingsmill's house in Hastings. By June he was so deeply absorbed as to be refusing all invitations, and the more the novel preoccupied him the more he neglected Vera. This self-imposed seclusion banished all previous ideas of moving permanently to the country. 'It would always be possible as an alternative', he wrote to Clara, 'to rent some waste land at £10 per annum and erect the simplest kind of huts which they advertise in the D. Express at £6–7 a piece—each hut being a separate room; and thus for some £60–80 erect quite a miniature village with the simplest kind of furniture—camp beds and deck chairs—and have this as a country retreat to visit and stay the night in fine weather.'

To his relief, the nosy housekeeper Edith at last gave notice. He advertised in the *Daily Express* for a kitchen-maid and shortly afterwards engaged 15-year-old Lucy. Her habit of washing the kitchen floor three times a day but leaving greasy plates piled in the sink was exasperating, and she always insisted upon unfolding his napkin and placing it in his lap, convinced that this was the duty of a well-trained parlourmaid. Vera attempted—with little success—to teach her to cook William's breakfast porridge and his lunch. Instead he purchased a 'three tier dinner carrier' consisting of enamel saucepans fitting into each other, which Lucy carried to and from Admiral Volkoff's Russian Restaurant where an excellent three-course luncheon was obtainable for 1/9. When Dolly and her family visited London they dined there together on Russian specialities, and William noticed that Dolly had grown 'so terribly fat in the face that it looks as if she were wearing it sideways'.

When Lucy left, the whole flat had to be sprinkled with flea-powder. Then came Lily, 14 years old, quick, anxious to learn, and very trying because—rather in the manner of his mother—she kept running in to ask him 'What next?' 'I do wish you had a dear good little wife to look after you', wrote Clara, who wished nothing of the kind. Besides, he had Patsy, whom no 'wife' could surpass.

Gerhardie at last succeeded in engaging a young cockney maid named Frances Champion, 'such a nice, modest girl. There is simply nothing wrong with her.' At the interview he had been attracted by her pretty face, with its 'set expression of sullen rebellion lighting up suddenly into a trusting pathos'. She was small and slight, 'with an elaborate coiffure of coils which unrolled and fell over her eyes at the slightest inclination of her head', and her movements were jerky, erratic, uncertain. 'And she was always in trouble—to-day jammed her finger, which had to be bandaged. Yesterday somebody had stepped on her in the street. Tomorrow she will have trodden on her own corn.'[14] Frances was very proud of her cockney habit of 'sticking up for oneself' and 'telling off' people, and she regaled Gerhardie with stories of rows she had had with her previous bosses to show that she 'won't be sat upon'. 'If I don't stick up for myself, who will? I'm as good as you any day. We're all made alike', she used to say. Then, if Gerhardie made a particularly unreasonable request she would cry 'Blessèd chee-eek!'

Frances was wonderfully industrious and polished the silver until it shone. She cleaned the carpets, removed blobs from his suits, pressed all his clothes, and even brought her own sandwiches. 'The new maid is really one of the seven wonders', he wrote to Clara, who quickly became as enamoured as William and Patsy. Frances kept her family informed of events in Rossetti House, and vice versa. While cleaning Gerhardie's Venetian glass chandelier she announced: 'I told me mother that this chandelier came from—where was it—Siberia was it?' She quickly grew attached to her new boss, and in imitation of him set up a little table in her kitchen with an inkstand, a pen, a rubber and pencil, and a pad on which she would make lists.

Things I have to do to-morrow:
1. Dust properly
2. Dust and clean thoroughly
3. Turn out bedroom and wash hair brushes and also wash odds and ends which don't go to laundry.

She always informed him with deliberation of her activities on his behalf: 'I've done a lot of work to-day. I've washed all the walls in the kitchen and bathroom and all behind the kitchen stove and put new paper in the cupboard.' If he was too preoccupied to listen she told it to anyone who happened to come along. She required frequent praise and appreciation, and from time to time, looking thoughtful, she would say: 'Mr Gerhardie, I want to ask you a question. Do you like me? Do you think I'm nice?'

Resurrection continued to absorb him. And then towards the end of the year outside events intruded: Vera's husband, suddenly sensible of his wife's infidelity, filed a divorce petition citing William as co-respondent. Though accustomed to amorous entanglements, this particular affair caused him the acutest anxiety, not least because of the fear of being landed with costs. Hourly he and Vera plotted how to avoid the case. Reluctantly, Vera threatened to reveal in court embarrassing details of her sex-life with her husband. 'My book has gone to bits and I will never be able to finish it this year . . . I'm in debt all round . . . All my time is spent in preparing the defence. And everything seems as bad as it could be.' 'Sleuths' skulked around Rossetti House waiting to see a dishevelled Vera emerge, and Gerhardie caught one in the act of attempting to bribe his porter. Evidence claiming that William and Vera had been spotted canoodling behind the Ancient History shelves in Hatchard's bookshop was obviously invented—Gerhardie insisted he had never set foot in the place—and to crown it all, it transpired by an unfortunate coincidence that these detectives set to watch him were the same detectives employed by his own defending lawyer.

In the end it was Vera who saved the situation. When her husband came round to her flat to collect his belongings, she enticed him into the bedroom and seduced him. The case was nullified through 'condonation'. But now that the divorce had collapsed, three of the parties involved—husband, wife, and husband's father—realized that they were all keen for it to take place, and agreed to pay all costs themselves if Gerhardie would let it go through undefended. William, still reluctant to become involved, suggested to Vera that if her husband were so set on divorce he could provide his own co-respondent:

'Don't be silly!'

'I'm not being silly. He could disguise himself as somebody else, stay at the flat with you and get his own sleuths to surprise him—and there's a co-respondent for you. And what's more, one who'll stay put! Name unknown. Or he can invent a foreign name, prefixed with *de*, to lend it distinction. Anonymity, however, has a *cachet*, I think, that you can't beat. Co-respondent back across the Channel before sleuths could nab him. Adultery, nevertheless, proved to the hilt—with man unknown.'[15]

Inventive though it was, this plan did not go into operation; Gerhardie escaped costs but he was named as co-respondent. Thereafter he practised extreme caution with married women.

Now Vera, who previously had been deeply, almost irritatingly, in love with the preoccupied William, began at last to show interest in another man. William, suddenly susceptible, woke up to what he had missed and promptly fell passionately and painfully in love with Vera. Months of torture followed as Vera earnestly sought his counsel over her (not very happy) relationship with his rival.

> 'Now Jim, though he isn't anything to look at, I admit, has the most extraordinary charm which—'
> 'He has a smile, certainly, which is as charming as a shark's.'
> 'If ever I found myself in any trouble I'd sooner go to him than anybody.'
> 'That's what you used to say of me.'
> 'Well, perhaps; and it was true in the days when we liked each other.'
> '"Liked"? Loved!'
> 'Well, loved, if you like.'
> '"If you like." You mean when you were terribly, in fact, quite insanely in love with me.'
> 'You're imagining it all!'[16]

Gerhardie, quite besotted and desperate to win her back for himself, granted Vera's every wish and lingered outside her flat gazing up at her lighted windows just as he had as a youth in St Petersburg. In response, she infuriated his passion by valuing above all else his kind friendship. She had a habit of telling him the most distressing details—in all innocence—on the Tube or walking down a busy street, so that William's face would work convulsively as he gnashed his teeth to stem the emotion and the rising tears.

> 'I thought we'd get married.'
> 'It's too late now. You should have thought of it before.'
> 'I did.'
> 'Well, if you did you kept it to yourself.'[17]

He sent her notes, flowers, chocolates, peaches. He telephoned constantly:

> 'When shall I see you?'
> 'I don't know. Ring me up some time.'
> He lingered desperately. It came back to him how in the early days when she loved him anxiously she used to say: 'Be nice to me.' He had thought nothing of it. It had struck him as a gratuitous exhortation to one who was the milk of human kindness. And now he said, with heartache, with an imploring, sinking hope: 'Be nice to me.'
> 'Here is Jim. Good-bye.'[18]

Advised by a friend, he pretended to be in love with another, imaginary, woman, who was not only more beautiful than Vera but had the intelligence to prefer him to a man like Jim. But as he could not stop ringing Vera up and visiting her to tell her he no longer cared for her and how deeply he loved the other woman, his plot had not the desired effect. It seemed a hopeless suit. 'We search, and search in vain', Gerhardie at length confided to his diary, 'hoping to find heaven now in this being, now in that, but always baffled because of an inexorable law that no human being can wholly identify himself with another—except for a brief moment. These brief moments, however, are like glimpses of immortality, pledges of a life we may know in another world, or never know at all.'

Financially he was as desperate as ever. He succeeded in getting his rent reduced from £232 a year to £200, but still had most reluctantly to borrow from Clara to pay it. Considering—and at once rejecting—Beaverbrook as a possible source of a loan, Gerhardie commented bitterly that he would 'make such a fuss of it if I went to him'. Thus, for all his intelligent interest in the original form which *Resurrection* was to display, Gerhardie could not altogether keep his thoughts away from the chance of financial success, and *Resurrection*—dealing as it does with the subject of life after death, the paranormal—promised an irresistible means of attracting public interest on a grand scale: 'If one could be sure of catching the eye of those wild enthusiastic lady adherents of the various movements generally—whose name is legion—we would indeed get the ball rolling.'[19] At the very start of the new year something happened which, to Gerhardie's mind, offered a way to increase interest in the book, whilst retaining its literary integrity.

John Holms dislocated his wrist falling from his horse on a rainy day on Dartmoor. The joint was set, very badly, by a local doctor. Months later the wrist was still painful and Holms arranged to have it reset under chloroform at their new house in Woburn Square. The evening before, he and Peggy Guggenheim gave a dinner party for a group of friends, including Kingsmill who had reappeared only four or five days earlier, after a three-year estrangement. Gerhardie, full of his recent experiences and very talkative, attempted to allay Holms's fears about the anaesthetic by pointing out that there was the exciting possibility he might temporarily leave his body for its astral counterpart. 'What if I never come back?' said Holms. Unappeased, he stayed up drinking very late. When warned, he replied, 'I am generally in a fairly alcoholized condition, which is normal for me.' At the end of the evening he came out on to the step to say goodbye to all the guests, and awoke the next morning, 19 January 1934, with a terrible hangover. Three eminent doctors arrived to operate—a general practitioner, a surgeon, and the King's anaesthetist. When at last they reappeared from the bedroom Holms was dead, his heart had given out. They had desperately cut open his chest and injected adrenalin, and attempted massage, but to no avail. The fastidious Holms had simply 'disdained to come back'.[20]

An autopsy found that Holms's organs were badly affected by alcohol and he was deemed to have died of a perforated liver. Guggenheim bitterly blamed the doctors for their negligence, but at the inquest they were exonerated. She was too distraught to attend the cremation. Only Muir, Kingsmill, and four others were present. Gerhardie was upset that he was not asked. To some extent, however, the deep grief and shock that he felt were lessened by his new-found inclination to believe in the immortality of the soul, and by deciding, as he now did, to incorporate into *Resurrection* not only Holms's death but an imagined posthumous meeting with Holms, during one of his own astral projections. By doing so he not only promised Holms a literary immortality, but also made his novel that much more appealing to the public. At the very end of the novel the narrator (who is Gerhardie), undergoing a further astral projection, meets the dead Bonzo (who is Holms). Rosamund Lehmann, who, after the death of her daughter, was especially interested in the subject of reincarnation, wrote to ask whether this meeting with Bonzo was 'all statement of sober fact?'[21] 'It is fact—but not sober', replied Gerhardie. 'My own experiences out of the body are, however, completely genuine. The Bonzo meeting at the end is imaginatively conceived, though I did on one occasion just catch a glimpse of Bonzo.'[22]

By March the book was nearing completion, but shortly before publication a crisis occurred when the editor of the *Daily Express* published, on its front page, details of the Boys divorce. Vera was delighted at the publicity. But Gerhardie, distraught lest it have a detrimental effect on the religious public whom he had hoped to impress, once again appealed to Beaverbrook, demanding why, at such a lean time, he should have allowed his editor to print the story. Beaverbrook, who had been away at the time, wrote briefly back saying he would certainly have suppressed it had he not been absent. 'I prize you greatly as a friend and look upon you as one of my intimates',[23] he added. The regal tone of Beaverbrook's letter was well answered by Gerhardie:

I am extremely honoured that you should look upon me as an intimate of yours, and I have the greatest natural affection for you. But when you advise me to cultivate fruitful relations with your editors, it is as if omnipotent God, who had favoured me with his omnipotent friendship, said to me: 'Now I will tell you something which will confer on you the greatest benefit. I have a son Jesus Christ who has a number of apostles and disciples under him. There is, among others, one Luke. Now it is my desire that much benefit accrue to you from your getting round Luke, and I wish you joy'.

In view of Luke's resemblance to Cain on the one hand, and God's omnipotence on the other, the advice is not heartening.[24]

Dedicated 'To the Memory of John Holms', *Resurrection* was published in the autumn of 1934. Gerhardie himself described the book as 'an autobiographical novel recording a true experience out of the body, followed that night by a London ball at which, against a background of social comedy, the theme is taken up and developed into a passionate argument for the immortality of the soul, illustrated by the spontaneous recollection of a year rich in travel and having the power to evoke a vanished lifetime in a day'.[25] It is the story of his life as a 'changeling', a man who feels himself a ghost in the world, paradoxically made more real by his ghostly astral projection.

All so strange. Being born was strange. Childhood was strange. Even my mother, strange. Childhood, parents, brothers and sisters, youth, school, army—it was all as if I had entered a strange spirit world peopled by ghostly strangers who had no *real* concern for you. How strange our early travels. . . . Then friends. Friends were such strangers, hiding their mystery from us because they, poor things, knew not themselves what they were. 'Tell me what is concealed in your innermost soul.' But there was really nothing to tell. One wasn't quite there, you know. And they called it real life!

As autobiography, *Memoirs of a Polyglot* had succeeded only in 'delineating the surface of events, not tapping the vase, not releasing the hidden perfume'. *Resurrection* develops those hitherto neglected aspects. Its epigraph, characteristically ambiguous, places the book in a region between fiction and fact:

Even though this book dispenses with invention, it resorts, for greater freedom, to a modicum of literary convention which unavoidably places it in the category of 'fiction'. It therefore devolves on me to make it clear to the reader, to whom this fact may be of moment, that the experience of which it treats is, incredible as it may seem, a true experience.

The critics took this as an assurance to the reader that the astral projections are true. Yet the circumlocution of this epigraph does anything but 'make it clear'. What are the fictive 'conventions' that are not 'inventions'? Gerhardie supplies an answer: 'Fiction is merely a question of arrangement—it deals, likewise, with real life, but on a freer and therefore more profound plane.' *Resurrection* raises many questions about literary 'truth', the writer's own identity, and, in turn, the reader's assessment of where the author stands. It is particularly important, when reading Gerhardie's works, to recognize the convergence of truth and fiction, and the subsequent labyrinth of nebulous, potential identities that abound. That Gerhardie the character is himself in the process of writing a novel called *Resurrection* suggests an idea first explored in *Memoirs*, of personality as comprehensible and perceptible only as part of a constant process of change. In Gerhardie's posterity-conscious vocabulary, *Resurrection* 'inherits the conclusions arrived at by Proust'.[26]

As in *A la recherche du temps perdu*, the novel opens with the subject in bed, about to sleep, and suddenly unsure of the status of his own identity. Gerhardie becomes, quite literally, his own audience, more efficiently than Georges in *The Polyglots* who perpetually strove to see himself in the looking-glass. In *Memoirs* the *reader* found himself in a voyeuristic relation to the author: in *Resurrection* Gerhardie becomes the watcher. His astral projection, itself a metaphor for his life's vocation as a writer, gives him the ability to move freely without restriction of time or space and, if not (like Satan) to actually *enter* individuals, then to silently observe them. 'Ah, if I could persuade you to become a novelist!' he wrote to Beaverbrook. 'To experience that rare feeling of walking outside and beside life.'[27] The whole point about an original writer, he declares, 'is that you cannot see him, do not know in what corner he is concealed'. We cannot *place* Gerhardie bodily, socially, nationally, culturally, or linguistically because his real territory is the territory of the past. His present is constrained by Habit and Anxiety:

We cannot live in the present because we cannot keep our thoughts in the present. Living, we want to know what awaits us . . . For the future we hope for, and which sustains us, is but a reverie improvised on congenial themes from the past. The past alone yields up the bounty. With the past alone I am concerned as a living man. The present moment I reserve for catching a train, satisfying my bodily appetites, signing a note: 'Yours in haste', perhaps waving a hand to another immortal caught in the shallows.

'It is in these waiting hours, while waiting for death, that we live.' What he chooses to do is to evade company and relive his past by narrating his experiences to Bonzo, who does not appear to be listening.

The metaphysical basis of the book is complemented by its setting at a most mundane (*mondaine*) event, the society ball. Here the senses predominate, guests are concerned with their appearance, their appetites—reminding us that at the start of *Resurrection* 'William Gerhardie' was anxiety-ridden by the consideration of his own (ageing) body: 'One grows older furtively. . . . It ill becomes my thirty-seven years, I thought, to vie with dashing young fools in getting away with the prettiest débutantes at the ball.'

And like all his work, *Resurrection* maintains an element of high comedy. Arriving at the ball, Gerhardie attempts to convince others of his new-found belief in the immortality of the soul. But instead of proving a topic of universal interest, he finds himself in the position of the Ancient Mariner, compelling his often reluctant audience to hear him out.

> 'I have an important announcement to make,' I said to the girl at my side.
> 'Engagement?'
> I shook my head.
> 'What?'
> 'We do not die.'
> 'Pf! . . . I don't know what has happened to men,' she said. 'There's no vitality in them these days!' And she brought down her fist in emphasis of her scorn.

When the ladies leave, and the men gather for their murky talk, Gerhardie is again tackled 'on this business of getting out of the body which, some believed, must have a sexually hilarious background'.

> 'Now do come and tell us about it.'
> 'I've had an amazing experience,' I found myself feebly repeating.
> 'Yes?'
> 'We—it seems—we don't die, you know. I've seen.'
> 'What have you seen?' They were convinced that I was trying to be funny, and that they were entering into the spirit of the joke.
> 'Oh, well—my own body, you know. In bed, you know.'
> 'Have a drink,' said the big hulk of a man who sailed in windjammers.

The humour is almost always at the expense of the Gerhardie-figure himself—just as in *The Polyglots* Georges's absurd philosophizing was interrupted by Sylvia's trivia and Captain Negodyaev's requests to borrow money. The double I, the formal enactment of Gerhardie's comic-ironic voice, generates comedy from the self. There is, too, a fleeting satire on Huxley's novels in the ponderous propounding of philosophical ideas. But there is more to this treatment of the self than mere humour, for when Gerhardie starts to talk at the party, his own sense of self-parody begins to undermine the readers' 'privileged' view of the veracity of the astral projection (we were 'there' when it happened: it is our fictive habit to take such things on trust). And so the question of who will believe him becomes increasingly important. The reader, after all, has a vested interest in immortality.

Then there are different levels of belief. Though he was apparently convinced of the actuality of the astral projection, we can never be sure what *status* Gerhardie assigned to it. He claims he is convinced of the immortality of the soul, not least because the astral projection overrules his chief obstacle to that belief by showing *how* survival of the senses independent of the body may be possible. However, the achievement of *Resurrection* is to convey levels of belief and scepticism simultaneously. It is a characteristic double-effect of tone: the scepticism of the guests challenges the status of the experience, but the experience challenges the status of their scepticism, which tends paradoxically to reinforce the reader's conviction. Whilst the faith is passionately upheld in Gerhardie's argument, his scepticism is also conveyed through the conception of the character Bonzo. Bonzo, silent, mysterious, is, like Lord Mark in *The Wings of the Dove*, deemed to be brilliant. Yet Bonzo's 'significance', the status of his silent, ineffable, implied wisdom is never settled. Do his minimal gestures denote endless sagacity or emptiness? They have their counterpart in Gerhardie's strivings for significance in his art:

But the moment when my overheated imagination seemed to hold within its grasp the heart and secret essence of my book, it over-reached itself, my vision dwindled, and I was left grasping a few loose and arbitrarily connected statements. Where had it gone? My book? The Resurrection and the Life? I stood there, troubled with reflections on the merits of a contemplated work seemingly bereft of all that constitutes a book. And the title? Was it, or was it not, the right one?

In literary-historical terms, Gerhardie still evades categorization: viewed in the context of the 1930s' drift towards belief and commitment, he is representative (though eccentric). Yet there is a strong suggestion that the ultimate 'truth' of the astral projection is, after all, incidental—a notion confirmed by the persuasive views of the bishop in Chapter Twenty-Two. Whether Gerhardie's beliefs are founded on religion or an appreciation of imaginative potential is not settled.

For Gerhardie, death as a parting from the self is equated with nostalgia. His preoccupation with survival—be it actual, as the astral projection seemed to promise, or metaphorical, in the creation of a literature which will outlive him—involves him in an attempt to duplicate that self. *Resurrection* crystallizes all Gerhardie's previous identifications of self in fiction by taking the book itself as a metaphor for his life. And this is why he calls it 'the crucial book of my career'.

What am I, I asked myself, who walk through this shifting sand of the present and carry my past on my back? I am memory. I live to the extent to which I remember. If something has not occurred to me I am less alive by that extent. I have carried the past on my back. Now let the book carry us both. . . . It was the book itself, I realised, who was my hero. It was the resurrection of my life that was the theme. And it was my past which was the material.

If I were allowed to write one more novel only, what would I say, what would I put into it? I would resurrect my life, make it live . . . My book, then, I thought, must be the story of a day out of my life; and of my life. Also it will be the story of my death because, slowly now, I am folding my tent.

Instead of linear, historical narrative, Gerhardie's is mimetic: the form *represents* the content, the life, the consciousness, that is spatially and temporally boundless: 'Though the whole book is but the narrative of one day, it contains the essence of a life, and that life is given new facets and a new understanding in its resurrection.' He uses his two selves—that is, his astral projection and his actual body—as a metaphor for subjective and objective modes. Whereas *Memoirs* concerns itself with the problems of *writing about* the 'unknowable metaphysical abstraction' that is 'me', *Resurrection* confronts the self itself and conjures Gerhardie in both body and spirit. *Memoirs*, with its spontaneous sense of 'present', conveys the vital, but essentially non-enduring, idea of a 'performance' while *Resurrection* strives for permanence: though the personality may fluctuate, there is always a personality. In fact, Gerhardie resists interpretation, even to himself, because the self is constantly changing. As Proust saw, and Beckett here explains:

Yesterday is not a milestone that has been passed, but a daystone on the beaten track of the years, and irremediably part of us, within us, heavy and dangerous. We are not merely more weary because of yesterday, we are other, no longer what we were before the calamity of yesterday . . . The aspirations of yesterday were valid for yesterday's ego, not for to-day's.[28]

Like Beckett's Krapp twenty-five years later, Gerhardie seeks to accomplish a resurrection through recounting his own past: both personally (at the ball, to Bonzo) and publicly (through writing).

Hugh Kingsmill was not alone in praising *Resurrection*. It was, he said, the book out of all of English literature that he would most like to have written. He carried it everywhere with him and when he lost his copy, had a set of proofs bound. Yet to Gerhardie's irritation he made no response at all to the astral experiences. His characteristically localized and emotive praise took the form of (for example) finding individual passages 'very beautiful indeed, really poignant and exquisite'; he also made the ambiguous remark '*Tristram Shandy* is accepted as a permanent masterpiece, and *Resurrection* is worth ten of it.'

Edwin Muir considered the book 'easily the best' of Gerhardie's work 'and also, I think, one of the most remarkable that have appeared in our time', comparable to the work of Sterne, Proust, and Gide.[29] But like many critics, Muir failed to appreciate the deliberate effect of incongruity occasioned by the fusion of social and metaphysical. Graham Greene praised it, but not unreasonably observed that there were several '*longueurs*',[30] while H. E. Bates scathingly referred to the novel as 'a kind of literary minestrone'.[31] It was typical of the author's 'effrontery' to pick another's title, said *Time*,[32] whilst the *Daily Herald* pointed out that Gerhardie was 'still the terrible child of contemporary novelists'.[33] H. G. Wells, with mixed feelings, wrote kindly and not unjustly to Gerhardie:

I liked the book but then I like you. But—the old man's voice quavered affectionately—it isn't good enough. You wrote it . . . but what you didn't do was to sit down to it afterwards and edit it like hell. . . . You have forgotten your tie, your flies are unbuttoned; one side of your face is lathered but not shaved—to speak symbolically.[34]

'*Resurrection* was met with a kind of dumb astonishment', Gerhardie later admitted. 'Nobody knew how to handle it. The critics lifted it gingerly and dropped it with a witticism about hanging on a chandelier.'[35] 'The sleep-walking book', as one acquaintance remarked. J. B. Priestley, however, was most supportive and told Gerhardie that *Resurrection* had given him the idea for writing his 'time' plays. If the book was 'too difficult' for the critics, it was certainly too difficult for the general public, and despite the fact that, as Gerhardie sadly noted, it had received 'probably the finest reviews of all the books I have ever had', it was selling very slowly indeed. He suggested that the publishers send it to heads of theosophical and spiritualist societies, to bishops and clergymen such as Dean Inge ('the old boy, I believe, is rather dead. But . . . he has a first-class mind'), in fact to any organization interested in survival and death ('I do not, however, suggest undertakers').[36] At length, realizing that in spite of all his optimism *Resurrection* was not going to sell, Gerhardie wrote miserably to Cassell: 'I feel like never wanting to write another book, but, alas, I have got to.'

17

OF MORTAL LOVE
September 1934–December 1936

> *Authors should not expose themselves in public. Their mystery is their capital. Once seen, nobody wants to see them again. If they must show themselves, let it be at a distance—at the end of a long corridor, at the top of the stairs.*[1]

'Everybody depressed as usual', Gerhardie wrote cheerfully to Clara in the autumn of 1934, shortly after Vera had first refused to marry him, then deserted him. 'I am still very sad about Vera, and seem quite unable to get over it.' He presented Vera with copies of two of his books, inscribed. In *Memoirs of a Polyglot* he wrote:

> To Vera,
> The loveliest woman of our era,
> (a little in the style of Norma Shearer,
> as difficult as de Valera)
> Whose treacheries I was the bearer,
> And whom I loved in eror,
> from William
> (One-in-a-Million).
> 1934

And in *Resurrection*:

To-day, Thursday, is the publication day of my book, and I thought that, in spite of all, you might like to have it. While I wrote it we were together. How many times I discussed it with you and, thoughtless and inconsiderate as I was, I wearied you with reading pages and pages of it when I should have concentrated on you. There is even the passage about Max which—do you remember—you offered to take down for me in longhand. There are all the Bonzo pages we had shared, and the whole theme of astral projection I owe to you, Vera dear. The whole period of writing this long and difficult book is associated with you, and it is a sad day today that it should see us parted. 20th September 1934. William.

But he continued to see her. When she was taken ill with diptheria and—unaccountably—placed in the children's ward of the hospital, Gerhardie visited her regularly, together with two other suitors and her brother.

'Which of 'em is 'er 'usband?' asked the doorman.

'I'm blowed if I know!' replied the nurse.

Clara, sympathetic to her son's distress, wrote in turn: '*I* try to console myself that all is for the best and that sorrow and trials are sent us with a reason to try and prepare us for the wonderful life which awaits us—Does it hurt as much as parting with Terry?'

As for the wonderful life awaiting us, Gerhardie was reading widely on all aspects of astral projection and the paranormal, including J. W. Dunne's influential ideas in *The Serial Universe* and *An Experiment With Time*, which he then lent to J. B. Priestley. He found the subject to be an unexpectedly profitable source of journalism, and over the next few years wrote a number of articles: 'What is the Twin Body?', 'Voluntary Projection of the Astral Body', 'Nocturnal Thoughts from my Bedside Note-book', and such titles for the *Daily Mail*, the *Modern Mystic*, *Psychic News*, and even (on Beaverbrook's instigation) the *Evening Standard*. Far from adopting a cranky, evangelical approach, Gerhardie discusses the scientific and philosophical implications of current theories with admirable clarity and detachment, so that Dunne wrote and praised one article as 'a very clever piece of work'. And of course they were not without humour. In 'You, Too, Can Walk Out of Your Body', he warns that 'the motive, sometimes frankly monetary, may be the wish to locate Uncle Arthur in the fourth dimension to find out from him where he has put his will'. Other people wish to project 'to the scene of a secret board meeting in order to obtain information convertible into ready money. At the extreme of innocence, the motive may be to recover a lost umbrella. On the romantic side, it is invariably to pay a nocturnal visit to a girl friend. And there is the malicious motive of surprising somebody in an indecorous situation.'

Soon Gerhardie, now viewed as something of a guiding light, was receiving all manner of letters and telephone calls, especially from the recently bereaved. One avid science-fiction fan suggested that Gerhardie project to the moon to report on conditions there. Dennis Wheatley, who greatly admired William's novels and asked him to autograph his collection of Gerhardie first editions, introduced him to a number of mediums and occult figures. Wheatley, Gerhardie, Tom Driberg, and two anonymous Africans drove one evening to visit the black-magician Aleister Crowley in a dingy hotel room. Facing them propped up in a narrow bed, the Great Beast 666 turned 'a sad, jaundiced, rueful eye' upon Gerhardie—'One's impulse was to dial 999'—and wailed that this newcomer had hit the headlines with only one-and-a-half astral projections, whilst 'I've had *'undreds!*—and no notice. No notice at all!'

Denis Bradley, the author and dramatist, helped Gerhardie to study mediumship, and presented him with an aluminium trumpet used in direct voice seances, but died suddenly whilst reading *Resurrection*, only to reappear (vocally) at a spiritualist gathering. At one seance a fat, matronly woman spoke aloud as Albert, King of the Belgians; at another 'histrionic' event Gerhardie was addressed first by Robert Louis Stevenson, then by an unknown individual describing himself as Company Sergeant-Major Thompson, who patted his knee with the trumpet and remarked: 'I see you've got that other suit on.' If this was a phoney medium's method of alighting on a message that could not fail to strike a chord, it was ill-chosen for Gerhardie, who did not possess two suits.

These excursions were amusing but they failed to convince William, who later professed 'very little interest in spiritualism and very grave doubts about its manifestations'.[2] Furthermore, after his initial pre-occupation with his own extraordinary experience, he no longer felt the need to convince others of its veracity. Years ago he had told John Rothenstein that he believed in spiritualism of a sort simply because there was not sufficient data *not* to believe in it. 'It is more likely than not that the incredible should happen because, when all is said, all life is a miracle. It would be incredible, since life is a miracle, that only the credible things should happen'[3]—a view which had close affinities with his literary imagination and his notion of humour.

In the past, if pressed, he would have admitted a nominal affiliation to Christianity. Since the projection, his interest and faith had increased considerably, and he began to describe himself as following Jesus 'at a distance'. But his concentrated attempts to induce further such experiences—and to get the rest of the family to join in—worried Clara: 'I hope you have not been projecting, for I am certain it can do no good to your health. Your nerves have sufficient strain as it is.' She preferred the familiarity of the Christianity she had been schooled in, and since Charles's death had grown increasingly spiritual. *Resurrection* she read and reread, but she told William not to bother to send his *Modern Mystic* articles, because '*au fond*, I am not really clever and do not possess a flexible brain and mysticism is some strain to me and I get bewildered and all would be wasted'.

Gerhardie's old preoccupation with death was now exaggerated not only by the loss of John Holms but by concern for his mother. She had travelled alone to Antibes to attend to Daisy, who in addition to her continuing financial troubles was suffering from chronic pleurisy. On the way there the train crashed and Clara, unhurt but badly shaken, began to have trouble with her heart. When she returned to England her doctor advised a complete rest. She booked into a Blackpool boarding-house run by Russian exiles where William, greatly alarmed, wrote to her:

I couldn't bear to think we might suddenly lose you if, God forbid, your heart gave out. I am crying at the very thought of it because, as you know, I think there is no one in the whole world like you or fit to lace your shoes. My life simply wouldn't be worth living if anything happened to you. . . . I so wish I had a little success with the next book so that I could provide you with a little comfort . . . *you know* I love you more than anyone in the world, though I do not often have the opportunity of saying it. . . . I feel so sorry now about the times when I have been so unkind to you.

He too was not in the best of spirits. 'I am rather exhausted. I used not to be. Probably my brain is drying up.' None the less he took up two new projects. The first was a reworking of an early, discarded novel entitled *About Love*, begun in 1922 after the painful separation from Terry. Now 'the charm of Vera's character' was to replace that of Terry, and in writing a semi-fictional account of their time together he hoped to exorcise the painful ghost of Vera. The book was retitled *Of Mortal Love*.

The second venture was a collaboration with Bianca's husband Prince Leopold von Loewenstein Wertheim-Freudenberg—'Poldi' as he came to be known. Together they conceived of a mask of thin rubber which, conveniently pulled over the head, with the loose ends tucked away into the neck of the collar, 'would make any old mug look like a new one'. This idea seemed too beset with difficulties. They turned their attention to a scheme they had been discussing for several years, an imaginative concept which Gerhardie described as 'an idea of mine, perfected by him', whereby books would be printed so as to give the reader the possibility of choosing his own version according to an infinite number of combinations of pages. Such a method might lend itself to an entirely new kind of detective story in which the reader himself, as it were, took part in following the clues and finding the right solution, or to a particular kind of children's book, or to one enabling the reader to read his own future. In fact none of these possibilities was utilized, but the basic idea was adapted into a complex type of psychological parlour game in book form, eventually published as *Meet Yourself*.

Faber offered an advance of £400 and Gerhardie was optimistically referring to the scheme as one promising 'really big money'. The book was based upon a series of questions—on the subject of family, environment, education, sexuality, health, intelligence, and talent—which lead eventually to specific character-readings. 'The only book in existence', as Gerhardie remarked, 'which reviews the reviewer before he reviews the book.' Poldi sat around Rossetti House, gold-rimmed spectacles on the end of his nose, reading psychology books in half-a-dozen languages, in order to make out plausible situations and responses, which Gerhardie then composed into mildly humorous English. In addition to which William had undertaken the devilishly complicated organization, so that he, Patsy, and Frances spent endless hours assembling and reassembling the charts and card indices—the most complex yet—which covered every available surface and half of the walls in the flat. 'It's really the most atrocious book of any that I've ever had to deal with—there seems no end to it—one alteration after another!' lamented Gerhardie. And, like all his collaborations, it occupied a ridiculously disproportionate amount of time, so that the riches to come appeared to be light-years away. Come December, bills dropped from the sky. 'I am approaching the ocean-bed of my resources', he lamented when *Resurrection* had stopped selling altogether. 'My own idea of spending Christmas is to go to sleep for five days.'

In the new year, after a long illness, King George V died: 'To-day we have buried our dear, good, King George', wrote Clara, 'and I am glad it is over, for it has been a great strain. It is as though one has lost a very close and dear friend and for the last week one could think of nothing but that loss.' She continued to worry about William, urging him to eat hot food, and sending through the post parcels containing apple dumplings, meat pancakes, teacakes, Oxo cubes, potato-cakes, corned beef, and boiled eggs. 'I wonder how your brain doesn't give way with all the thinking', she wrote. 'I sometimes think mine is giving way—or is it simply that I am getting old and tired.' Tamara, she informed William, had taken a room on her own, which made things easier for Clara. But there was little respite, for now Auntie was getting helpless, 'She wants so much done for her, and she is so dreadfully jealous of my children . . . every morning she has her breakfast in bed. And who is there to bring it up to her? Only me.'[4] One day William surreptitiously asked Sissie if she really insisted on having her breakfast in bed, and she, 'in her quaking old voice of perpetual astonishment', replied firmly: 'I don't. Only your mother won't let me come down . . . so what am I to do?'

Still William and Clara attempted to get Rosie out of Russia, all the more urgently now, for Stalin had instigated a cruel purge after the recent murder of his rival Kirov. In answer to Gerhardie's request for help, Maxim Gorky made the gesture of forwarding a letter of appeal to the Soviet State Press, who transferred to Rosie the 960 roubles due from the Russian translation of *The Polyglots*, from which she was enabled to pay the fee for an exit permit. Gerhardie wrote to H. G. Wells a slightly embarrassed, apologetic letter, enclosing a copy of *Resurrection* and asking if Wells might *once again* use his influence with Stalin. His own relation to Rosie was, he explained, very much that of the hero of Wells's novel *The Dream* to his sister. Wells, however, had made public his dislike of Stalin's regime, and his intervention, he regretfully admitted, would likely do more harm than good. Leslie Hore-Belisha, after hearing Rosie's complicated history, replied kindly that it was 'a story of human vacillation with which I have sympathy' and wrote at once to the Foreign Office. At long last, after further innumerable influential interventions, Rosie was granted permission to leave Russia and enter England.

On 24 March 1935 she and Galina set foot in England. Vowing never to return to Russia, Rosie at once entered the Bolton Infirmary for an operation. When she was well again William visited Bolton, where all the family gathered in Clara's house. He had not seen his 'beautiful' sister for fourteen years, and he was shocked to find that she looked as old as her mother, but her impulsive, loving embrace was very different from Dolly's sober greeting. William, in a rush of feeling, wanted to tell his sisters about his unhappiness with Vera, but reflected that Dolly would never understand, and that Rosie 'would be sure to over-understand'. Galina, 8 years old and badly crippled, was an oddly handsome child, and exceptionally clever. She also possessed a prodigious memory for reciting verses and delighted her uncle by 'reeling off poems by the yard in three languages'. She and Aunt Sissie were crammed together in Sissie's room, Rosie and Clara in the tiny spare room, and William walked in and out of all the rooms preparing for bed and chatting as if they had never been apart. They talked emotionally of the St Petersburg house which now accommodated the families of the mill workers.

Unlike the rest of the family Dolly apparently felt no regrets. Practical and content, she had even become accustomed to the English weather, believing that it heightened one's powers of resistance. Rosie found the English fog and damp intolerable, laid her astrakhan fur coat over her bed to keep warm, and looked longingly back at the Russian snows.

When the novelty of reunion wore off, Rosie began to miss Leonya and Galina cried for her father. William began to notice that when anybody praised England Rosie replied: 'We have the same kind of thing over there—only bigger.' Food was plentiful in England, and the atmosphere quite safe, but Bolton seemed so dull and sedate. The more they talked of the past the sorrier Rosie grew. William, always her favourite, was stern with her for pining. All the trouble taken to get her out; all the trouble she'd face if she went back; all the misery; all the poverty; all the cold. But one damp afternoon as they sat huddled over the fire they began to talk of Russian stoves. Gerhardie had to admit that England was dull by comparison with Russia—what could ever compare with their early years? However, he added firmly, he was English now and it was too late ever to go back. By writing he had tried to forget: 'My memories of Siberia, put to rest by *Futility* and *The Polyglots*, are now pale ghosts.'[5] To add to Rosie's troubles she could not find a job, though she applied for secretarial and translation work, and had instead to sell a diamond pendant given her by Leonya's mother. For all its uncertainties Russian medicine was free and Galina, disabled as she was, would have a chance of employment if they went back. Victor offered to help, but Rosie realized that were she to stay in England she would be dependent upon his charity which, in view of his uncertain temper, was not a cheerful prospect.

When William, now back in London, heard that she was contemplating a return to Russia he wrote to her, at first a 'stinker' letter pointing out that she was being absurdly premature, then a letter of great sympathy and kindness:

I never suggested for a moment that we did not 'want' you. What I said was that I foresaw and foretold you that you would not find life in England such a paradise as it seemed to you in Russia . . . We all have, I have it myself, a great deal of the 'pending heaven' complex about us, but I feel that you have it more strongly developed than anyone I know . . . I have a very tender feeling for you and I have always considered you as a woman of exceptional sensibility, generosity, endowed with a noble heart and the best of intentions.

Her return seemed a dismal reproach to himself. He planned to build her a timber house, centrally heated, in the quiet English countryside, with a maid to care for Galina, if she could only hold on until *Meet Yourself* was published. If, however, she was set on going back, in the current political climate it would only be safe to do so if she severed all communication with England. She and Clara must resist all temptation to correspond. Eventually, after much anxious indecision, Rosie and Galina departed. She had been in England only seven months. Her mother, her brother, her sister, and her daughter came to the station to wave goodbye. This was the last time she saw them.

In spite of emotional crises, lack of money, and the tribulations of 'that damned book' *Meet Yourself*, Gerhardie remained optimistic. 'You do keep your spirits up so bravely,' said Clara. 'You and Daisy are very much alike in that way.' Much of his energy during the mid-1930s was directed towards trying to write for the films, and the perpetual and endless deferrals were to be comically described in *My Wife's the Least Of It*. Gerhardie had recently spent a pleasant afternoon at a 'Beautiful Babies' competition, organized as a publicity stunt by British Gaumont in an attempt to find promising young starlets. Gerhardie, covering the event for a magazine, had been particularly taken with some of the women and sidled up to the man in charge asking in his rather foreign, elegant manner: 'Will you introduce me to your babies?' Alan Hyman, scenario editor for British Gaumont, was only too willing to oblige. He had read *The Polyglots* and by the end of the day the pair agreed to adapt the novel for the films.

'Are you a homosexual?' enquired Gerhardie as they sat down to work on the first day of the synopsis. Hyman lived only a few minutes' walk from Rossetti House and visited frequently. When London palled, he, Gerhardie, Patsy, and Frances took trips to Hyman's parents' house in Buckinghamshire. Hyman provided the prototype of Harold Burke in *My Wife's the Least Of It*, just as the character of Mr Baldridge is based loosely upon Gerhardie himself. 'Mr Baldridge could not help liking this agreeable and good-looking youth who combined so much deference for Mr Baldridge with a modest but dogged determination to succeed himself in the field of authorship, on a lower level than Mr Baldridge, yes, but in a wider field.'[6] Hyman was tall and good-looking (Frances quickly fell for him), and he tended to speak with a 'mixture of esteem and parody' and was always immaculately polite—'perhaps over-polite. Every time Mr Baldridge got up, just to stretch his legs, up popped Harold. When Mr Baldridge sat down Harold plomped down as if in sympathetic awareness. If Mr Baldridge took three paces to the right, Harold Burke took three paces with him. If Mr Baldridge turned round and took three steps to the left, Harold did likewise.'[7] Hyman instructed his new pupil in the intricacies of the film industry, the delicate difference between 'a First-Treatment', a 'scenario', a 'synopsis', and if they argued it was because Gerhardie was reluctant to adapt his novel to the lowbrow mentality which, Hyman insisted, was the average filmgoer's. 'I see your point', Hyman used to say patiently. 'It is undoubtedly the best way when writing a book. But it won't do in the films . . .' Unlike Brian Lunn, Hyman never lost his temper. If Gerhardie became abusive he merely chewed his pencil 'as if waiting for a regrettable manifestation of Nature, such as a sudden shower of hail, to pass'.[8] Then they continued from where they had left off, before ending the day 'with a special stress of friendliness and mutual regard'.

Undeterred by the fact that the book was 'too morbid . . . too restricted in action, and too cynical for the screen', as well as the consideration that the 'wedding' night of Georges and Sylvia would be impossible on account of the censor, they eventually produced a completely altered screen synopsis, entitled *Love in Four Languages*. In great excitement they submitted it to the relevant departments. Suspenseful weeks passed. Eventually it was rejected as '*below* the current intelligence of cinema audiences'. Some months later Gerhardie sent both the synopsis and the original novel to Robert Donat, a popular and distinguished British stage actor who had been successful in Hollywood. Donat, for whom the part of Georges was suggested, was 'absolutely enthralled' with the book, which struck him as 'a wonderful opportunity for a really perceptive and imaginative producer'. Donat was, however, a very indecisive man, and he also suffered from severe asthma attacks which to some extent dictated his career. After weeks and months of uncertainty, suspense, and high hopes, the plan was abandoned, although this was not necessarily Donat's decision.

Gerhardie's ultimate failure to have a book accepted by the film industry makes it difficult to gauge his attitude to the cinema, for he was growing increasingly subjective. As a *potential* source of artistic achievement he envisaged history made real, the screening of *War and Peace*, the Battle of Waterloo, the integration of epic moments with private emotion. But most of the films that he saw—and apparently he had rather bad luck in this—he thought 'bad, stupid and worthless'. Instead of enhancing, they tended to blunt sensibility: 'A whole generation has been fed on faked emotion supplied by Hollywood and has grown up to accept it as genuine life, with the result that even American love is rank journalese.' Much of his information came from Frances who, film-struck, went every week, bought all the film magazines, and regularly consulted the *Hollywood All-In Compendium* which had a picture of Greta Garbo on the cover. Cinematic technicalities held a certain fascination for William: the stream of independent flickering imprints, the notion of running film backwards in order to go back in time; in *Resurrection* he writes that 'it would be a wonder if our life in Time, like the cinema reel composed of so many independent imprints, could be anything more profound than a cinema film'.[9] But at best he simply did not take the new medium seriously, and wrote an amusing article on 'Taking a Girl to the Pictures'. There were many advantages to be gained in developing the correct technique for your love affair, he pointed out, and advised observing the girl's reactions to the hero and *his* love-making. For the tongue-tied it provided endless opportunities for conversation as well as for the silent game of 'holding hands' ('Those who sneer at it merely prove that though they may have held hands, they have held the wrong hands').[10]

Gerhardie's increasing domestic comfort was, in some measure, compensating for his literary and financial disappointment; he was settling easily into a loose routine. Patsy and Frances invariably arrived before he was awake ('The self-respect which other men enjoy in rising early I feel due to me for waking up at all'),[11] then Frances carried in his early-morning tea and hung about chatting. Occasionally she would arrive as much as three hours late, explaining, 'a man that never keeps punctularity, that's why his maid doesn't'. Once she told him that she had had to walk all the way 'what with them buses being so long-winded'. After the cup of tea William would take a slow bath. 'Mr Gerhardie, you take ages over your bath', Frances admonished him. 'Once you get in you sit there ages and ages, right through the middle ages into our own ages.' On emerging he always wrapped a towel round his waist, loose ends at the back, 'since if the towel came loose my back (I reflect) is more like a woman's than my front',[12] before dressing for a long walk in the park. Only after an hour's solitary roaming was he ready for work, when he would sit down to answer letters and dictate to Patsy, who 'chews gum, talks a language of her own, with a strong American intonation derived from the movies, and reports the business of the day in gruff monosyllables: "Old Clingham has called. Old Bonzo has 'phoned. Old Bachelor has sent in his account."'[13] Patsy was also busily compiling scrapbooks of all her boss's articles and press cuttings. 'As you know, my happiness lies in this absurd flat with all its ups and downs', she told Clara. 'Willy is unchanged and shows no signs of growing up. He locked himself in the bathroom for ages the other day with my scissors and I couldn't think what on earth he was up to. At last he flung back the bolt and let us see the result of his terrible hair-cutting. It was terrible, just as though a goat had been chewing at it.' Often Gerhardie worked in his dressing-gown, pacing the two corridors of the flat as he did so. Lately he had taken to eating in the bedroom or sitting-room because the dining-room was not only icy cold but crammed with several dozen life-size plaster busts of himself, produced for the *Satan* publicity. In the afternoons William or Patsy read aloud, either from the work in progress or from favourite books. Frances now not only requested 'Love' books from the library, but borrowed her boss's poetry and fiction; she had acquired a taste for 'long words' and pronounced them at every opportunity with great relish which particularly intrigued William, for he remembered his own early attempts at English. When the reading was over Frances would dash off to the kitchen to make tea, which they drank to the music of Beethoven or Wagner on the gramophone, William conducting, sometimes throughout a whole symphony.

Frances was learning to cook from a Woolworth's book, singing in the kitchen, and calling out periodically to Patsy, 'My darling Honey', as though to check she was still close by. Gerhardie observed her as she moved around the flat, and made notes of her idiosyncrasies which were, happily, many. Every time she went out, even just to cross the road or in high summer, she put on a long, thick coat reaching to her ankles. If she permed her hair or bought a new outfit ('I thought I'd put on me black suit: it shrieks of Regent Street') she invariably requested her boss's opinion. She presented him with a photograph of herself fetchingly got up in her Sunday best, with beret and silk stockings. Whenever she and he came to blows—a 'bust-up' as she called it—she cried 'Blessèd chee-eek!', removed all her things from the little table in the kitchen, and folded it away in protest. Gerhardie had borrowed her Bible, and she took pride in seeing it on his desk and dusting it. But when they argued the Bible disappeared and the biscuits which she fed him with his tea were abruptly discontinued. 'I'm very highly annoyed', she would announce. 'Me mother thinks I'm simple—that I allow anyone to wipe the floor with me.' Then the following day they would be as affectionate as ever, bidding farewell to each other thus:

'Good-bye, dear boss.'

'Good-bye, sweet Frances.'

'Good-bye, my precious.'
'Good-bye, my little Champagne grapes.'
'Good-bye, my dream man.'

Sometimes when she went home she left little notes for her boss: 'I see, Mr Gerhardie, you have been and broken a glass, you naughty man.' When William had flu they nursed him, and Patsy rubbed camphor oil into his muscles. When he was in particularly bad financial trouble Patsy took on the role of adviser while Frances kept a stern eye on his spending:

'Mr Gerhardie, you've been at the sherry!'
'None of your business. You're not my governor, Frances!'
'I govern your life, don't I? I look after you. I'm you're governoress, aren't I?'
'Of course.'

She told him that to make money he ought to buy 'them things what go up and down'.

'Aeroplanes?'
'Nah! Them things what go up and down. *You* know.'
'Lifts?'
'Nah!'
'Yoyos?'
'Nah! Shares.'

They both took a very lively interest in William's women. One day Alan Hyman arrived unexpectedly early and noticed a dog whip on the floor. Frances quickly picked it up: 'Mr Gerhardi, you're a wicked man', she admonished him, shaking her finger. William looked mildly sheepish and concurred.

'I have found it convenient not to seduce either my secretary or my parlourmaid, but live with them in amity', wrote Gerhardie—an arrangement that suited everybody, not least Patsy who was a lesbian. Where once she had off-handedly sought William's advice about Ronnie or Lawrence, now she enthused over Jane's long fair hair, the seductive appeal of Beatrice. Always attentive to her own appearance, Patsy took more and more to tweed suits of a masculine cut. She worried about her sloping shoulders, and instructed her tailor to build up her jackets accordingly. And as for Frances—'Our dear little Frances, whom we both love so much', William wrote to Clara. 'Frances to us is like a child.' Frances seemed to have plenty of troubles without William adding to them. One day, after she had appeared with a black eye and made ready to leave early, she explained, 'Mr Gerhardie I left my bathroom and that as I wanted to get home and see if my boyfriend really meant what he did.' And family troubles too. Frances adored her mother who was bedridden with arthritis, and her brother, but her father was rather too fond of the 'little brown jug', all of which William found very interesting. 'He is a great man and I'm sure I'll never find a dearer sweeter man who listens to you when you are fed up.'[14]

Clara, of course, valued a ménage which ensured her son's health and happiness whilst presenting no threat to her own supremacy. When William was too busy to write, Patsy did so, relating all the news and ending affectionately: 'take care of yourself, angel, and don't forget that we love you dearly and think of you all the time', and when Daisy visited she and Frances took her baby son Claude for camel rides at the zoo.

Having at last recovered from the loss of Vera (now secretary to Beaverbrook and adviser on women's dress, cookery, and such matters) William had fallen in love with a society girl called Marjorie Glasgow to whom he periodically proposed marriage ('having another go at Marjorie'). But when she took a holiday in Germany she wrote to him not with affection, but to describe the indigenous political situation; Gerhardie, exasperated, wrote back with details of Lloyd George and mortality in Africa.

Gerhardie now seldom saw Beaverbrook: 'Max, with all his magnetic charm is merely a mental twister.' 'You will find him very agreeable', he told an acquaintance about to meet Beaverbrook. 'Not unlike Nero.' Though he rarely ventured out on social visits, Gerhardie kept in touch with a core of close friends about whom he liked to make notes (and who, incidentally, always seemed to share his financial plight). Perhaps his most unusual choice was Bunny Tattersall, a dilettante, rather smart journalist who wrote on racing and fishing and had published a book about the idle rich.[15] He had the great advantage over many of William's friends of being clean, but was quite unable to distinguish between the literature of Gerhardie and that of Somerset Maugham, and if anything discriminated in favour of Maugham. Not over-endowed with sensibilities, he tended to treat William with genial condescension. 'You may very well be right' was his habitual comment. Tattersall had once had money and, though now in debt to the tune of £2,000, none the less lent Gerhardie £20 and sent him six bottles of vintage port at Christmas. He was a great connoisseur of food and wine and therefore—in William's opinion—a sore trial to dine with. Gerhardie turned him into the bluff trencherman Job Devonshire in *My Wife's the Least Of It*:

Devonshire ordered a waiter to call the wine waiter and instructed him to remove a cucumber from the jug of champagne cup. 'The slice of cucumber should be there, you're quite right,' he said, 'I *did* say so. But you're quite wrong in *keeping* that slice of cucumber in the jug. A cucumber gives the champagne cup a fresh country-air flavour. *True*, my friend, *true*. But if you leave it there after the first ten minutes it taints the cup and that's to be avoided by all possible means.' . . . Job leaned sideways over his guest's glass, examining critically its contents. 'Have it as cold as you can stand it, by all means, I say; but don't have lumps of ice floating in your glass. It's a fallacy of the worst order and in the long run it's you who are the loser.' . . . 'By Jove, old boy, one does enjoy a quiet meal without women, two intelligent men by themselves, what?'[16]

But, Tattersall apart, Gerhardie was doomed to mucky friends. Not only Brian Lunn, but his brother Hugh, 'that great tight-fisted altruist, who, though clean, is clumsy, can't find his handkerchief and sneezes over my papers and cushions'. Bill (actually Arthur) Sykes, son of the Canon of Liverpool Cathedral, who had written appreciatively to Gerhardie after reading *Memoirs of a Polyglot* and thereafter put in regular appearances, 'though like Brian and Hugh a *relatively* free spirit, wears sandals with socks soaked in *both* human and canine urine into which he steps freely in public urinals and on the pavements, has only one shirt and wears it continually, no teeth, and is a drunk'.

Gerhardie's own once-immaculate wardrobe was growing a little shabby, but he was no less fastidious about his appearance—'a tall, fair-haired, youngish-looking man in a long black overcoat and white scarf, with a lost, unaware look in his blue eyes under a soft black hat set at a slant', as he portrayed himself.[17] He continued to experiment with diverse inspired concoctions to prevent his hair from receding, but even on this sensitive issue he was—like Frank Dickin in *Jazz and Jasper*—optimistic:

As his hair fell out more and more, he neither lost courage nor faith, but interpreted this as a process preparatory to new growth. The new hair which was to make its appearance must, he argued, have room; and the old hair was making room for it—with alacrity. When, after a time, it had entirely disappeared, he judged that now at last the field was clear for a fresh crop.[18]

After a year or two of Admiral Volkoff's hefty Russian lunches William discovered—and then only because Clara had requested his measurements for a new pair of pyjamas she had designed—to his horror that his waist 'at rest and expanded' had reached a portly 38½ inches. Out came the rubber vacuum roller that had so startled a woman customs officer at Boulogne. And in accordance with the latest theories he began to diet: two fried eggs and a glass of milk for breakfast ('milk is not fattening, it appears, nor is cheese or butter, because they are easily digestible'); half a pound of steak with gravy and tomatoes at four o'clock, followed by two or three thin slices of brown bread and butter and honey; raw carrots and milk in between meals ('if the truth were known, I drink heavily—three pints a day—but only milk'). An excellent new laxative, 'a cereal called Kellog (All Bran)', morning and evening with some liquid paraffin helped things along and he lost still more weight with a new patent brand of slimming pills—until Clara wrote to tell him that she had learned from her doctor that the active ingredient was tapeworm eggs.

After the sad departure of Rosie, William joined his mother in Bolton for Christmas, making a mental note that he would lay off the pudding. Christmas Eve was a cold, dark day of sleet and fog; he travelled by the midnight train, dozing in the crowded carriage. At Crewe a passenger suddenly said aloud 'Merry Christmas', and after that his companions, all Northerners returning home for the holiday, never stopped talking. At 5.00 on Christmas morning the train drew in, and Bolton, shrouded in yellow mist, looked like 'the bottom of a pond with the water drained off'.[19]

Another year had gone by and little achieved. As before, the new year found him sorely tested by 'the almost total absence of money'. One grand film hope after another floated before him, tantalizingly out of reach. Robert Donat picked up *The Polyglots* again: then decided that only Hollywood or Alexander Korda could do justice to the story. Basil Dean, who had filmed *The Constant Nymph*, seemed keen, wavered, and backed out. One by one the script went the rounds of the American companies, week after week, month after month of suspense. Patsy saw the whole thing as a big adventure and wrote delightedly to Clara of a youthful millionairess who had miraculously appeared on the horizon. She was the spring and summer of love and finance; the supple, irrepressible, boundless, and gaily laughing joy, and she lasted a week and then disappeared.

William's life was gradually becoming more and more solitary. In the evenings, when Patsy and Frances had departed, he would pace the London parks and streets at great speed, then return to the empty flat and play Wagner; then a piano sonata of Beethoven, and then he would enjoy putting away the records, closing the gramophone, and sitting in silence. He wrote a scenario for a short story: a country house is occupied by a ghost. A lonely man buys the house. At first he is very frightened of the ghost, then they make friends. They have innumerable conversations together, 'and everything else by the test of their friendship becomes unreal'. Gerhardie's was a melancholy loneliness, one he was both unable and unwilling to shake off. Passing the Royal Academy of Music one day he saw the students going in together chatting and laughing and felt sad because he was solitary and excluded. But he remembered how he had missed his chance of 'belonging' at Oxford, and passed the days alone. 'He was one of these people who really remained a foreigner', said Anthony Powell. He 'had no kind of feeling for living in England. I think he'd have been much more at ease in some continental capital.'[20] Now he felt he belonged nowhere. Blasé about praise when it was offered, when it was withdrawn he felt distressed and isolated.

The 'disembodied correspondence' continued. 'This kind of mysterious acquaintance is the ground from which a new book grows, I always feel', he wrote to one (as yet unknown) admirer. 'That is, the writer is in the position of the reader—but knows *nothing* as yet. But there is the book which contains it all. The imagination stands still for want of data.'[21] To another:

I am honoured by your invitation to lunch, and a little puzzled. Can you tell me why you wish me to lunch with you? I cannot recall our having met before; can you? How do I know that the luncheon is not a trap to kidnap and release me against heavy ransom? Are you the famous author of that name or am I mistaken?[22]

A Dutchman asked for 'a "waste paper" in your writing' which would be enough to keep him happy, and an anonymous individual requested some of Gerhardie's underclothing; he replied that he had just been completely cleared out of almost *all* his clothing by needy relations.

Another admirer, Carlotta Pinto, enclosed a glamorous photograph of herself and asked Gerhardie to become guardian to her little boy, Henry Vincent Quique Pinto. He politely declined: 'You see, you derive your idea of me from my books, which display me as being so fond of children—which I am. But it does not follow that on the practical side I am at all the ideal guardian. My own nephews and nieces find me sadly deficient on that score.' And he pointed out that people in the future would be bound to assume he was the father of the child. He would have far preferred to be Carlotta's guardian, and paid her a surprise visit but found her not at home.

Gerhardie was irritated by pedantic criticism of his books and particularly irritated by pretension: 'Don't write rot', he told one convoluted would-be writer. 'Tell me *simply* about your life and send me a snapshot. I'd like to know what you look like.' Another received a curt note which ended: 'Your being a cousin of Matthew Arnold is not interesting.'

But to most he was kind and considerate. Gladys M. South wrote in hearty appreciation of Gerhardie's humour, which induced 'not mere smiles, chuckles or titters, but real hoarse belly-laughs, such as one only hears when there is some good, dirty fun going around. I hope you will pardon my vulgarity, but if you had ever heard my laugh you would know that I had used *le mot juste*.' Gerhardie, intrigued, telephoned her to ask if she were young and beautiful; she burst into delighted laughter and told him that she most certainly was not. Moreover she pined for her professor. Ms South wrote back again and for a while the two of them kept up an exuberantly saucy correspondence. Her long typed letters relate in hilarious detail her life and love affairs:

I have now lent you to my young man, but I doubt if he will enjoy you to the full as he is inclined to be ponderous . . . We shall probably have a row about you. But it doesn't matter, we are always having rows. He is so sensitive, and I am so crude, what's in must out, sort of business. But I think you would care for my young man, he is bizarre, really quite unique. About 6′ 4″ in height, and that thin you would never believe. I am in perpetual expectation that his pants will fall right off (but no luck so far!) because they are without visible means of support and he has no hips at all, absolutely none. And he is most aesthetic, living for the ballet and all like that, wearing shirts of peculiar hue and a strange tie like a face-flannel.

And of course, intruding into this imaginative world, was his correspondence with Clara ('How I wish I could see you kiss you and talk and listen to you', she wrote).

Meanwhile he was having trouble finding a publisher for *Of Mortal Love*. Cassell, after losing £800 on *Satan* and over £600 on *Resurrection*, refused to pay anything like the old advances; William was reluctant to let the book go cheap and entered into negotiations with Arthur Barker. Barker, however, 'humiliated' Gerhardie by asking to see the finished novel before signing a contract. 'I haven't in the least bit weakened in my confidence in you as a writer', explained Barker when Gerhardie pointed out that only with *Futility* had he had to do this. 'On the other hand I don't think that there is any doubt, mainly due to your collaborations, you have adversely affected the possible sales of any new book of your own.' Somehow an agreement was reached. Gerhardie was to produce three books over the next three years: the first, *Of Mortal Love*, to be finished by 1 July, the second by January 1937, and the third (tentatively entitled *Our Square*, and probably the germ of *My Wife's the Least Of It*) to be completed by July 1938. Barker would pay an advance of £500 a year in quarterly instalments for the next three years, with the option to break the contract after the first year.

This caused great excitement in the flat. For the first time since the army Gerhardie could anticipate a guaranteed income, which he hoped, amongst other things, would enable him to repay the 'hefty sum' owed to his mother. 'The fact that we have to work to time makes all the difference', wrote Patsy to Clara, 'because we simply have to get a move on, "mood" or no mood. And I'm surprised how Willy can get into the mood for writing if only he is forced to do so! Willy has at last tumbled to the fact that money doesn't necessarily come from heiresses and that it is much more certain to come from hard work than Irish sweepstakes which is something I for one have been telling him for years but which he thinks he has thought of all by himself! You really have borne a funny child, you know.' In a genuine effort to meet the deadlines he cut himself off from all distractions: the telephone no longer registered incoming calls. 'Mr Gerhardie is indisposed', said Frances sternly when friends tempted with personal visits and, if they demurred, gave them a dragon scowl. She permitted him to leave the flat only for evening walks in the park. One night very late a little boy, too small to pull the bell at the front-door of an imposing house, asked Gerhardie to do so. 'And now let's beat it, Uncle', said he, 'or we'll get it in the neck!' They both ran like hell. On warm days William and Patsy worked out of doors. William told his publisher that *Of Mortal Love* absorbed him more than anything previously, and was convinced that in addition to being a work of literature it would be his most popular book.

Too busy to visit Bolton, they celebrated a Russian-style Easter in the flat, placing a white tablecloth on the dining table and arranging food sent by Clara: traditional eggs coloured with onion skins and brightly painted, cold roast beef with Russian salad, pork, cake and chocolates, bread and peanuts. Admiral Volkoff supplied an expensive *pashka* which they ate with sherry and port. After which Gerhardie decided to abandon the 'sawdust stuff' breakfast cereal in favour of Ovaltine and croissants at Lyons' Corner House.

For much of this time they also had *Meet Yourself* on their hands. When at long last it was completed, after unending months of frustration, Gerhardie gave it a ceremonial blessing with the sign of the cross and he, Patsy, Frances, and Poldi sang in unison, 'For it's a jolly good riddance', as it was borne aloft to the post office. When in June 1936 it was published, the response looked promising. Selfridge's arranged a splendid display: 'WILLIAM GERHARDI' and 'PRINCE LEOPOLD LOEWENSTEIN' appeared in neon lights on the roof, and the largest window featured their photographs a yard high, with Gerhardie's popping out of a gigantic mirror and vanishing every ten seconds. All the Oxford Street windows sported photographs, and inside the shop was a special stand with two hundred copies of the book and a glamorous girl to sell them. Crowds gathered where William and Poldi sat waiting to sign copies; hundreds fingered the books, nodded, conferred approvingly amongst themselves—and went away. All week they sold less than sixty copies. The profit for Selfridge's was a mere £3, and the window display alone had cost £4. 10s. a day. Bitterly disappointed, Gerhardie could not help but see the humour of it. 'Difficulties and setbacks, his own and other people's, were always a source of amusement rather than concern to Gerhardi', noted Brian Lunn.[23]

Besides, the end was not yet in sight. The critics wrote at length with great enthusiasm of *Meet Yourself*, tempting the *Daily Mail* into offering £600 for the serial rights. It was, they later told the authors, their most successful serial for three years. William and Poldi received scores of letters, many detailing personal character traits, recounting dreams, and asking advice about the future. An Oxford undergraduate wrote to say that he had worked out the answers for a number of famous men in history and found the readings to be perfectly correct. Years later Mr Charles E. Sprague, who had given the book much serious attention, asked Gerhardie to explain its 'scientific framework', 'symbolic connections', and 'guiding principles'. He was especially interested as he himself had translated a book of ancient Egyptian temple teachings. Gerhardie replied gravely: 'The work you have translated, of course, derives not from an Egyptian but much earlier Assyrian source having its beginnings in early-Mexican eschatology. Yours sincerely but not truly.'

Despite its inauspicious start, *Meet Yourself* sold 4,000 copies by Christmas, short of expectation but not an unrespectable sum. Curiously enough the American edition did not do well, until republished in an Americanized version entitled *Analyze Yourself*, in 1956. By then Gerhardie had quite lost interest in it, though due to Poldi's perseverance it eventually sold more than 200,000 copies in England, America, and in translation abroad, and provided its authors with some badly needed income.

In October 1936 *Of Mortal Love* appeared. It is the story of Walter

Smith, an aspiring young(ish) composer, and his love for the beautiful but dim-witted Dinah, unhappily married, thrice-courted, and unable to make up her mind between her suitors. It had long been Gerhardie's ambition to write a 'story of a simple heart', a 'simple love story', something he considered to be extremely difficult to achieve without resorting to sentimentality. He approached the subject from an unusual angle, telling 'how a casual love affair grew and blossomed into real love—in the opposite direction of conventional fiction'.[24] 'The seriousness is *implicit*', he explained to H. G. Wells. 'There is no *show* of seriousness.'[25]

Its strength lies in its delicacy and candour, and its hero and heroine are the most vivid of all Gerhardie's fictional characters. Walter's love is not a 'one-melody' emotion, but a shifting, elusive orchestration of feelings, so that *Of Mortal Love* becomes 'a novel containing fresh love-lore and treating of the succeeding stages of transmutation of love erotic into love imaginative; of love entrancing into love unselfish; of love tender into love transfigured'.[26] 'There have been cases,' he told his publisher, 'when biography masqueraded as fiction—the very opposite of what I in effect propose to do. Mine is a novel claiming to be classified as a biography, all the more appealing to the public imagination because it is a story of a real woman.' This synthesis of fact and fiction in the presentation of a living individual—'imaginative biography' as Gerhardie called it (the book was originally to include a 'scholarly preface' explaining such ideas)—goes back to his earliest writings. For not only is this love story a result of a long-cherished idea, but it embodies his childhood preoccupations of love, death, and a beautiful heroine who shares many of his own characteristics. Gerhardie has created Dinah out of a fusion of Vera and himself, and in so doing displays a delicate sympathy towards her.

Of Mortal Love is, in fact, far more than just a *simple* love story. It is the narrative of Walter/William's attempt to 'capture' the elusive Dinah/Vera. In the telling the story becomes increasingly complex, almost impossibly elusive. Art—either (Walter's) music or (William's) literature—is revealed as a surrogate, idealized form of experience, both superior to and inadequate for human communication. And yet, as Gerhardie also believed, 'It is the inadequacy of all human contacts that throws one back on oneself, and makes the artist.'

Walter and William are identifiable with each other because, apart from sharing certain qualities, they are both faced with the problem of first understanding, and then presenting Dinah/Vera: Walter within the confines of the plot and story, Gerhardie as 'real' author, who has known the 'real' woman. But from the start Walter is confounded by the very difficulty of perceiving his love as a person. Fiction seems always to intervene. Her past before he knew her—what is it but a series of stories? After learning of an amorous episode in Hungary he feels (mistakenly, as he realizes later) that he knows her better, that this somehow draws him closer to Dinah:

By a sudden flash of intuition into her being Walter understood that if he had, for instance, never known of Dinah's Hungarian interlude his conception of her reality would have been at fault; and he thought how many small happenings and people he had never heard of must at one time or another have entered into her existence, adding their quota to that savour she experienced as her life but could never communicate to him in full; and for the first time he was jealous.

It seemed incredible to him that here he was walking with the heroine of that Hungarian romance; that he and she now stood leaning over a fence together and looked at the shepherd's dog chasing a flock of sheep.

And Dinah herself is quick to appreciate the different turns her life might have taken—she constructs separate plots for herself: '"This is perhaps what I too would have had if I had married Mark . . .—Or," she added, more credibly, "if I had remained on that film".' Indeed she still has not made up her mind about how her life is to be plotted, keeping the ending open by assuring Walter that she may still go back to him. Walter too perpetually attempts to impose simple stories on a complex world. He falls for Dinah originally because she reminds him of the wicked—and fictional—Eleanora. Like Proust's narrator, he desires the symbol above the actual and so his unfulfilment is a foregone conclusion—anticipated in the very title of his book.

Infatuated, Walter is drawn into a misdirected attempt to see events in Dinah's life in a novelist's terms of a denouement.

All these had seemed loose ends. But were they? They seemed, these ambitions, to be turning and losing themselves like footpaths in a forest, yet somehow coming back again to the main avenue of her life stretching like a broad belt through the park. He was convinced that everything that happened in her life was to the ultimate enrichment of her being.

Yet the presence of Lord Ottercove, still concerned with his theistic plotting, is enough to ridicule any notion of rational destiny. We remember Andrei's lament when, towards the end of *Futility*, he comes to *reject* the identification of 'novel plot' with 'life', and Gerhardie's praise of Chekhov for his affirmation of the 'loose-end nature' of our existence, his rejection of the notion of 'personality'. And sure enough, Dinah's attempts to plot her own life go wrong both for her and for those around her.

Walter's eventual awareness that he is in fact quite ignorant of the Dinah he thought he knew, dawns with her rejection of him—only one of a series of rejections and misplaced, shifting passions. A chance move of Dinah's that Walter cannot 'place' (she visits Cambridge to decide the fate of some apples) precipitates his realization:

It came to him, in a rush of thought, how little he knew her, a cross-section at most of the trunk of her life, cut here, cut there, today, tomorrow. But there was all the greenery of the tree she felt in every twig and leaf, and how she did feel it she alone knew: it was her mystery of being, incommunicable, her leafy life. He could not see it . . . There was her unknown life of which he had merely seen the face, the dear familiar hieroglyphics he knew so well but could not read—the voucher, faithful and exact, for her unknown life. In the midst of her emotional preoccupations, she had suddenly seen fit, seen necessary, to go to Cambridge with her aunt to see about those apples. Consequently he, Walter, had omitted from his stock of observation, something wide of his knowledge of her. He understood, with a shock, that he could not know Dinah, that he could never know her, however much he listened to her and stared at her or for the rest deduced by reference to his own emotions and experiences, his private store of apples. He could never know her.

The 'simple' story has proved impossibly complex, and the precarious nature of Walter's perception of Dinah is his only certainty. Perception of another remains, to a large extent, a fiction constructed by the self, hardly more intimate than the stories of people Walter hears casually related on a train journey. And memory itself offers a perpetually elusive contact. But in spite of this, in an alienating world, art restores the contact. Walter/William relives Dinah/Vera by writing *Of Mortal Love*. His failure to 'grasp' her creates, paradoxically, a greater sympathy between Walter and the reader. For Gerhardie is creating a sophistic-ated relation between hero, heroine, and reader. He does not, like so many novelists, present a heroine we may identify with and like. We may love Dinah or we may hate her (opinions varied on this): what is of value is the shifting relations between the three of us. 'The real test of a novel,' Gerhardie wrote, 'is perhaps how close the reader has come to the people whom the author has made him meet, the link between the people in it and ourselves and those others whom we want to read the novel in order to enlarge the link of our common humanity.'

Yet the majority of reviewers did not respond to Gerhardie's intricate challenge to his readers' sympathies. A novel, they insisted, should provide an unequivocally likeable heroine. 'Alas! my love has been for women who were not my intellectual equals,' lamented Gerhardie, 'and the average reader, being a snob, always felt: "If he doesn't respect (intellectually) the woman he loves, why should *we* respect her, or respect *him* for that matter for loving her?" '[27] Many condemned Dinah's vanity, lack of intellect, 'irritating' mannerisms, and above all her 'immorality', judging the novel as a whole on their antipathy to one character and on their own narrow, sexist expectations. Yet Dinah is the victim of men, and in creating her Gerhardie has displayed a very delicate sympathy on this point. 'As the quality was new and the theme was new,' he wrote to Desmond MacCarthy in despair, 'I left undefended and exposed the moral parts, thinking that they would feel as you feel about Dinah and would not take advantage of her candour and frankness. But they have all thrust their swords through the breach in the breastplate.'

Clara rallied to the defence. 'It is a great masterpiece Vassinka and a man who can write like that *must* be proclaimed and acknowledged an outstanding genius. Just a little more patience, lovie.' Despite the reviews, she was not alone in her judgement. Over the years, *Of Mortal Love* commanded a loyal body of admirers and is to this day considered by many his finest work. Edwin Muir in *The Listener* said as much, comparing it to Sterne's *Sentimental Journey*,[28] and C. P. Snow lauded it highly. H. G. Wells thought the book excellent in places, but 'the texture is too uniform. It ripples gaily—good for 30 pages but not for 300. It's like a composition that is all allegretto. I think a novel should be more moody . . . About it all is something not quite flesh and blood. One of your ancestors was a transparent tinted creature of Venetian glass and you show it and the quality affects all your characters in what is after all a very real story.'[29] Kingsmill was full of praise ('genius my dear William, that is the only word for the book'), naming Dinah as 'far and away the most complete character in any of your books, except of course yourself'. Desmond MacCarthy's daughter Rachel, wife of Lord David Cecil, was so intrigued by the novel that she wrote to ask Gerhardie about the *real* Dinah. 'Only the other night we drove to a party together,' Gerhardie replied, 'and she leant forward impulsively and knocked on the glass to tell the taxi-driver not to drive so fast. Then, leaning back, she said, "How awful if there had been an accident. I might have injured my face." I pointed out that, apart from the driver who, if he had engineered the accident, was not perhaps entitled to so much pity, there was still myself. "Yes," she said. "And you, too."'

But the book did not sell, realizing less than £200 of its advance. Clara remained unpaid and Barker apparently terminated the agreement. Desmond MacCarthy caused a slight revival of interest several weeks after publication following an appreciative review in the *Sunday Times* in which he referred to Gerhardie as 'the gentlest of debunkers'. Again William's hopes rose when, a few days after publication, Edward VIII abdicated and a newspaper photograph appeared in which the Duchess of Windsor stood holding a book which, by its distinctive square shape, convinced him that it was *Of Mortal Love*. Then, early in 1937, he learned that it had failed to find an American publisher. That this was due in part to the after-effects of the Depression was small consolation: 'It is completely unreasonable that America should have entirely refused to publish *Of Mortal Love*, my *best book*', he wrote to Clara. 'Sooner or later I am bound to have a real success and then all the publishers who have not felt inclined to continue giving me an advance big enough to enable me to write at all, will regret their not having gone on a little longer and cutting their losses.'

Even in old age Gerhardie considered *Of Mortal Love* his favourite —possibly even his best—novel, and stressed how much harder it had been to write than the early books. It was with the greatest difficulty that he now kept his spirits buoyant, and he admitted that he was 'beginning to sag a little under the latest attack from the air on my tender, whimsical and delicate *Of Mortal Love*. . . . I used not to care much about reviews, but this sort of patronizing attitude and misjudgement from totally stupid people is beginning to wear me down and I don't see any prospect of appreciation except from a few rare friends.' This letter to Oliver Stonor was in fact the opening of another 'rare friendship'. Stonor, himself the author of one novel,[30] had recently written praising *Resurrection* and bemoaning the difficulties of composition. Gerhardie encouraged him in his work and spoke of his own: 'I am, in fact, in the same glum mood about my future book. I can't even find an adequate plot to suit the accumulated material. I feel entirely weak and uninspired. I haven't been so dead and resourceless for a long time, so please forgive me for this brief note. Christmas is a depressing time.'

18

MOVING PICTURES
January 1937–September 1939

There is nothing like lying in bed except perhaps lying in one's coffin.

In the new year Gerhardie, in a gloomy mood, wrote to Kingsmill: 'The bottom seems to have fallen out of literature. There are neither critics nor readers, neither publishers nor money, and I am also at a loose end. I am, however, applying for a patent in respect of a certain article I have invented; and our hopes are centred on it—which is the thing to do with hopes: attach them to something.' The 'article' was a disposable self-pasting toothbrush, a badly needed innovation embodying a number of advantages: no more fiddling with toothpaste caps, no more unhygienic old toothbrushes, no more danger of swallowing bristles because you keep forgetting to buy a new brush, and withal very modern. Just as the fountain-pen had supplanted the pen and nib, so this would take over from the brush and tube. 'I'll shortly send you an icing bag and ask you to make a little receptable out of it for the toothpaste to fit into a handle I will send you', he wrote to Clara, who responded with alacrity. But the pendulous bag dripped. Dolly's husband Lot, less imaginative but considerably more mechanical, suggested a tube with a key mechanism, not unlike that on a sardine tin. But tremendous pressure was needed to force out even the thinnest paste. The toothbrush occupied Gerhardie throughout 1937 and eventually, after a number of mishaps, he paid £5 to patent a prototype. The Merseyside Society of Inventors elected him to its ranks, where Mr Wigglesworth advised that the maximum price for such an article should be 1s. 3d. Macleans and Odol both asked to see a model, and Boots the Chemist said that they would be interested in selling the finished item, but not in manufacturing it themselves.

The toothbrush proved deeply inspirational and, after a couple of hours of welding, gouging, and squeezing, Gerhardie's mind was abuzz with new ideas. The market for novels was much depleted but he was drawn to writing a life of Queen Mary, against which he would present, humorously, a general picture of English life encompassing without bias every class and faction. Peggy Guggenheim's tentative invitation to edit the letters of John Holms eventually revealed itself as a 'thankless and profitless task'. Guggenheim objected to his introduction of Holms in an 'ironical light', and he was irritated by the 'inapproachable veneration' in which Holms was held by his various women admirers. 'Jenkinson', a story about Russia with reference to the political situation in Spain, was read on the BBC, and Gerhardie made elaborate but ultimately fruitless plans to found 'a new advertising weekly paper'. Beverley Nichols, with his enviable knack of producing second-rate best-sellers, had recently made a great deal of money with a book about Christ, *The Fool Hath Said*. With this in mind Gerhardie considered writing about religion in Communist Russia (hardly best-seller material), then 'a book about Christ from a modern angle—a very reverend book, at the same time the book of a novice who has only come to understand the teaching and philosophy and life of Christ late in life'. And, most promising of all, he considered a work encompassing such disparate events, historical and fictional, as Goethe falling in love with Charlotte Brontë, Queen Christina attempting to seduce Mr Darcy and Byron killed by Bolsheviks at Vladivostok. 'The idea is that while differences of environment are of enormous influence, differences of the age we live in are negligible. I want to show that there is really no such thing as modernity.'

What he actually sat down to write began as an idea for a newspaper serial in which a number of his old fictional creations—Uncle Emmanuel and Aunt Teresa from *The Polyglots*, Mary Brandon from *Perfectly Scandalous*, and others—gather in London for the Coronation. When he decided to incorporate into the story his own vicissitudes with the film industry, the serial turned into a novel. Gerhardie was unexpectedly 'overjoyed' when, on the strength of a sample, the 'distinguished' firm of Faber and Faber offered him a contract: '£500 advance, on top of a succession of *financially* unsuccessful books, shows my name alone is still worth something', he told Clara, explaining that they had also agreed good royalties and an option of £500 advance on each of his next two books. For most of the year he remained in very good spirits, writing the book with not only a card index but a complicated chart that enabled him to see the plot development as a whole. Patsy and Frances thought it his funniest book yet—'We nearly die laughing'—but for William it was, as all his books had been, 'hard labour'. 'I had occasion to look at *The Polyglots* the other day', he told Clara. 'The ease and good humour of it suggests as if it had been sheer effortless pleasure to write it. But the tears and blood I shed over it.'

Yet there is little doubt that he was finding it increasingly difficult to write. Patsy no longer simply typed his manuscript, but undertook the whole organization of it, from start to finish, even having to urge William to sit down and work. 'Excuse this short note but I must go and see what your naughty son is doing—quite likely he is fast asleep!' she wrote to Clara. 'Sometimes I think the easiest way to move him on would be to give him a big biff. I've always felt that you spared the rod on him as a child. I've tried everything else—coaxing, raving, nagging. In fact, he now calls me "nag Rosenstiehl", if you please. But nagging has not the slightest effect on his slowness. The only thing left to me now is beating!' The 'Proustian shutters' were taking their toll. Gerhardie had spent almost every day of the last seven years at a desk in Rossetti House. The 'glorious uncertainty' that had so stimulated him, kept him from other professions, held him to literature alone, was inexorably transmuting itself into 'dead certainty'—no money, no new experiences, no inspiration—'truly deadly'.

Whilst dissociating himself from any literary movement or group, Gerhardie had always kept abreast, in a haphazard fashion, of contemporary literature. But as years went by this became more and more of a chore. 'If writing wasn't such an exhausting race between trying to reach the winning post in advance of one's creditors and at the same time breed one's yearlings with regard to other qualities as well as speed into self-respecting horses decently proportioned, one might attend to the whole field of contemporary critical output with a wider benevolence: subscribe to all current reviews in several languages and be in contact with all the latest publications'.[1] The success of others became increasingly hard to accept. He declined an invitation from the University of London School of Slavonic and East European Studies to a small reception for 'a brilliant young Russian novelist, Vladimir Nabokov-Sirin of whom you may have heard', who was to read from his autobiography and from his novel *Despair*.[2] Though Gerhardie admired Nabokov, this was hardly likely to appeal, and must have hurt him a good deal. The wound was reopened two years later with a further invitation to meet 'the most interesting Russian author writing today' whose 'almost desperate financial plight' necessitated an admission charge of 2*s*. 6*d*. Successful women novelists aroused his jaundice most of all—at times it was almost rabid, as when Patsy left a copy of Virginia Woolf's *The Waves* lying around which Gerhardie picked up: 'I began to read—here and there—and, finally, overcome by nausea, I feel positively *ill*; and quickly drank several glasses of port in the hope of neutralizing my disgust. I have never yet read an author that nauseated me to such an extent. . . . The literary adjective to describe it accurately is—*fucking* awful! . . . she presents us with a tedium never known on land or sea, a tedium multiplied by her own bloodless, fuckless anaemic self—oh, the bitch!'[3] Dorothy Kingsmill, believing that Gerhardie's hysteria was often a sign of envy, thought that at heart he recognized Woolf's talent, and indeed in calmer mood he went so far as to admit that she wrote 'carefully', displaying a 'marvellous gift for observation of little things, but all drowned in a pretentious form of presentation'. Gerhardie claimed that he had it on good authority (Leonard Woolf, in fact) that Virginia Woolf's aloofness towards his own work was due to social factors: being a snob herself she envied him his patronage by the aristocracy.

Yet he was surprisingly sanguine when other writers 'borrowed' from him. Evelyn Waugh was introduced to Gerhardie's work whilst at Oxford, years before writing his own, but his (understated) acknowledgement—'As no doubt you recognized I learned a great deal of my trade from your own novels'—pleased William enormously.[4] In the mid-1930s, Hazel Lavery reported to Gerhardie Waugh's admission that he was 'envious' of him: 'I shall never be as good as he. I know I have great talent, but he has genius.' In a rather more tenuous connection, Gerhardie light-heartedly claimed to have had a hand in the conception of *Animal Farm* for, whilst walking with Oliver Stonor, he outlined his idea for a novel about animals in revolt against man. Stonor wrote such a book—*A Star Called Wormwood* (1941)—which was reviewed by George Orwell, who four years later produced his masterpiece. What did rankle with Gerhardie was the critics' persistent habit of comparing whatever he wrote unfavourably with his past work, because,

Though a perfect work by another author is a joy for ever, the best of one's own work ceases to mean very much when one has grown out of the state of being which had inspired it. . . . After all, it is delightful to behold a youth, a child, a babe; but the contemplation of oneself as a babe, a child, a youth is a little disgusting. The reason being that the umbilical cord which binds us to our diverse selves is not severed in our various works in which we have buried our contemporary conceits and faults. When we re-read a book of our own we are conscious of the timely aspect of ourselves, so different from the timeless contemplation of the past which cleanses and sanctifies the self in time for perpetuation in eternity.

Continuing expectations of a film success kept spirits buoyant at Rossetti House, whilst also providing material for the new novel —which novel in turn, when published, caught the attention of the film magnates and thus fuelled further expectations. New film companies seemed to be springing up like mushrooms all over England and America—even Poldi was attempting to inaugurate one, having 'at long last found a fool to put a £1,000 into it!' Again Robert Donat picked up *the Polyglots*; and again changed his mind. Gaumont British tantalized with a sudden interest in *Of Mortal Love*, and William, imagining Bette Davis in the role of Dinah, sent her the book. Urged on by the knowledgeable Frances, letters went out to every film-star in Hollywood.

In May Gerhardie watched the Coronation of King George VI and Queen Elizabeth from the balcony of Bunny Tattersall's West-End flat. All London was peppered with temporary lavatories set up in the streets and parks. The procession sprang into view led by a mounted officer who could not manage his prancing steed. 'The horse sidled, refused to walk on, and finally about-turned altogether and for a while led tail forward.'[5] Gerhardie leaned on the balustrade, breakfasting on champagne and smoked salmon, while Edwina Mountbatten's sister pointed out her brother-in-law as he passed below. Clara, detained in Bolton, put her eulogy for the new king down in a letter, praising him for the 'brave manner in which he has met and is trying to carry through a most unpleasant ordeal'. And Gerhardie recalled a pre-Abdication ball at Londonderry House when the then Duke and Duchess of York appeared, and 'suddenly all the people drew up awkwardly and unnaturally . . . Lord Londonderry suddenly looked like his own lackey, and the Duke as he went dancing with the hostess had a strange hunted expression. He is a miserable looking specimen of humanity with a chauffeur's type of face, small, hunched, chinless, effete.' Tattersall was a very efficient and bossy host, shepherding his guests about—William in particular—exhorting them to stand up, sit down, kneel, according to whether they were singing, listening, or praying. Troop after troop, band after band, passed below, 'bunches of assorted Royalty, foreign and home-grown', all the armed forces of the Empire, 'a trifle too many of them, perhaps; too many weapons. One might have wished to see thrown in a few painters and intellectuals, Bloomsbury types in loose flannels, even a golfer or two in plus-fours. Something more representative.'[6]

Shortly after the Coronation, Clara left for a summer holiday in

Finland. Victor, recently recovered from the economic depression and again doing well, paid for his mother to sail first class: manicures, pedicures, massage, hair-waves, and unprecedented luxury marred only by the constant fog-horn. Victor lived in great style and comfort, with a flat in Helsinki and a handsome country house with servants' quarters, stabling, garages, and workshop, as well as a private beach on the lake where the mosquitoes gave her a very warm welcome.

After an adulterous love affair Victor's home life had considerably improved. At the time Clara, deeply shocked, had begged William to intervene. William desisted, and Victor's new wife Joan, a fine horse-woman, made 'a happy wife'. Victor had won prizes with his horse Black Prince and his rooms were strewn with medals and rosettes. In recognition for his services towards Anglo-Finnish trade relations he had received the order 'Knight of the White Rose of Finland, First Class'. 'I think he wanted his mammie to know that he could also excel in something', said Clara with some satisfaction when she relayed all this back to William, for her own diagnosis of her elder son was that he suffered from an inferiority complex.

Victor still took a great interest in the career of his brother and ordered his books direct from the publisher. Like Clara his rooms were strewn with photographs—to her surprise five of William alone. And to her even greater astonishment he now freely admitted that he had persecuted William as a child. 'You know I have told you again and again, how Victor admires you', Clara reminded William, ever anxious for peace in the family, 'and this generous acknowledgement of his unkind treatment of you in your boyhood proves he is genuinely sorry.' William was sympathetic—up to a point. There was something 'wrong' about Victor. 'He may be ever so well intentioned, but his sensibility is ill-informed, and so he does and says everything wrong, and everyone hates him.'

William, too, was planning to go abroad, probably to Paris where the exchange-rate was still favourable and where Clara could join him. She might spend several months there, before visiting Daisy. 'Then in the hot months you could visit Victor in Helsingfors, see Dolly again in Bolton, (en route), stay in your own house, then go to Helsingfors, then to Rosie's, then back to Victor, to Bolton, to Paris, again to see Daisy, and so remain in perpetual circulation and circumlocution through Europe!' Like so many of these plans, it never flowered. Prudential Insurance, his new and excellent landlords, agreed to reduce his rent to £160 a year and installed an expensive new electric boiler in the bathroom. And so Gerhardie, his Parisian longing somewhat abated, remained comfortably ensconced in Rossetti House. For his forty-second birthday Aunt Sissie sent chocolates, and Clara a dish of pork and gravy, and his own special favourite, boiled eggs and anchovies. Frances was still learning to cook from a book and still 'not up to much'. They experimented with some tinned food, but rather cautiously: medical opinion was divided as to whether or not tins were unhealthy. William had always hated the killing of animals for food—the nicest thing about horses, in his opinion, was that they were clean and herbivorous—and earlier in the year he had changed to a vegetarian diet. 'I could no more eat meat or fish now than if I were offered a dead mouse. Even when I dine with my friends I insist on a special vegetarian cuisine, and if they want me to come they have to go to a great deal of bother!' He and Bill Sykes had discovered an excellent restaurant nearby, which offered three-course nut cutlet meals for around 2s. When Clara heard of this she begged him to be careful crossing the roads.

At length the new novel was complete. 'I have never that I can remember been *so completely fagged out* by a book. I'm all nerves and irritation! I can't help thinking it's good and, in a way, the most completely *original* book in idea and construction I have ever done. There is really nothing of that kind in existence.' But there was trouble with the printers again, for instead of taking extra care over foreign words, 'they seem to let themselves go, thinking: "Ah! Any sort of spelling will do!" . . . rather as if a motorist on seeing the sign: "School" increased rather than decreased his normal speed.' Furthermore, the proposed title, *My Wife: A Study in Insanity*, horrified Faber. Not only was it intimidating, they hurried to point out, but people would also assume the book to be some ghastly scientific treatise. Eventually retitled *My Wife's the Least Of It*, with a dedication to Arthur [Bill] Sykes, the book was published in April 1938. 'A novel depicting humorously the tragedy of protracted patience',[7] it is the story of the attempts of an elderly man, Charles Baldridge, to write a successful film script, and thus save himself from insolvency. Baldridge, 'a projection, a sinister foreboding of my old age', appears as a once-famous, now forgotten writer, rather fussy, somewhat put upon by others, though not without guile himself, and very, very different from the young, rather debonair heroes of the earlier books. Gerhardie had conceived his novel 'in the Pickwickian vein', with a group of characters who 'meet with day-to-day adventures which amuse the reader because he sees the characters he has got to know so well in characteristic situations ... [they] are mouthpieces of comically divergent opinions in our world to-day which we see through their eyes'. His earlier (and more appropriate title), *Moving Pictures*, expresses his interest in the form of this novel, whereby the overall result 'depends on the cumulative effect of placing a great number of little incidents and characters in the right order'. Individual scenes, differing very slightly on each occasion, suggest not the totality of a film but the minute progression from one frame to the next. As in *Futility*, the repetitions—of manuscript rejections, inconclusive meetings with film directors, deferred promises—leads *My Wife's the Least Of It* from comedy to tragedy, though nightmare and back to farce. Michael Holroyd has most aptly praised the book as 'an illustration, detail by dire detail, minute by minute, of our life in time. The film world symbolizes the visible surface of things divorced from all poetic implications. It is actual, but unreal.'[8] Oliver Stonor acknowledged the novel's 'imperfection', but none the less recognized in it Gerhardie's characteristic

capacity for taking the commonplace and the usual and exhibiting it as the wildly strange—strange in the philosophically terrifying manner in which a two-sided triangle or a circular square would be strange. ... To him, nothing appears common or ordinary, because, to him, balanced on a point of space in the midst of infinite and inconceivable mysteries, everything has preserved the wonder, the unreason, and the oddity of nightmare. Mr Gerhardi is one for whom the visible world hardly exists, or, if it does, does so in a way essentially no more real than that of his dreams or his imaginings. He is at once both poet and philosopher.[9]

T. S. Eliot who, as a director of Faber, read the novel in proof, was apparently attracted by Gerhardie's definition of humour as 'the clairvoyance of this life', though what else he thought of the book remains tantalizingly unknown.[10] To some extent, as in *Pending Heaven* and *Resurrection*, Gerhardie's ambitious formal interest is not matched by the content; the book is often very funny, but it is too long. L. P. Hartley recognized the interest in the depiction of Baldridge's deferred hopes, but warned that 'the reader must not be allowed ... to share in the despairing tedium of the victims'.[11] The characters taken from previous novels do not sparkle, there is a sad sense that Gerhardie is attempting to rework old successes and failing, but the introduction of Baldridge's maid Marigold, a lively individual based upon Frances, won many admirers. Despite its faults, the book seemed to get 'first place in all the reviews, and high praise everywhere', with the exception of the all-powerful *Daily Express* reviewer, James Agate ('that old Agate wants drowning!' responded Clara). Gerhardie thought of suing the *Times Literary Supplement* for mis-labelling him a German which, at such a critical moment in history, he considered would prejudice sales. Self-ridge's decided to risk another go at Gerhardie and gave the novel a special display, and the *Daily Mail* chose it as their Book of the Month for April. But yet again it soon became clear that *My Wife's the Least Of It* was not going to sell well: by early May only 2,500 copies, out of the 5,000 necessary to exceed the advance.

Then one night in the middle of February the secret police came pounding on Rosie's front door. In they burst, ransacked the flat for nothing in particular, then dragged the half-naked Leonya away with them. Nothing was said about his crime; still less about his punishment. Rosie, hysterical with terror and grief, intimated to Dolly and Tamara that she was ready to kill both herself and Galina, then begged them to keep a promise made earlier to look after Galina should anything happen to her. She was left with only a handful of roubles and expected to be arrested at any moment. The British Subjects in Russia Relief Association dared not help for fear of provoking yet further reprisals against her.

William, exasperated beyond endurance, wrote furiously to Clara, reminding her yet again of his warning: 'All this *writing* backwards and forwards, informing her *quite uselessly* of Tamara's illness, and all the drivel that women write about their own and each other's health, backwards and forwards—it's this that has got poor Leonya into prison. *Stop writing to her.*' He worked 'like a Trojan' to get her out of Russia and to help set Leonya free, putting everything else aside and concentrating only upon innumerable letters, visits, and telephone calls. But it seemed an impossible task, for so many of those previously sympathetic and influential had been alienated by Stalin's policies. Bernard Shaw wrote regretfully: 'The notion that I am persona grata with the dictators is one of the Shaw myths. . . . I am loth to pass by on the other side; but I do not see how I can act with any beneficial effect', signing himself 'Callously, alas!' The Foreign Office warned that due to general distrust of foreigners in the Soviet Union it was useless for them to plead with the Soviet Government, and the British Ambassador in Moscow feared that any intervention would lead to Rosie's exile in mid-winter. In October she was ordered to leave for Chelyabinsk, a town on the fringe of Siberia. Somehow, through some mysterious and convoluted intervention,

William was able to secure Rosie a reprieve. She remained in Leningrad but saw no hope of ever leaving Russia.

Politics did not, it seems, come easily to the Gerhardis. For while Rosie was trying to leave her country, Uncle Willy's son Sasha, whom William had last seen in Petrograd fleeing from Smolensk and was now living in Germany, was trying to remain in his: the Nazis had suddenly demanded that he prove his Aryan ancestry. He wrote to William asking for copies of their grandparents' birth and marriage certificates. It was a fruitless search that occupied many hours of Patsy's time. Sasha fled from Germany on 24 August 1939, ten days before the outbreak of war, leaving everything he owned.

Yet despite the upheavals, Gerhardie was already dedicated to his next project, an idea that had been mooted back in September 1937 when Curtis Brown reported, vaguely, that 'somebody wanted a book on the Romanovs'. William greeted the suggestion enthusiastically, quickly signed a contract with Rich and Cowan, who offered £500 advance and 'excellent royalties', and rushed off to the British Museum reading-room in order to incorporate the latest facts from post-Revolution sources scattered all over obscure Russian publications. 'I'm soaking myself in the Russian tsars in preparation for writing the new book. I tell Patsy that I'm the weak-kneed Tsar Nicholas; she's the strong-willed Empress Alexandra; and Frances is the all-powerful Rasputin.' But the magnitude of the task soon depressed him, and by August 1938 he was complaining of 'these Romanov skunks, twits and whores weighing heavily on me'.

Oddly enough, *My Wife's the Least Of It* had not yet disappeared without trace. The editor of the *Daily Mail* now suggested that Gerhardie write a series of articles (at twenty guineas each, plus expenses) in a new form combining fiction with journalism: pretending to be an intimate friend of Charles Baldridge, he and Baldridge were to report on various topical events. What looked at first like an excellent opportunity quickly became a chore. After dashing at short notice to a pig market in Norfolk, then to a cricket match in Nottingham, Gerhardie complained that he was kept on tenterhooks, never knowing from one day to the next when and where he would be sent; and when sent, he had to slave all night over a hot typewriter to produce the piece in time for the latest edition. 'This feeling of being on tap is hardly the atmosphere in which I can write my Romanoff book steadily without interruption', he groused. Added to which there were four pneumatic road-drills outside his window going full blast throughout the summer from dawn till dusk.

A move to the country seemed once again appealing, and he attempted to sublet the flat at seven guineas a week. Patsy and Frances packed up his riding-breeches and boots (now covered with mildew inside and out) and the trio departed to a Norfolk cottage at six shillings a week. They returned two days later, for the cottage lacked essentials such as electric light and drains, but abounded in inessentials such as rats. Gerhardie, sinking fast in his 'Baldridgean quagmire' of debt, the overdraft itself overdrawn, was reduced to filling in the football pools at 6*d*. a time. The one bright spot on the horizon was a new bank manager, Mr Hope, a fan of Gerhardie's who happily received inscribed copies of *Of Mortal Love* and *My Wife's the Least Of It*. Mr Hope had been 'revelling in the pictures of the film magnates and their satellites, who, exactly as you draw them crowd into my own office quite frequently with the most wonderful schemes which only require a few thousand pounds of the Bank's money to make fortunes for all of us!' After a sympathetic visit to the bank, where Gerhardie was treated with the greatest reverence, they agreed to extend the overdraft from £219 to £300. But Mr Hope died suddenly at Christmas.

That Gerhardie's creative potential was undermined by poverty was a burden he felt he shared with Kingsmill, who was still living with his wife and children in Hastings, comfortable though in debt. The only difference was that Kingsmill had a knack of doing well for himself, and though impoverished somehow managed to occupy a large and very well-furnished house. His father had recently died: he left no money but he did pass on a smart set of clothes so that Kingsmill could stroll about at the weekend looking very dapper. Fielding, he pointed out, would only venture into the streets on a Sunday, on which day duns were legally prohibited from serving writs, and for the same reason he too preferred not to be seen about too much on a weekday.

Gerhardie visited Hastings and put up at a boarding-house close by, where, much to his consternation, they persisted in waking him at 8.00 a.m. After breakfast he would stroll over to Kingsmill's house and listen to Beethoven on the gramophone. William drank coffee by the pint, Kingsmill tea ('he was an indefatigable tea drinker—the sight of what tea did to the pot not being apparently sufficient to detract him to some less corrosive beverage').[12] Then they would take a walk by the sea, before joining the rest of the family for lunch. The afternoon passed in a similar fashion, talking, listening to music, and taking the odd nap. They continued to spend many hours plotting ambitious new publishing ideas. A sample exchange of letters on subjects such as Mussolini and

Hitler entitled *Pickled For History* was rejected by a publisher as dreadfully dull, but Gerhardie contributed a chapter to Kingmill's anthology *The English Genius*: 'Climate and Character' joined Rebecca West's 'Snobbery' and Hilaire Belloc's 'English Verse'.

Gerhardie continued to revel in Kingsmill's 'marvellously vitilizing' conversation, his extraordinary power to make one feel happy. 'I *do* so enjoy, for a change, the society of an intellectual equal', he wrote to Clara. 'This sounds conceited, but you know how I mean it. It's such *misery* always to be consorting with a lot of pretentious second-rate people. A few days in the proximity of a great genius—and he is that, even though he has not produced anything on his own level for a long time owing to poverty—is such a solace, such a pleasure, that I can't find anything like it elsewhere.' Beaverbrook, 'though jolly enough, is a crude piece of work by comparison with Hugh, who *is* "a great spirit" in the real sense—I mean quite of the Goethe calibre—and completely simple and unaffected—no pretensiousness, no pose at all'. But Kingsmill, dispirited by lack of success, was growing embittered and quick to take offence, hating the world for not recognizing him as a great literary figure. Even Dorothy admitted that at times it amounted to a persecution mania. Alec Waugh asked him to dinner alone, because he so enjoyed his company, and Kingsmill at once took umbrage and began to berate Waugh: 'So I'm not good enough to meet your friends . . .' Gerhardie found Kingsmill's choler trying but amusing:

Max Fisher sat very dazed in a chair and said nothing. But when Eudoxia mentioned that some author had been paid £40,000 for a film, Max Fisher suddenly writhed up like an eloctrocuted felon rising in the chair and flopping down in collapse. 'Come, come,' I strove to render first-aid. But he would not have it. 'It's not envy, it's longing,' he said. 'Can't you distinguish envy from longing, you fathead?'
'I'm sorry: it's longing. How stupid of me.'[13]

But their relationship was on the wane, and by 1939 they had all but ceased to correspond—Gerhardie at the best of times found Kingsmill's letters, written in a minute curly hand, 'clipped, constipated and niggardly', and quite unrepresentative of his expansive personality. Dorothy, of course, was still a central feature of their enmity. Whereas once William had been jealous of Kingsmill over Dorothy, now he was jealous of Dorothy's influence on Kingsmill, for Kingsmill found his wife the greatest comfort and support and had grown intolerant of Gerhardie's anti-feminine prejudices. 'You are completely impervious to any view of women which does not flatter your illusion of your own superiority to them,' Kingsmill bristled. 'You don't wish to have a detached view of yourself, and so you avoid the kind of, admittedly rare, woman who would help you to see yourself from the outside.' Dorothy, he explained, had helped him 'to objectify life and myself more than all the other persons I have met put together. You talk of my "drivelling sentimentality" about women. Certainly I have had a lot of it to work out of my system. That I have succeeded better than you may, I suggest to you, be seen if you compare the heroine *Of Mortal Love* with any woman in my books.' Gerhardie rather sneeringly blamed Dorothy for not being more welcoming to her husband's friends. The truth was that such visits (numerous and often unheralded) simply prevented Kingsmill from working, and unless he worked they could not eat.

The dwindling communication with Kingsmill was to some extent replaced by that of Oliver Stonor. After Stonor's first laudatory letter Gerhardie invited him to the flat. Stonor proved to be 'a very nice character', with a number of worthy attributes: he was extremely intelligent, enthusiastic, well-read, had a private income, and most important of all 'the highest opinion of my literary abilities . . . he would do anything for me, and might be useful'. Clara approved of him because he so obviously admired her son. Tamara was unnerved by his long, girlish eyelashes, and Patsy 'can't stand the sight of him and thinks he is a ninnie and a sap and a zanie!' Though Stonor never stimulated or amused Gerhardie as Kingsmill had done, he was companionable, dependable, and a good deal more generous—instead of borrowing money he frequently donated it.

In particular Stonor helped Gerhardie to finish *The Romanovs*. The book continued to occupy him throughout 1939, eliciting an unpleasant correspondence with Putnam's, the American publishers who, impatient with the delays, wrote a letter couched in peremptory language demanding the manuscript or their money back. 'The tone of their letter is that of an aggrieved shareholder to a crook who had escaped with his savings. I have never read anything like it. I replied rather in the fashion of Hitler's Reichstag speech in answer to Roosevelt's cable.'[14] Harassed by lack of time, lack of money, and mental exhaustion, Gerhardie relied not only (as always) on Patsy but increasingly on Stonor as well, a debt which he was only too ready to acknowledge: 'Your attitude to me and my work, dear old chap, has always been warm and tender and imaginative and exquisitely sensitive. You have sustained me, far and near, with advice. You devoted untold labour and exertion and time in going through my weary *The Romanovs*. You have been my host: I have had gifts; you sprang swiftly and unhesitatingly to my side with loans of money when I was at my last gasp.'

Large chunks of *The Romanovs* which, in the pressure of the moment, had been lifted almost verbatim from other sources, had now to be painstakingly rewritten. Gerhardie, by this time highly uncomfortable with the project, bemoaned the fact that he had done it too hastily and without imagination, and his letters to Stonor betray almost embarrassment at what he terms 'my often execrable prose . . . at this stage of acute exhaustion when I often write drivel'. Whilst collecting material Gerhardie had found the work intensely interesting, 'but as the subject was immense, the size required enormous, the time short and my treasury empty, I never felt I could do more than give a journalistic account of it all, sufficient to satisfy the publishers and the kind of public which finds nothing so interesting as the daydreams of Hitler . . . My book is as meaningless as history.'[15]

There was little time for other ideas, although Gerhardie considered a book on the Prime Ministers of England, and almost signed a contract for one on Hitler. The *Evening Standard*[16] paid a spectacular thirty-five guineas for an article describing his Mediterranean boat trip with Herr Himmler, now apparently none other than Hitler's Chief of Secret Police. A photograph of Himmler striding across the page towards a large Bovril advertisement heralded

MY STRANGE ADVENTURE WITH EUROPE'S MAN OF TERROR

'Measly Little Man'

And yet, despite the threat of war and worries about *The Romanovs*, it was really rather a happy time, perhaps the last truly happy period of Gerhardie's life. He visited Stonor at the village of Woodbury in Devon, where he lived with his sister Margaret Penn in a resplendent old house with a 'somewhat flabbergasted' garden and enclosed courtyard with rambler roses on the white walls. Photographs show Gerhardie, rather stout, clad in pale trousers, a stripy double-breasted blazer, and bedroom slippers, relaxing on the lawn. Margaret Penn was an excellent cook and a most kind and thoughtful hostess, although she and Stonor found William an exacting guest. 'They began by having set hours for meals,' he told Clara. 'But I have cured them of all that. Only once Stonor called out to me: "How long will you be?" I told him that never—*never*—but *never*—since I left the Army has anyone put such a brutal question to me. So now we no longer have meals by the clock. They just try to guess by my face whether I am hungry or not.' They took long invigorating walks by the sea while Gerhardie busily tried to persuade Stonor to write a book about Gerhardie. Stonor seemed willing; Gerhardie told him exactly what to say; Stonor seemed less willing. Patsy kept in touch by post, and she and Penn undertook the boring job of compiling *The Romanovs*' index, whilst Frances spring-cleaned the flat. 'But we do miss you, angel,' Patsy wrote to him. 'And though you talk too much the place is dead without you, which is worse.'

Brian Lunn took to dropping in to Rossetti House to see Patsy and Frances, but he was growing increasingly dotty, muttering to himself, making curious gestures, and rolling his eyes. 'He has,' one friend noticed, 'that curious air of physical well-being and prosperity which madness brings.'[17] Twice that year he met with a drunken accident. First he tumbled on to the railway lines at Charing Cross, then he fell off the top of a bus on to his head and cracked his skull. He recovered consciousness in hospital, but not much of his memory: 'I shouldn't stay in this place, old man: it gives you the headache,' he said when he saw his brother Hugh at the bedside. Then he asked for some whisky. Kingsmill, much moved, was inspired to write a novel—published the following year as *The Fall*.

In July Tamara married Frank Tipping, a young BBC employee who, enchanted by her Russian accent, refused ever to correct her wayward English. Clara, who was now receiving 10s. a week old-age pension, continued with enthusiastic lament to busy herself with Aunt Sissie. At the slightest sign of illness Sissie would be put to bed with a glass of hot sugared Burgundy, and the herbalist consulted. 'She is simply snowed up in blankets wadded quilt eiderdown and 4 hot water bottles during the day and night. Besides 3 coats, 1 a fur one and all the woollies and undies that one can heap on her. Her little head is nowhere to be seen.' William was tormented by the fact that he had not yet been able to provide his mother with a maid: 'But I will look after you when my ship comes home—and God knows it's been a long time cruising around now without heaving-to with the goods!' He tried to ease her troubles by insisting that she be a frequent visitor at Rossetti House that summer. '*I have a great longing to see you* and think of you every day and night before I fall asleep and pray for you' he told her. Whenever she arrived she joined Frances in the kitchen to cook her son's favourite meals of beef stroganoff, *filet mignon*, *sole veronique*, and *le pie cottàge*.

After Clara left, Frances, rather less adulatory and a little more parental, would take over once more. 'But Frances,' William protested, 'you treat me as if I were a child.' 'That's all you are,' she retorted firmly, and the flat would ring with her laughter 'in a high sustained treble, like a burglar alarm let loose'. She had now learned how to make cauliflower 'grattong' ('God! how it smells! The whole flat stinks like a sewer'). Patsy, whose father was chef at the Waldorf and always cooked elaborate dishes at home, craved this simple fare, but when the smell became too much for William he got himself taken out to an oriental supper by a young Sinhalese admirer who had conceived a grand scheme for starting a chain of Woolworth-type shops in India, Burma, and Ceylon. All this was to be based upon a Lawrentian-style 'undying bond of friendship' with Gerhardie who, having learned that the Sinhalese's father was worth a million pounds, was not altogether averse.

After what seemed an eternity *The Romanovs* was completed. Gerhardie enjoyed but two weeks of respite. On 3 September 1939 war was declared.

Damn it all, one World War is enough in one's lifetime! . . . Sometimes I feel as though I will presently wake from this oppressive dream into freedom. It is as impossible to ascend to any height of thinking as it would be for German aeroplanes, which would find themselves driven down by British aircraft to flounder in a forest of barrage balloons. It's *no use*—I CAN'T WRITE ANY MORE.

19

WAR
September 1939–January 1946

Who wants to write—who wants to live in a world like this?[1]

The outbreak of war plunged Gerhardie into the most profound gloom. Throughout the early war years his letters express constant misery, despair, and frustration: 'This is a sordid life . . . and there is no safety in life except in God . . . My "will-to-write" has completely disintegrated, and I am half-paralyzed.'[2] The realization—so long suspected, now confirmed—that the idea of 'a war to end all wars' had been illusory caused him the bitterest grief. He had never understood why it was often said that D. H. Lawrence suffered more than any man in the previous war. Now William felt that he himself was in that position, and admitted that he was undergoing agonies at the thought of the sufferings of men, far in excess of anything he had experienced in the First World War.

Politically, he nursed unrealistic hopes that the Allies would negotiate peace and undertake 'a complete reorganization of the world on a federal basis—the pooling of our sovereignties in one world-sovereignty;—in fact a United States of the World on a thoroughly democratic basis . . . a world-wide order of equal opportunity, education and federation, the pooling of resources, etc. etc.'[3] He was irritated by Kingsmill's attitude of complete indifference, 'as though the war were a natural phenomenon like rain or thunder', and by his refusal to discuss it. Gerhardie, by contrast, could talk for hours, ceaselessly speculating on when, how, and where it would end. The war offered, in his view, only two benefits: the public might read more, and he could take girls for taxi rides in the blackout.

A number of people, including his mother, offered him a home away from London, but as always he was reluctant to alter his routine. 'For my own part, I feel that there is nothing to be done: and that I am the very man to do it', he wrote to Clara. 'London with its balloon barrage—a veritable forest—is perhaps the safest place in England. If this war is going to last it will be so unendurably dreary that I don't think the astral world would be a bad exchange.' Two months later she visited for his birthday, and she, Patsy, and Frances sang the forty-fifth year in while he held a *levee à la Roi Soleil*. Stonor and Penn had sent port, Devonshire cream, grapes, eggs, honey, apples, and unripe pears, and Clara invented a new pudding by mixing the port with sweetened whipped cream. Then the four of them finished the bottle and lay around comatose for the rest of the day.

Though voluble in lamenting the horror and tragedy of the war, Clara derived a certain satisfaction from the adverse conditions and the camaraderie it inspired, and she promptly became even more busily efficient. She made a will and agonized over the best place to deposit her few remaining jewels. Then she took to sleeping on the ground floor of Forton Avenue, and always sat underneath the stairs during air raids, or hurried into the shelter next door. 'I hope that nasty old Hitler gets his come-uppance soon,' she remarked. 'His treatment of the Jews is perfectly inhuman.' She found Englishmen more gentlemanly when employed as soldiers, and the introduction of rationing in January 1940 gave an added purpose to her food parcels, for she often sent William her own sugar and butter allowance.

He too made a will, leaving all to Clara and, in the event of her death, to Patsy. Though he declined Stonor and Penn's offer of more permanent accommodation, Gerhardie agreed to spend Christmas in Devon. Before he went he drew up a long, mildly humorous and detailed list of 'rights of the individual' so as to be quite free and under no obligation to get up, go to bed, take meals, or talk. At Christmas lunch they served a goose—a favourite meal of his—but altogether the visit was not a success. Although he was inspired by the winter landscape he was dismayed to find how cold and damp Devon could be. He was annoyed by Margaret's ceaseless cough and noises in the nose and the constant attention of the dogs who killed a song thrush when they were out for a walk. Stonor had begun work as a surveyor and spent most of his days measuring drains, a job which left him tired and intolerant of Gerhardie's living hours. A further crisis occurred when William, who had announced he was going for a stroll, returned unexpectedly to the house to fetch a scarf and found Stonor and Penn in a passionate embrace—at which Stonor rather irritably admitted that Margaret was not, as everyone in the village believed, his sister but his lover, unable to divorce her present husband. Relations did not improve and after less than two weeks they put him on the train home again.

On 30 November 1939 the Russians invaded Finland. Victor, in a near-repetition of twenty-two years before, fled from his Helsinki home with just twenty-four hours' notice. He crossed through mined waters to England, accompanied not only by his new wife Joan and her two children, but by his first wife Olga and daughter Christina—rather like Nikolai Vasilievitch and his dependants, Gerhardie remarked admiringly. 'They are,' retorted Clara, 'really always involved in some sort of misfortune there is no end. It is either themselves, the horses, the dogs, the children or loosing their homes.' But Victor had a good deal of money saved and bought Shiplake, a handsome house on Dartmoor with seven acres of land, whence he rallied with enthusiasm to the British cause. When William, deeply gloomy, visited him, he was as surprised at Victor's cheery attitude and his devotion to the Home Guard as he was at the few unexpectedly agreeable evenings they spent together. Yet for most of the war 'diplomatic relations' between the two brothers were minimal, thus ensuring peace all round. 'I consider it sheer economy in nervous force to make one quarrel do the work of several', wrote William.[4] None the less, Victor, he noticed, showed 'a touching deference towards his brother' and was flattered when William introduced him to some literary friends. Impulsively generous, he insisted on buying William a walnut radiogram, the most up-to-date model, which enabled eight records to be played in succession. He, Patsy, and Frances listened avidly to Hitler's speeches while they worked.

Clara was glad to have more of her family in England but she regretted that as she gained Victor so she lost her last link with Rosie: 'I wonder what other blow my old and tired heart has to be prepared to meet. There seems no end and I am getting weary. This winter seems to have put the lid on me somehow.' With the fall of France, Daisy too disappeared.

After considerable delays, not the least of which was caused by the sudden bankruptcy of the publishers, *The Romanovs* appeared in 1940.[5] It was an unusually handsome illustrated edition priced at 30s., and dedicated 'To Patricia, In undying affection, gratitude and regard.' Subtitled *Evocation of the Past as a Mirror for the Present*, *The Romanovs* was prefaced by a twelve-page Historical Credo, described as 'the vindication of the priority of the individual man's rights.'[6] *The Romanovs* is a vivid and highly entertaining account of the Russian dynasty, presenting history 'with singular dramatic power and with an easy command of all the authorities', as the *Daily Telegraph* observed.[7] The book was popular, and adverse comments came chiefly from academic quarters, the *Times Literary Supplement* typical of the more scholarly critical reaction: 'Whatever the entertainment value of many of these pages, it is surely fair to suggest that the mixture [Gerhardie] provides here of biographical anecdote . . . and somewhat flippant comment can only loosely be styled history.'[8] The *Sunday Graphic* paid 120 guineas for 20,000 words which appeared during February 1940 in six very success- ful instalments, extravagantly billed, 'The Greatest Biography of Modern Times'.

But by May *The Romanovs*, in unenviable pursuit of all Gerhardie's works, had sold only 1,450 copies and was clearly not going to exceed the advance. The timing was wrong, the volume altogether too expensive. 'Things are not cheerful', wrote Gerhardie. 'Like Count Keyserling, I am sustained only by my own secret fount of humour.'[9] Again his thoughts turned to marriage. Alexander Korda's first wife had tele- phoned to say that she thought *The Romanovs* would make good film material, and she entertained him lavishly for two weeks. Gerhardie, sceptical of the results, was none the less pleased when she introduced him to a wealthy widow, Mrs Maria Phillips. William discussed the details freely with Clara. Mrs Phillips had been a ballet dancer from Tallinn in Estonia before marrying an English lord, upon whose death she inherited £50,000. She had then married a Bond Street jeweller, from whom she inherited a second fortune. She was now 51, childless, but possessed of two London houses and a flat, a small country house, a Rolls-Royce, a chauffeur, a secretary, and was, she hinted during a spectacular Russian dinner at her house, rather lonely. 'She is a very simple, quiet, nice unostentatious woman who speaks five languages all badly, though she has lived for over thirty years in England.' Gerhardie envisaged a pleasant 'marriage of companionship', while he got all the other delights he required 'discreetly on the side', he told Clara. 'Also, and chiefly, I would be at last able to help you financially in a really effective way and your troubles, too, would be over.' Patsy thought it worth a try and Clara also seemed not displeased with the idea, particularly on account of Mrs Phillips's maturity.

He dined with her a second time and suggested marriage. As her previous husband had courted her for four years she thought the proposal a little sudden but was, he judged, agreeably surprised. He told her that, like Hitler who believed in the *Blitzkrieg*, he believed in the '*Blitzheirat*'. There remained just one question:

'And do you . . . ?'

'I'm sorry?'

'Do you still . . . ?'

'Oh, that! Oh, yes, certainly,' she replied coquettishly and with a flutter.

Gerhardie was considerably alarmed. For despite her 'really sweet nature' he found her general appearance 'pretty damping', not least on account of her yellow teeth. 'The nearest I can describe her is to compare her with that slatternly old Frenchwoman in Toulon.' Then he began to notice a few more undesirable features: she was rather 'tight-fisted', and he thought it a bad sign that when she asked him to tea she gave him only black bread and radishes. She also had an unsavoury collection of stray cats and dogs, and he discovered that should she predecease him her income would stop, and should she postdecease him it was of little consequence anyway. 'There seems', he wrote in summary, 'little doubt that the old girl despite her age has not yet renounced the idea of sex, and as she appeals to me about as much as my tattered bedroom curtains this would seem a tough proposition . . . Perhaps even the army is a better proposition than Mrs P, for at least *you* will be getting an allowance.' When the following year (their romance of the year before having suffered an embarrassed decline) she reappeared in Gerhardie's life, Clara had quite gone off the idea: 'she strikes me as being an old humbug'.

The uncertain publishing situation, his own lack of inspiration, and extreme financial hardship motivated Gerhardie to seek employment. He first volunteered for the Army Officers' Emergency Reserve, a pool from which officers could be drawn to meet requirements as the need arose. At the medical examination three of the doctors recognized his name and said they looked forward to reading a description of themselves in a future book, before pronouncing him no longer A1, as before, but Grade 2 on account of slightly imperfect eyesight. Clara cleaned and sent his Sam Browne belt, his boots, revolver, and (reluctantly) his spurs ('with the hope that you will not use them. They are *very cruel*. It is bad enough to handle them but to use them on a horse is as bad as a bayonet on a human. You who would not hurt a fly!') The idea of active service did not appeal to Gerhardie, more than ever the '*insane* individualist', but worse still was the prospect of the jovial mess life he had glimpsed when spending a day at interview. 'When you see me again', he wrote dismally to Stonor and Penn, 'you will behold a sozzled irascible idiot with brick-red complexion and reeking of double-whiskies. You will be irritated by my wandering look seeking something as we stroll together through the lanes of Exeter; and then, with the satisfied grunt of one who has found what he wanted,—"Ah! there it is!"—disappearing, followed reluctantly by yourselves, in a pub or a bar. My poetic life is over.'

He did, however, try very hard to get a more definite job, offering his services wherever possible. When last he had met Brendan Bracken he had offended him, which recollection optimistically inspired William to make contact again because he considered it 'better to ask a favour of a man you have offended, as he will want to show his generosity. Whereas a man you have befriended might consider you required the return of an old kindness.'[10] He wrote to the British Council, the Colonial Office, the Ministry of Intelligence and the Ministry of Information, where he envisaged a job in 'propaganda or censorship or some other rot of that kind'. His lack of success was testimony to administrative conditions: far fewer people were absorbed into government service than in the previous war, and the Foreign Office in particular was glutted with staff gradually driven out of foreign missions by the German advance.

In 1941, after being closely interviewed and examined in his languages, Gerhardie was offered a job by the Intelligence Corps examining suspected spies. But he detested the idea and declined. 'To accept such a job would mean for me to lose all faith in life and to be haunted for the rest of my days by spectres of doomed men, the victims of my intellectual adroitness,' he explained to Margaret Penn. 'With Tchehov, I believe that there are always enough accusers in the world and that for a writer the role of Paul is anyhow more suited than that of Saul . . . in such a job there would be nothing for me except a reputation of growing incompetence if I gave way to my natural humane instincts, while my success could only be measured by the number of people I had succeeded in stringing up . . . No: I would finish as a Dostoievsky character relating to casual wayfairers in pubs: "Shall I tell you how I ruined my soul?"'

In the meantime he began an '*indescribably dreary*' job as a fire-guard, for which he was issued with a new and very heavy tin helmet, and obliged to attend lectures at the Royal College of Music before patrolling the streets round Rossetti House once a week from 7 p.m. until 11 p.m. (Clara was upset when she read in the newspaper that London's 'Blackout Ruffians' had knocked on the head a 'celebrated literary man' in Piccadilly.) The rest of the night William was to remain in the public shelters 'to bolster morale'.

On 7 September 1940 Hitler began bombing London: the Blitz lasted almost a year, at one stage continuing for fifty-seven consecutive nights and days. Fires raged everywhere. On the night of 10–11 May almost fifteen hundred people died, with more than fifteen hundred injured. Stornoway House was hit and now lay in ruins half a mile away, no longer the most exclusive club in London. Throughout, when not on duty, Gerhardie remained closeted on the fifth floor of Rossetti House, busy with his manuscript and reading Samuel Butler, La Roche-foucauld, H. G. Wells, and Oliver Goldsmith. 'I intend to "stay put"', he wrote to Stonor and Penn. 'Yes! shake your heads over my reckless bravery, my almost incredible bravado, deplore my heroism in the face of a thousand perils, my spirit, typifying that of the nation at its highest remains undaunted and unshaken!!' He tried using the air-raid shelter in the basement corridor of the block, but found the cold, the discom-fort, the bad air, and 'the unbelievable snoring' so unpalatable that he preferred to remain upstairs. 'Anyway, I doubt whether this rodent life is worth the preservation.' With fuel rationed, the flat was colder than ever, but he sat up in bed well swathed in nightshirts and pullovers. Clara was ever encouraging: 'To produce beautiful thoughts with bombs falling around must take all one's courage and will power and I am sure that *very few* indeed can do it. God bless you my brave boy.' Gerhardie remained grim but humorous. 'I say,—there has been *one blitz after another since I began this letter yesterday* . . . I was, I once was—dear Sir and Madam, an author. I have now degenerated into a target!'[11]

He was particularly worried about the possible Nazi incineration of *English Measles*, his new comic play on the subject of snobbery. As each act was completed he deposited one copy in his own steel filing-cabinet, posted another to Stonor and Penn in Devon, and a third to Clara. At last the work was complete, and himself still intact. 'I can only assume,' he reflected, 'seeing that we have been bombed all around within a radius of fifty yards, that God is interested in modern drama.'[12] He was immensely confident that *English Measles* would be a big commercial success as soon as the theatres were able to reopen. But when at last he sent it off to Curtis Brown it was returned with the comment: 'People stopped talking like your characters about 35 years ago.'[13]

When another birthday came round, Stonor and Penn sent three bottles of port and three of sherry, after which Gerhardie remarked that he was now contemplating celebrating the day of his conception as well as his last day in the womb. Throughout the year they had regaled him with fruit, fresh eggs (sent through the post), and other such luxuries and at Christmas dispatched another case of port. Gerhardie sat up in bed with a bottle, got quite uncharacteristically drunk, and scrawled his diatribe against Virginia Woolf in the thank-you letter.

One morning in March 1941 Patsy, composed as usual, telephoned to say that she would not be coming in to work that day. Her parents had recently acquired an Anderson air-raid shelter, she explained. Her father, her girl-friend Jane, and she were about to get into it when a large bomb hit the ground an inch or two away. Nothing whatever remained of the shelter. Her parents' home was in ruins. But somehow the three of them had been left unharmed. She paused, and then, to the sound of the passing trains, he heard a muffled nose-blowing. Clara, deeply sympathetic, wrote to console her, 'for you Darling are "the family" and we all share our sorrows and joys'. Patsy survived another two bombings, but later that year her father died. He had begged to be allowed a last drink of his own vintage brandy, a request which the hospital, with one eye on the sober regulations, had steadfastly refused. His latest appointment had been as chef to the mess of an air-force regiment who gave him 'a rousing funeral—if funerals can be rousing'.

Shortly afterwards, with the conscription of women, Patsy left Gerhardie's employment to become secretary to Christina Foyle at Foyle's Bookshop—considered to be war work, because Foyle's supplied books to the forces. 'Now that I have left,' she told Christina Foyle, 'Willy will never write another book, because I always had to chase him to get down to it.'[14]

Following Patsy, Frances also left. Not long after visiting her aunts in the cold and damp of Barnstaple she began to lose weight and started to cough. Then she began to spit blood. By the time she entered the Central Middlesex Hospital with tuberculosis she seemed far beyond the reaches of wartime treatment. Even at the best of times, contemporary medicine offered no cure, no antibiotics or chemotherapy, but only an attempt to improve natural resistance. Operations could in some cases help, but at six-and-a-half stone Frances looked far too weak. So for months on end she lay flat on her back, not even getting up to visit the bathroom. She underwent regular pneumoperitoneums, the pumping of air into the pleural cavity so that the lungs be allowed to relax. But because the lung adhered to the chest wall air had also to be pumped into the abdominal cavity, pushing up the diaphragm—and as the air was gradually absorbed, so the gruesome procedure had to begin again. 'I cried my heart out first time I was so frightened,' she told Gerhardie.

Every week she wrote to him, long loving letters, signed 'your Little

Frances Marigold xx'. She took immense trouble with these letters. For days on end she jotted down fragments of thoughts she had had in the night, verses of poetry she composed in her long hours alone, and when she could not write herself she dictated to friends. Then she would carefully rewrite, adding relevant inserts, until she had a perfect top copy. Most of all she wrote about missing Mr Gerhardie:

thank you dear one if I didnt have you I dont know what I should do, you have done such a lot for me and I dont quite know how I shall ever repay you, I often lie and wonder if you did suddenly leave me, I just shouldnt want to get better, I lie planning what Im going to do for you when I get out of here, oh how I wish I were not far away, so I could help you in lots of ways so you wouldnt have to have all the worry I want to share it all with you, there are plenty of little things I can do for you, so please relieve my mind and tell me you still want me back with you, it was just like heaven being in your flat once again.

He, in turn, wrote long affectionate, encouraging letters back. He enclosed books of verse (Browning, Rupert Brooke, Coleridge), a leather notebook for her to write her own poems in, a bed-jacket, and odd items she particularly requested: a French grammar, a looking-glass, and a book of shorthand. She kept a framed photograph of William so that 'If I get lonely I turn round to you . . . Oh why did we three "Muskerteers" have to be parted, what have we done to deserve such a penalty.' He urged his friends to write and visit. Frances, better for the rest, began to grow vain, to brush her hair with great care and put on lipstick, so that her doctor said that she looked like Scarlett O'Hara. Alan Hyman brought her a book on birds and, though they had never met, Margaret Penn wrote and sent her regular parcels of food and cigarettes to give away to her nurse. William visited most Sundays, often with friends—Bunny Tattersall, now a colonel in the army, and Alan Hyman who was shortly to go off to sea. Vera had recently married and given birth to a baby for whom Frances made toys. But sometimes, despite the tumult of good will and hospital life, when visitors arrived to chat she would gesture hopelessly at the blank hospital walls, saying, 'What is there to say?'

After declining the Intelligence job, Gerhardie was offered employment at the BBC who planned to start broadcasting to Russia. In fact no Russian section was formed, but in June 1942 he began work as a sub-editor of the Czechoslovak Section, a mysterious appointment that had come about, so he believed, as a result of somebody having read in *Who's Who* that he had been awarded the Czech War Cross. He adapted and edited the general English news for broadcasts to Czechoslovakia, and then, as 'my sole qualification for the post is that nobody knows any Czech to appreciate that I don't know any either',[15] he simply distorted his Russian in the hope that it might resemble the language. News poured in all day long, right up to the very last minute. There were three separate bulletins and therefore, Gerhardie lamented, three separate crises to overcome each day. He found the effort almost unbearably strenuous, involving his 'practical brain, atrophied from long disuse'. The need for punctuality was a constant source of anxiety. He also had to attend meetings and conferences throughout the day and, worse still, endure the 'unceasing affability and courtesy, self-effacement': 'I should imagine that the BBC has the best-mannered people in Europe.'[16]

In October 1942 conditions improved when he was transferred to European Productions as a script-writer to compose pen portraits (neither humour nor irony were permitted) of newsworthy celebrities or short items of political significance—commemorating China's National Day, Czechoslovakia Independence Day, Woman's Suffrage Anniversary—and a series on English writers (into which he managed to get some wit past the censor):

If you asked Evelyn Waugh how he pronounced his name, he would say: 'Evelyn Woff'. But that is just his way of being funny; for he is essentially a humorous writer. His name is not unlike the sound made by English milkmen to halt their horses when delivering milk from door to door: 'Wo-a!'

In 1943 he helped to start 'English By Radio' ('which absorbs the interest of all but me'). This project was a technique, 'just short of fatuous', involving dialogues illustrating different usages of 'I telephoned', 'I was telephoning', and 'I have telephoned'. Gerhardie, paralysed with boredom, was confined to a stuffy room artificially lit. He would arrive at six in the evening, go to the office, and hang up his coat in the naïve belief that people would think he had been there for hours, then take dinner in the canteen before sitting down to work. He did not, in truth, work very hard; it was the *fact* of work which hung over him all day. And though his colleagues were still '*exquisitely*' polite' ('this being on one's best behaviour all day wears one down'), one young script-writer had an unpleasant habit of scratching his head whilst leaning over Gerhardie's table. Then his morale was sapped by his boss's Cairn puppy, 'a bitch in both senses', who worried his trouser-leg, messed on the floor, and sniffed at his crotch.

Gerhardie now found himself with his old problem in reverse, earning a good salary of £640 a year, but with no time to work. 'I loathe being "employed"', he wrote to Stonor, who was himself busily involved with the Home Guard. 'The sudden forcible ban on my contemplative life is really an agony: *I can't endure it* . . . This is to tell you how unhappy, bewildered and *helpless* I am.' He particularly resented the lack of solitude, complained that he suffered 'intellectual impotence', and with uncharacteristic melodrama feared that he was on the verge of a nervous breakdown: 'You see, all my life I have marched out of step with my fellow-men, and at 47 I am no better fitted for the collective life than I was at York.'

He found it harder than ever to keep in touch with Frances, who had been moved to Harefield Hospital, a two-hour journey away. Year after year she lay, with very few visitors, watching other patients get well. She did not know how ill she was and, as her letters seem to show, was sustained only by the belief that she would one day return to Rossetti House.

Thank you once again dear one for all you have done for me I shall never be able to repay you, the grandest, sweetest man in the whole world even better than MY DEAR Doctor. I don't want to go any where else I just want to look after the sweetest man for alway's and alway's.

She continued to worry about William from her hospital bed, urging him to eat properly and wrap up well, knitting him socks and gloves and scarves.

I hope you arent to busy and get home at a reasonable hour at night—and go straight to bed and not try to write books, you must wait until we three 'Muskerteers' are all together once again.

And once again please dont miss your meals you worry me honest you do, I lie here wondering how you are managing, you are just a little boy to me, Im very fond of you, more than anybody else Ive known.

Altogether, it was not a cheerful time. Bill Sykes was imprisoned for refusing to wear military uniform, and released only after a great many people had written a great many letters. He grew smug in his newly appreciated liberalism, riveted to 'his *principles*', and he appeared to 'hanker after prison'. In July 1942 Aunt Sissie died, heavily muffled, a glass of pepper vodka within reach. 'We were the last members of the old brigade and now I stand alone', sighed Clara.

William was not finding it easy living entirely alone for the first time in his life. He improvised a hot-water bottle by filling three empty beer bottles with boiling water: the bottoms fell out and drenched the bed. His letters are full of lamentations that he was going without food because he was too busy or too exhausted to queue for his rations. 'I'm absolutely famished, aren't you?' he wrote to Margaret Penn in 1942. 'I'm now as thin as when I was a youth—just a reed; Patsy's new nickname for me is—"Skinny One". It's the difference between three pints of milk *a day* and two pints *a week*.' And, once the food arrived, there were the hazards of cookery. He described in tortuous detail to Penn how Patsy had procured for him a 'stake', his whole meat ration for one week, which he had planned to eat for his Sunday dinner. For two days he meditated on the pleasure in store, whilst roaming the London parks in the snow and rain, developing an appetite like a wolf of the steppes. 'I particularly dwelt on the indescribable delight of mixing it with pepper and mustard and scrapping the pan when the fat had gone cold and congealed; this struck me as the most delicious thing in the world.' At last he put the meat on to cook, went into his bedroom to arrange his pillows in the most comfortable fashion, and returned to find the food burned to a cinder.

Half-way through the war, Gerhardie, unable to endure his domestic ineptitude any longer, procured Jenny, 'a talkative and extremely boring charwoman'. Fortunately, he soon became deeply interested in details of her marital problems. His life changed very much for the better: he no longer had to shop or cook for himself, as Jenny would prepare his breakfast and his lunch which she took to serving, quite formally, not in his bed but in the dining-room. And it was Jenny who, quite inadvertently, brought Gerhardie what was to be the most enduring friendship of his life. One morning late in 1942 there was a knock at his door. The young woman who stood outside, of middle height, slender, '*so so* fetching', and not, Gerhardie appreciated, above her twenties, had come to end an acrimonious dispute between her charlady and Jenny over the possession of a broom. William invited her in, settled the dispute in seconds, then followed her back into her own flat where they remained talking for the next few hours. Anne Allan, he learned, was a young actress who had recently moved into Rossetti House; within a few days Jenny was shopping and cooking for both of them, running the two flats almost as one. Anne was by her own admission enjoying all that the war had to offer for those of a rather reckless disposition: the exhilaration and mystery of bombs and blackouts, parties by the score, dancing through the night with fighter pilots wearing dark glasses, the strange excitement of never knowing when and if you would meet again, untold chaos and freedom. For Anne, but recently liberated from the strictures of family life, society had suddenly and wonderfully lost its compartments.

Much of her enthusiasm she communicated to William, lifting to some extent the gloom that had settled upon him in 1939. They were regularly to be observed at private views standing silently and wisely sipping wine, nodding sagely at the paintings, and saying nothing. One evening William spied Anne's sister arriving in full and resplendent VAD uniform. Affecting disapproval of Anne's civilian status, he gouged out a white feather from his own eiderdown and, placing it in an envelope, pushed it through her letterbox, signing it 'Intrepid Londoner'. With money to spare for the first time in years, they visited theatres together, parties together, dined out together. Gerhardie, when his fire-watching duties allowed, would fetch her from the theatre on the way home from Bush House, often accompanied by Kingsmill. He, now literary editor of *Punch*, was a much more appealing guest now that his state of mind had improved somewhat, after having had an unexpectedly good time as a schoolmaster, first at Marlborough then at the Merchant Taylors' School in Middlesex.

With the exception of Dorothy Cowan, Anne was the first intelligent woman whom Gerhardie had known intimately. He enjoyed advising and encouraging her literary tastes, lending books and discussing them with her afterwards. Their relationship developed into one of the greatest mutual affection and candour. They never quarrelled. And, remarkably, William was for all his great affection entirely without jealousy. 'I have never felt that I have the *right* to *expect* anyone to love me,' he later wrote. 'On the other hand, when *I* love, I love a human being with all her *being*, and would not be jealous if she fell in love with another man any more than I would be jealous because she had extended her horizons by, say, acquiring a love for the Swiss mountains and a taste for, say, oysters.'[17] Strangely enough—at least by earlier standards—this was not self-deception: Anne cried on his shoulder over an unhappy love affair and received only sympathy. Perhaps the greatest ingredient of their relationship was independence. Anne had her own life, her own flat, her own money. They discussed marriage. Anne was not insensible to the difference in age, especially since her own parents had married with a large age difference and had not been happy. Yet unlike his elderly friends, William never seemed to her at all old; Kingsmill, on the other hand, treated Anne like a sweet child and in his extraordinary way took her out to an ice-cream parlour. William was

also wary, not least on account of his mother, whom Anne thought very
kind and gracious, rather the *grande dame*. Marriage was rejected, at
length. William wrote to allay Clara's fears. Thanking her for sending a
pair of shoe-laces, he goes on to tell her that, after all, Anne was about to
marry not himself but a viscount.

Anne *pretends* that she does not want to marry him—as he is an awful fool,
though he dresses beautifully—and says she'd much rather marry me. But I am
urging her to marry the Viscount—he is better able to stand the *obvious
disadvantage* of having a wife, whereas I cannot afford to forfeit the one pleasure I
have in life—to live alone, and have a housekeeper to look after me, and no
nagging and no scenes or quarrels, inevitable with *all* women . . . ![18]

Despite his mental inertia, Gerhardie had, at the start of the war, begun
another project born of his dissatisfaction with *The Romanovs*. This was
to be 'a history of our time, starting from 1900 and including everything
to date, even the present war', expressing 'a loathing of war, of class, of
violence', which he eventually called *God's Fifth Column*. He had already
read over eighty books in preparation and secured from Methuen a very
small advance of £135, but good royalties.

'To-day, after three glasses of port, I began to dictate', he wrote to
Stonor in November 1940. 'Very heavy going, a muddled brain, a
sagging soul. Another glass, and another . . . Mind utterly paralysed. No
good. Try again to-morrow.' And so the book progressed, slowly and
painfully, until by 1942 it was substantially complete. Gerhardie,
however, now felt it expedient to delay publication, because it was too
critical—of politicians, of nationalism—to be popular during the war.
By the end of the war his enthusiasm was channelled elsewhere. The
book was never finished. After his death the manuscript was found by
Michael Holroyd who, together with Robert Skidelsky, edited it for
publication in 1981.

God's Fifth Column: a Biography of the Age 1890–1940 is an ambitious
and idiosyncratic work of history, 'perhaps Gerhardie's masterpiece', in
Holroyd's opinion. The author takes his title from an episode of the
Spanish Civil War: in 1936 four columns were advancing on Madrid
under the command of General Mola who boasted in a broadcast that
the soldiers of his four columns would be welcomed by a fifth column of
friends awaiting them within the capital—and so the term 'fifth column'
entered the dictionaries. Gerhardie sees God's Fifth Column as (in
Holroyd's words) 'the sabotaging agent in life, the destructive element
without which nevertheless life could not progress. It exists as comedy in

a self-important age; as tragedy in times of superficiality; and, in a materialistic society, as spirit within the gate of matter. It is the eternal corrective—even against itself.'[19] As Gerhardie described to Margaret Penn:

I decided, on the model of *War and Peace*, to select a few key characters, whose story would recur at regular intervals and progress through the decades. Grouped round them would be a multitude of other minor characters. To get the richest results I selected four representative figures: Mrs Asquith, William II, Hitler and Tolstoy, to represent the social, royal, neo-political, and intellectual worlds.

Having structured it thus he skilfully plots one view against another, a parallel history through personal lives. Much of Gerhardie's interest in the subject had been generated by observing at close quarters the private foibles of politicians. These 'men of action' necessarily take an over-simplified view, recklessly sacrificing the individual, the 'suffering unit'. Yet the power-mad seem to him not so much wicked as ludicrous. 'As a moral indictment of the half-century under inspection, Gerhardie's argument carries complete conviction', wrote one reviewer,[20] although in truth these attacks on the vices of humanity are the most conventional, least interesting, aspect of an otherwise entirely individual work.

   As an exposition of the notion 'that Providence sabotages the complacency in man', the book gives historical expression to Gerhardie's preoccupation with ironical narratives, first glimpsed in *Futility*: 'I felt indeed I was on the summits of existence. Why should *I* be treated to such stupendous depths of irony? There beyond the clouds the gods were laughing, laughing voluptuously.' The subtitle intentionally suggests a commerce between the personal ('a biography') and the larger perspectives of history ('the age'); and the age in question is, almost exactly, Gerhardie's age. If *God's Fifth Column* is history through personal lives, it presents, by extension, another autobiographical aspect of Gerhardie. He has recreated the milieu that created him, and in doing so has shifted his motivation for self-perpetuation into another sphere.

   'I hold that it behoves a real writer not to express controversial opinions', wrote Gerhardie to Stonor, 'without at least having the decency of clothing controversial statements, no more intrinsically true than another's, in pleasing epigrammatic language.' Gerhardie's language is not merely pleasingly epigrammatic, but lyrically labyrinthine, an achievement in keeping with the multi-dimensionality of the subject. On the death of Proust:

Nobody would believe that a man only fifty, who had suffered from asthma since he was a child, was going to die now at the height of his fame. His personal friends brought their wives to his bedside, unaware that their scent, more surely than the pollen, threw him into a welter of choking. Céleste, *alias* Françoise of the epos, who had been cook and maid to his mother, his aunt and his grandmother, and seemed to perform all these functions still, as well as tackling his manuscripts with the sewing-needle when he had insertions to make, though she had been complaining (in the novel) that, when he was but a child, her feet were already giving her trouble, was being sent backwards and forwards to the Ritz for iced beer, as though that was the only place where he could get it and Céleste the only one to obtain it. Although the doctor had insisted on his giving up all idea of work, Proust went on with his proofs and, to propitiate the doctor, as he thought, sent him expensive bouquets of roses to make up for defying his orders.

The book was widely praised—'a continuously readable, stimulating, and impressive work',[21] 'highly remarkable' in the 'wonderful variety of his thoughts and his portraits'.[22] 'This extraordinary work will amuse, alarm and instruct even if its mysterious thesis will not necessarily satisfy the fact-grubbing historian despised by the author.'[23]

On 31 March 1945, with the German surrender only weeks away, Gerhardie left the BBC. For three years, with little time to write, his ideas had accumulated so that he felt as confident and fertile as when he had left the army in 1920. Clara, like Gogol's mother, now thought office life good for her son and wished he would keep his job and write in the evenings. She begged him not to continue sending her money; he ignored this, and also took out a life insurance lest he should die before her.

At the same time Frances Champion was given up as incurable. She did not know the prognosis, but suspected it. 'She looks more like a fox-terrier than a human being', said William after visiting. 'Her face is so sharp, so pinched—a sharp triangle.'[24] She returned to her family in West Kilburn. Her mother had died two years before; her father, unemployed, missing his wife and suffering from asthma, none the less had attempted to make the rooms nice for her return and to act as a dutiful parent. Although for four years Frances had dreamed of this moment, she had almost forgotten that without her mother it would never be the same. She sank down on her bed and cried, while her father, misunderstanding her grief, berated her harshly for being 'a misery'. William, over the telephone, urged that she should have confided in her father. Then he told her that she must ring off and get back to bed, otherwise she would find herself back in hospital. 'Oh wouldn't that be wonderful,' she sighed.

Clara, accustomed to the idea that Rosie had perished in the siege of Leningrad, was overjoyed to learn that her daughter had survived relatively unscathed. When the siege began Rosie had been working in a fever hospital for soldiers. As food became scarcer and thousands died of starvation, Galina was taken into hospital; as Rosie was leaving to return home Galina suddenly remembered that an old leather belt of Leonya's still remained, which she instructed her mother to boil up and eat. Soon afterwards they were evacuated to the Altai region of Russia, three hundred miles from the nearest small town, where Rosie tilled the ground and lived on potatoes. There was no news of Leonya. Daisy too, after a silence of two years, was found to be alive and well, though Jean had been interned for nine months 'for his opinions'. On Clara's seventy-seventh birthday in January 1946 the house in Forton Avenue was full of her children, grandchildren, and great-grandchildren.

20

CLARA
1946–1958

I think life is best in retrospect. When I lie in my grave and remember my life back to the time I was born, as a whole, perhaps I shall forgive my creator the sin of creating me.[1]

For the next three decades Gerhardie published no new book. Throughout these years he was working with a languid fervour on the most ambitious project of his life, a fictional tetralogy entitled *This Present Breath*, 'my magnum opus'. 'I love nothing so much as my own quiet interior', he wrote, propped up on a pile of cushions and pillows in bed. 'My own work is the result of what I discover by throwing a wide net of associations. I let my mind roam in assumed idleness, association adding to association, the net spreading wider and wider, while I am genuinely under the pleasurable impression that I am not working:—and so a fish is caught, and another, and yet another. They let themselves be caught when I am not looking.'

Shortly after the war, at the instigation of admirers in the publishing world, Macdonald began a reissue of his books—the Collected Uniform Edition of the Works of William Gerhardi, published between 1947 and 1949 in an inexpensive rexine-covered edition priced at six shillings each. Post-war paper shortage reduced the planned ten volumes to eight: *Futility*, which included two new items, 'What they said at the time', a reminder of his early fame, and 'My Literary Credo'; *The Polyglots*; *Anton Chehov*; *My Sinful Earth* (a retitling of *Jazz and Jasper*, which title increasingly 'grated' on Gerhardie); *Pending Heaven*; *The Memoirs of Satan*; *Resurrection*, containing an intelligent preface by Hugh Kingsmill; and *Of Mortal Love*, the only one to have undergone considerable alteration. At the end of each volume was a numbered list of all the author's published works, and a short digest of each. Preceding this list, a 'Bibliographical Note' designed by Gerhardie to deal with the 'casual newcomer' and his 'chilling' demand, 'What are your books *about?*' The answer, he habitually retorted, depends largely on what the reader is 'about', literature being a two-way relationship. But in deference to public demand the Bibliographical Note concludes with an ironic list of his subjects:

I have treated of love (15, 9, 10, 12), children (3, 9, 10), youth (*passim*), ambition (17, 10), hope deferred (1, 9, 16, 4), snobbery (10, 15, 13), delirium (9), death (15, 10, 9, 3, 5), immortality (10, 13, 15, 9), music (1, 7, 9, 13, 15), and even sex (*passim*).

Reviews of this new edition were not unfavourable, but Gerhardie's reputation was slowly evaporating, and as a reprint it attracted little attention.

Life for Gerhardie after the war grew increasingly solitary. In 1947 Anne Allan fell ill with pneumonia and was fetched home to Roehampton by her father. Her doctor hurried to St Mary's Hospital in Paddington, where Alexander Fleming had his laboratory, and begged some penicillin (at that time available only for the armed forces), then sat up all night on the sofa giving four-hourly injections. By the time she had recovered it was clear that her father was himself ill. And so, as it happened, she never returned to Rossetti House; the following April she married, not the beautifully dressed viscount but a television and film director, Julian Amyes. William, bereft after her departure, none the less kept in touch through numerous telephone conversations and occasional visits.

Patsy continued to telephone every week, but her return was never an issue. Gerhardie could not have afforded to pay her salary, and as Christina Foyle's private secretary she had grown adept at organizing Literary Luncheons, 'putting Dowager Duchesses at their ease'. The work was demanding and as ever Patsy put her life into it. She and Christina Foyle shared a love of animals, and Patsy reported stories to William of Christina's enormous poodle Sambo, and Larry the lamb (later a sheep) who demanded a tin of Fortnum and Mason biscuits for his supper. But she was an exacting boss. 'As for my life with Christina— well', wrote Patsy to William. 'Sometimes I adore her, and sometimes I don't. She and her father both think I'm not all there—I can tell by the way they laugh—but they treat me very kindly just as you might a nice lunatic. I don't much like this, but it's preferable to being in their bad books. I still can't get used to their wicked ways, such as sacking such nice people for no reason at all.'

Soon Jenny the housekeeper also left Rossetti House, finding that factory work was very much better paid. A few weeks later her replacement made off with Gerhardie's laundry, shopping-basket, fountain-pen, ration-book, and identity-card. Frances, who would have worked for nothing, was too ill even to look after herself. She regularly haemorrhaged from violent coughing, and needed the constant attention of a nurse. She kept in intermittent touch with William, and whenever wheeled to a shop to telephone her old boss she insisted, in a voice no more than a croak, that she was 'fine' and everything was well. Her father had died at the end of the war, and her brother, himself suffering from tuberculosis of the kidneys, now cared for her. He bought her a second-hand bookcase which she filled with the works of all her friends: Gerhardie, Hugh Kingsmill, Brian Lunn, Bunny Tattersall, Oliver Stonor, Margaret Penn; every now and again she added a new volume.

By the end of 1947, Frances could barely get out of bed. In February of the new year she caught a mild influenza, but recovered. 'Cheek them doctors and that pink stuff to swallow', she mumbled defiantly. In March her appetite improved. April was a stable month, and early in June she was rushed to Middlesex Hospital suffering from an abcess on the appendix. She lay in the brightly lit ward and explained that, as she was not going to die, and therefore must recover, could her brother please stay at her bedside to keep her from accidentally passing away through boredom. On the second day he arrived again, but she was cross because she wanted just to sleep. So he sat quietly by and held her hand for the night. On the third day, though very weak, she improved a little and asked for water. Her brother fetched some from the hospital kitchen and wetted her mouth with it. Shortly afterwards she lost consciousness and, her face twitching with pain, at 8.30 that evening she died.

Clara was growing weaker—'My brain is so *very very tired*.' She celebrated her seventy-ninth birthday in January 1948 with family and neighbours, and proudly surveyed her gifts: a lampshade, a purse, writing-paper, a cake, some new-laid eggs, and a pot of jam. William had given her a silky bed-jacket as a Christmas present a week or so before and she, to prevent him spending money again so soon after, put it away until her birthday when she wore it for the first time. In May she took a holiday by the sea. 'I am not well', she wrote, her usual spirit quite absent. 'My strength has forsaken me I cannot recognise myself at all—and am hoping B'pool will work it's usual spell upon me though I fear not this time.' Two months later, still weak and sleepy and helpless, she now had some abdominal pain and discomfort. The doctors suspected an obstruction in the lower bowel near the colon, possibly malignant, but they were reluctant to operate, for she was old and the illness would certainly develop only very slowly. And then to William's relief the X-rays showed nothing.

In mid-July, two elderly Jewish admirers of Gerhardie, Mr Dunitz and Mr Benjamin, wrote and invited him to join them on a motor trip through Yorkshire. Dolly, who was caring for Clara, urged him to accept ('Let the Jews do something useful for a change'). The trip could not have been a jolly one; the photographs show William preoccupied and troubled, a painful contrast to the carefree days in Stonor's garden before the war. When he returned a week later Clara was no better, and by September so weak that she was often confused for hours on end. None the less, she continued to write letters to him right up until he moved to Bolton to be with her.

Anne wrote to ask if she might visit, but Gerhardie declined: 'Sometimes she doesn't even recognise us. It would be too sad if she didn't recognise you. Dearest Anne, life is very grim, isn't it.' A district nurse came twice daily and a doctor once a day. The neighbours proved remarkably supportive, and William engaged a young Irish companion-help who managed to cheer them up a little. Clara herself had always taken a placid view of death. 'Ah well, one more friend on the other side to greet me someday', she exclaimed after the demise of a contemporary. Dolly and Tamara were almost constantly in attendance, Victor visited and Daisy arrived from France. Clara would sometimes call for one of her children, adding to the others, in an echo from their youthful days in Russia, 'Now don't be jealous', and as they gathered for meals it seemed to William that for a moment they were all back in the St Petersburg house.

Her face looked a little waxy now and puffed out, but less lined than usual; her articulation was indistinct and her memory and concentration wayward. In her lucid moments alone with William she explained how much Dolly admired him. He did not know whether to believe her or not, for although she liked to make things romantic, she seldom lost her eye for truth. Even at her weakest she worried that he would get cold sitting in her room, and once called to him from the depths of a confused dream.

A year later William wrote the play based closely upon his own life, *The Fool of the Family*. In the last scene the Gerhardie-figure, Jamie Wadsworth, attends his dying mother. Whether or not the following exchange—or anything like it—ever took place, is impossible to say:

JAMIE. Everything has gone badly, Mama.

MRS WADSWORTH. Has it been our fault?

JAMIE. It must have been mine.

MRS WADSWORTH. Perhaps we hoped for too much.

JAMIE. I made you hope for too much . . . I forced you to take the way I wanted—and it has come to this . . .

MRS WADSWORTH [*sadly*]. You're so much like me, Jamie. You can hope and hope and hope. And so can I—*even now*—but sometimes I think we have fooled ourselves with hopes . . .

JAMIE. Believe what I tell you, Mama.

MRS WADSWORTH. I don't want to die fooling myself with hopes. I don't want to die without knowing that all will come well.

JAMIE [*desperately*]. So you can't believe me?

MRS WADSWORTH. Not now . . . Well—perhaps success would have spoiled you. Perhaps you wouldn't have been the same dear loving Jamie. [*After a long pause*] I shouldn't have wanted you other than you are.

JAMIE [*he swallows his tears*]. I don't know what to say.

MRS WADSWORTH. I have been blessed.

[*another pause. Mrs Wadsworth starts panting for breath. Jamie tries to hold her up, shouts for his sisters. They come in and hold her in a sitting position.*]

Don't let me go. Hold me—tighter—Oh let me go. Let me go.

[*Lucy (Daisy) stretches out her hand to Jamie so that he can support her. Mrs Wadsworth opens her eyes—her mind is wandering and she misunderstands.*]

Jamie, why are you hitting Lucy? Go away.

LUCY. He's not hitting me, Mama, he's helping.

MRS WADSWORTH. Jamie's always been a nuisance. Go away.

JANE (Dolly). No. No.

MRS WADSWORTH. Yes. Yes. He's always been a nuisance. He's always been a nuisance. He's always been the fool of the family. Papa said so.

JAMIE [*bitterly wounded*]. Won't you lie back against your pillows now?

MRS WADSWORTH. Yes, I think I will. And none of those hot clammy hands, please.

[*They settle her as if to sleep. She wishes Jane and Lucy goodnight, and kisses them.*]

By the middle of September Clara was having trouble sleeping: the draughts had ceased to work and she struggled for breath. Late in the evening of the 19th the doctor arrived to inject morphia in an effort to relieve the exhaustion. Clara kissed Dolly and Tamara and William goodnight, 'very tenderly as though merely settling for the night'. The next morning she slept on; the doctor would not wake her. She slept through the whole of the day. The following morning her breathing became faint, then erratic. At 3.10 it ceased, she drew her breath once, then again, and ceased.

To William she looked, laid out on the bed, 'incredibly beautiful and young, with a smile on her lips and—it seemed—beneath her eyelids'.[2] A service was held at the house, which almost the whole of Forton Avenue attended, and Clara was buried in the Wadsworth family grave in Bacup, beside her father and mother, her sister and her husband. A fragment of William's own writing, the beginning missing, reads:

. . . sorrowfully attending his own funeral.) Now I followed my mother's coffin, the chaplain leading ahead, his scanty hair blown in the autumnal wind, and in the hearing of it uttered the holy words raised to the inclement skies:

I heard a voice in heaven cry: now to release the hibernating powers of the astonished soul, in what are perhaps the most pregnant lines in all literature:

I am the resurrection and the life.

Later he sat alone in Rossetti House and placed in a black-edged envelope 'The last letter written to me by my Dearest, sweetest, unforgettable Mama'. It is a shakily written, slightly garbled note, and ends: 'I do so love you . . . I am fighting on Your worthless old Mama.' William did not, as he had hoped that January day back in 1925, die with her. He lived on alone in Rossetti House another twenty-nine years.

'I just cannot get used to it', he wrote, utterly inconsolable, to Anne. 'We wrote to each other every week. She replied to *everything* I told her; every bit of news, the rejection or acceptance of a MS was of the same interest and concern to her as to myself. I can't believe that there will never be another letter from her. I feel that I have no more ambition to succeed, and that if I do it will be a bitter irony.'[3] Two months later he told Stonor, 'I don't know or care where I am or what I do', and the following year described himself as 'like Queen Victoria after she had lost the Prince Consort'. He declined Stonor and Penn's invitation to Devon and spent Christmas in London.

Hugh Kingsmill, in rather good spirits since the war, continued to drop in to Rossetti House occasionally in the mornings. He had left

Punch and was now literary editor of *The New English Review* ('which seems all at once to have become staffed with many of the people who in past years had found themselves employed by the Lunn Travel Agency').[4] He had romantic ideas of consoling William with a happy marriage, and suggested Peggy Guggenheim who, approximately the right age, had recently ended an affair with Man Ray and was about to buy an Italian palazzo. Kingsmill, Gerhardie, Guggenheim, and Anne Amyes met for dinner at the Café Royal, Hugh a jolly and exuberant matchmaker. But the idea was unreal. Neither William nor Peggy seemed the least bit enthusiastic.

The same year Gerhardie dined with a party of friends whom he entertained with a maliciously amusing impersonation of Dorothy Kingsmill, mocking her loyalty to the Indian guru Meher Baba and her more fanciful beliefs in reincarnation. Amongst the diners was Antonia White, who felt a certain loyalty to Dorothy—not only were they friends but Dorothy, though not a trained analyst, had recently succeeded in lifting a long-standing writer's block from Antonia by psychoanalysis. On top of this, Antonia was a notorious troublemaker. The following day she telephoned Dorothy and Hugh and related the full story. Thus began the final Kingsmill–Gerhardie rift.

Throughout 1948 Kingsmill had been in bad health, in and out of hospital with vomiting and haemorrhages, and suffering from 'fatigue and general fed-up-ness'.[5] In mid-1949 Gerhardie learned that he was dangerously ill. From his hospital bed Kingsmill spoke kindly of William and sent a message of reconciliation. Inexplicably—even to himself—Gerhardie did not visit. Dorothy, who always considered that for all the turbulence theirs was a truly great friendship, was desperately sorry about this. Meanwhile, Kingsmill was visited regularly by Hesketh Pearson, Malcolm Muggeridge, and other close friends who found him (outwardly at least) very cheerful and amusing—the prospect of his own demise, he told one, made him feel like an evacuee who was told that arrangements had been made for him, but who much preferred to stay where he was. 'I am holding on to life like grim death', he remarked shortly before he died, on 15 May 1949.

The funeral took place in Brighton. Neither Pearson nor Muggeridge was present. Gerhardie arrived, late of course, wearing a heavy black overcoat and running like mad; within a dozen yards of the crematorium he was overtaken by the hearse bearing his friend. As the coffin disappeared into the furnace Dorothy turned and saw tears streaming down William's face. He had thought—wrongly—that after Clara's death he was so numb nothing could affect him. 'My dear—oh _infinitely_ missed—Hugh,'[6] 'I feel his loss increasingly', he wrote to Stonor. 'Don't die, Oliver, or I'll have no one left soon.'

'William never really got over losing Clara', wrote Stonor. 'His decline dates from her death.'[7] The years following the demise of his mother were Gerhardie's worst years of poverty and seclusion. Anne noticed that whereas before he had always been known as 'Willy', now he became 'William'. He had exhausted his wartime savings, and after the lukewarm reception of the Macdonald's reissue found his work nowhere in demand. 'I am probably the least influential of men now writing.'[8] Troubled about suffering increasing general unpopularity, he entered into an acrimonious correspondence with Collins who had published a novel, Margery Sharp's _Britannia Mews_, containing a dubious individual known as 'the Jew Gerhardi'. William worried that he might be mistaken for this character, 'leading my readers to suppose that I have fallen on evil days and taken to hawking dolls in a sack'. His letters to family and friends at this period fluctuate between profound depression and wry amusement—he told Stonor how his landlords, the Prudential Society, on hearing that he was a novelist, had enquired with the utmost charm, 'Mr Gerhardi, what pen-name do you write under?'

He was not always so easy-going. Dorothy Kingsmill's young son telephoned and offered detailed and elaborate praise of _The Polyglots_. Then he mentioned a mild criticism. There was a deadly silence on the end of the line. 'Are you there, William?' he enquired, a little embarrassed. There was a splutter of rage, followed by a stream of abuse. The boy put the receiver down in terror. But such moments were rare. All in all Gerhardie kept his spirits up as best he could by recalling how other great artists had suffered neglect in their own lifetime. How much of a comfort this really was is doubtful, for _The Fool of the Family_ expresses a rather different view. The character Charles Wigmore (who is based upon C. P. Snow) admits to Mrs Wadsworth that

on the face of it Jamie's chances are worse than most. Because, though everyone likes to think that there are forgotten geniuses, whom no one recognises in their own life-time—in literature it has happened very rarely . . . it is more likely than not, that Jamie's work hasn't made sufficient impact to be picked out of the flood that goes into oblivion.

Gerhardie's income continued its downward spiral. 'My illness is financial', he told Penn in 1952. 'In fact, I have no prospect of survival after Christmas—except by a miracle', describing himself as a complete recluse who habitually dined alone out of a tin. Alan Hyman rarely saw more than a bottle of milk in the fridge. He often went hungry, either through lack of money or lack of organization, and lived in an uncomfortably haphazard fashion. Not only was he immensely frugal with the electricity, but when eventually the power sockets began to go wrong he was obliged to work in the kitchen with the oven and two hotplates on, wrapped up in a padded pilot's suit, and signing himself 'the icicle who yet was once no other than William Gerhardi'.[9]

Though he sought solitude, William had always been gregarious. Now he went for days at a time without seeing a soul. When the outside of Rossetti House was redecorated he took a keen interest in the activities of the workmen.

There is the nearest thing to a mecano at one side of my flat, and to gallows with cradels lowered from the other. Caledonian and Cockney voices call across from the courtyard to one another to exchange their impression of last night's TV; and a voice from the Hebrides interjects each sentence of his pal with a brief 'A-a'—a sound that is neither interrogatory nor yet affirmative but seems to express total disassociation from what the other fellow is saying.[10]

The telephone, mysterious, disembodied, and above all hygienic, usurped more and more of his day. Michael Ivens described him as 'a Telephone Master of the first, nay absolute class', and conversations —for he was both a great talker and an avid listener—had 'the humour and humanity of a short story by Chekhov or Gogol and the solid length of a Tolstoy novel'.[11] There was a tragi-comic intensity to these communications. In the middle of a long, involved, and invariably humorous story (very often against himself) he might suddenly break off with an anguished 'Oh God' before resuming the narrative. Friends could—and did—telephone him at any time, day or middle of the night, and he would talk, talk, listen and talk for five or six hours at a stretch. Many still argue as to who holds the record for the longest call. When the new system of charging calls by the minute was introduced, Gerhardie was particularly hard hit. He had skilful means of disposing of any suggestion that he was deaf. 'You know', he would say confidently, 'the strange thing is this new receiver is not as good as the old one in the bedroom. Let's both shake our 'phones—that sometimes works. Spell it, would you. Yes, now I can hear you perfectly. You weren't speaking into the telephone properly before.'[12]

Gerhardie's small but loyal body of friends and admirers helped to support him during these difficult years. Hilda Leyel, founder of the Herbalist Society at Culpeper House, supplied him with the potions, herbs, pills, and tablets that were to be found all over his bedside floor. Gorley Putt, a Fellow of Christ's College, Cambridge, visited America soon after the war when food in England was still scarce, and delighted Gerhardie by the present of a tinned duck:

My dear Gorley,

The first of the ducks arrived safely the day before Christmas, but was not followed by a second duck. I realise, of course, that it is difficult to time these things and that allowance must be made for unpunctuality in a weekly delivery service of ducks between our two Atlantic countries. Still, this sort of thing puzzles me. What am I to make of it?[13]

When Putt lent Gerhardie £50 he received as collateral the enormous cavalry sword which, he remarked, would be useful when Christ's started admitting women; it hangs to this day in his room. Margaret Penn sent chocolates every birthday without fail. 'My well-known *prudence*', he wrote in acknowledgement,'in delaying my thanks to you until the last chocolate has been lingeringly consumed, *in case one of them should prove defective*, has this year been complicated by my near-diabetic state, in consequence of which I have been permitting myself only *one* chocolate a day.'

Stonor, after living so many years with Penn, abruptly left her. He had kept secret for years not only his affair with another woman but also their 5-year-old child. Gerhardie, incensed, berated him noisily for his cruelty and refused ever to speak to him again, but maintained an affectionate correspondence with Penn, signing himself 'ever, and always and forever William'.

'Any fame I ever had was fanned by readers indignant at my obscurity', wrote Gerhardie—which in the later years was certainly true. C. P. Snow was one such, who worked hard to promote William's work, mentioning him whenever possible in his *Sunday Times* reviews. Shortly after Clara's death, Snow suggested that they collaborate on a play— Snow had recently had one of his own put on and later televised, and optimistically thought a second would be easy. *The Fool of the Family* is, as Gerhardie explained, the story of his life: a man who in the first act is regarded as a fool, in the second act as a genius, and in the third reverts to being a fool. As in the past, the collaboration was not entirely free from friction: when Snow wrote something William did not like, he received a telephone call from the housekeeper Jenny who terrified him out of his wits with her torrents of natural indignation. The play, curiously lifeless and flat, was never produced. Gerhardie thought little of Snow as a writer, but he felt a great debt of gratitude, and for this reason supported him (with considerable skill) after F. R. Leavis's savage attack on Snow's Rede Lecture, *The Two Cultures and the Scientific Revolution*.[14] Their friendship faded eventually when Snow and his wife Pamela Hansford Johnson invited William to a splendid meal of roast goose and all his favourite dishes. William, utterly disorganized, telephoned at 10.00 p.m. to say that he did not think that he could manage to get there.

Dining out was always something of an event now. William, agitated at the mere thought of moving from the flat, liked to make full enquiries about the menu beforehand, and, if possible, to bring a friend along with him, 'whose atmosphere, he urged and argued, was indispensable for his well-being, but to whom in reality he was returning hospitality at the expense of his host'.[15] More than once he sent out a reply worded thus: 'Mr Gerhardie thanks Lady Razzle for her kind invitation but is unable to come to a decision as the arguments for and against appear to him overwhelming.' Then, if he did accept, fastidious as ever, he had to put in train several days of elaborate preparations to ensure that he had clean clothes. For although he still took great trouble with his appearance in public, he had neither the finance nor the organization to do it properly. At dinner with C. P. Snow one evening William walked into the room and the sole of his shoe fell off. Alan Hyman and his wife noticed when Gerhardie dined with them that he was wearing his pyjamas beneath his suit. This was not, as they believed, absent-mindedness but common good sense. For he attempted to wash and iron his own shirts 'with, on the whole, unsatisfactory results'. The blobs on his suit he cleaned with liberal doses of a miraculous new preparation called Dabitoff—so marvellous that Gerhardie could not put it down and the suit was left a little soggy. In the ice-cold flat, with the shirt still damp, the pyjamas were an obvious precaution against pneumonia. Outdoors he wore a hat, despite their being long out of fashion, because of his thinning hair; and any photographs he found in which he appeared bare-headed he would carefully adjust with a little pencil shading. The stage directions of Act III of *The Fool of the Family* describing Jamie Wadsworth provide a clear impression of how Gerhardie saw himself in late middle age.

He is . . . baldish, with pouches of strain under his eyes. But he is not grey and his hair is full at the sides. When we hear him speak . . . he is sadder and subdued, though there are sometimes flashes of his old spirit. He has known much disappointment and fallen on bad days. But this effect must not be overdone: there should not be any indication in his appearance that he is seedy or down-at-heel or helpless. His suit is a little shabby, but well-cut and well looked after.

In 1956 Michael Holroyd, a young man doing military service, had come across Gerhardie's books by chance and read most of them. As coincidence would have it Holroyd's mother knew Gerhardie's niece Christina. 'I thought William Gerhardie must be dead', Holroyd later remarked. 'In fact I discovered he was merely buried alive.' William, fearing yet another fan who had 'read all his books' but overlooked 90 per cent of them, delighted in the truth of this new man's boast and kept him after dinner so long that he missed the last train home. It was to be a most fruitful friendship. Gerhardie, who heaped praise and encouragement on young writers, whether or not it was due, was a still better master to those who, like Holroyd, truly merited the compliment. That Holroyd had been educated not at Oxford or Cambridge but Maidenhead Public Library was even more of an incentive to William, who took an ambivalent view of the value of university education. With the encouragement of William, Holroyd produced the first critical biography of Hugh Kingsmill. Unfortunately, Gerhardie used this opportunity to further his virulent anti-Dorothy campaign, with the sad result that Holroyd could not draw on the material he had hoped for, and both he and Dorothy (in their very different ways) were unhappy with the book. Perhaps William, who would of course have preferred Holroyd to write about him, stirred the fury (either deliberately or subconsciously) so as to prevent Kingsmill outdistancing Gerhardie.

After the war he also developed a friendship with Olivia Manning, whose radio adaptations of _Futility_ and _The Polyglots_ were broadcast by the BBC. Most astonishingly of all, Gerhardie, long fond of declaring that no woman could write, became an ardent admirer of Manning's work. She did much, with Anne Amyes, to dispel Gerhardie's prejudices about female intellect.

Olivia Manning has been called the foremost woman novelist writing today. Why this gratuitous division into men and women novelists—as though the dears were in purdah? As soon divide again and speak of Marcel Proust as the most eminent homosexual (between reluctantly consenting males) author since Oscar Wilde.[16]

At about this time too, in the early 1950s, Gerhardie embarked upon his last love affair. Dolores, the illegitimate granddaughter of a Spanish marquis who had had an affair with an English maid before dying in the Spanish Civil War, was a model and dancer: dark-eyed, raven-haired, curvaceous, and more than thirty years his junior. Though she was a little unpredictable in her behaviour, William became deeply attached and wrote scores of passionate letters whenever she went on tour to the Middle East. But Dolores had a tiresome way of arriving at the flat and remaining for two weeks at a time. Gerhardie professed that he was fond of his lover, but preferred on the whole to have 'middle distance friends'. When this passionate liaison had run its course William, who liked to match-make, introduced her to a friend of his whom in due course she married; and thereafter he happily visited the family and lavished attention on the children.

For the first time since the unhappy affair of the red-haired secretary William's sentimental attachment to children was asserting itself. He took very seriously his role as godfather to Anne's son Sebastian, who when small regularly rang up with little quizzes and guessing tests. William carefully considered the clues before putting pen to paper with the answers. 'I think it is a Musical box. Have I guessed right? If so, have I won a prize?'[17] Though to some he had once appeared aloof and ungiving, with Anne and her family he was not only generous, but infinitely loving and affectionate. With Clara gone, he confided in Anne and she to him. 'You could say anything you liked to William, *absolutely anything at all*', she later stressed. 'He was the most reliable friend I've ever had in my life.'

Gerhardie held a particular fancy for mail-order catalogues, and at Sebastian's instigation became quite hooked on *Exchange and Mart*, spending hours consulting each page for the myriad wondrous bargains to be had. He was always very fortunate in his purchases. 'Invariably the curtains, bedspreads and step-ladders he ordered not only actually arrived but, against all probability, turned out to be bargains. Toys, games and even a microscope all turned out to be splendid.'[18] Any kind of gadget attracted him: a special plastic reading-stand for Anne and her daughter Isabelle, a waterproof cover for Sebastian's Mini and a revolving Lazy Susan for his own chaotic kitchen. When his ripped and battered dining-room curtains at last fell to pieces he joyfully sent off for some frightful gold velour replacements. And when a dog from another flat fouled his back doorstep near the milk bottles William promptly sent off for an extra dust-pan, specifying that he would prefer a model with a very long handle ('longer than the jumping distance—a large distance, I believe—of a canine flea').

The single exception to these bargains was the curly black rugs in his hallway. Gerhardie's old acerbity asserted itself by return of post.

I write to say that I am bitterly disappointed in the 12 rugs I recently ordered. They are not a success. They get hopelessly matted and lose their sheen. They do not stay put. People fall over them and break crockery. I am being continually reproached by my family who were against the idea from the start.[19]

A refund, he suggested, would be in order. He was not silent either when Bloomsbury County Court somehow contrived to propel black smoke from their chimney into his bedroom window so that he had to seek shelter in the streets.

Throughout these lean years Gerhardie worked day and night attempting to muster interest in his work. 'I am in bed, not because I am ill, but because nowhere else do I feel equally well', he told Penn. 'London just now is a yellow-eyed monster, exuding an all-drenching bitter fog, and bed is about the only place where I can have my back to the wall.' Indefatigably he suggested adaptations, dramatizations, reprints, and new projects, writing to theatre managers, actors, directors, publishers, journalists, and authors, offering to make cuts, alterations, and rewrites. He submitted a comic play on the subject of reincarnation, *I Was A King In Babylon*, to Kenneth Tynan who found it 'maddeningly brilliant' in parts, the dialogue 'often wildly funny', but (justly) felt that ultimately the work was 'an author's comedy, rather than an actor's or an audience's'.[20] Michael Redgrave admitted how much he had been helped in his work by having read *Anton Chehov*, but pointed out that this play lacked the delicate poise of the novels because the author seemed to be laughing *at* his characters. Despite a facility for dialogue, Gerhardie was not a gifted dramatist. His novels achieve humour and tone through the presence of the narrator, the authorial voice. And what many directors then saw as ignorance of stagecraft would perhaps today be appreciated as modernity. His play *Rasputin* was, however, successfully broadcast by the BBC and later produced at the Vanbrugh Theatre in London in 1960. Peter Hall thought it was 'conceived with real insight and imagination', but found much of the dialogue 'trivial or repetitive, and sometimes curiously stilted'. It was produced twice in Africa (once in Afrikaans), and Granada eventually paid £1,000 for a television option.

Gerhardie conceived of a serial, each chapter to be written by a well-known author, then forwarded to another author of their choice. Gerhardie opens the story with the hero lying in bed, transformed suddenly into a large grey wolf. His pretty young wife, far from being put out when he jumps up and bites her playfully on the throat, explains to two disapproving onlookers, 'This is how I like him best. This is what

Bob always was, before a wicked fairy had turned him into a man.' Strangely enough, Evelyn Waugh found the tale resistable and returned it with the comment: 'Alas, I haven't the energy to accept.' One day William was rung up by an old gangster with fourteen years' prison experience, who offered to collaborate with him in writing his (the gangster's) life story.

Occasionally Gerhardie put in an application for a job: as Professor of Russian History at London University, as a Programme Assistant in the Russian section of the BBC. He survived on odd items, paid intermittently: a grant from the Royal Literary Fund (paid over three years), another of £300 from the Royal Bounty Fund, a reasonable sum for a film option on *The Polyglots*, and so forth. It was a painfully uncertain existence, a constant nagging anxiety. But he bore his penury cheerfully. With no money to buy Christmas cards he simply sent on those he had received the year before:

> To dearest Patsy and Sonya
> Greetings and best wishes from
> Willy,
> to say nothing of
> [and here followed the original signature]
> Michael Ivens and all other Ivens

Then Gerhardie was courted by Jaques Schwartz, an American dentist who dealt in modern manuscripts as a sideline. 'I am coming over with a pocket of new notes and want to exchange them for literary items . . . so try your best to tempt me . . .', he wrote, knowing full well that Gerhardie was in no position to refuse 'new notes'. 'I *easily* have enthusiasms—but just as easily cool off . . .', he added ominously. 'Right now I am immersed in your talents.' For several days in succession he visited Rossetti House and quickly ascertained what was valuable (Gerhardie's letters from Wells, Bennett, and Wharton, for example). Then, if his client appeared unwilling, he removed a wad of bank-notes from his pocket and began to count them on the table. He offered William fifty pounds for the original manuscript of *Futility*. Gerhardie pointed out it was no longer in his possession. Schwartz told him to sit down and rewrite it. Be careful to make it look authentic, he warned, with plenty of revisions: 'You should be able to knock that off in between more serious efforts as an exercise in a race against boredom.' Reluctantly, Gerhardie complied, and the manuscript was sold in America.

In 1953, after a sixteen-year estrangement, Gerhardie and Beaverbrook met once again. Beaverbrook, 74 years old, was standing over a lectern in his flat with his back to the door reading John Galt's *Annals of the Parish* when his guest entered. He turned and came slowly forward, 'as though stepping straight out of the frame of the famous Sutherland portrait'. They talked lengthily over a glass of whisky. Beaverbrook was a little quieter than before, perhaps more sad and meditative. But he was still spirited; he had had, unlike Gerhardie, an exhilarating career during the war as Minister of Aircraft Production. He showed William round the penthouse, pointing out the nearby bomb-sites and, though seventeen years Beaverbrook's junior, Gerhardie's arthritic hip prevented him from keeping up.

Gerhardie suggested he write an article entitled 'If I were Lord Beaverbrook'. But Beaverbrook shook his head: 'That fellow gets too much space in *The Standard.*' Gerhardie offered to write Beaverbrook's biography, an idea first mooted in 1932 when he and Valentine Castlerosse contemplated a collaboration. This appealed to Beaverbrook; he drew up a contract stipulating that he was to pay Gerhardie £50 a month for six months, and reserving the right to reject any or all material that did not meet with his approval. Gerhardie set to work, but the result was a curious mixture of excellence and irrelevance: 'There are good pages, excellent paragraphs, pithy sentences', wrote a critic friend of Beaverbrook's (not unjustly). 'But the thing doesn't so much flow as spread—and so becomes not a stream but a marsh. It has so little tendency to direction that one has a sense of losing one's way. Rather surprising from such a good writer.' 'You must take this as kindly criticism', said Beaverbrook.[21] But it was criticism that revealed an increasingly common characteristic of the later Gerhardie. As with a projected biography of Kingsmill, his fine facility for capturing a personality was often swamped by sentences so long and involved that, though a joy to the ear, they convey little to the intellect. The project was abandoned. Nine years later Gerhardie learned of Beaverbrook's death. 'I always loved the dear old boy.'

William kept in intermittent touch with his own family. Dolly, now widowed, saw Victor often and William occasionally, and stayed for two weeks to nurse him over a bout of flu. Daisy, also widowed, had achieved great distinction in the library at Antibes and been made a *Conservateur honoraire*. She was still plagued by ill-health and told William that she now resembled an old war veteran, seeing with only one eye, walking with a military stick, a dachshund at her heels. She sometimes found it lonely living in a 'strange country' with nobody to share her early memories, and she thought often of their days in Russia, and the miniature villa and garden they had shared in Sestroretsk.

Even Victor and William were on better terms. In an attempt to alleviate Gerhardie's financial crises Victor gave him £100 and appointed him to the board of his company, for which he received £150 a year. Occasionally, William would pass a varyingly pleasant weekend visiting his brother's new and rather grand house at Hythe in Kent, high on a hill overlooking the sea. Victor, always slightly obsessional about privacy, continually bought land all around to keep the neighbours away. One day Victor noticed with horror that his brother's shoes were full of holes, and ignoring his daughter's retort that artists never worried about such things, surreptitiously got hold of the shoes and resoled them himself in his workshop. Then they took a walk by the sea together. Victor confided to William that he was worried about creeping paralysis, though he had only pulled a muscle while weeding the garden. He worried about his shares which had recently dropped in value. And he worried about retiring. William, on the other hand, envied Victor his adoring wife, his central heating, and the gardener who looked like Montgomery. Yet it was as it had always been, an intermittent friendship, and they soon quarrelled again.

One weekend in 1958 Dolly visited Victor and noticed that he seemed unusually humble and mild, only ran himself down, and pitied all those he had formerly abused. 'Poor Willy—I don't know *what* he lives on; and I can't help him now.' He said he had ruined the life of his first wife, of his second wife, and of his daughter. Dolly urged him to turn over a new leaf, but he simply replied: 'No, dear; my song is sung.' He went to fetch the car to take Dolly to the station and when he did not return she followed in search of him. She found her brother on the garage floor, lying next to a letter to his wife written five days before, his head shattered by a shotgun blast.

William attended the funeral. 'For me, who had not seen or spoken to him since our quarrel last Easter, to see him suddenly in his closed coffin, was unbearably poignant, and all St Paul's words about the two bodies the Chaplain uttered at the funeral service somehow did not square with that self-mangled body about to be consigned to the flames', he wrote to Penn. 'Where did he get the courage?' he wondered, and while showing little grief outwardly, nonchalance even, William spent many private hours contemplating Victor's life, his difficult disposition, his impulsively generous and kind nature.

But his habitual occupation was to run down everyone in turn . . . When the list of relatives and friends ran out, he relieved himself by abusing whole nations, saying that Englishmen were only better than Russians because there were fewer of them. There were, he said, 200,000,000 blackguards in Russia, but only some 40,000,000 in England.

'He took his life because he had nothing to do. I'd *give* my life if I had nothing to do. But he was a restless man who could not endure his own company and, by the same token, nobody, for long at a time, could endure his; and he felt unloved, unwanted.'[22] Rosie thought that Victor had killed himself because—as he once confided to her—he could never settle down.

And, after all these years, Rosie and Galina *had* settled down. They occupied a one-room flat, sharing with others the kitchen and bath-room, in a beautiful part of Leningrad. She wrote to William of their balcony, full of flowers in window-boxes, that looked out on to trees; the streets were well made and clean, and new houses were being built by the thousand. All trace of the famine was gone. Neighbours and friends helped with Galina when Rosie was ill, and sometimes they visited the country to stay with the peasants—old servants from pre-Revolution days, or those they had known during the terrible war years.

Despite her disability, Galina had a degree in mathematics, and now worked as assistant to her professor, researching and translating in six languages. She wrote poetry, read philosophy, ancient history, and art history, and occasionally earned money when the odd verse was pub-lished. She and her mother listened to Tchaikovsky, Beethoven, Bach, and Chopin on the radiogram. And then one morning a postcard dropped through the letter-box: Leonid Misernuik had died in an Arctic labour camp of 'natural heart failure'.

'I myself can say that the feeling which unites us brothers and sisters has greatly helped me in my darkest hours', Rosie told William, and went on to remember all those now dead. Every year on her wedding anniversary, 14 July, she took the train to Sestroretsk and walked all around the places she had grown up in, the casino, the seashore and the wooden dacha with the balcony where Charles had sat with his coffee and cigarettes. The St Petersburg house still stood on the desolate quay, lacking the caryatids and kneeling angels supporting the Gerhardi shield, and other baroque embellishments lost during the siege of Leningrad, but otherwise unaltered. William often dreamed of the house, of his coming back to it. And every time he came back it was different. 'You have left me, but I have a soul of my own, and I shall live even when you will not', it seemed to say to him. Then one day Rosie walked down Vibourg Quay and the space was empty. William was happy when he learned. 'Now no one will ever live in it again.'

21

DOOM
1958–1977

I dreamed that I died and rose beyond the grave. I was astonished and I asked What is the secret. Tell me what is it all for? And they said: 'We don't know. Can you tell us?'[1]

'Most people imagine I have died long ago,' Gerhardie told a newspaper reporter with some relish. When he heard that the Humanities Research Center at Texas had purchased Evelyn Waugh's library and furniture he wrote and suggested they do the same for him, including his embalmed body so that he might sit forever behind his own writing table. 'That would result in the most neglected author of his time suddenly becoming the most famous writer who ever lived.' He had never quite relinquished the idea that in order to be well known he must have a label. Having viewed with dismay his own literary demise, he had for many years styled himself 'best-known forgotten author of the century', 'celebrated unknown'—epithets that surfaced with irksome regularity in the later decades.

For much the same reasons, on 4 January 1967, an announcement appeared in *The Times*:

After spelling his name 'Gerhardi' for seventy-one years, Mr William Gerhardie has decided to 'revert to an earlier ancestral spelling' of his name and add an *e*. He tells us this is how his great great grandfather, a printer in Amsterdam, spelt the name—a fact he discovered recently from an old letter.

Why go to the trouble of changing a name he has made famous? Mr Gerhardie said 'Dante has an *e*. Shakespeare has an *e*. Racine has an *e*. Goethe has an *e*, and who am I not to have an *e*?'

Then, having, he hoped, jogged people's memory, he waited for the publishers to besiege him with offers. A single letter dropped through the letter-box: from the bank manager requesting a specimen signature. The change was not, however, entirely for publicity purposes, but something of an Anglicization. Gerhardie had never lost his sensitivity about belonging nowhere, 'neither fish nor flesh', and now after so long in Britain the delicacy was acute. 'Being born in a stable does not make you a horse', he wrote (quoting the Duke of Wellington) in some exasperation to the *Sunday Telegraph* who had referred to him as 'the "Russian-born" writer'.[2] 'One might as soon speak of the Persian-born Harold Nicolson, or French-born Somerset Maugham—born, respectively, in Tehran and Paris.' He hotly denied, for example, Holroyd's assertion that he spoke with a distinctly foreign intonation, or that his manner in greeting people (especially women) was too extravagant, too elaborate, too full of hyperbolic praise ('You look so very very beautiful today . . .') ever to let him pass as a chilly Englishman. Anthony Powell spotted him in Regent's Park late in life and noticed that he still carried a distinct aura, 'odd and rather indefinable'.[3]

In Rossetti House Gerhardie continued to write. The small scraps of paper, three inches by five, multiplied and proliferated, now filed neatly in cardboard boxes: on the left side the tentative sketches, on the right the finished version, and all (as Holroyd observed) 'resoundingly labelled'

DO NOT CRUSH

He telephoned friends to read out extracts, no more than two or three sentences at a time, and he regularly consulted his porter and his milkman as to their opinion of the best version. There is an almost poetic intensity about the way in which Gerhardie strove for the ideal sentence, the perfect cadence. The whole was to represent 'a new departure in fiction . . . a logical and necessary (r)evolution of the Novel'.[4] *This Present Breath: A Tetralogy in One Volume* (the four books 'corresponding in their cumulative progression to the four movements of a symphony and calling for integration in a single volume') is both a development from and a rejection of his old preoccupations, a shifting of focus from 'the comic agonies of procrastination to the imaginative power of time regained',[5] in an

attempt to lift art into a purified life presented as *unallayed felicity*—not by sugaring life, or 'escapism'— but by arranging the pleasure which, Wordsworth says, is in life itself so focused that all blurring spots are removed from the face of life. I consider that *is* art: to make life *life*, and not the purgatory it seems by our not evading the *superficial* irrelevancies which prevent us living . . .[6]

The idea, though briefly put, is intriguing. But it is difficult to conceive how such a work could avoid becoming meaninglessly subjective. In

1962, a fourteen-page extract appeared in *The Wind and the Rain: An Easter Book For 1962*. Edited by Neville Braybrooke, this journal had been founded in 1940 to 'interpret the Christian order in the light of current affairs, philosophy, literature and the arts', and had also published the work of Robert Musil, Simone Weil, Mary McCarthy, and William Sansom. Gerhardie's piece is not encouraging although, with his emphasis on cumulation for artistic effect, publication of only the opening and closing chapters makes criticism problematic. A section taken at random:

And whomsoever I look at, and whatsoever I yearn for, I instantly am. For I am that I am. I'm a signature testifying, as I ever sign away my delimiting 'I', to the living breath of the abundant and untethered *am*. And there is no more 'that is I, but that is she or you or it or he'. All those egregious pronouns were but Time's sharpness slashed in air to split life's sweetness into heartbeats sealed in woe. Recurring decimals whittling away the immemorial verb into running minutes, seconds—unavailing milliards of our suffering unit strewn in space forelorn, they beat no more. They beat no more, illusory, sad symbols of division, now bright toys to play with at a game not learnt before, that to distinguish is not to divide.

Instead of conjuring the ineffable *out of* concrete images and contrasts, he is now attempting to write *about* the ineffable, which provoked Philip Toynbee's remark: 'But I *still* feel that even a very high-flown passage should be somehow *pegged down*—I mean tethered to earth rather than a free-flying balloon.'[7] Gerhardie's distinctive humour and narrative voice are lost; his definition of 'form' as 'a lens focusing dispersing rays of light' is not elucidated in this subjective, rambling, and often sentimental flow of words, neither poetry nor prose. His pleas for individuality had turned, in his own life, into a non-creative isolation. 'That was his ironical tragedy.'[8]

He was considerably cheered when, in 1959, he was awarded a Civil List Pension in recognition of his services to literature, and seven years later received £800 from the Arts Council to enable him to continue his tetralogy.[9] From now on he received intermittent publicity, and not a few offers for publication of the new novel. 'The legend of your work in progress is on the point of exceeding the solid fame of your published works', observed Olivia Manning. 'I think of myself', he replied, 'as the author of my work in progress, my magnum opus, the tetralogy in one volume. I live and dream in this great mass of infinite crystallization of hundreds of thousands, perhaps a million, fragments into a rapturous, colourful mosaic.'[10] Michael Ivens gave him a new typewriter, but he refused all offers of a secretary with, 'No, no, the typing it out is the exciting part' (though he was not above generating a little pathos by bemoaning this lack to a journalist). The boxes piled up around him, but without Patsy to organize and chivvy him he had not the energy; and without Clara, the burning ambition for financial success was gone. Somehow the contemplation of the work gradually shifted to pride of place; but it was an agreeable and rewarding experience, almost an achievement in itself. Now that he had accustomed himself to the loss of Clara, perhaps for the first time in his life William was savouring his isolation, free from anxiety and obligation.

Like Proust, I have learnt the austere lesson that it is not to beings we must attach ourselves, that it is not beings who exist in reality and are consequently susceptible to expression, but ideas. It is ideas which are real in this phenomenal world, not persons—ideas which are but the coin, the currency, the intellectual assignations, the promissory notes, the spiritual equivalents of some other existence.[11]

He both wanted to finish the work, yet feared to do so. 'He came to feel that if he finished it he would die because his work would be over'[12]—Holroyd's analysis of *God's Fifth Column* is perhaps more apt for *This Present Breath*. 'My last book must be in the nature of a Confession', he had written in *Resurrection*. 'This must be the story of my life. Also it will be the story of my death.' For he had now passed the three-score years and ten, and felt indeed that what he had left was a gift. 'Do you think I might have another five years?' he asked a young woman six years before his death. 'Well, it's rather a lot to ask', she replied.[13] He was not, he insisted, afraid to die but he was in no hurry.

Accustomed now to the fact that he had failed to attract the attention of 'that d——d public which buys my own books so sparingly', he abandoned the dream of a wide readership. He wrote, he insisted, for his *ideal* reader. After all, 'the books stand, the reader evolves', he pointed out. To one critic of *The Polyglots*, overgracious in his faint praise, Gerhardie retorted: 'As if *you* conferred something on it! All you confer is a lack—showing up what you haven't got!' In fact, Anne Amyes believed that he learned at last to come to terms with adverse criticism of his work. He placed his hopes for the future on there being always a select core of admirers who might keep his memory alive. Graham Greene was one such. 'You know how much I have always admired [your work]', he wrote to Gerhardie, and, in an article for *The Times*: 'To those of my generation he was the most important new novelist to appear in our young life.'[14] Anthony Powell and Olivia Manning both acknowledged that they too might well be classed as 'disciples', whilst L. P. Hartley admitted that Gerhardie was always more of a literary 'pioneer' than himself. Gerhardie himself believed that his greatest achievement was the development of the 'humorous tragedy, the highest literary expression in our time'.[15] He was greatly amused that an enormous tome, published under the auspices of the Russian Academy of Sciences and devoted to scholarly work on Chekhov, defined his own approach as 'neo-psychological-philosophical relativism'.[16]

He was always conscious of the difficulties of such early success. 'An author's subsequent books can never please as well as the mere memory of his first. People are tired if he gives them the same type of book, and annoyed if he gives them another.'[17] Of his own works he considered *Of Mortal Love* and *Resurrection* the most satisfying, though he believed that the three early books had been remarkable achievements for such a young man. There has, however, never been a consensus about his novels. Wharton loved *Futility*, hated *The Polyglots*, and loved *Pending Heaven*. Arnold Bennett, surprisingly, preferred *Jazz and Jasper* and *Pending Heaven*. Altogether *The Polyglots* was probably Gerhardie's most generally popular work, although he never reached a really wide audience. Gorley Putt suggested that this was partly due to the books' plotlessness: 'You can just as easily read a Gerhardie novel backwards as forwards.'[18] By comparison Evelyn Waugh, also a fine comic writer, had elaborate and exuberant plots which helped to endear him to a larger public.

As testimony to Gerhardie's continuing popularity in the literary and publishing worlds, Macdonald's agreed to a second reissue of his books: the Revised Definitive Collected Edition of the Works of William Gerhardie, to be published between 1970 and 1974 with an advance of £4,000. The 'as good as posthumous definitive edition', as William termed it. At once he set in motion meticulous plans, the cause of innumerable—and often very acrimonious—letters between himself, his editors, his publishers, and Michael Holroyd, who was to write a preface for each. Since the spectacular success of *Lytton Strachey* and *Augustus John*, Holroyd's distinguished literary reputation was to help sell Gerhardie.

William of course agreed—but found it well-nigh impossible to keep his fingers out of the pie. With great zeal he helpfully told Holroyd exactly what to write. But his suggestions were for the most part wildly unsuitable: written in the sort of elaborately labyrinthine prose that had sunk the Beaverbrook biography, picking up and weaving in obscure references, and tiresomely self-congratulatory, they could not be used. Patiently Holroyd struggled to produce his own, harangued and coerced day and night by William's 'improvements'. There were particular ructions when Holroyd, feeling that a preface must be not meandering and poetic but entertaining and incisive, wished to include an amusing anecdote about Gerhardie's agitation over his Oxford scout stealing the marmalade. Gerhardie, indignant, felt it exhibited him 'in a mean, ridiculous, pernickety, fussy, "agitated", hysterical light', the scout as a common thief, and was altogether libellous.[19] Holroyd persisted. Gerhardie persisted. Holroyd modified and persisted. 'With you, it is always a question of bargaining and haggling', fumed Gerhardie. 'You're not going round the bend, by any chance?' The books, he explained, were not impersonal objects to be purchased by anonymous readers, they were living objects for him, now. 'The novels *ipso facto* carry on the story of [my] life up to date in the voluminous tetralogy of novels; fiction, according to Thackeray, containing more truth in solution than autobiography in lump.'[20] 'I love my definitive edition and like to *caress* them as my bedside books. Anything in the prefaces that jars on me would kill this happiness in my last years.'[21] Eventually Holroyd came to understand, or at least accept, this point of view. The Oxford scout was withdrawn, other compromises reached, and William was satisfied.

Gerhardie also had strong ideas about the appearance of the books and now adopted the ampersand as his personal cipher: 'on symbolical, mystical grounds; the all-embracing "and", not "but"', it is a figure for forgiveness and tolerance. And by closely resembling the treble clef, it reminds the reader of Gerhardie's aspirations to music, symbolic of the inarticulate. The '*exquisite* curves' of the ampersand eventually appeared on the title-page and preceded each chapter heading—but not before Gerhardie had questioned the size, the spacing, the proportions, and the very form of it, rejecting a dozen printer's attempts at perfection ('after actors, printers are notoriously the worst misinterpreters of genius'). For the dust-jackets he selected two photographs—one (to be placed left of centre) taken when very young and 'representing the romantic auto-biographical hero of the novels when I lived and wrote them . . . fittingly contrasted by the old ruin on the right to which I have come'. The latter was, he thought, 'decidedly someone not to be trifled with'.[22]

The order in which the books were to be issued was crucial, too, so that they 'follow a symphonic sequence according to *leitmotiv* and motto-theme', creating a harmonious whole, 'a thematic evocation running through the entire corpus of his work, as though it were one vast symphonic poem',[23] though what this motto-theme is remains a mystery. The ten volumes were the same as the 1940s edition, with a few improvements: *The Memoirs of Satan* was omitted, *Pretty Creatures* and *Memoirs of a Polyglot* added, and *My Sinful Earth* (originally *Jazz and Jasper*) at last appeared under Gerhardie's original title *Doom*—once deemed too gloomy, now, he suggested, a prophetic understatement.

The edition attracted a good deal more publicity than the previous one, and a lot of appreciative reviews. But once again sales were modest and many were remaindered. Gerhardie, though bitterly disappointed, had at last grown accustomed to such results. 'Don't let it hurt you, Mama,' says Jamie Wadsworth to his mother. 'Deep down it doesn't hurt me. I sometimes grumble because I've been unlucky, but I've always known that my time will come, sooner or later, perhaps not for a hundred years.'

Although the reissue was not a spectacular success, gradually new readers were emerging; articles peppered the newspapers and journals (albeit sparsely), Gerhardie was elected a Fellow of the Royal Society of Literature, and visitors to Rossetti House became more frequent. The flat had come a long way from Brian Lunn's recollection of pristine modernity. 'Bell out of order. Please use knocker', announced a sign on the front door—the knocker itself a Dartmoor pixie, 'to discourage the burglars'. After a long silence the gold net curtain would be cautiously drawn back so that the face behind the glass could make quite certain of who was calling, before disappearing again for ten minutes to 'put on more clothes'. Now followed the sound of bolts being drawn back, and the door opened a little; the visitor was admitted, the door relocked and bolted and tested several times.

A musty smell hung in the hallway, which was cold and darkish, for the curtains in the flat were now never opened. Olivia Manning visited and remarked that it was a lovely day outside. 'Is it?' said William eagerly, but he did not get up to look. The visitor would pass along the corridor where cardboard boxes were stacked nearly to the ceiling, past the plaster bust of Gerhardie when young, past Patsy's empty study awash with papers from floor to ceiling, past the kitchen, a-tumble with dirty saucepans and with a cooker so old that the Electricity Board replaced it free of charge in the interests of safety. The whole was 'like Miss Havisham's house', said Patsy's friend Sonya, whose name William pronounced with a 'romantic' Russian accent, when they visited. Sonya was entranced by the huge dull mirrors, curtains hanging in dust, the threadbare rugs, the chaos and cold, the books and unread newspapers piled high. Patsy was appalled by the transformation since the days of Frances, the dingy drabness.

The sitting-room where William worked was like a rock-pool with circles of yellow lamplight on the purple carpet, and with the ornate gilded looking-glass above the sofa that Gerhardie pretended to have rescued from the St Petersburg ballroom. When, in the 1960s, Anne Amyes and her husband Julian painted this room cream, William asked them to pick out in gold the door panels, the mouldings, and the ceiling cornice, and some little cane chairs, all to re-create the ballroom. Here too the walls were stacked with cardboard boxes, not only the myriad components of the tetralogy, but food ordered in bulk from Selfridges, whatever happened to have caught Gerhardie's fancy that month. One caller saw only Coca-Cola and meringues, another several score tins of Beef Italienne, yet another punnets of mouldering strawberries, and a fourth vast quantities of celery and mayonnaise. Each month he ordered a box of chocolates 'for Anne', every one of which he ate himself.

Here and there was evidence of Gerhardie's inventive handiwork— an armchair raised on four coffee jars; an electric hotplate rigged up on the sofa by a friendly electrician. Full-looking paper bags abounded on the floor and all about were elastic bands and biro pens. 'With my arthritic hip I can't be running around looking for these things when I need them', he explained. 'The solution is to have one to hand wherever I happen to be.'[24] June Turner, another devoted friend who shopped, cooked, and generally assisted him (and who, incidentally, William introduced to her husband) would be sent out periodically to buy in bulk aspirin, quinine, several dozen more black biros ('make sure you test each one') and money in crisp new germ-free notes or fifty-pence pieces that could be easily washed.

In the midst of all this was Gerhardie himself, a huge pile of brocade cushions supporting him as he sat at his typewriter, zipped, according to one visitor, into a sort of waterproof tracksuit or parachute outfit. He had just bought a brand new suit, he explained, and already it was full of moth, which made him furious. 'Mr Gerhardie manages to convey a combined effect of decrepitude and well-being.'[25] When, late in life, a hernia proved very painful he remarked with a kind of grim cheer that it took his mind off the arthritis. He talked eagerly, his presence as 'dazzling, confusing and stimulating' as ever. 'Each question released a rambling account of some meeting, long quotations from conversations once held or literature once read, associations, allusions, evaluations.'[26]

The guest would be offered a drink of Gerhardie's own invention: in his leaner days it was All's Well, a patent concoction of either tepid water or weak tea into which raspberry jam was stirred, so called because, of course, it ended well, the jam getting denser towards the bottom of the glass. This was not so much wild eccentricity, as some claimed, as a Russian upbringing—the Ambassador's daughter Merial Buchanan had noticed 'the invariable custom of Russian soldiers, who put everything one gives them into the beloved cup of tea, from oranges, lemons or apples to jam and sweets'.[27] Later he was immensely proud of having devised Sherrivapa, sweet sherry mixed with evaporated milk:

> That I have written marvellous novels is neither here nor there. Other men, before my time, have written marvellous novels. And men after my time will write, perhaps, even more marvellous novels. Though I doubt it. But that I should be the first in the field to invent Sherrivapa—that is an achievement. And an ambition beyond anything I have ever dreamed, and it is one that cannot be taken away.[28]

Had he had the energy he would probably have taken out a patent. He never offered food, and those who knew what to expect arrived very warmly wrapped and bearing a picnic. Any guest who asked to use the telephone would be conducted to a special extension which she or he might freely contaminate. The lavatory was rather more serious: Gerhardie would first prevaricate (he even took a visitor to use the next-door neighbour's) then reluctantly consent, but go mysteriously ahead first.

Female callers were, of course, particularly welcome, and even a census collector was pressed to stay for a drink, which she declined only because she had another 185 collections that day. If young enough, Gerhardie would thoroughly inspect them, top to toe, from all angles like a sculptor, commenting aloud about features he particularly admired: 'a very Proustian profile' or 'ankles in the style of Margot Asquith'—and when they had left perhaps, 'nose a trifle sturdy', 'mouth a little awry'. Having for so long himself felt shy and out of place in the world, now in the warmth of his seclusion, his world, his rules, William enjoyed putting others in his place. Those who did not know him sometimes found his insistent interest in them (or their womenfolk) offensive. Worried lest female companionship should flag, he conceived of a female shop mannequin to stand perpetual vigil in the sitting-room dressed in a maid's uniform.

His correspondence had been all but replaced by the telephone, although he occasionally replied to appreciative letters: 'Thank you again for writing so warmly and cheeringly. In another forty years I shall be 108.'[29] In 1972 Vera rang him up. She was 65, about to marry for the fourth time, and had taken a fancy to the idea of seeing her old lover. No, said he, 'I want to keep my illusions'. For much the same reason he declined, in his sixties, an invitation from the *Daily Telegraph* to visit Russia to write a series of articles, although very badly in need of the money. His visit might, he explained, endanger Rosie. By now this was unlikely. 'I cannot think of anything so sad as re-visiting the places of one's youth', he had written in 1931. 'I once made the mistake of re-visiting Oxford . . . From an emotional point of view, a place should not be re-visited except in the imagination.'[30]

But Daisy's son, Jean-Jacques, kept in touch with his aunt, visiting Russia and sending books to his cousin Galina. In 1969 he went with a French delegation to Leningrad and found Rosie in hospital, very ill, attended by Galina. Delirious, Rosie called in vain for the English chaplain. Jean-Jacques sat beside her bed and they repeated the Lord's Prayer together in English, a few days before Rosie died.

Patsy had set up house with Sonya, somewhat younger than herself, who worked on the perfumery counter at Harrods. Still in her old job, Patsy was also busy writing a book about Christina Foyle, *The Bog Rose*, using Gerhardie's card-index system. She had always been a difficult person, quiet and shy in company, often awkward and domineering in private. Now she grew increasingly possessive with Sonya, her rages more forceful, more frequent and more random. After a particularly nasty row she swallowed a bottle of sleeping pills and a bottle of whisky and was removed to hospital for a stomach pump. She wanted to live an enclosed life with Sonya, to prevent her from seeing others. Sonya, deeply fond of Patsy, could no longer bear this, and left for Spain.

Left alone, and corresponding only intermittently with Sonya, Patsy now more than ever spent hours on the telephone to William. At work she began behaving rather oddly—she sent Christina Foyle's laundry lists to Lord Brabazon of Tara; on the way home she walked round and round certain streets, repeatedly missing her turning. Christina Foyle came round to her flat one day in 1965 and banged on the door to find out why she wasn't at work; and when she got no reply she pushed a cheque and her notice through the door.

After almost two years away, Sonya returned to England. She made her way to the flat and, though she realized there was someone at home, she found the doors were heavily bolted. At last she climbed through the window. Patsy was lying on the floor, drunk and emaciated and surrounded by empty bottles—so many that it took three months to dispose of them. Their two cats had almost starved to death. Pat, a friend of Patsy's who also worked at the bookshop, realizing that something was wrong but unaware of the extent, had left food outside the door whenever she passed by. Patsy had taken it in and left it to rot. At once Sonya telephoned the doctor and the social worker, and that very evening Patsy, making no protest at all, was removed to the hospital.

William had known none of this, incredibly. Patsy's psychiatrist diagnosed pre-senile dementia, Alzheimer's Disease, which, in her early fifties, had begun tragically early. For the first week in hospital she suffered terrible alcohol withdrawals and hallucinations and had to be locked up. Later she was removed to an open ward at Napsbury Hospital near St Albans. In the early years there she continued her telephone calls to William until gradually she became more and more remote, and the world outside the hospital seemed to be of less and less concern. She no longer read, and though she seemed happy with visitors when they were there, she lost interest in them and their visit the moment they left. She never mentioned coming out. But, confused and with little memory, she appeared neither distressed nor unhappy. Sonya and Pat loyally visited twice a week until, after six years in hospital, she suffered a brain haemorrhage. They sat with her for several hours, even when she was unconscious, and three days later she died.

William, who missed Patsy's cremation because he didn't know either the time or the place, had no driver, and withal a hernia attack, wrote instead to console Sonya: 'We are all going in the same and *only* direction—to a state of being where there are no sighs or tribulations.'[31]

Excursions of any kind were now rare for William. The world outside was a depressing place and, moreover, one which could bring only dismay. When, for example, his play *Rasputin* was performed at the Vanbrugh Theatre, Gerhardie was rung up by the *Daily Express* and told, with only a few hours to spare, that a reporter would be there to photograph him and give half a page over to the play. He had no clean shirt, so quickly washed one and put it on wringing wet. He and Holroyd duly turned up at the theatre, applauded vigorously, and then, William very nervous, they stood and waited. And waited. There was no reporter, because the pound had been devalued instead. They returned home. Gerhardie thought this quite typical of life: you pin your hopes on outside things and are bound to be disappointed. The solution was, he felt, not to go out. Michael Ivens gave him a television set, but he preferred to read, and told the story of how Proust, when dying, his sight and hearing enfeebled, explained that what he liked best was to put his hand on his books. Speaking of his own published works and of his new tetralogy, Gerhardie explained: 'I feel these books have more to do with me than my life. I get so depressed when I go out to post a letter. But there are so many people in these books.'[32]

Yet he continued his walks in Regent's Park, well wrapped up in overcoat and scarf, with hat and powdered face. Christina Foyle passed him in Piccadilly in the 1970s looking 'like a person from another age, pale, and very old-fashioned clothes and rather woebegone; very different from the witty, debonaire man I knew as a girl'.[33] In 1973 he attended a royal garden party, looking *extremely* debonair in top hat and tails, and was given special permission to enter by the Electricians' Gate so as to avoid the stairs. He was very taken with the Queen, 'this slip of a girl with a *gorgeous* neck. You can see it on the postage stamps. I've never felt so well since that outing.'

A year or two later Gerhardie telephoned Anne one Monday morning, but found her out. The call was answered by her daughter Isabelle who noticed with surprise that he sounded slightly drunk. Knowing the alcoholic content of Sherrivapa to be almost nil, she consulted a medical dictionary instead and concluded—correctly—that William had suffered a stroke. He had sensed that something was wrong with himself the previous Friday, could not exactly say what, and found that he was unable to make a telephone call. In this state he had sat alone all weekend.

Gerhardie's full power of speech eventually returned, but the stroke left him very weak and he was never again so lively. Now more than ever he relied upon assistance from friends and relations—some to do his laundry, clean up a little, shop, or cook. Tamara arranged meals-on-wheels three days a week and sometimes shopped and cleaned, while Victor's daughter Christina brought provisions. Every weekend Anne cooked a substantial casserole to last several days. William would never permit anybody to help him wash and dress, but whenever he had a bath Anne remained in the next room so that if he fell and called out she could fetch help. She and Julian arranged for parts of the flat to be spring-cleaned and for the Dickensian wiring to be made safe. And they put in train a plan to purchase for William the freehold of Rossetti House. The following year an eighty-first birthday celebration was organized. He lay in bed, very fragile, greeting visitors one by one.

In the new year he asked Anne to have a look at a lump on the back of his neck. She was appalled to see that it was the size of a golf ball—he told her that many years ago his herbalist Hilda Leyel had advised him it was nothing to worry about. Gerhardie went in to the Middlesex Hospital to have the tumour removed. Here the doctors became interested in his case for teaching purposes, and persuaded him in the interests of medical science to allow a group of students to examine him. But for this William had to be removed in an ambulance to another hospital. Anne was very much against it—he was so weak and frail. William, however, had given his consent and he was adamant. At the other hospital he suffered a massive heart attack; only the immediate presence of the ward sister saved him.

Back at the Middlesex, Gerhardie's diabetes needed stabilizing before the operation. He knew he had not long to live. He told Anne that he was content with what he would leave behind, but he asked her to do two things: to try to keep his books in print so that posterity would have an opportunity to judge him, and to give mementoes of himself to a few close friends.

The tumour, malignant, was removed and Gerhardie transferred to a National Health convalescent home in Highgate. Whilst there he refused to get up and dress, and told Anne that he disliked the man sitting opposite him who was speaking about him in Russian. He was very glad when he was allowed to go home; Tamara had made up his bed and tidied the flat. Now he told Anne that he believed in an after-life and so did not fear dying. 'I am convinced that, as we pass into a higher dimension, perception and imagination become more identified', he had once written to Rosamund Lehmann.[34] A few days later he was put back into the Middlesex Hospital in a geriatric ward and—again to Anne's regret—given vigorous physiotherapy, about which he complained.

On 15 July, June Turner visited and sat holding his hand. 'What have you been thinking?' she asked after a while. 'Not for me to say'—he faintly shook his head—'not for me to say.'[35] Later the same day Anne stopped at the hospital on her way to the theatre. She sat alone with him for about a quarter of an hour. William tried to speak to her, as if wanting to say something specific and important—he said it twice—but she could not hear. She told him not to worry, and to tell her tomorrow. William Gerhardie died that night.

EPILOGUE

Gerhardie's will left all he had to Anne Amyes. He asked that his body be cremated according to the rites of the Church of England, and his ashes scattered in Regent's Park.

And what of the *magnum opus*? He had amassed something in the region of 85,000 pieces of paper, three inches by five. Most are in his own hand, in pencil or fountain pen, sentences, quotations, a line of poetry, brief impressions, overwritten here and there, opinions, memoranda, thoughts and scenes of fifty years before, moods, reviews, stories, a line of French, trivia, half-thoughts, new projects, Russian and German, reveries, now in biro, red crayon, months and weeks before his death, letters, revisions, descriptions, shopping lists, ideas for the future.

There is no narrative, nothing that could remotely be construed or reconstructed as a novel. But out of the chaos emerges something infinitely more suggestive. Gerhardie had faithfully pursued his early plans to 'card-index' his thoughts, a method far 'better than a notebook, for it corresponds to the process of the brain'. And he who saw his life as 'a vocation', who strove to preserve the self from extinction, who so distrusted the streamlined interpretation, the all-illuminating analysis, has left behind a body of material that in its fragmentary, stimulating, baffling, and sometimes secret sense approaches the jigsaw of human consciousness.

NOTES

This biography is based, to a very large extent, upon Gerhardie's own literary estate. This was purchased in 1981 by the Cambridge University Library, where it is now housed. The fact that this material—all 59 large boxes of it—has yet to be catalogued makes precise noting very difficult indeed. With this problem in mind, and because each chapter makes such extensive use of quotations, I have adopted the following, rather spare, policy.

All unpublished material quoted in the biography is derived from this estate, unless otherwise indicated by the following abbreviations:

> [AA] in the possession of Anne Amyes
>
> [BB] in the possession of Beaverbrook Library
>
> [DD] in the possession of Dido Davies
>
> [MH] in the possession of Michael Holroyd
>
> [GP] in the possession of Gorley Putt

Although original letters from Katherine Mansfield, Edith Wharton, and H. G. Wells were sold, photocopies are held in the Gerhardie Archive.

In the case of quotations from Gerhardie's own published works, I have used not the first editions (now very hard to come by) but the more readily available Revised Definitive Edition of the Works of William Gerhardie published by Macdonald between 1970 and 1974, abbreviated thus:

AC	*Anton Chehov*
Doom	*Doom*, but note that this is the 1974 version of *Jazz and Jasper*
Fut.	*Futility*
GFC	*God's Fifth Column*
MP	*Memoirs of a Polyglot*
MWL	*My Wife's the Least Of It*
OML	*Of Mortal Love*
PC	*Pretty Creatures*
PG	*The Polyglots*
PH	*Pending Heaven*
PS	*Perfectly Scandalous*
Res.	*Resurrection*
Roms.	*The Romanovs*

All Gerhardie's novels draw largely on his own experiences. From his earliest days he jotted down not only ideas, but scenes from his life, conversations, observations. Many readers familiar with his books will recognize some material that here appears as biography. This is not presumption or guesswork: Gerhardie's notes make quite clear that such material is indeed biographical.

I. ANCESTORS

1. Gerhardie to *The Literary Digest*, 6.7.1934. However he was not above, later in life, confusing the issue by pronouncing it on the radio 'gair-háardi' and 'gur-háardi'.
2. *MP* 29.
3. 'Memories of St Petersburg', *The Listener*, 25 June 1953, p. 1049.
4. *Fut.* 64 and 67–8.
5. Carroll, 86.
6. Murray, 407.
7. Murray, 400.
8. Murray, 410.
9. Murray, 397.
10. *MP* 74.
11. *MP* 74.
12. *MP* 39.
13. *Roms.* 475.

2. NIGHTS IN ST PETERSBURG

1. *Fut.* 181–2.
2. *MP* 48–9.
3. *Res.* 338.
4. Patsy Rosenstiehl to Gerhardie, 6.10.1948.
5. *MP* 71.
6. *MP* 74.
7. *MP* 71–2.
8. Ibid.
9. Ibid.
10. *MP* 71.
11. *MP* 55.
12. *MP* 56.
13. *MP* 49.
14. *Res.* 134–5.
15. 'My Idea of Utopia', typescript article. Published version not located.
16. *MP* 53.
17. Rodzianko, 45.
18. *MP* 36.

19. *MP* 75–6.
20. *MP* 76.
21. *MP* 52.
22. Nabokov, 25. Nabokov, born in 1900, was from a celebrated Liberal landowning family.
23. Nabokov, 77.
24. Field, 105.
25. Gerhardie sometimes writes this as 'Espiobeheonargi'.
26. To Horace Richards, 20.1.1932.
27. Gerhardie to Curtis Brown, 24.5.1938.
28. *MP* 76–7.
29. *Res.* 194–5.
30. *Res.* 24.
31. Nabokov, 19–20.
32. *MP* 57–8.
33. *MP* 46.
34. Nabokov, 79.
35. Quoted by Gerhardie in *MP* 229–30.
36. *MP* 71.
37. *MP* 75.
38. *GFC* 183.
39. Baring, 256–7.
40. *MP* 66.
41. *MP* 67.
42. *The Fool of the Family*, unpublished play.
43. *Res.* 124.
44. *MP* 81.
45. *MP* 82.
46. Unpublished poem, translated by Patrick Miles.

3. ENGLAND

1. *PG* 206.
2. *MP* 95.
3. *MP* 96.
4. Unpublished poem 'London 9/11 November 1913', translated by Patrick Miles.
5. Unpublished poem 'London November 1914', translated by Patrick Miles.
6. *MP* 96.
7. A. Simpson to Gerhardie, 20.12.1934.
8. *MP* 98–9.
9. The title of a play (1884) by Alexander Ostzovsky, 'guilty without guilt' is also a Russian proverb having the sense 'more sinned against than sinning'.
10. *MP* 100.

11. *MP* 103–4.
12. *MP* 101.
13. *MP* 105.
14. *PG* 307.
15. To Oliver Stonor, 23.3.1941.
16. *MP* 114–15.
17. *MP* 125.
18. *MP* 124.
19. *MP* 118.
20. *MP* 120.
21. Gerhardie to John Fletcher, 30.7.1931.
22. *MP* 122.
23. *MP* 131.
24. *MP* 132.

4. PETROGRAD

1. *Fut.* 74–5.
2. Petrograd, a Russianized version of the Germanic St Petersburg, was deemed more patriotic.
3. *MP* 134.
4. *MP* 137.
5. *MP* 105.
6. Lockhart, *Memoirs of a British Agent*, 116.
7. *Fut.* 71.
8. Lockhart, *Memoirs of a British Agent*, 117.
9. *Fut.* 72.
10. *MP* 140.
11. Knox, xxvii.
12. Knox, xxxi–xxxiii.
13. Knox, xxxiv.
14. Lockhart, *Memoirs of a British Agent*, 160.
15. Knox, 514–15.
16. *MP* 149.
17. Knox, 558.
18. Knox, 561.
19. *Fut.* 73.
20. Knox, 575.
21. Knox, 582.
22. George Buchanan, 31.
23. *MP* 135.
24. *MP* 156.
25. *MP* 140–1.

5. THE GHOST WAR

1. *Fut.* 91.
2. *MP* 159.
3. *MP* 158.
4. *PG* 126.
5. Luckett, 206.
6. *Roms.* 36.
7. Rodzianko, 169.
8. *PG* 3.
9. Hodges, 53–4.
10. Hodges, 57.
11. Quoted by Rhodes James, 50.
12. Hodges, 56.
13. Ibid.
14. *Roms.* 530.
15. Hodges, 38.
16. Hodges, 88.
17. Hodges, 23.
18. From W. E. Harris, 2.2.1958.
19. *Fut.* 146.
20. *MP* 167.
21. Hodges, 59.
22. *PG* 55.
23. *PG* 76–7.
24. *Fut.* 123–4.
25. *Fut.* 124.
26. *Fut.* 132.
27. Bernard Hughes to Gerhardie, 29.8.1928.
28. *Fut.* 110.
29. *Fut.* 148.
30. *PG* 249.
31. *Fut.* 190.
32. *PG* 321–2.
33. *PG* 326–8.

6. OH, *FUTILITY*

1. *MP* 206.
2. *MP* 205–6.
3. *MP* 183.
4. Evelyn Waugh, *A Little Learning*, 173.
5. Rothenstein, 94.
6. *MP* 192–3.

7. *MP* 190.
8. *MP* 204.
9. Rothenstein, 78.
10. *MP* 184–5.
11. Rothenstein, 54–5.
12. Evelyn Waugh, *A Little Learning*, 164.
13. *MP* 200.
14. Rothenstein, 56–7.
15. Rothenstein, 77.
16. Nichols, *Sweet and Twenties*, 120.
17. *PG* 64.
18. *MP* 195.
19. 'A Sunday Morning Survey of the World', *Sunday Referee*, 9.8.1931.
20. *PG* 113.
21. *Res.* 183.
22. *MP* 192.
23. *MP* 189.
24. Rothenstein, 56.
25. 'Felony', *Oxford Fortnightly Review*, 3 Nov. 1921, 245–8; 'The Proposal', *Oxford Fortnightly Review*, 27 Jan. 1922, 316–18; 'Tact', *Oxford Fortnightly Review*, 26 May 1922, 409–13; 'Of Hypocrisy', *Oxford Outlook*, June 1922, 199–201.
26. *PG* 2666.
27. Alpers, 88.
28. *AC* 8–9.

7. AUSTRIA

1. *MP* 127.
2. *Adelphi*, July 1923, in a review of Gerhardie's next book, *Anton Chehov*.
3. Rebecca West sent Gerhardie a verbal message.
4. *Times Literary Supplement*, 20.7.1922.
5. *London Mercury*, Aug. 1922.
6. *Daily Telegraph*, 7.8.1922.
7. *Nation and Athenaeum*, 12.8.1922.
8. Quoted in a letter from Cobden Sanderson to Gerhardie, 17.7.1922.
9. To Gerhardie, 21.5.1936. 'Amy' is Amy Johnson.
10. Lewis, 443.
11. To Michael Holroyd, 12.9.1971 [MH].
12. To Gerhardie, 14.2.1923.
13. The Preface first appeared in England in Duckworth's New Reader's Library edition of 1927.
14. 23.4.1923. Gerhardie received a £15 advance for *Anton Chehov*. The American edition was published by Duffield (New York, 1923).

15. 'Why Men Remain Bachelors', *The Golden Hind* (Boot's Magazine). (Published version cut out and therefore no date visible.)
16. Gerhardie to Macdonald [1970].
17. Eliot, 15.
18. Steiner, 48.
19. Woolf, 194–5.
20. *Res.* 113.
21. *PG* 280.
22. To Cass Canfield, 8.3.1930.
23. 'Turning Over New Leaves', *Vogue*, 18.4.1928.
24. Unpublished lecture delivered at the Royal Academy of Dramatic Art, 1960.
25. *Weekly Westminster Gazette*, 5.1.1924.
26. Proust, 255.
27. Rothenstein, 57–8.
28. 23.8.1923, quoted by Rothenstein, 59–60.
29. *MP* 221–2.
30. *MP* 225–6.
31. *MP* 226.
32. Lewis, 462.
33. November 1923, June 1928, May 1925, respectively.
34. Retitled *The Vanity Bag*, published by Ernest Benn (London, 1927) in a limited edition.
35. *A Bad End*, published by Ernest Benn (London, 1926) in a limited edition.
36. *MP* 241.
37. *MP* 242.
38. *MP* 245.
39. *MP* 236.
40. *MP* 250.
41. *MP* 249.

8. WATER IN THE TEAPOT

1. Gerhardie received a £50 advance. The American edition was published by Duffield (New York, 1925).
2. *Spectator*, 1.8.1925.
3. To Mrs Kurath, 23.11.1931.
4. Tchehov, Act 1, p. 162.
5. Bradbury, 143.
6. Powell, 85.
7. *MP* 164.
8. 19.6.1925.
9. *MP* 248.

9. 2/6 A DAY

1. *MP* 265, also quoted in Taylor, *Beaverbrook*, 234.
2. *Daily Express*, 19.10.1925.
3. Taylor, *Beaverbrook*, 7.
4. MP 271, also quoted in Taylor, *Beaverbrook*, 234.
5. Taylor, *Beaverbrook*, 216.
6. Donaldson, 63.
7. Taylor, *Beaverbrook*, 241.
8. *Res.* 57.
9. Taylor, *Beaverbrook*, 137.
10. Taylor, *Beaverbrook*, 237.
11. *MP* 309.
12. Bennett, vol. iii, p. 11 (14 Jan. 1926).
13. *MP* 297.
14. 'The "Society Hostess": A Queer Bird', *Graphic*, 26.5.1928.
15. *MP* 278.
16. Ibid.
17. Ibid.
18. *MP* 328.
19. *MP* 281.
20. *MP* 273.
21. *Doom*, 96.
22. *OML* 142.
23. *Doom*, 223.
24. *Doom*, 131.
25. Enclosed with letter to Gerhardie, 23.9.1926, but published version not located.
26. 5.12.1922.
27. *MP* 269.
28. Unpublished notes [AA].
29. *Doom*, 66.
30. *Doom*, 97.

10. A MOST UNPLEASANT SORT OF LUNATIC

1. *PH* 23.
2. *MP* 255.
3. *MP* 314.
4. *PH* 58.
5. *Res.* 191.
6. *PH* 86.
7. *MP* 315.

8. 1.1.1925 [BB].

9. 27.12.1926 [BB].

10. *MP* 310.

11. *PH* 63.

12. Gerhardie to Beaverbrook, 24.12.1926 [BB].

13. Gerhardie's unpublished introduction to Michael Holroyd's *Hugh Kingsmill*.

14. Ibid.

15. Holroyd, *Hugh Kingsmill*, 56.

16. Holroyd, *Hugh Kingsmill*, 70.

17. Ingrams, 68.

18. Ingrams, 69.

19. Ingrams, 11.

20. Alec Waugh, 94–5.

21. Muir, 172.

22. Guggenheim, 122.

23. Holroyd, *Hugh Kingsmill*, 58–9.

24. Alec Waugh, 74.

25. 'Portrait of an Unknown Man', *Daily Express*, 11.10.1934.

26. Holroyd, *Hugh Kingsmill*, 56.

27. *Sunflower* was posthumously published. Both H. G. Wells's *The Autocracy of Mr Parham* (1930) and Arnold Bennett's *Lord Raingo* (1926) had characters based upon Beaverbrook. Evelyn Waugh denied that Lord Copper in *Scoop* (1938) was modelled on Beaverbrook.

28. Gerhardie to Beaverbrook, 14.9.1926 [BB].

29. Glendinning, 105.

30. *OML* 10.

31. *MP* 321.

32. *OML*, 1st edn. (1936), 230.

33. American edition published by Duffield (New York, 1928). Later issued in England by Duckworth as *Donna Quixote or Perfectly Scandalous* (London, 1929).

34. To J. B. Priestley, 9.1.1935.

35. To Beaverbrook, 26.9.1926 [BB].

36. *The Daily News* (a notably Liberal paper), 29.2.1927.

37. 23.6.1927.

38. Gerhardie to Konni Zilliacus, 10.6.1930.

39. *PH* 152.

40. 'A Ghost in a Ghost World', eventually published as 'Ghosts', *The English Review*. (Published version cut out and therefore no date visible.)

41. 24.12.1926 [BB].

42. *Res.* 300.

43. 26.9.1926 [BB].

44. *Res.* 305.

11. LONDON

1. 30.6.1927.
2. *MP* 372.
3. Holroyd, *Hugh Kingsmill*, 160.
4. *MP* 326.
5. *MP* 327–8.
6. *PH* 52.
7. *PH* 49.
8. Gerhardie's unpublished introduction to Michael Holroyd's *Hugh Kingsmill*.
9. 20.12.1927. (The Harry Ransom Humanities Research Institute, University of Texas.)
10. *PH* 52.
11. American edition published by Duffield (New York, 1928) as *Eva's Apples*.
12. 'My Literary Credo', published as an introduction to the Collected Uniform Edition of *Futility* (1947), xvi–xvii.
13. Jules Verne (1828–1905) and H. G. Wells (1866–1946) depicted the plausible aspects of adventurous scientific progress. The first publication of *Amazing Stories* (New York and Leicester, 1926), a monthly journal edited by Hugo Gernsback, helped to revitalize the popularity of this genre.
14. Review of *Jazz and Jasper*, in the *Evening Standard*, 19.4.1928.
15. Taylor, *Beaverbrook*, 167.
16. *English History: 1914–1945*, 260.
17. Garnett, xiii. In retrospect Garnett admitted, 'the whole foundation of those years . . . was an illusion . . . an illusion as beautiful and as foolish as that which underlines Christianity: the belief that men naturally love one another' (xi).
18. Hynes, 42.
19. 2.12.1926.
20. 18.4.1928. (University of Texas.)
21. *Punch*, 2.5.1928.

12. DIGRESSION ON WOMEN

1. *Doom*, 180.
2. *MP* 349.
3. Holroyd, *Lytton Strachey*, 540.
4. *MP* 275–6.
5. Cohen, 83.
6. *Res.* 313.
7. *Res.* 310.
8. Sieveking, 110.
9. 'The Hermit of Hallam Street', by June Turner, *London Magazine*, Apr.–May 1981.

10. Mannin, 246.
11. Ibid.
12. Ibid.
13. Gerhardie to Kingsmill, 18.11.1930.
14. *MP* 346.
15. *Doom*, 119–20.
16. 'The Attractive Woman', *Graphic*, 14.4.1928.
17. *Res.* 351.
18. *MP* 142.
19. *MP* 358.
20. To Edith Wharton, 25.12.1928.
21. Nichols, *Twenty-Five*, 44.
22. Quoted in a letter from Curtis Brown to Gerhardie, 1.12.1926.
23. *Richmond Leader*, 12.2.1930.
24. In a letter from Alan Parsons to Gerhardie, July 1928. I do not know if the advertisement was ever used.
25. *Vogue*, 18.4.1928.
26. *Bookman*, Feb. 1930.
27. *Nash's Magazine*, May 1927.
28. *Daily Express* (*c.*1928).
29. *Daily Chronicle*, 30.11.1928.
30. *London Opinion*, 31.1.1931.
31. 'Why I Am Not a Best-Seller' (*c.*1928). Published version not located.
32. 'Truth About Social Climbers' (*c.*1928). Published version not located.
33. 'Should We Fight Like Gentlemen?' *Evening Standard*, 24.5.1929.
34. 'Are We So Very Naughty?', *Daily Mirror* (*c.*1928).
35. Nichols, *All I Could Never Be*, 35.
36. 'Wives Who Love Too Much', *Daily Mirror*, 9.8.1928.
37. 'What Women Have Taught Me', *Daily Chronicle*, 30.11.1928.
38. Ibid.
39. 'Let Women Rule the World', *Daily Mirror* (date not visible).
40. Lockhart, *Diaries*, 21 June 1929 (p. 92) and 29 Mar. 1933 (p. 252).
41. *MP* 41–2.
42. Gerhardie's unpublished introduction to Michael Holroyd's *Hugh Kingsmill*.
43. Ibid.
44. *Res.* 49.
45. Ingrams, 125.
46. Unpublished introduction to *Hugh Kingsmill*.
47. Alec Waugh, 93.
48. To Oliver Stonor, 6.2.1941.
49. Unpublished introduction to *Hugh Kingsmill*.
50. Gerhardie to Rosie, 9.9.1929.
51. To Thomas Balston, 2.10.1929 [MH].

13. INDIA AND AMERICA

1. *Res.* 126.
2. The Short S.8 *Calcutta*, which carried fifteen passengers, served *en route* by a steward dispensing meals from a buffet, was the only British commercial flying-boat then capable of crossing the Mediterranean. It had cost £20,000 and was a big improvement on the older flying-boats and passenger aircraft: comfortable and, as all petrol was carried in the wings, smoking was allowed. The plane was 66 feet long with a 93-ft wingspan; cruising speed 97 m.p.h., range 650 miles, ceiling 13,500 ft.
3. *MP* 364.
4. *MP* 365.
5. 3.12.1929.
6. *Res.* 127.
7. *Res.* 135.
8. *MP* 368.
9. *MP* 373.
10. *MP* 365.
11. *MP* 378.
12. *Res.* 139.
13. *Res.* 144.
14. 25.4.1928.
15. *MP* 380.
16. *Brooklyn Eagle*, 16.2.1930.
17. *MP* 382.
18. *MP* 385.
19. From Florence S. Peple, 12.2.1930.
20. *MP* 384.
21. *MP* 145.
22. To Edith Wharton, 23.6.1930.
23. The American edition was published by Harper (New York, 1930) with a £400 advance. As American librarians had recently been attempting to suppress as indecent Waugh's new novel *A Handful of Dust*, the publishers warned that they might have trouble with the 'amorous portions' of *Pending Heaven*.
24. 26.3.1930.
25. Gerhardie's own synopsis in the 1940s edition.
26. Berlin, 141.
27. 27.2.1930.
28. Allen, 52–3.
29. 23.2.1930.
30. 27.3.1930.
31. 20.2.1930.
32. *Manchester Guardian*, 25.2.1930.

33. From Arthur Wellings, 30.5.1930.

34. 4.8.1930.

35. *MP* 284.

36. To Mrs Foss Allen, 20.3.1938.

37. 'Wanted: A Personality', typescript article. Published version not located.

14. MARRIAGE?

1. *Res.* 337.

2. *Res.* 192.

3. *MP* 402.

4. *Res.* 195.

5. *Res.* 163.

6. *PH* 208.

7. To Messrs Cox and Co., 30.9.1931.

8. To Margaret Penn [Jan. 1966].

9. *Res.* 138.

10. Gerhardie to Hugh Kingsmill, 17.7.1930.

11. Holroyd, *Hugh Kingsmill*, 127.

12. Sieveking, 117.

13. The American edition was published by Knopf (New York, 1931). Gerhardie inscribed Kingsmill's copy: 'To Hugh Kingsmill gratefully: may every faulty comma, a misplaced full stop, burn a hole in his guts! gratefully—William Gerhardi. June 1931.'

14. Beckett, 14.

15. Ford Madox Ford, 282–3.

16. Beckett, 15.

17. *Sunday Times*, 12.7.1931.

18. *Glasgow Herald*, 27.8.1931.

19. *Observer*, 28.6.1931.

20. *Sketch*, 19.8.1931.

15. SATAN

1. *Res.* 327.

2. Gerhardie to Thomas Balston, 29.5.1931 [MH].

3. Gerhardie to Beaverbrook, 25.6.1931 [BB].

4. Lockhart, *Diaries*, 24 July 1931 (p. 179).

5. Taylor, *Beaverbrook*, 24.

6. Unpublished interview with Olivia Manning.

7. Evelyn Waugh, *Letters*, 634.

8. *Doom*, 162.

9. *MP* 277.

10. *GFC* 307.

11. Most of these were politicians who, having shown early promise, amounted to nothing. None had achieved anything comparable to Gerhardie. Others included Arnold Ward (1876–1950), foreign correspondent and MP; C. F. G. Masterman (1873–1927), Liberal politician; George Mair; Ellis Ashmead-Bartlett (1881–1931), war correspondent and Conservative MP. 'Most of the Splendid Failures were collected and exploited by Max', wrote Bruce Lockhart in his diary. 'He got 'em cheap.' (21 June 1932; p. 220.)

12. *MP* 44.

13. *Res.* 206.

14. *Sunday Times*, 12.7.1931.

15. *Fut.* 91, my italics.

16. Typescript article. Published version not located.

17. *Res.* 106.

18. 'Talent, Blue Blood or Money?', *Good Housekeeping*, Jan. 1932.

19. To Oliver Stonor, 14.6.1946.

20. Letter to *News Chronicle*, 17.5.1932.

21. To Prince Leopold Loewenstein.

22. Antony Powell to Dido Davies, 6.4.1987 [DD].

23. Gerhardie to Miss McNeight, 18.11.1931.

24. 'How A Maharajah Lives', typescript article. Published version not located.

25. Lunn, 218.

26. Lunn, 229.

27. Gerhardie's own synopsis in the 1940s edition.

28. Lunn, 230.

29. Lunn, 231.

30. Gerhardie to Hugh Kingsmill, 9.7.1930.

31. Lunn, 231.

32. To Brian Lunn, 7.10.1934.

33. Lunn, 231.

34. *OML* 245.

35. Oliver Stonor to Gerhardie, 22.10.1939.

36. *OML* 256.

37. *PH* 32.

38. *MP* 85–6.

39. The American edition was published by Doubleday Doran (New York, 1933). The dust-jacket of this edition is a work of art: a white naked woman reclining provocatively away and facing a green Satan; behind him the New York skyscrapers rise, and turn into flames as they meet the sky.

40. Hugh Kingsmill to Gerhardie, 20.11.1932.

16. RESURRECTION

1. 7.12.1932.

2. To Doubleday Doran, 30.12.1932.

3. Holroyd, *Hugh Kingsmill*, 143.
4. Holroyd, *Hugh Kingsmill*, 144. The book was *Sentimental Journey* (1934).
5. *Res.* 54.
6. Ibid.
7. *OML* 27.
8. *OML* 41.
9. *Res.* 177.
10. *Res.* 18–20.
11. *Res.* 32.
12. *Res.* 33.
13. *Res.* 36.
14. *MWL* 40.
15. *OML* 130.
16. *OML* 190.
17. *OML* 191.
18. *OML* 196.
19. Gerhardie to Harcourt Brace, 18.7.1934.
20. 'Portrait of an Unknown Man', *Daily Express*, 11.10.1934.
21. 2.11.1934.
22. 13.11.1934.
23. 13.4.1934.
24. 18.4.1934.
25. Gerhardie's own synopsis in the 1940s edition.
26. Gerhardie to Simon and Schuster, 3.11.1933.
27. 1.1.1925 [BB].
28. Beckett, 3.
29. *Listener*, 17.10.1934.
30. *Spectator*, 5.10.1934.
31. *New Statesman and Nation*, 6.10.1934.
32. 29.10.1934.
33. 27.10.1934.
34. 13.2.1935. (University of Texas.)
35. To Oliver Stonor, 5.11.1936.
36. To Cassell, 27.6.1934.

17. OF MORTAL LOVE

1. *MP* 296.
2. Gerhardie to Victor Gollancz, 26.8.1940.
3. 23.8.1923, quoted by Rothenstein (p. 60); Gerhardie's letter dated 23.8.1923.
4. *OML* 246.
5. *MP* 174.
6. *MWL* 64.

7. *MWL* 64.
8. *MWL* 80.
9. *Res.* 106.
10. 'Taking a Girl to the Pictures', *Film Weekly*, 26.11.1928.
11. *Res.* 16.
12. Ibid.
13. *Res.* 22.
14. Frances Champion to Gerhardie [1942].
15. *Europe At Play* (London, 1938).
16. *MWL* 200.
17. *OML* 40.
18. *Doom*, 178.
19. 'Climate and Character', in *The English Genius* (ed. Hugh Kingsmill), 80.
20. 'My Life's the Least of It', by John Stevenson, broadcast on BBC Radio 3, 25 February 1981.
21. To Oliver Stonor, 5.11.1936.
22. To Rupert Gleadow 8.2.1934. Gleadow had written on magic and astrology.
23. Lunn, 218.
24. Gerhardie to Desmond MacCarthy, 13.11.1936.
25. 12.2.1937.
26. Gerhardie's own synopsis in the 1940s edition.
27. To Oliver Stonor, 7.8.1938.
28. 25.11.1936.
29. 9.2.1937.
30. *The End of Mr Davidson* (London, 1932), published under the name of Morchard Bishop, taken from a town in Devon.

18. MOVING PICTURES

1. To Oliver Stonor, 31.5.1941.
2. From Gleb Struve to Gerhardie, 20.2.1937. Nabokov used Sirin as a *nom de plume*.
3. To Oliver Stonor, 3.12.1940.
4. 10.5.1949. Evelyn Waugh, *Letters*, p. 298.
5. *GFC* 310.
6. *GFC* 311.
7. Gerhardie's own synopsis in the 1940s edition.
8. Introduction to the Revised Definitive Edition (1973), 17.
9. 'The Method and Vision of William Gerhardi', *Nineteenth Century*, June 1949, pp. 387–8.
10. 'Author's Epilogue' to 1973 edition (p. 545).
11. *Sketch*, 4.5.1938.

12. Gerhardie's unpublished introduction to Michael Holroyd's *Hugh Kingsmill*.
13. *Res.* 314.
14. To Oliver Stonor, 11.5.1939.
15. To Oliver Stonor, 24.5.1939.
16. 10.2.1940.
17. Muggeridge, 210.

19. WAR

1. To Oliver Stonor, 8.2.1940.
2. To Oliver Stonor, 16.4.1940.
3. To Oliver Stonor, 28.9.1939.
4. To Oliver Stonor, 23.3.1945.
5. The American edition was published by Putnam (New York, 1939).
6. To Rich and Cowan, 16.1.1940.
7. 24.1.1940.
8. 27.1.1940.
9. To Hugh Kingsmill, 30.3.1940.
10. To Oliver Stonor, 10.10.1940.
11. To Oliver Stonor and Margaret Penn, 14.9.1940.
12. To Oliver Stonor, 14.11.1940.
13. Quoted by Gerhardie to Oliver Stonor, 24.8.1941.
14. Christina Foyle to Dido Davies, 18.8.1985 [DD].
15. To Oliver Stonor, 2.5.1942.
16. To Oliver Stonor, 23.6.1942 and 15.7.1942.
17. To Dolores Hutchinson, 5.2.1953.
18. Gerhardie to Clara [AA].
19. BBC2 'Arena' programme, broadcast 1971.
20. Piers Brendon in *Book Choice*, Apr. 1981.
21. William Haley in *The Times*, 9.3.1981.
22. Nigel Dennis in the *Sunday Telegraph*, 1.3.1981.
23. K. G. Robbins in the *Times Higher Education Supplement*, 20.3.1981.
24. To Oliver Stonor, 23.3.1945.

20. CLARA

1. *PG* 22–3.
2. To Oliver Stonor and Margaret Penn, 5.10.1948.
3. 29.9.1948 [AA].
4. Holroyd, *Hugh Kingsmill*, 201.
5. Holroyd, *Hugh Kingsmill*, 210.
6. To Margaret Penn, 30.11.1953.
7. To Dido Davies, 23.7.1985 [DD].

8. To Margaret Penn, 8.10.1947.
9. To Gorley Putt, 2.1.1951 [GP].
10. To Edward Sammis, 12.6.1959.
11. Michael Ivens, 'Gerhardi and the P.M.G.', *Spectator*, 7 Apr. 1961.
12. 'The Hermit of Hallam Street', by June Turner, *London Magazine*, Apr.–May 1981.
13. To Gorley Putt, 2.1.1951 [GP].
14. *Spectator*, 16.3.1962.
15. *OML* 74.
16. 'Valedictory', typescript article. Published version not located.
17. To Sebastian Amyes, 26.2.1956 [AA].
18. 'The Hermit of Hallam Street.'
19. To Brentford Nylons, 10.1.1966.
20. [1951]. It was produced by Jerome Kilty at the Theatre Workshop of Harvard University in October 1948 where it ran for the stipulated week with average success.
21. Quoted in a letter from Beaverbrook, 26.1.1956.
22. To Oliver Stonor and Margaret Penn, 30.1.1958.

21. DOOM

1. Draft journal.
2. 15.3.1967.
3. 'My Life's the Least of It', by John Stevenson, broadcast on BBC Radio 3, 25 Feb. 1981.
4. To Margaret Penn, 4.4.1941.
5. Introduction to *GFC* by Michael Holroyd and Robert Skidelsky.
6. To Oliver Stonor, 4.3.1941.
7. To Gerhardie, 7.2.[1961? 1962?].
8. BBC2 'Arena' programme, broadcast 1971.
9. C. P. Snow acted as referee. This began in 1959 at £150, increasing regularly to keep pace with inflation so that by 1972 it was £700. At 65 Gerhardie qualified for half the Old Age Pension.
10. Unpublished interview with Olivia Manning.
11. *MP* 355.
12. 'My Life's the Least of It.'
13. 'William Gerhardie at 75, and ready for a great revival', by Janet Watts, *Evening Standard*, 25.5.1971.
14. Graham Greene in *The Times*, 28.6.1973, p. 15.
15. To Oliver Stonor, 7.10.1946.
16. *Literaturnoye nasledstvo. 60. Chekhov*, Moscow, 1960, 801–34.
17. *Res*. 100.
18. Conversation with Dido Davies, 1985.
19. Gerhardie to James MacGibbon at Macdonald, 30.8.1970.

20. Gerhardie's own suggestion for Michael Holroyd's preface [MH].
21. 17.7.1980 [MH].
22. To Susan Hodgart of Macdonald, 2.3.1970.
23. Gerhardie's own suggestion for Michael Holroyd's Preface [MH].
24. 'The Hermit of Hallam Street', by June Turner, *London Magazine*, Apr.–May 1981.
25. 'William Gerhardie at 75, and ready for a great revival.'
26. Bo Gunnarsson to Gerhardie, 6.11.1975.
27. Meriel Buchanan, 42.
28. BBC2 'Arena' programme, broadcast 1971.
29. To Professor Ashley Montagu, 27.5.1964.
30. To Miss McNeight, 18.11.1931.
31. Sonya Crooks, 4.9.1971.
32. 'William Gerhardie at 75, and ready for a great revival.'
33. To Dido Davies, 18.8.1985 [DD].
34. 13.11.1934.
35. 'The Hermit of Hallam Street.'

WORKS BY WILLIAM GERHARDIE

Fiction

'Felony', *Oxford Fortnightly Review*, 3 Nov. 1921, pp. 245–8.

'The Proposal', *Oxford Fortnightly Review*, 27 Jan. 1922, pp. 316–18.

'Tact', *Oxford Fortnightly Review*, 26 May 1922, pp. 409–13.

'Of Hypocrisy', *Oxford Outlook*, June 1922, pp. 199–201.

Futility: A Novel on Russian Themes (London: Cobden Sanderson, 1922; New York edition containing a Preface by Edith Wharton: Duffield, 1922; first English edition to contain Wharton's Preface: London, Duckworth, 1927).

The Polyglots (London: Cobden Sanderson, 1925; New York: Duffield, 1925). Russian translation published as *Nashestvie Varvarov* (Moscow, 1926).

'The Big Drum', *Calendar of Modern Letters*, Apr. 1925, pp. 147–52.

A Bad End (London: Ernest Benn, 1926).

The Vanity Bag (London: Ernest Benn, 1927).

Pretty Creatures (London: Ernest Benn, 1927; New York: Duffield, 1927).

Perfectly Scandalous; or, The Immorality Lady. A Comedy in Three Acts (London: Ernest Benn, 1927; New York: Duffield, 1928). Republished as *Donna Quixote* (London: Duckworth, 1929).

Jazz and Jasper (London: Duckworth, 1928); published in the United States as *Eva's Apples* (New York: Duffield, 1928); republished as *My Sinful Earth* (London: Macdonald, 1947); republished as *Doom* (London: Macdonald, 1974).

Pending Heaven (London: Duckworth, 1930; New York: Harper, 1930).

The Memoirs of Satan by William Gerhardi and Brian Lunn (London: Cassell, 1932; Garden City: Doubleday Doran, 1933)

Resurrection (London: Cassell, 1934; New York: Harcourt Brace, 1934).

Of Mortal Love (London: Barker, 1936).

My Wife's the Least Of It (London: Faber & Faber, 1938).

'This Present Breath, a Tetralogy in One Volume', *The Wind and the Rain*, edited by Neville Braybrooke (London: Secker and Warburg, 1962).

Non-Fiction

Anton Chehov: A Critical Study (London: Cobden-Sanderson, 1923; New York: Duffield, 1923).

'Introduction', *From Double Eagle to Red Flag*, by P. N. Krassnoff, translated from the second Russian edition by Erik Law-Gisiko (London, 1928).

'Epilogue', *The Technique of the Love Affair*, by A Gentlewoman (London, 1928).

Memoirs of a Polyglot (London: Duckworth, 1931; New York: Knopf, 1931).

The Casanova Fable: A Satirical Revaluation by William Gerhardi and Hugh Kingsmill (London: Jarrold, 1934; New York: Jarrold, 1947).

'The First Time I Scaled the Heights of Nature—and Plumbed the Depths of Human Nature', *The First Time I . . .* , edited by Theodora Benson (London: Chapman and Hall, 1935).

Meet Yourself As You Really Are, by William Gerhardi and Prince Leopold Loewenstein (London: Faber & Faber, 1936; Philadelphia: Lippincott, 1936).

'Climate and Character', *The English Genius: A Survey of the English Achievement and Character*, edited by Hugh Kingsmill (London: Eyre and Spottiswoode, 1939).

The Romanovs, including a preface, 'My Historical Credo' (New York: Putnam's, 1939; London: Rich & Cowan, 1940).

'My Literary Credo', *Futility* (London: Macdonald, 1947).

God's Fifth Column, a Biography of the Age: 1890–1940, edited by Michael Holroyd and Robert Skidelsky (London: Hodder and Stoughton, 1981; New York: Simon & Schuster, 1981).

Collections

The Collected Uniform Edition of the Works of William Gerhardi (London: Macdonald, 1947–9).

The Revised Definitive Edition of the Works of William Gerhardie, containing Prefaces by Michael Holroyd (London: Macdonald, 1970–4).

Gerhardie's own extensive scrapbook collection of his published journalism is available in the Gerhardie Archive, Cambridge University Library, although many of the items have no reference.

SELECT BIBLIOGRAPHY

An asterisk indicates that Gerhardie is mentioned by name. Place of publication is London unless otherwise stated.

*ALLEN, WALTER, *Tradition and Dream: The English and American Novel from the Twenties to Our Time* (1964).

*ALPERS, ANTONY, *The Life of Katherine Mansfield* (1980).

*ASQUITH, EARL OF OXFORD AND, *H. H. A.: Letters to a Friend*, Second Series, 1922–7 (1934).

BAINES, EDWARD, *History of the Cotton Manufacture in Great Britain*, second edition (1966).

BARING, MAURICE, *The Russian People* (1911).

BECKETT, SAMUEL, *Proust* (1931).

*BENNETT, ARNOLD, *Journals*, edited by Newman Flower, 3 vols (1932–3).

*—— *Journals*, edited by Frank Swinnerton (1971).

BERLIN, ISAIAH, *Russian Thinkers* (1978).

BLACKLOCK, MICHAEL, *The Royal Scots Greys* (1971).

BLACKMORE, SUSAN J., *Beyond the Body: An Investigation of Out-of-the-Body Experiences* (1982).

BLUNT, WILFRED, *Lady Muriel* (1962).

*BOOTH, WAYNE C., *The Rhetoric of Fiction* (Chicago, 1961).

—— *A Rhetoric of Irony* (Chicago, 1974).

BRADBURY, MALCOLM, *Possibilities: Essays on the State of the Novel* (1973).

*BREWSTER, DOROTHY, *East–West Passage: A Study in Literary Relationships* (1954).

BUCHANAN, GEORGE, *My Mission To Russia*, 2 vols (1923).

BUCHANAN, MERIEL, *Petrograd: The City of Trouble* (1918).

—— *Diplomacy and Foreign Courts* (1928).

—— *Ambassador's Daughter* (1958).

CAMROSE, VISCOUNT, *British Newspapers and their Controllers* (1947).

CARR, E. H., *The Bolshevik Revolution 1917–23*, 3 vols (1950–3).

CARROTHERS, W. A., *Emigration from the British Isles* (1929).

CHAPMAN, S. J., *The Cotton Industry and Trade* (1905).

CHEKHOV, ANTON, *Letters*, edited by Avrahm Yarmolinsky (1974).

Chekhov: The Critical Heritage, edited by Victor Emeljanow (1981).

CLARK-LOWES, NICHOLAS, *Books on the Paranormal: an Introductory Guide*, pamphlet published by the Society for Psychical Research.

*COHEN, HARRIET, *A Bundle of Time* (1969).

COOCH BEHAR, THE MAHARAJAH OF, *Thirty-Seven Years of Big Game Shooting in Cooch Behar* (1908).

DEVEE, SUNITY, MAHARANI OF COOCH BEHAR, *The Autobiography of an Indian Princess* (1921).

DONALDSON, FRANCES, *The British Council: The First Fifty Years* (1984).

ELIOT, T. S., *The Music of Poetry* (Glasgow, 1942).

*ELLIS, G. V., *Twilight On Parnassus: A Survey of Post-War Fiction and Pre-War Criticism* (1939).

ESSLIN, MARTIN, *The Theatre of the Absurd* (1962).

FARRAR, DAVID, *G—for God Almighty: A Personal Memoir of Lord Beaverbrook* (1969).

FIELD, ANDREW, *Nabokov: His Life in Part* (1977).

FORD, FORD MADOX, *Mightier Than The Sword: Memories and Criticisms* (1938).

GARNETT, DAVID, *The Familiar Faces* (1962).

GEORGIAN STORIES 1925 (1925).

*GLENDINNING, VICTORIA, *Rebecca West* (1987).

*GUGGENHEIM, PEGGY, *Out Of This Century* (New York, 1946).

HARRIS, MURIEL, *The Seventh Gate* (1930).

HENDERSON, W. D., *The Lancashire Cotton Famine, 1861–65* (Manchester, 1934).

—— *The Industrial Revolution on the Continent: Germany, France, Russia, 1800–1914* (1961).

*HODGES, PHELPS, *Britmis: A Great Adventure of the War* (1931).

HOLMS, JOHN, 'A Death', *Calendar of Modern Letters*, June 1925, pp. 297–302.

*HOLROYD, MICHAEL, *Hugh Kingsmill: A Critical Biography* (1964).

*—— *Lytton Strachey*, 2 vols (1967–8).

—— *The Best of Hugh Kingsmill* (1970).

*—— *Unreceived Opinions* (1973).

HOWARD, PETER, *Beaverbrook: A Study of Max the Unknown* (1964).

HYNES, SAMUEL, *The Auden Generation: Literature and Politics in England in the 1930s* (1976).

*INGRAMS, RICHARD, *God's Apology: A Chronicle of Three Friends* (1977).

JOUBERT, CARL, *Russia As It Really Is*, second edition (1904).

*KELLY, LAURENCE, *St Petersburg: A Traveller's Companion* (1981).

KINGSMILL, HUGH, *The Will to Love*, published under the name of Hugh Lunn (1919).

—— *The Dawn's Delay* (1924).

—— *Blondel* (1927).

—— *Matthew Arnold* (1928).

—— *The Return of William Shakespeare* (1929).

—— *After Puritanism* (1929).

—— *Invective and Abuse* (1929).

—— *More Invective* (1930).

—— *Behind Both Lines* (1930).

—— *The Worst of Love* (1931).

KINGSMILL, HUGH, *Frank Harris* (1932).

*—— *The Table of Truth* (1933).

—— *Samuel Johnson* (1933).

—— *The Sentimental Journey* (1934).

—— *What They Said At the Time* (1935).

*—— editor, *The English Genius: A Survey of the English Achievement and Character* (1939).

—— *The Fall* (1940).

—— *The Poisoned Crown* (1944).

—— 'William Gerhardi', *New English Review*, Sept. 1947, pp. 269–72.

—— *The Progress of a Biographer* (1949).

—— *The High Hill of the Muses* (1955).

KNOX, SIR ALFRED, *With The Russian Army, 1914–17*, 2 vols (1921).

KOHL, J. G., *Russia and the Russians in 1842*, 2 vols (1842).

*LEWIS, R. W. B., *Edith Wharton* (1975).

*LOCKHART, R. H. BRUCE, *Your England* (1955).

—— *The Two Revolutions: An Eye-Witness Study of Russia, 1917* (1957).

*—— *Diaries*, 2 vols (1973–80).

—— *Memoirs of a British Agent*, new edition (1974).

LOEWENSTEIN, PRINCE HUBERTUS, *Conquests of the Past* (1938).

LOEWENSTEIN, PRINCE LEOPOLD, *A Time to Love—A Time to Die* (1970).

LUCKETT, RICHARD, *The White Generals* (1971).

LUNN, BRIAN, *Switchback* (1948).

*MACCARTHY, DESMOND, *Criticism* (1932).

MCKAY, J. P., *Pioneers For Profit: Foreign Entrepreneurship and Russian Industrialization, 1885–1913* (1970).

MACKENZIE, F. A., *Lord Beaverbrook, An Authentic Biography* (1931).

*MAIS, S. P. B., *Some Modern Authors* (1923).

*MANNIN, ETHEL, *Confessions and Impressions* (1930).

MANSFIELD, KATHERINE, *Collected Stories* (1945).

—— *Journal 1904–1922*, edited by John Middleton Murry (1954).

*—— *Letters and Journals*, edited by C. K. Stead (1977).

*MEYERS, JEFFREY, *Katherine Mansfield: A Biography* (1978).

MUGGERIDGE, MALCOLM, *Like It Was*, diaries selected and edited by John Bright-Holmes (1981).

MUIR, EDWIN, *An Autobiography* (1954).

MULDOON, SYLVAN, and HEREWARD CARRINGTON, *The Projection of the Astral Body* (1929).

Murray's *Handbook for Northern Europe*, second edition, Part II, Finland and Russia (1849).

NABOKOV, VLADIMIR, *Speak, Memory: An Autobiography Revisited*, revised edition (1967).

*NEHLS, EDWARD, *D. H. Lawrence: A Composite Biography*, 3 vols (Madison, Wisconsin, 1957–9).

NICHOLS, BEVERLEY, *25; being a young man's candid recollections of his elders and betters* (1926).

—— *The Fool Hath Said* (1936).

——*All I Could Never Be* (1949).

—— *The Sweet and Twenties* (1958).

PEARSON, HESKETH, and MALCOLM MUGGERIDGE, *About Kingsmill* (1951).

PENN, MARGARET, *Manchester Fourteen Miles* (Cambridge, 1947).

—— *The Foolish Virgin* (1951).

—— *Young Mrs Burton* (1954).

*POWELL, ANTHONY, *Messengers of Day*, vol. 2 of *Memoirs* (1978).

PROUST, MARCEL, *Time Regained*, translated by Andreas Mayor (1970).

*PUTT, S. GORLEY, *Scholars of the Heart: Essays in Criticism* (1962).

RHODES JAMES, ROBERT, *Victor Cazalet* (1976).

RODZIANKO, PAUL, *Tattered Banners: An Autobiography* (1938).

*ROTHENSTEIN, JOHN, *Summer's Lease: Autobiography 1901–38* (1965).

SETON-WATSON, HUGH, *The Russian Empire 1801–1917* (Oxford, 1967).

SIEVEKING, LANCE, *The Eye of the Beholder* (1957).

STEINER, GEORGE, *Language and Silence* (1967).

STONOR, OLIVER [under the pseudonym MORCHARD BISHOP], *Two For Joy* (1938).

—— [under the pseudonym MORCHARD BISHOP], *Aunt Betty* (1939).

—— [under the pseudonym MORCHARD BISHOP?], *The Green Tree and the Dry* (1939).

TAYLOR, A. J. P., *English History: 1914–45* (Oxford, 1965).

—— *Beaverbrook* (1972).

TCHEHOV, ANTON, *The Cherry Orchard and Other Plays*, translated by Constance Garnett (1935).

TREWIN, J. C., *Robert Donat* (1968).

TURGENEV, IVAN, *Hamlet and Don Quixote*, translated by Robert Nichols (1930).

UNWIN, STANLEY, *The Truth About Publishing*, third edition (1929).

*WAUGH, ALEC, *My Brother Evelyn and Other Profiles* (1967).

WAUGH, EVELYN, *A Little Learning* (1964).

—— *Diaries*, edited by Michael Davie (1976).

*—— *Letters*, edited by Mark Amory (1980).

*—— *The Cultural Heritage*, edited by Martin Stannard (1984).

WILLIAMS, HAROLD, *Russia of the Russians* (1914).

WOOLF, VIRGINIA, *The Common Reader*, First Series (1925).

INDEX

William Gerhardie's main published works are denoted by an asterisk.